René Berger   Discovery of Painting

1. Romanesque Art. *The Martyrdom of St Margaret* (detail), panel, 12th century. Vich (Spain), Episcopal Museum. Photo Held.

Discovery of Painting

René Berger

453 illustrations, 47 colour plates

A Studio Book · The Viking Press · New York

Translated from the French by Richard James

This edition © Thames and Hudson, London, 1963

© 1958 La Guilde du Livre et Editions des Fauconnières, Lausanne

Reproduction rights reserved by A.D.A.G.P. and S.P.A.D.E.M.

Printed in Switzerland

Published in 1963 by The Viking Press, Inc.

625 Madison Avenue, New York 22, N.Y.

Library of Congress catalog card number: 63-11815

CONTENTS

Contents

Contents

Contents

PREFACE

This work would never have seen the light of day if the *Fonds national de la recherche scientifique suisse* and the *Département de l'instruction publique du canton de Vaud* had not granted me their support. I am happy to express my gratitude to them both. I am also indebted for his advice to M. Etienne Souriau, professor of aesthetics at the Sorbonne, and to MM. Vladimir Jankélévitch and Pierre-Maxime Schuhl, professors at the Sorbonne, all three of whom accepted the substance of this work in the form of a thesis. The documentation of the book posed many problems, and I wish to express my gratitude to all those artists, art historians, art critics, museum and gallery curators, librarians, collectors and publishers who have helped me in its compilation. Most of the photographs from which the coloured and black-and-white illustrations have been made were taken by M. André Held. I thank him, and also M. Nicollier, whose care and patience in the preparation of the sketches and diagrams have been beyond all praise.

The production of the book raised a number of technical difficulties. I had expressed the wish that each illustration should closely follow the relevant passage of the text, so that the reader should have both before him as he followed the argument. *Arts graphiques Héliographia* surmounted these difficulties and granted my wish to the limits of possibility. Finally, I do not forget the friends who have helped me in research and in the correction of proofs. It is not merely a duty, but a pleasure for me to thank all those who have helped in this enterprise.

Introduction

It can safely be said that public interest in the visual arts, and in painting especially, is growing from day to day. Art books, almost unknown fifty years ago, are now abundant. People buy them, look at them, give them as presents. Reproductions are published in their thousands, and even the humble postcard

forgets its tradition of the landscape 'view' to be the proud emissary of a Van Gogh or Matisse. As a result 2 of all this, paintings no longer seem to be imprisoned in the museums, but break loose to roam the world. Wherever they stop they are contemplated by innumerable eyes, and exhibition galleries prove too small for the crowds who throng them . . .

Moreover, it is something more than mere curiosity that draws people to painting with the force of a flood-tide. Consciously or unconsciously the public takes an interest in works of art, an interest that reaches fervour in the young, most of whom wish to possess in reproduction the picture they love. From deep in the Louvre the Mona Lisa broods over her 3 countless effigies, which spread her subtle radiance through the world. By definition unique, this is the masterpiece endowed with the power of ubiquity. Painting has become for our age a 'presence' from which, one may dare to say, some sort of *revelation* is expected.

But, although the need for art is unanimously felt, there is no unanimity in what the public appreciates. Anyone passing through Florence makes it his duty – and pleasure – to visit the Uffizi. Thousands emerge, enriched, from the Louvre and the Rijksmuseum every day; and the Prado, like the Alte Pinakothek, has its own enthusiasts. However, if one were to question these wide-eyed visitors, one would find that their minds are by no means always at rest.

So long as painting at least appeared to respect the exterior world as we know it, the spectator's attitude could take advantage of a certain ambiguity: for sure, Rembrandt was admired – but were the reasons for 4 admiring him distinguished from the reasons for admiring, say, Aert de Gelder? In both of them one 5 could observe the same religious emotion and the same conflict of light and shadow. The achievement of modern art is to have got rid of this ambiguity. Since Impressionism, more or less every important form of artistic expression has been met with hostility, and yet, despite the condemnation of critics and public alike, has triumphed in the end, to take its place in the history of art – visibly in museums and galleries, and more securely still in the hearts of succeeding generations.

Modern art has made clear what before was only suspected or hinted at – *that the worth of a work of art depends not on one's taste for it, nor on the respect*

2. Vincent Van Gogh (1853-1890). *Boats at Stes. Maries-de-la-Mer.* Amsterdam, coll. V. W. Van Gogh. Photo Viollet.

11

which it displays for the exterior world or for tradition, nor on its qualities of ornament or entertainment, but on what is proper to itself, expressed by its own proper means. That being so, there is no real obstacle to understanding.

But does one have to *understand* painting? Is it not enough to look at it – to experience it? Well, it is one thing to observe or to experience, but it is another to appreciate, that is to say *to know and to love with discernment.* Although painting has never been so popular as it is today, it is a fact that the public has never felt so urgent a 'need to understand'. This book is an attempt to answer that need.

Let me make myself clear, for books on art are legion. Without considering the plethora of picture-books and albums of plates, it is fair to say that most works of art-history, criticism or aesthetics, however useful they may be, are concerned hardly at all with that initial query of the spectator: 'How should I set about knowing this work; how do I equip myself to pass a valid judgment on it?' A fundamental question, which we all ask ourselves, but on which there reigns a curious silence.

None the less, one cannot doubt that there *is* a 'way of setting about it'. Though specialists in the field of art are silent, their silence does not deny its existence – or prevent them from practising it themselves, consciously or unconsciously. If they denied its existence, or even doubted it, how could they form opinions or pronounce judgments on the quality of works of art? We thus arrive at the distinctly bizarre conclusion that the thing most neglected is the very thing we need at the outset!

This desire of a growing public to appreciate pictures makes it the duty of anyone concerned with art to explain himself honestly and simply.

Contrary to what people suppose, it is becoming ever clearer that a work of art is not just a thing – albeit a 'thing of beauty' – but that it has somewhat the nature of a *text,* which must be apprehended – its sense grasped and its quality felt – before it can be appraised. In other words, works of art need to be 'read', according to their nature. There is a way of 'reading' form which, under its different conditions, is as precise an exercise as reading literature, and requires similar initiation and practice.[1]

Though no-one would seriously deny that the faculty of discerning beauty is common to all, we

3. Leonardo da Vinci (1452-1519). *Mona Lisa.* Paris, Louvre. Photo Held.

---

[1] From infant school to university every child is trained to read literary texts; but, through an oversight of which the effects are only now beginning to be realised, the 'reading' of works of art has been almost totally neglected.

4. Rembrandt (1606-1669). *Saint Peter Denying Christ*. Amsterdam, Rijksmuseum. Photo Rijksmuseum.

5. Aert de Gelder (1645-1727). *Abraham Entertaining the Three Angels*. Rotterdam, Boymans Museum. Photo Boymans Museum.

are bound to admit that there is no end to our disagreements on the subject. From what do they arise? As Descartes said of our search for truth, 'because we conduct our thoughts along different paths, and do not consider the same things'. His observation carries no less weight when transferred to the domain of art. If we bear it in mind we may hope – if not to put our finger on 'beauty' – at least to direct our steps purposefully instead of groping in the dark, first trying by all the means at our disposal to lead our minds onto the right track. This is the theme of the two central sections of this book. In the first of these we study in turn line, space, colour, tone and light; in the second, composition, structure, tension, proportion, movement and harmony. Note, however, that these are nowhere studied in isolation; colour or rhythm have their existence not in the absolute, but in works of art. Since our minds are unable to grasp all at once, we need landmarks to guide us; and these two sections are intended to show how the spectator, through the study of composition, light, colour and proportion, can find that approach which gives him the feeling of being both fair to the work and honest with himself.

It is no part of my intention to involve my personal taste in this inquiry, and I have no polemical motives. The book is a vindication neither of ancient nor of modern art. I have sufficient respect for art *tout court* to hope that I may serve it without recourse to factitious contrasts.

I believe that to seek the road to aesthetic values is a legitimate activity, but to pronounce judgment on behalf of others is not. The conditions of judgment are a proper object of study, but the act of judging is a matter of individual liberty. However, nothing could give me more pleasure than to be able to show that such conditions do exist, and that there is a road we may follow together, untroubled by disagreements or misunderstandings!

Intellectual thought long ago forged logic as its instrument of communication. True, logic invents nothing; it is sterile, if you like; but it does have the great advantage of obliging anyone engaged in argument to be consistent. As a widely respected discipline it allows men, if not always to agree, at least to oppose their views intelligibly. Why must our artistic judgments be nothing more than vague, capricious or contradictory opinions? Logic cannot provide the remedy, but we are surely justified in looking for a method of art appreciation that could be applied with similar precision, and that would encourage a similar sense of responsibility.

One may wonder that it has not been looked for sooner. The answer is that there are many obstacles of many kinds; and for this reason it seemed necessary to begin with a preliminary section, which I have called *Orientation.* The reason why some people resist art, or hold extravagant views about it, is that, in the phrase of Descartes, they 'do not consider the same things'. So many still complain of an El Greco 6 that the body and neck are elongated, the limbs too thin . . . only to be quite satisfied, however, when ingenious members of the medical profession tell them that the painter suffered from defective eyesight! This can only mean that where some see an ensemble of formal relationships, others are looking for a transcription from life, though it is the same picture which they have before their eyes! And, of course, there are those who still prefer to imagine they are being duped, and that there is nothing to understand anyway!

It would be a waste of time to propound a system to one who believes the ultimate objective of the system to be without validity, or the system itself to have no useful purpose. But, when we examine it, we see that this state of mind is due chiefly to ignorance and to prejudices of various kinds, which either prevent people from seeing, or cause them to see imperfectly, or cause them to see something else. The first section of the book attempts to expose these prejudices so that the reader (if he has need to) may discard them and be ready to collaborate in this research.

Finally, I have added a fourth section, entitled *Application,* in which several outstanding paintings of different periods and styles are studied in detail. These studies are in no way meant to be models. In writing them my one concern has been to apply the principles established in the second and third sections, with the idea not of advancing my personal views in a devious way, but of upholding my responsibilities to the end. The statement of a method is one thing, and its application another; but, in the spirit in which this book has been conceived, the one is worthless without the other.

The book has, to all intents and purposes, imposed its own plan, but I must confess that its execution has presented considerable difficulties. How expound the principles of such a method without making the reader feel that this is a theoretical treatise: how persuade him to use it without making him feel that his liberty is being encroached upon, or without tempting him to apply it as a rule-of-thumb?

Steering a course between those two shoals has been a formidable task, for although in intention

6. El Greco (1541-1614). *Saints John the Evangelist and Francis of Assisi.* Madrid, Prado. Photo Held.

there is nothing contradictory in the avoidance of both, there is some contradiction in practice – by virtue of the fact that things do not appear in the same light at the end as they do at the beginning; they are not the same for the uninitiated as for the experienced. In the unavoidable perplexity of this situation I thought it best to proceed by measured stages, both in the book as a whole and within the individual chapters.

If I may be allowed a final reference – this time to Socrates – I would say that what I hope to produce is not simply an elegant dissertation, but a body of solid evidence. The need to consolidate my progress, step by step, has caused me here and there to repeat myself and to reconsider the same works of art.

Another difficult decision has been whether or not to include abstract art in the discussion from the start, for undeniably it is one of the most active expressions of our own times. However, not wishing to add to the difficulties, I have confined myself to figurative art in the main body of the work, reserving non-figurative painting until the end. Both present us with the same formal problems, but, since the public is more accustomed to figurative art, it seemed wise to use it alone for the purpose of establishing my basic premises.

The third difficulty is a literary one: in what style to write a work that is neither an essay nor a textbook. Here too I have had to make a choice and, as befits my purpose, have done my best to exclude any specialised vocabulary or jargon. Now and again, it is true, I have had to coin a word, but I have done this only with the utmost discretion. As to style, I have aimed at clarity and precision: philosophical or lyrical utterance would be out of place, and I have tried to use only straightforward, everyday language.

This book is not addressed to specialists, nor to artists, nor to art historians, but solely to the general public. Its object can be precisely defined: to establish the conditions under which works of art, and more particularly paintings, can be 'understood'. In method it proceeds by stages with a constant concern that the reader should share and enjoy the processes of research. In character it aims at a practical result.

The main objection will no doubt be that I have paid no regard to history. Only in appearance, I would reply; for although the standpoint of this book has been set deliberately outside the passage of time, I trust that no-one would impute to me the folly of *denying* history! But, while the history of art concerns knowledge of works according to their evolution through the centuries, the fact remains that the artistic consciousness of our own age is distinct from that of the past. Never before have purely aesthetic qualities been so keenly appreciated by so many people, and in all the arts equally. History is indispensable as a point of reference, but a method of appreciation such as we propose has the undeniable merit of answering the needs of our present consciousness. We should help the spectator to recognize that a work of art belongs to an order other than that of reality, and that it demands of him a different attitude of mind if he wishes to experience it actively.

Possibly there is something a little naïve in wishing to make all these points so precisely; but, whether or not I have here achieved it, it is worth indicating the extent of the programme that can legitimately be aspired to. A new discipline is taking its place beside art history and pure aesthetics. With its starting-point in the works of art, it aims to base aesthetic knowledge on the qualities which are proper to the works themselves. Resulting from this discipline, which one might call *Applied Aesthetics,* we may hope for a new way of establishing contact with works of art, and we may even hope that it may enrich traditional art history by inviting it to place greater stress on the life of forms than on their succession in time. At the risk of parodying a writer whose authority I shall be invoking on more than one occasion, I would wish this book to be – in so far as art is concerned – 'a discourse on the method of guiding one's reason and searching for truth'. Perhaps, with a healthy regard for caution, this is not too immodest an ambition.

Orientation

First contact

The prejudice of reality

Let us be frank about it: the moment a picture deviates from reality, whether or not we like it, something in us rebels. And when an international jury awards first prize to Reg Butler's project for the *Monument to the Unknown Political Prisoner,* and 7 instead of the expected prisoner we discover an empty framework – 'a somewhat ambiguous form', as one of the jury commented, 'with suggestions of jail, scaffold, cross and guillotine' – we may justly wonder if we are not being fooled. The same writer's assertion that the empty space of the platform 'expresses the instrument of execution much more than the act itself' increases our suspicion rather than allaying it. We cannot bear to be made fools of, and the artist who sets out deliberately to disconcert us inevitably rouses our resentment.

However, instead of getting worked up about it, let us try to see clearly what this *reality* is on which we rely for our judgments. Easy enough – it is that image of the creatures and objects about us which we receive through the processes of our senses and our minds. A man changes with age, a fruit with the season, but a photograph is expected to fit its description. If we are to be shown the portrait of a seated woman, we know pretty well what we expect, so it is only after a struggle that we submit to Picasso inflicting on us, under this title, monsters 8 that our common sense rejects. There is surely no need to define at greater length the reality to which we appeal.

Now, we feel that this reality is worthy of art. We refer art to it as to a model – its model – and the artist who ignores it arouses our suspicions at once. 'Why the devil can't he paint what he sees?' One may read this nettled exclamation in the looks of a great many ordinary people at any exhibition of modern art. And since people are reluctant to believe in a purely gratuitous act, they end up by supposing that the artists' intentions must be malign, if not downright wicked, and that they deserve not merely our smiles (which cost us no effort anyway) but also our indignant protests. Some even go so far as to contemplate reprisals! . . . 'Ah!', think others, 'If only we were still in the age of Zeuxis, who, according to the ancient writers, painted a bunch of grapes so lifelike that even the birds were deceived and came to peck at them!' A most significant nostalgia! Reduced to imitation, the artist would excel in the

7. Reg Butler (b. 1913). *Monument to the Unknown Political Prisoner.* First prize, International Sculpture Competition, London, 1953. Photo F. L. Rennett.

precise degree that he was faithful to nature; perfection would be attained when the work of art displayed the highest possible power of illusion; and the layman, possessed of an infallible criterion, would need only to compare before pronouncing a judgment beyond all risk of error, simply by measuring the effect of the illusion upon himself – without waiting for confirmation from the birds.

We should not treat this attitude lightly. It shows a sincere desire on the part of the man-in-the-street to understand and to have a secure basis for approval. His fear of being fooled really matters less to him than his wish to have a clear conscience in his judgment, and one cannot hold it against a man that he wants to be honest with himself.

Do people in fact have any such clear conscience? If we examine ourselves and, strong in our conviction that art should be the mirror of reality, turn to the works of former ages, we cannot help noticing that many of them, while respecting this idea, do not espouse it unconditionally. Though many people 9 may at first sight be captivated by Ciseri's *Entombment,* it will soon dawn on them in the light of 10 experience that Raphael's work, or Michelangelo's, has something more to it. On first entering the Sistine Chapel, do we not experience an incomparable thrill in the presence of this race of giants that occupies the vault? And are we not stunned with awe 11 at the sight of the *Last Judgment* on the far wall, sounding its ominous trumpet-blasts over the damned? It is thus that we come progressively to feel – even if not straight away – that art is not *only* the image of reality, but that it can be, and has the right to be, something else.

The more we think about it, the more strange doubts begin to arise. Have we perhaps been rather too hasty in our condemnations? When Modigliani 12 in his portrait of Leopold Zborowski presents us with an elongated body, with shoulders and neck like a bottle, is he really doing it to bewilder us? Can we still maintain with assurance that Braque, Picasso, Matisse and Léger – men like ourselves – are capable of spending their lives, each minute of their days, producing pictures whose sole object is to shock us? Think of the patience and trouble it would require! And for what? A success which they themselves would not believe in? No, it would be too absurd.

As our doubts increase, we wonder if perhaps it might be that the people who are scornfully described as 'advanced' are called so with good reason – because they are indeed in front, while we lag behind! For sure, the most important thing is to be honest

8. Pablo Picasso (b. 1881). *Seated Woman.* Farmington, James Thrall Soby coll.

with oneself; but we must be honest with other things, too. And there our clear conscience is called in question again: *is* art the copying of reality? *Can* it be? Has one the right to judge a work on resemblance to reality? Anyone with a grain of honesty must admit to a doubt.

Now, although most people react with hostility to art which they find disconcerting, it can be shown that this does not apply equally to all the arts. The form of a house may be discussed, but no-one takes it into his head to criticize the architect for lack of resemblance – for the very good reason that there are no such things as 'natural' buildings; all issue from the hand of man. For the architect, then, the problem does not arise. Thus we already have one exception from our decree that art is to be tied down to nature. And there are others. We do not object to a vase or a medal being decorated with stylized 13 animals. It seems perfectly 'natural', and we should more likely be offended by a brooch in the form of a bee that was too convincingly life-like! Wall-paper, carpets, ceramics and other decorative arts do not as 14 a rule have us looking for references in nature. The pleasure we derive from the shape of a vase, the

9. Antonio Ciseri (1821-1891). *Entombment*. Locarno, church of
the Madonna del Sasso.

10. Raphael (1483-1520). *Entombment*. Rome, Borghese Gallery.
Photo Anderson-Giraudon.

11. Michelangelo (1475-1564). *Last Judgment,* fresco in the Sistine
Chapel (detail). Rome, Vatican. Photo Anderson.

12. Amedeo Modigliani (1884-1920). *Portrait of the poet Leopold Zborowski*. São Paulo, Museum of Fine Arts. Photo Held.

13. Gallic art. *Horse with stylised head,* medal, 1st century B.C. Paris, Bibliothèque Nationale. Photo Corvina.

texture of a material or the design of a carpet seems sufficient in itself. It is not that we place little value on such things; on the contrary, we are attached to them because we find them beautiful, and the fact that they belong to the so-called 'minor arts' does nothing to diminish them in our estimation. So, with architecture we do not think of looking for natural models; and with the decorative arts, although models exist, we do not in fact resort to them. Our attitude to them is different from that which we feel bound to adopt towards painting and sculpture. Only these, apparently, oblige us to refer our judgments to reality. Clearly we must add to our former questions the following: *why* do we treat them differently? How have we come to apply to them a rule which we would not think of applying to architecture or the decorative arts?

Turning to history, we soon discover that men hardly ever have expected painting or sculpture to be a mirror, and that this is a quite recent notion, dating more or less from the Renaissance. But what are five centuries compared to the thousands of years during which art offered man not merely the likeness of his mortal frame but – transcending it – the rare flowers with which religion excited his imagination, as for example the manuscript page on which the figure of Christ is not so much crucified as enveloped 15 in a remorseless arabesque, stretching out his feeble arms above his puny legs, as if the painter's genius lay in weaving for him the most intricate of prisons! And it will not do to argue that this particular flower is a monstrous one. The whole of early Irish art is contained in a vision which forsakes human resemblance to spin a thousand and one variations of linear pattern, ceaselessly twisting and twining, and which finally exhausts itself when calligraphy becomes a substitute for the symbol it was originally intended to serve. For thousands of years the guardian genius of Egypt imposed its fertilizing 16 tyranny to represent the human image, not as a puny creature, at the mercy of the seasons, age and death, but as a fluent silhouette graced with the purity of good design and the durability of stone, the face in profile, eye drawn back, the shoulders full-face, hips three-quarters and legs in profile – men and gods triumphantly summarized in a body which is a living challenge to reality!

Though the Celtic art of Ireland endured but a while, and the art of Egypt for thousands of years,

14. Romanesque art. *Norman ship,* Bayeux Tapestry (detail), ► 11th century. Bayeux, Ancien Evêché. Photo Giraudon.

15. Irish art. *Crucifixion*. Book of Saint-Gall, 8th century. Saint-Gall (Switzerland) monastery library. Photo Hildegaard Morscher.

16. Egyptian art. *Tomb of Tut Ankh Amon* (detail), 14th century B.C. Egypt, Valley of the Kings. Photo Viollet.

neither was a slave to imitation. And from the ends of Asia to Easter Island, from cave-painting to the frescoes of Tavant, all the works of other civilizations bear the same testimony.

Certainly, it is a far cry from Raphael to a Negro 17 fetish, but the mere fact that neither is a product of 18 imitation warns us that they may have something in common. We cannot accept the fresco and reject the fetish, on the pretext that the one is closer to nature than the other, without grievously troubling that clear conscience which is our support. Already it has become a question, not of the work of art being the image of reality, but simply of being *near* to it, *reminding* us of it. Once this point is admitted, that is the end of the assurance which we thought we derived from our attitude. It is just what we were afraid of. We are unwilling to run the risks of the adventure to which art invites us, for, if we yield a little more ground, the most outrageous excesses of our contemporaries will soon be entitled to our admiration! Is it not true, after all, that the usual preference for the 'classical' is largely due to the fear of being led by modern art on to ground where one is all too likely to stumble? However, though it is true that art should never be confounded with reality, it does not follow that if one digresses as far as possible from reality masterpieces are bound to result. That, as you will have realized, is not the problem.

All this should be enough to clear our minds, were it not for the fact that history since the Renaissance (roughly from the 15th century to the dawn of modern art at the end of the 19th) has helped to aggravate the misunderstanding. First comes the invention of perspective, throwing open the picture like a window, pouring the whole world of visual appearances onto the canvas and turning the formal work of art into a 'view'. The human body, so long flattened to the picture-plane, is suddenly awarded volume, density and even the illusion of living flesh. Light, air and the play of shadows join in the fun, and reality soon becomes as fascinating as the Mona 19 Lisa, whose too celebrated smile is not only a symbol but a snare. Small wonder that so many painters and sculptors have been deceived by it!

Nevertheless, none of the great Renaissance artists, before or after Leonardo, fell into this temptation. We do not need to study Piero della Francesca's 20 figures for long to realize that, although they are recognizable and identifiable, they are only distantly related to reality. This emaciated old man is Adam, this man in his prime is Seth, and this withered old woman is Eve, yet, in spite of the drama they evoke, all this is of less importance than the grave pattern in which they are grouped. The human form is here a motif which the artist employs to conduct a kind of subtle ballet, where the 'inward eye' may take delight in what is beyond the outward eye's vision: movement, rhythm, harmony, the secret ferment of the art – sublime logic in which, enraptured, the inward eye learns to participate. Even while utilizing perspective and representing the human figure in the round, no true artist fails to subordinate them to aesthetic ends. If Renaissance art seems sometimes to be limited by naturalism, it is only so at its rim; it never succumbs to it.

But naturalism, royally instated among the higher forms of art by such men as Uccello, Masaccio, Piero della Francesca, Leonardo, Raphael and Michelangelo, is at the bottom of this misapprehension, whose pernicious effects have persisted to our own times. On the one hand, numerous 'artists', professing to follow in the steps of the masters, set them-

18. Raphael (1483-1520). *The Mass of Bolsena,* fresco (detail). Rome, Vatican. Photo Anderson-Giraudon.

17. Negro art. *Fang head,* carved wood, Gabon. Paris, Musée de l'Homme. Photo Thiriet.

19. Leonardo da Vinci (1452-1519). *Mona Lisa* (detail). Paris, Louvre. Photo Held.

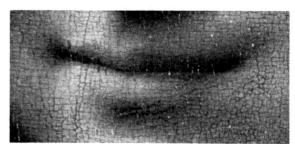

25

20. Piero della Francesca (1410/20-1492). *Death of Adam,* fresco, detail of the upper part of the *Legend of the True Cross.* Arezzo, church of St. Francis. Photo Anderson-Giraudon.

selves to vie with reality, giving imitation of form precedence over its disposition; on the other hand the public, beguiled into error by such constantly repeated (and applauded) dexterity, first accepted and then demanded that art should submit to it. Mediocrity flourished, academism moved in, and the colour-print sellers did the rest; the prejudice had taken root. Under the pretext of paying homage to Leonardo or Raphael, public favour was accorded to a Guido Reni or a Bonnat, to the worst products

21 of Saint-Sulpice or of 'official art'.

Ambiguity is so subtle a poison that even the art with which the Renaissance claimed kinship has suffered from it. It used to be believed that Greco-Roman sculpture alone possessed the secret of beauty, and it was praised, not as one of the loftiest expressions of human genius, but as an affirmation of the triumph of reality – a crudely grotesque error which fortunately has now been recognized as such, but which is still widely enough accepted to pass on some of its malign influence. Yet when we compare

22-23 a Greek statue with the photograph of an athlete in the same pose, the differences strike us at once. In practice one finds that no statue ever exactly follows the model. Thus the argument supposedly based on Renaissance and Greco-Roman art is a false one, used more often than not as an excuse.

Let us be clear about this. It appears that over the centuries art oscillates between realism and non-realism, but, through some mysterious sense of its own nature, avoids overstepping either limit. At the limit of realism it is rubbish: at the limit of non-realism it is nothing whatever – and Renaissance naturalism does not escape this law.

History confronts us with a fact: art is never identified with reality, in the commonly accepted sense of the word. But opposing this fact is another: works of art which move too far from reality antagonize us. It makes no difference to us whether or not

24-25 the Aztecs, the Chaldaeans, the Egyptians or the Chinese experience the same difficulty. We are concerned with our own reactions, our own problems. In short, we want *reasons* rather than facts. We are not immovably obstinate, but we want things at least to be explained, even if we are not persuaded.

It is worth noting here that we react differently to the art of a civilization and to an individual work. If we are perplexed and irritated by Reg Butler's project for a monument (page 19), it is above all because the design seems purposeless, its meaning eludes us. But supposing we go to a museum and linger among the Egyptian antiquities – in the Louvre, perhaps –

21. ... to the worst products of official art. E. Sonrel (b. 1874). *To Immortality*. Photo Braun.

27

we cannot help being impressed by a sense of under-lying unity. Despite the many differences between one object and another, we are aware of something which links them, a kind of spirit emanating from them, and we gradually come to feel it cannot be simply by chance – or by the arbitrary choice of the artists – that these works, spread over thousands of years, assert themselves through their own unique and appropriate characteristics. We see this persistence in representing man by *conventions* which withdraw him from reality, more and more as the result of considered reflexion, as a conscious decision. And if we get that far, we can scarcely avoid the idea that these conventions, far from being pointless, have a meaning. This is a crucial revelation, for the moment we allow that there is a *motive* for such a procedure we abandon our hostile attitude and cease to insist that reality must be the model for art, and our own criterion. At once works of art appear in a new light. It no longer seems necessarily perverse to modify the image of man, or indeed of nature itself. Once we are satisfied it is *legitimate,* then we are neither surprised nor upset to find that man may express himself in his works otherwise than he sees. The image he chooses seems to respond to an inner truth no less valid than that to which our senses bear witness. Nowadays we are not shocked by African idols, because we have ceased to look on them as clumsy or derisory *representations*. Deep in our being we become aware of a growing respect for the symbols which the myths of each race have called forth, and though we no longer believe in Horus, Gilgamesh or Zeus, we remember in all fairness that for centuries, and for countless human beings, they were the sovereign reality which both transcended and illuminated the everyday world.

We now see that the problem of art cannot be contained within the terms which we laid down at the beginning of this chapter. Reality as perceived by our senses and defined by our common sense is not the only thing that matters: the profounder reality of myths counts for much more. When one has grasped this, one no longer expects artists simply to imitate,

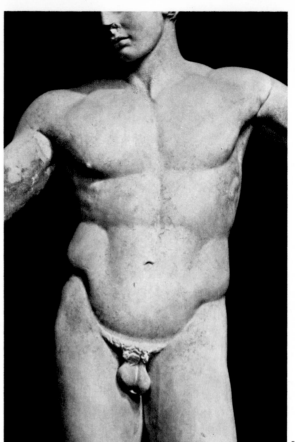

22

22. Polycletus. *Diadumenos* (detail of an antique copy), 5th century B.C. London, British Museum. Photo British Museum.

23. *When we compare a Greek statue with the photograph of an athlete in the same pose, the differences strike us at once.*

23

28

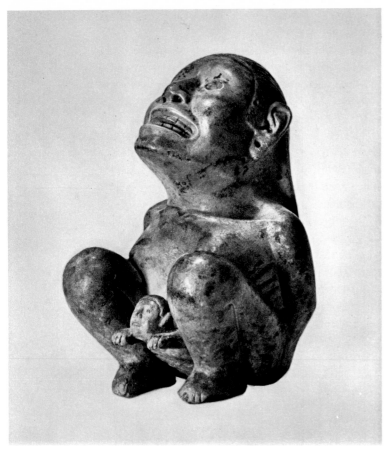

24. Aztec art. *Parturient woman,* probably a goddess of childbirth, 15th century. Washington, private collection. Photo Josi Oster, Paris, Musée de l'Homme.

25. Egyptian art. *Nut, Goddess of the Sky,* Dynasty, about 350 B.C. New York, Metropolitan Museum. Photo Metropolitan Museum.

for the reality they aspire to is of a higher order, to which we also may aspire through their works.

But what are we, as men of the twentieth century, to make of the art which is now produced all around us? It must be confessed that the guiding myths, which once were so vital, have either disappeared or survive only in the impotence of decline, but, curiously enough, the artists have shown no sign of capitulating, for all that. In fact it is doubtful if they have ever been more numerous – Paris alone, it is said, harbours close on fifty thousand of them! Could they really be expected to live on a moribund past, to suffer privation for the sake of a futile nostalgia, to invite contempt and sarcasm in a spirit of humility or of expiation? Obviously not. Deprived of the myths which inspired their ancestors, they seek to invent new ones, which they feel they can give shape to in their art, and they do so in the unconquerable hope that other men will consent to share them. From the beginning of time the artist's function has remained the same: to express the invisible reality

which – beyond our physical existence – is the true essence of man. The art of our own age is making a prodigious and heroic effort to preserve the spirit which former ages have bequeathed to us.

This effort could not be made without some surprises and dissensions. There was hardly time to digest Impressionism before Fauvism appeared, then Cubism and so on, until it almost seems as if art is gaining speed on us, and suffocating us instead of bringing us new life. Also our fear of being misled naturally warns us not to seize the shadow for the substance, not to let go of the reality we know in favour of the unknown which is offered us, even if the latter is more highly prized. It is in times of crisis like our own that one is most liable to cling to the prejudice of reality and relapse into error.

Are we, then, going to turn back in the face of this obstacle? Since we do not find any immediate sense in the artistic endeavours of our contemporaries, are we going to decide once and for all that there is none? Are we going to condemn them in the name of a reality which we have seen to be incompatible with art? Are we to take refuge in ignorance or shall we accept arbitration in the matter? Is there *no* way to be both just and clear-sighted? This is perhaps the place to recall the distinction which I made above. With regard to architecture and the decorative arts, we remember, there is no impulse to refer to natural models. The appropriateness of a building and the attraction of its form, the taste which makes us choose a particular carpet, jug or jewel, convince us that aesthetic pleasure is self-sufficient. Now this pleasure, which we experience in different ways and degrees, is always felt to be connected with *quality*. Might we not employ it in the same way with respect to painting and sculpture? If the significance of a picture or statue does not strike us right away, is it not reasonable, before rejecting it out of hand, to see if it has anything of this 'quality' by which we recognize a work of art? In the last resort it is *aesthetic value* which constitutes the work of art and comprises its reality.

The problem of Art and Reality as traditionally propounded is a false problem. No art at any time has been merely imitative, but has always been a process of adaptation and redisposition, through which man is made aware of an image distinct from that of his senses. Past civilizations show that art depends on myths. In our age it is seeking them. Both ancient works and modern ones can contain a *quality* which gives them life, and which it is in our power to comprehend.

Therefore, in the presence of a work which troubles us, we owe it to the artist (and to ourselves) to examine it. Clear conscience will depend neither on acceptance nor refusal, but on a balanced judgment, that is to say a judgment one believes in because one has reasons for doing so. Only quality can provide material for this judgment.

26

26. Chinese art. *Green Dragon,* ritual object, 6th-5th century B.C. Paris, Musée Guimet. Photo Musée Guimet.

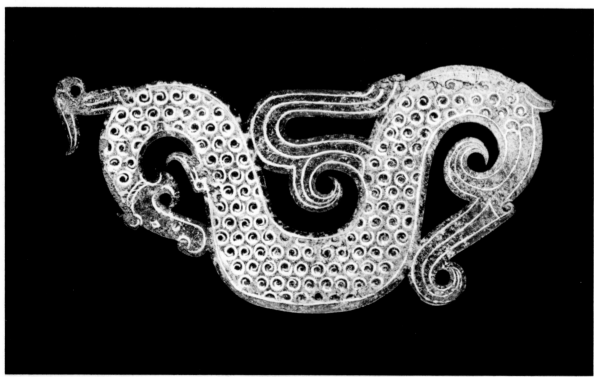

First contact

The work of art
and the spectator

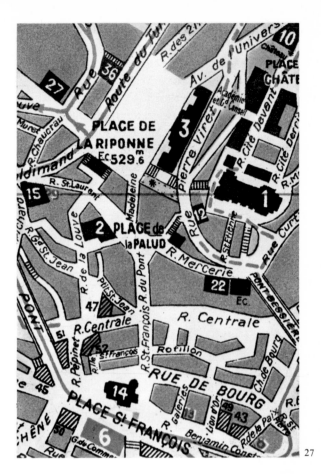

Since it is our attitude that is in question, let us try to define it. The very confusion that prevails around us and within us obliges us continually to take stock of where we are, and we are grateful for anything that can provide a point of reference. When I enter a strange town, I look first of all for the names of the 27 streets, and the streets themselves are real to me only in so far as they help me to find my bearings. Until I have done so, they have no pictorial attributes, and the whole town is reduced to the plan which I hold in my hands. But when I have got to know the place a little, and am no longer afraid of losing my way, my attitude changes. Wandering at random, I observe the people, the shops and the houses. From being the mere landmarks which they were when I arrived, the 28 streets have become an animated landscape, full of movement, sounds and smells, adding up to a total impression in which I share, and of which I am myself a part. Of course, it was all there just the same when I first entered the town, but I was too preoccupied with finding my way to take it in. Thus the image which I form of things does not depend solely on the things themselves. My state of mind is equally important.

It is worth while inquiring into this relationship with external objects, which permits them to appear in such different guises. Surely the misunderstandings that arise over works of art are largely due to our approaching them in the wrong *attitude of mind.* By

27. *The streets are real only in so far as they help me to find my bearings.*
Plan of Lausanne. Photo Held.

28. *From being mere landmarks the streets have become an animated landscape.*
Lausanne, place de la Palud. Photo Held.

definition, painting and sculpture consist, in the widest sense, of images. Let us examine a few examples of how we approach them.

Consider a passport photograph. What is its function? To confirm the classic description of profession, place and date of birth, height, colour of hair and special peculiarities. That is all it is for the customs officer – a means of information and identification. A passport photograph (which is, in its way, a portrait) exists for a precise purpose, apart from which it is of no interest or importance to anyone. Its sole object is to provide information, serving to identify an individual by showing his distinguishing features in the form of an image, just as a street-plan identifies the features of a town.

It need hardly be said that a work of art, while also presenting an image, calls for a quite different kind of approach, though we realize from common experience that this is far from being generally understood. What a lot of people still protest – with an insistence that is the measure of their sincerity – that a portrait 'misses' the sitter's appearance, and are shocked by what they are pleased to call the painter's 'distortions'. And this is not only true of portraiture; in other genres the prejudice is equally strong.

Now, the man who asks 'what does this represent?', and who *goes no further,* is merely acting like a customs official. So far it is just a question of error – a harmful error, maybe, but one which can be explained and, on reflection, redressed. Yet it is not as easy as all that! Since the spectator expects not only that a work of art should give him an image, but also that the image should possess quality, he goes on misguidedly to suppose that the quality depends on its documentary value. He is then guilty of a double mistake – first in not adopting a proper attitude of mind, secondly in presuming that his own erroneous attitude is the only correct one. That is why prejudices are so hard to eradicate; they are not just matters of opinion but virtually articles of faith.

None the less, when we stop being obstinate, we can readily agree that the true function of a work of art is not to impart information. The distinction we draw between a document and a picture is enough to prove it – the document can be reduced to its content, and the picture cannot. When information is extracted from the one, it loses its relevancy: once through the customs, the traveller is handed back his passport, now of no use to him, since a document only 'exists' in so far as it is of service. With a work of art it is quite the contrary: its virtue is in no way diminished by what we get out of it.

There are other attitudes, innocuous in themselves, which can be equally deceptive; for instance, our attitude to a family photograph-album. Happily turning its pages, conscious only of the echoes which these images evoke from our past, we share a sort of intimate complicity, from which any of our friends who may be present are not altogether excluded. They too begin to feel a gentle nostalgia as our memories stir their own, and gradually the same tender emotion is shared by all.

In this case the image is not regarded simply as a document. Certainly it does give information, but primarily it is an excuse for an effusion of sentiment. The attitude here is emotional, and the feelings evoked by the image are what gives it its value. We might say that here our response to the image is a response of the heart.

While not claiming that all human beings have exactly the same feelings, we cannot deny that they share a certain community of emotion. If you see a woman in tears, you do not need to know *why* she weeps before being moved yourself to sadness and compassion. If, on the other hand, you see someone in fits of laughter, you are hard put to it not to laugh yourself. In short, there is always something communicative in the expression of feeling. We put ourselves in the place of others; sadness or merriment become real for us when we have, so to speak, mimed their expression. Nor is there any need for the person to be present for the feeling to be communicated; an image is enough. Eric von Stroheim disturbs us; 29-30 Dany Carrel delights us. The former's photograph exhales an aura of damnation; in the other we see only a fresh and pert ingenuousness.

The emotional approach seems so natural that it is difficult to get rid of it even when it is irrelevant. It continually gets mixed up in our appreciation of art, especially in the case of painting and sculpture. Diderot, with the best intentions in the world, made it the basic principle of his aesthetic theory, and since this error is so widespread, it is worth quoting an example from his writings. Falconet's *L'Amitié* 31 enraptured him, and here is how he described it:

'It is the standing figure of a girl who holds a heart in her hands; it is her own, and she offers it tremulously. This is a piece filled with soul and sentiment; one's heart is touched and softened as one beholds it. Her face beseeches acceptance of the gift in the most lively, sweet and modest way. Poor child, she would be so disappointed if it were refused! The head is of the rarest character; I truly believe that there is in it a blend of eagerness and reverence such as has

29-30. *An image is enough. Eric von Stroheim disturbs us; Dany Carrel delights us.*

31. Etienne-Maurice Falconet (1716-1791). *L'Amitié,* marble. Paris, Maurice de Rothschild coll. Photo Held.

not been seen before. It is sensibility, candour, innocence, timidity and discretion all fused into one. The expression of these parted lips, these outstretched arms, this body that leans hesitantly forward, is beyond description. Her heart beats; she hears – and hopes! I declare that Greuze's girl mourning her little bird is a hundred leagues away from such pathos as this. How beautiful, and how novel it is!...[1]

Re-reading the *Salons,* one finds they are written almost entirely in this vein. The underlying fallacy is obvious. By a sort of *emotive contagion* Diderot appreciates Falconet's statue *by virtue of the sentiments which the young girl's figure awakens in him.* So far one does not altogether disagree with him; but when he takes this emotive contagion of the subject to be the very essence of the work's quality, one realizes that he is on the wrong track. Would not a 'statue vivante' (as one speaks of a 'tableau vivant') have been just as good, if not better? Which leads us to ask why Falconet should have gone to the trouble of fashioning his out of marble! If, as everyone in the long run must agree, a statue is something other than its model, it is because its *formal qualities* must be taken into account.

Even though we are less susceptible to errors of this sort nowadays, sentimentality is still very much alive. Plenty of people are still prepared to believe

32 that Andrea del Sarto's *Madonna of the Harpies* is one of the highest summits of art. Crowds gather in the room where it is displayed, the guides never fail to devote the best part of their time to it, and the spectators go into raptures – rather as if they were being privileged to peep into the Virgin's family album – and end up by feeling that they, along with Saint Francis and Saint John the Evangelist, have been admitted into the intimacy of the Holy Family...

After the *Madonna of the Harpies* the *Madonna del*
33 *Granduca* seems somewhat unapproachable! The Virgin's face has lost its motherly expression, the infant Jesus no longer shows off in front of the visitors, and the Madonna's robes no longer seek to catch the eye with a contrived *negligée.* Raphael deals squarely with us.

[1] Diderot, *Salon de 1765.*

32. Andrea del Sarto (1486-1531). *Madonna of the Harpies.* Florence, Uffizi. Photo Held.

33. Raphael (1483-1520). *Madonna del Granduca.* Florence, Palazzo Pitti. Photo Held.

We may conclude that a work of art offers a relationship that is different from our relationships to the touching episodes of daily life. If we ignore this, then we take into account only the subject and the superficial emotion which it communicates. So doing, we affront the true nature of the work and commit the further injustice of measuring its quality by an element that is foreign to it. The *emotional approach* to a work of art is no more appropriate than the *documentary approach*.

Need we then despair of finding the right one? In spite of so many causes of misunderstanding, the signs of an increasing general interest in artistic knowledge are even more numerous. Venice and Rome absorb their seasonal influx of visitors; can we believe they come only to pay homage to vanished glory, or to enjoy the novelties of foreign travel on the cheap? Gondolas are all very well as a tourist attraction, but no-one who has ever seen the crowds in the Accademia delle Belle Arti could suppose that they are motivated only by curiosity and a taste for the picturesque. Paris, Rome, Venice and Florence are all called 'cities of art'. Well, people do not flock to a place of their own free will for nothing; one has to admit that where they gather in such numbers *something* must be going on. It is perhaps to the point to recall that the Greek word for church, 'ecclesia', signifies an 'assembly'. This is not to suggest that art is a new religion, but to point out that its devotees grow in number because it offers them something they can get nowhere else, that it alone can give. Perhaps it is in its power to give us even more . . . and that is not so bold an assertion as it may sound.

Consider how the retrospective exhibition of Paul Cézanne was received when it was put on by the *Salon d'Automne* in 1904. The leading art critics seized on it as a chance to put paid to the artist's reputation for good and all . . . 'As for M. Cézanne', fumed Camille Mauclair in *La Revue,* 'his name will be remembered for the outstanding artistic joke of these last fifteen years.' Though less violent, Arsène Alexandre in *Le Figaro* was no less categorical: 'What strikes any impartial mind on examining a painting by Cézanne is that, alongside an indisputable nobility of conception at the point of departure, there is an utter incapacity to follow the road to its end.' *Le Petit Parisien,* through the voice of Valensol, made condemnation more effective by the use of comparison: 'The fellow does landscapes, seascapes, still-lifes, portraits, in a hit-or-miss, random way, and the process reminds one rather of the pictures which schoolboys make by squashing flies in the folds

of a piece of paper.' The wrath of Marcel Fouquier in *Le Journal* even called on the future to bear witness: 'His still-lifes, which have been extolled to the skies, are crude in technique and heavy in effect. We have been told they will one day hang by the Chardins in the Louvre – but that happy day is not near!'

We need not pause to pour contempt on this chorus, so presumptuously and prematurely chanting the funeral dirge of Cézanne. As Bouyer commented in *La Revue Bleue*: 'Ah! Cézanne! Blessed are the poor in spirit, for theirs is the kingdom of art!'

Let us go back to the facts.

'The unfinished appearance of Cézanne's canvases' 35 writes Elie Faure, some twenty to thirty years later, 'gives those who have not encompassed his mind the impression of a wayward character, that restricts itself to jotting down notes from nature – authentic notes, maybe, but summary, caught by instinct on the wing. In truth each one of them represents an enormous labour, a spiritualization slowly and painfully extracted from the purely sensual elements that were its origin.' And he ends with these words: 'The shadow which closes in on us from our fortieth year 34 may have weighed on his heart, but did not deflect him from the mission which he felt was all important. Nor did his tardy and qualified success deflect him. *He knew that he was the greatest painter in Europe.*' [1]

René Huyghe is no less emphatic: 'From this man and his oeuvre the whole of modern art is descended . . . the time has come to think of Cézanne not as the justification of a particular cause, but for his human importance . . . Never in the whole history of art has a man clung more steadfastly to what is immutable . . . He is the final offshoot of the Latin tradition, working to restore the certainties that had been undermined since the 17th century . . . Patiently, passionately, he seeks out what is solid, durable and permanent – the shapes, the substructures and the eternal foundations of reality and thought, of the outward and the inward life . . . He will always disturb those for whom life is quiet, normal and without problems; for the rest he will remain one of the most heroic adventures of the human mind'.[2]

Let us get this quite straight. Fact number one: in 1904 the majority of critics and of the general public deny any quality in Cézanne. Fact number two: thirty years later he is recognized as one of the great artists of all time. No need to meditate on this . . .

[1] Elie Faure, *Histoire de l'Art Moderne*. Ed. Plon.
[2] René Huyghe, *Cézanne*. Ed. Plon.

Instead, let us note a third fact, one so self-evident that I almost hesitate to draw attention to it: *Cézanne's pictures have not changed.* It requires but little thought to arrive at the conclusion that, if the paintings have remained the same, then it is the critics and the public who have changed; we *see differently* from our predecessors, we *feel differently,* and we *judge differently!*

This is surely very astonishing. *Are* we so different from the men of the beginning of this century? Who could persuade us that our thoughts and feelings have been modified to the point where these men are stranger to us than are the last of the New-Caledonians who have survived into our time? Yet, if we were really just the same as the preceding generation, how does it come about that we diverge from them on this point? It happens in this way: although we have not changed in so far as the problems of ordinary life are concerned, we have discovered in Cézanne – the conclusion is inescapable – *a quality that has become for us a new reality.* Thus quality in a work of art is neither a thing, nor an idea, nor a concept, nor a sensation; it is this power which makes us *change* ideas and feelings, and which finally *changes* our ways of looking at things. It is not (as is

sometimes lightly said) that it 'transforms the world'; we ourselves are what it transforms.

You will understand that this takes both time and trouble! . . . As the poet Reverdy (in *Self-Defence*) has lucidly expressed it: 'One is more accustomed to life than to art; hence the success of works which give an appearance of life. To present a work which rises above this appearance is to demand a formidable change of habit.'

The aesthetic approach requires us to relinquish our habitual consciousness – that which governs our contacts with the world and with other beings. Besides the response of the heart and of the mind there is also the *response to quality.* This is acquired at the price of a change of heart, of which the first effect is to make us accept that things are not only *what they are,* but also *what art makes them in our eyes.* We are not chained to our consciousness as to a perfected instinct. Without being God, we can none the less create forms of reality which raise us above our natural condition. Art does not usurp divine powers, but is the fulfilment of our humanity. For the artist this is *conquest,* for the spectator it is *discovery*; and it is on a voyage of discovery that we must embark.

34. Paul Cézanne (1839-1906). *Self-portrait with a Palette.* Zürich, Bührle coll. Photo Held.

35. Paul Cézanne (1839-1906). *Woodland.* Formerly Vollard coll. ▶ Photo Held.

Materials

There we are, then: contact with life is one thing, and contact with art is another. No *Montagne Sainte-Victoire* by Cézanne will be identical with the actual mountain of that name, for the artist adapts reality and recomposes it, while the spectator makes a corresponding adjustment of his normal consciousness. If we forget this we shall go astray, and art will remain no more than the occasion of much misunderstanding and bad reasoning.

Having got this clear in our minds, let us now examine the question of *materials*. One may imagine the most marvellous things, conceive the loftiest projects or the most exquisite harmonies in one's head – for all the world like a man of genius – without in fact doing anything. As there can be no art without works, there can be no works without material. It is as well to remember this, especially in an age like ours, when so many people put forward airy proposals, proclaim manifestoes or lay down programmes for this or that – *and* find other people credulous enough to follow them.

Yet, just as sound does not in itself make music, material does not in itself make a work of visual art. Through the one, music is made audible; through the other, the work of art is made visible. Thus

36

37

36. Paul Cézanne (1839-1906). *La Montagne Sainte-Victoire.* Zürich, Bührle coll. Photo Held.

37. La Montagne Sainte-Victoire, photograph of the motif. Document John Rewald.

38. Pablo Picasso (b. 1881). *Crane,* painted bronze. In the possession of the artist.

material is a necessary though not self-sufficient condition for the existence of visual art.

You may ask: 'What materials are we talking about?' Simply, the architect's stone, bricks, cement, marble and concrete; the sculptor's wood, bronze and (again) stone and marble; all the variety of pigments used by the painter – in short, of all the materials which nature and industry have put at our disposal, those which the artist commonly makes use of. Of course, artists make their choice from what is available, but sculptors and painters do not invent new stones and pigments, any more than poets invent new words. The artist's concern is not with the nature of material, but with the use that can be made of it.

How about the average layman? Does material count for much in his appreciation of art? Very little, I should say, for he tends to look for the more obvious factors, such as colour and the general effect. But, since material is as essential as form itself for a work's existence, we may as well see if our attitude towards it is all it should be.

'Iron', we read in the dictionary, 'is a bluish-grey metal'. That is scarcely saying anything we did not know already, for we are familiar enough with the *appearance* of most materials. We know sawn wood by its rough, lined surface, a pebble by its polished smoothness, and so on . . . indeed, we have no difficulty whatever in distinguishing a steel bar from a plank of wood. We take note of the appearance of materials in the first place *to distinguish one from another.*

The dictionary continues its description of iron by saying: '. . . serving a great variety of uses in industry', thus exhibiting our normal attitude to materials, which is to consider them (and matter in general) in terms of their practical qualities rather than their appearance. *Utility* is what primarily interests us, and we appreciate materials according to their usefulness.

Before inquiring whether or not works of art modify this relationship, we should first of all consider what the artist requires of his material. He needs it to take a shape and keep it – that is, to possess some degree of plasticity. For obvious reasons, water would be of no use to him; fluid in the extreme, it can be regarded either as too ungovernable or (and it comes to the same thing) as too docile. On the other hand it can be seen that materials of extreme hardness have never defeated the artist; carvings have been made since the earliest times in basalt, granite and diorite. Thus, there is another essential quality to be added to that of plasticity – *resistance.*

39. Michelangelo (1475-1564). *The Delphic Sibyl,* fresco on the vault of the Sistine Chapel, detail. Rome, Vatican. Photo Anderson-Giraudon.

40. Michelangelo (1475-1564). *Madonna and Child,* marble, detail. Bruges, church of Our Lady of Bruges. Photo Giraudon.

41. Romanesque art. *Head of Christ*, stained-glass, 2nd half of 11th century. Strasbourg, Musée de l'Œuvre de Notre-Dame. Photo Giraudon.

In fact, both these qualities would appear to be as necessary in industry as they are for the artist. The machine which makes car-bodies exploits both the plasticity and the resistance of the metal. But how is the metal itself regarded? Merely as a substance which will accept with indifference the shape in which it is to be moulded – so much so that nowadays the lighter and less costly 'plastic materials', derived from nylon, are invading every branch of motor-car bodywork. Here material is simply a *means*. Its quality is passive obedience, and in itself it is no more than the temporary frame for a certain shape, to be thrown on the scrap-heap when finished with.

The resistance which the artist meets – and seeks – is of quite another kind. Far from using matter simply as a means, he treats it as an element no less 'active' than himself, and therefore is not content to impose form upon it mechanically. One may say that a sculptor is 'worked upon' by his stone no less than it is worked upon by him; the block offers resistance to the blows of the chisel, and the artist feels this not as mere passivity but as a stimulus which can and should be reckoned with. While he collaborates with the stone, the stone collaborates with him, and from their mutual 'understanding' form is born.

While on this subject, we can dispose of certain legends, dear to the popular imagination (a sign usually of mental laziness), such as that of a frowning Michelangelo striding the hills of Carrara and in imagination peopling the whole landscape with living statues! . . . This is the old superstition which confounds the artist with the Creator: 'Let the dry land appear: and it was so.' But for mortals it is a long step from the subjunctive to the indicative! Unlike God, the artist does not create matter; he *works with it*.

Watch the hand of the craftsman – the coppersmith's fist; the potter's fingers on his clay; the engraver's palm, closed on his burin – and you will see that matter is anything but inert for the artist. Like himself, it has impulses and affinities – it has 'temperament'. Need I resort to the absurd to prove this? If it were just a question of giving shape to a material that remains indifferent, why – in view of modern technical progress – should people go on carving wood and stone, and why should people still want paintings? The machine has ousted neither the sculptor nor the painter because sculptor and painter bring to light in solid matter something which they alone can discover; and we still have the taste for works of art, preferring the original to the reproduction, because we are aware of this 'something' conferred upon matter by the artist's hand.

42. Renaissance art, *Saint Martin,* stained-glass, 17th century. Paris, Louvre. Photo Giraudon.

'Liberty' is of small value to the artist. The man who (like the machine) looks for a material that will be at his mercy – utterly compliant to his wishes – can at best turn out a standardized article. The point where the artist is content to use matter for a limited number of deliberate and well-tried effects is the point where mere virtuosity begins. Instead of being stimulated in his researches by each new encounter with material, he limits himself to a few variations in which vivacity of handling cannot conceal an intrinsic lack of character.

Picasso, menaced as he is by his astonishing talent, continually breaks new ground. He is accused of sensationalism – as if other people's disapproval could matter to him when he is aware (painfully so, no doubt) that the peril is within himself. As soon as one form seems in danger of exhaustion, he tears himself away to invent another, and in the same way he experiments with material for the renewal of his genius. Paint, stone, bronze, pottery – he lays his tireless hands on everything about him. Indeed, he has even called on the humblest of utensils – gas-tap, shovel, piping and table-fork – to yield up unsuspected secrets, so that a new affirmation of victory may rise in the shape of his *Crane*. The man seems 38 almost to be 'possessed' – as if the gods decreed that this too fortunate mortal should be tormented by a relentless gadfly, as a reminder that all his gifts avail him nothing unless he unceasingly probes and questions *matter* – so that they may find expression in a work of art.

True artists recognize at once the material with which they have an affinity. Can one imagine Michelangelo as a sculptor in wood? He would have reduced it to splinters! Yet, when the Pope shut him up in the Sistine Chapel, with what near-divine mastery he discovered the potentialities of fresco. One has only to compare one of his painted figures with one of his 39-40 sculptures to see how he avoids demanding of paint the polished surface, the caressing play of shadow, the *nuances* in the progression from one plane to the next, which he demands of marble. In the fresco the volumes are blocked out in strongly defined colours, to which the modelling imparts a monumental (and not, as is so often said, a sculptural) grandeur.

Whatever an artist's talent, he can do nothing worthwhile unless he is 'in sympathy with' his material. The history of art is littered with failures that have no other cause. Is not this what happened

43. Greek art. Column of the *Temple of Juno*, 5th century B.C. Agrigento. Photo Viollet.

to the Greek sculptors of the decadent age, when they ignored the rightful needs of bronze and marble, and tried to achieve the reflected lights and flesh-tones which were admired in the painters of their time? And think of the fate of stained glass! It was simple and robust originally, deriving its power from the actual substance of the glass, but when the Renaissance exalted the prestige of great pictorial compositions, that was the end of it! From then on, every stained-glass window emulated painting. Perspective and modelling became the rule, as we see in this 17th century window, which, for all its splendour, owes more to the resources of painting than to the radiance of sunlight shining through fragments of vitrified paste. Churches were embellished with pseudo-pictures.

I do not mean to suggest there should be anything restrictive in the relationship of the artist to his material. Neither ought to dominate the other, and one can no more predetermine the capabilities of the one than of the other. The all-important thing is that they should agree in 'temperament', for matter has potentialities which it is no use trying to force, and which it will yield only to patient and persistent questioning. Perhaps it is now more clearly understood that matter is the medium through which form becomes not only visible, but *tangible*.

In spite of technical progress and the daily discoveries of science, we retain mysterious links with the natural elements, as if those 'humors', to which our ancestors attached such importance, still flowed into us from down the ages. Gaston Bachelard [1] has made some fascinating observations on the subject of fire and water, tending to demonstrate that humanity's deepest roots are always in our natural surroundings, though we are usually unaware of the fact. Thus, wooden partitions 'act' on us differently from walls of stone or cement; a cottage has a warmth of atmosphere which is quite foreign to the buildings of a large town; and not without reason we say of certain houses, covered uniformly with some protective surface-coating, that they are 'gloomy', while those which have retained their original masonry never give us this feeling. A solid country farm-house

[1] See his stimulating books: *L'Eau et les Rêves; La Terre et les Rêveries de la Volonté* (ed. Corti); and especially the most recent, *La Poétique de l'Espace* (P. U. F.), in which the author, breaking with the rational tradition, shows how we project ourselves 'poetically' into the world, and the world into ourselves.

44. Byzantine art. *Attendant of Empress Theodora,* mosaic, detail, 6th century. Ravenna, church of S. Vitale. Photo Held.

45. Japanese art. *Head of Amida Buddha,* wood, end of 12th century. London, British Museum. Photo Bernard Juillerat.

can give us enduring pleasure through the splendour of its stonework, its colour and its grain. Have we not all at some time or another felt this 'something' in the quality of stone – when gazing at a church, a tower, or a column? The more we consult our own intimate experience, the more examples we will recall of 'sympathy' with inanimate matter.

Perhaps we see it most clearly inside our houses, where we describe this or that furnishing as 'cold' or 'heavy'. Interior decorators understand this well, and try to match things up to achieve a pleasant over-all impression: 'gay' curtains, a carpet that strikes a 'muted note', a 'warm accent' here, direct lighting that is 'hard', or indirect lighting that is 'soft' – and so on. Materials have many other 'virtues' that could be enumerated, but in fact we pay little attention to them, are only vaguely conscious that they exist, being content simply to experience their agreeable or disagreeable effects without analysing them.

Thus we can look at matter in several different ways: sometimes we are concerned with its *appearance* (when distinguishing one material from another), at other times with its *practical qualities* (which Industry exploits to ensure the efficacy of its products), and at times with a *mutual relationship*. In the first instance we are regarding it as the *sum of its characteristics,* in the second as a *means,* and in both as a *thing.* In the third instance, and only in the third instance, we regard it as an *entity* which has links with us and acts on us.

It is matter as an *entity* which art reveals, freeing it from the associations that normally veil it from our eyes. When we cease to look for its utilitarian quali-ties, we can recapture the retina's natural sensibility. Far from being disagreeable, the rough, unequal surface of mosaic is precisely what we like about it, giving to the image a flavour that is at once tart and full-bodied. Wood gives us the sensation of its compacted substance and of the uneven passage from one surface plane to the next, while stone makes us aware of the loose or tight-knit texture of its grain. Oil-painting satisfies us with juicy qualities that fresco and gouache do not possess, while these offer other qualities, of a drier kind as a rule, which we find equally enjoyable. Thanks to the way in which art treats matter, the whole world is invested with flavour. 'Everything is intelligible!' as the poet cried, repeating the words of Pythagoras. The work of art, releasing us from the habitual modes of thought which hedge us in, helps us to renew our conscious-ness of things by giving us a privileged experience of them. It is not that matter is imbued with life, as a facile pantheism would have it: no, there is not in stone a 'soul' of an inferior order (at least, I do not think so), but what we do know is that any material, when considered attentively, brings us into contact with an entity that is both definite and durable.

The work of art does even more. The only differ-ence between the block of stone in the quarry and the block which Michelangelo has carved is that the one speaks in the language of nature, and the other in the language of mankind. The former is to us a closed language; we hear it, but do not understand it. It is rather like listening to a Chinese or a Japanese speaking his own tongue; however hard we listen, the words remain unintelligible. That is not saying that they mean nothing at all to us; on the contrary, certain sounds may charm us, others surprise us, and others again strike unexpected chords of response in us. At all events, we are not indifferent to them. But the work of art permits us to hope for something more than this, for the artist is able to translate the 'closed' language of matter into an 'open' one, or, more precisely, to transmute the sparse and muffled sounds of nature into a human language.

Can we understand this language? Yes, if we are prepared to modify our normal relationship with matter. When considering only its appearance, we confine ourselves to the surface of things: 'iron, a bluish-grey metal . . .' When considering it in terms of objects we can use, we reduce it to the status of a means to an end. Fortunately many a half-buried memory and many a daily experience remind us that matter is no stranger to our sensibility, and that its 'presence' acts on us in many ways.

In art, then, matter is never merely the framework of a form. Wild and docile at the same time, it offers to the artist the resistances and the affinities that are its 'temperament', and he does not cow it into sub-mission, but woos it gently to his will. If he treats it indifferently or tyrannously, he will produce from it no more than sterile mimicry – or muteness. To make his material 'speak' he must first respect it. It is one of the lessons of art history that there can be no great work without respect for material.

Let the spectator show the same respect! Instead of 'serving a great variety of uses', let matter be for him the living substance in which each new reality takes on life before his eyes. One can no more appreciate a work of art without regard for its material than one can speak a foreign language with-out regard for pronunciation, articulation, and so on; for awareness of material is what makes our response an *experience,* and not merely an idea.

Form

It used to be said that 'Nature abhors a vacuum'. Science long ago exploded this particular myth, but without altering our way of looking at things. Nature still seems like an inexhaustible fabric from which we cut out the stuff of things. Every object occupies a portion of space, bounded by an outline. Such is the nature of our familiar world, of which memory is custodian; and men go about like snails, with the shell of their habitual world upon their backs – their dwelling, and their refuge at the least alarm.

This is not only true of the world of visible objects. The mind's world, too, has need of *familiar forms* in which we instal ourselves. For example, a man who respected neither grammar nor syntax would be doomed to silent isolation, since communication is made possible only by the forms of language. One realizes this clearly enough when attempting to think in a foreign language. How difficult then it is to formulate the ideas which, in one's own speech, would seem to 'run' of their own accord! Indeed, no foreign tongue can ever seem entirely 'natural'! It is the same with our thought processes. The logic taught in our schools has in the course of centuries moulded a western mentality, which is altogether alien to oriental and primitive peoples, who through long ages have been trained in other modes of thought, and vice versa.

Whether it is describing the external configuration of an object, or the sum of qualities belonging to a concrete or an abstract entity, we may say that it is *form,* in the first place, which establishes the *structure of the world* in which we live. Without it, all would be chaos. That is where habit stands us in good stead; by providing us with the 'double' of our familiar world, it succeeds in dispelling our anxieties.

It is not surprising, therefore, that in spite of every admonition we are so strongly tempted to confound the *forms of art* with 'natural' forms! Since we want, above all, to feel secure, why should we take unnecessary risks with artists? Unless, that is, they take pains to reassure us, like the host of still-life painters who flourished in 17th century Holland – Maria van Oosterwyck, for example, whose *Flower-piece* is tran- 46 quillity itself! Every bloom and herb is immediately recognizable; each is presented in the form which nature gave it – the sunflower with its ragged petals, the nasturtium with its trumpet-shaped corolla, the rose folded in upon its heart, the carnation in its petticoat-freshness – this is more than a copy, it is a

46. Maria van Oosterwyck (1630-1693). *Flower-piece*. The Hague, Mauritshuis. Photo Mauritshuis.

49. Marc Chagall (b. 1887). *The Cock.* Vence, in the artist's possession. Photo Archives Photographiques, Paris.

reconstitution of reality, as if at heart the painter wanted to be a gardener, and to be taken for one.

However, even in a case like this, where realism would seem to have attained its limit, one cannot escape one simple thought – the thought that the painting, for all its exceeding fidelity, is not nature!

No object can escape the destructive hand of time, and, in so far as it is an object, a picture is no exception to the rule, but suffers the common fate of all things. The stretcher disintegrates, the colours fade, changed by a subtle and pernicious alchemy. Nevertheless, whether the artist be skilful or unskilful, it is obvious that the time contained in the painting is *another* time, as if artistic form were able to arrest the flux of things, suspend the passage of the hours, even to conjure the power of death – as in this Saint Sebastian whom Memling offers, stripped yet 47 proud, to martyrdom; or Chardin's jug and pipe, 48 which have lain so long in silent communion.

I need hardly point out that if a work of art has to do with *another* time, it also has to do with *another* space. Whatever the artist's resources, he can never make the surface actually recede in depth. We know with what eagerness Uccello applied himself to mastering the laws of perspective, 'sweetest of mistresses' as he called it. While observing that Maria van Oosterwyck's vase 'goes round', that the rose has 'volume' and that the carnation is 'in front of' the sunflower, I am still aware that this play of volumes does not in fact extend beyond the picture-surface. Thus, while most forms in nature develop in depth, in conformity with the space in which we live, we have to recognize that the forms of art inhabit a *different* space, the complexity and mystery of which are expressed equally by stained glass and mosaic.

Still more obvious (if that be possible) – and this is merely remarked in passing – is the fact that the *material* of a picture is not that of nature. The painted flowers may indeed be the 'living image' of reality, yet the effect they produce owes nothing to the texture of their petals, nor to the properties of chlorophyll! Oil, water-colour, pastel – these are the substances which human ingenuity has employed to give them their existence in our eyes.

Should it finally be added that the sole *creator* of these flowers is the woman who painted them, and that to her they owe all that they are?

Now it would be quite pointless to recognize that forms in a work of art are concerned with a *different* time, a *different* space, a *different* material and a *different* creator from those of nature, if after all we are going to blind ourselves to these facts and insist that they are really exactly alike! Neither painting nor sculpture can deceive us – but we *can* deceive ourselves.

In our normal experience we tend to cling to certain stable forms which serve as co-ordinates; houses are vertical, water is horizontal; birds fly, animals and men walk on their feet . . . it is understandable that many people should protest when Chagall turns the habitual representation of the world inside-out! And what happens to our peace of mind when Hieronymus Bosch's monsters slyly come to life?

In general, what we ask of form is to *assure our practical existence:* I open the door, and I see the passage; in the town I keep to the pavements, while among the vehicles which pass on the roadway, I notice which ones are large, and which are speedy; at the pedestrian crossing I keep between the rows of metal studs; if I am in a car myself, I keep to my own side of the road and make the proper signal before turning . . .

What category of *existence* is this? It is that of my own person as a body in motion, exposed to all sorts of dangers. It is for my person that my image of practical reality is shaped, with its notions of high and low, upward and downward . . .

And what *world* is this? It is the world of objects that surround me, and among which I myself, in my body, am an object, subject like the rest to the forces of nature, to weight and duration, to the seasons, to

50. Hieronymus Bosch (c. 1451-1516). *Temptation of Saint Anthony,* detail of central panel. Lisbon, National Museum of Fine Arts. Photo Giraudon.

52

heat and cold and space. It is for my body, first and foremost, that the whole apparatus of my senses operates – a veritable instrument-panel, ceaselessly signalling information – the overall control-system which we call *perception.*

Now obviously one has to use one's eyes to see a picture, but one is not done with it as soon as one has registered what it represents; moreover, no-one thinks of it *only* as an *object,* and no-one considers himself simply as an object in relation to it. This shows that we are capable of a different attitude.

But from what is a man to form the idea of *different* time, *different* space and *different* material? Not from chance, assuredly, nor from heaven, nor any super-natural source, but from *himself,* and from himself alone. If we accept that art, for thousands of years and with tireless perseverance, has shown us con-ditions different from those which nature imposes on us, it means that besides being *conditioned* to existence within and through our bodies, as objects which obey the laws of 'natural' time, 'natural' space and 'natural' necessity, we are also, as human beings, *capable* of existence in *our own* time, *our own* space and *our own* liberty – and without resorting to magic or illusion.

Is this really surprising? No, for our minds have long been accustomed to forms which owe nothing to nature. We know there are geometries in six, seven or n dimensions, of which the figures could never be expressed as diagrams, but which nevertheless are the instruments of calculations no less precise than those based on Euclidean space. Does this mean that the forms of art have only an 'ideal' existence? One might be tempted to think so if experience did not show the importance to them of material, and the degree in which they are connected with sensuous pleasure. It appears then, that forms in art participate both in 'perceiving' and 'conceiving', but without being reduced to *natural, objective forms* on the one hand, or to mere *ideas* on the other. Intended to be both seen and spiritually apprehended, they demand an appropriate kind of understanding on our part.

If we were limited only to perceiving, we should doubtless be content to register representations unrelated to one another, or rather, related only to the existence of our own bodies. Like animals, our only concern would be the satisfaction of our bodily needs, and the world would be simply an assemblage of objects, among which we should trouble only to distinguish the useful ones from the useless, the dangerous ones from the harmless. If, on the other hand, we were spirit alone, we should doubtless need only to 'conceive' for reality to be born of itself, and the universe would be a supernal algebra, of which we were at once the equation and the key.

Of course we know very well that our condition belongs to neither of these extremes. We are not resigned to being *altogether* objects, nor do we presume to be *altogether* gods. Daily experience, no less than reflection, tells us that we are *mixed* or *intermediate* beings, and that *mixed* or *intermediate* forms are the most likely to satisfy our true condition – among them, the forms of visual art.

It is through them that we are granted the experience of that *imaginary yet real world* which is our own. Please do not misunderstand me: it is not a question of denying the world of objects or the world of ideas, but simply of realizing that we are situated in neither the one nor the other *exclusively*. Instead of seeking to define *the* truth, as an idea does, form seeks to convey the feeling, the *sensation* of truth. By its means truth ceases to be an abstract notion and becomes an *experience*.

This is why a stroke that simply follows the outline of a shape always seems static; but how exciting it can be to follow the living hand of the artist in search of a form! See with what imperious pen-strokes Raphael endeavours to snare it in a net of divine geometry – and see, too, how the drawing bears witness less to the 'kill' itself than to the spirited gesture of the hunter!

Thus – and this bears repetition – total realism and total abstraction are equally impossible in art, for in either of them the nature of man is mutilated. However much respect we pay to objects, we know that it is not through them that we live, though we remain among them; however much respect we pay to the spirit, we know that we do not live through it alone, though we cherish it within us.

Only the imaginary *and* real life shows us as we are in our deepest being, and the forms of art, halfway between the object and the idea, are our guides. They touch our senses and appeal to our minds at the same time; and in our consciousness meaning takes root, putting the seal upon the experience of our *complex unity*.

It would be vain to pretend that all works of art succeed in achieving this, yet all aspire to it. Sublime or mediocre, they give to mortal man an image which transcends him; which, though it cannot grant him immortality, can claim to demonstrate its possibility. Even the modest *Flower-piece* of Maria van Oosterwyck at least makes the attempt.

52-53. *The forms of art, halfway between the object and the idea, are our guides to the imaginary yet real world which is our own.*
Document Bernard Juillerat.

Leonardo da Vinci (1452-1519). The right eye of the *Mona Lisa*.

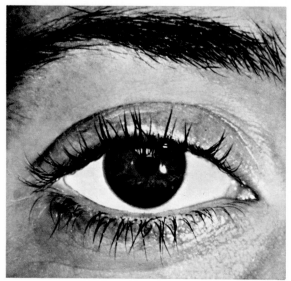

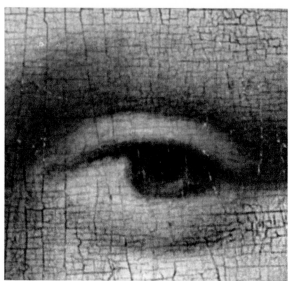

The work of art

Hand and tool

We forget all too quickly the books we read in childhood. Who, though, could fail to remember with delight his *Robinson Crusoe*? Escaping the murderous storm, swimming to the shore, landing on the unknown island, and trying to live . . .

Condemned to utter solitude (his prison has not even a jailor), Crusoe knows that he is cut off from other men, and he also knows – as days, then years, go by – that in all probability nothing will ever happen to relieve the bitterness of his lot. If only he could hear a voice! But there is none . . .

And yet, how energetically he strives to restore at any cost the contact with humanity which his shipwreck has severed. He needs to keep himself alive, naturally, but the most significant thing of all is the way he goes about it. As he strengthens his hut, or traps his animals, we see him transforming a patch of wild country into cultivated ground. The first shoots of barley sprout, grow and ripen. Never can harvest have seemed so blessed! . . . No, the need to satisfy hunger is not all. Much more important for Crusoe is the need to associate himself, even at a distance, with his fellow-men, his brothers, in performing their gestures, in rediscovering their forms (do you remember his joy when he managed to fashion his first pots, and his elation when he succeeded in making them water-tight by baking them?), in recording the daily incidents of his life in a diary through the medium of a language that was useless to him – dead almost, since there was no-one to speak it – but was kept alive by his writing it!

A modest and exemplary hero, Crusoe demonstrates in his every gesture, his every thought, that our condition here below is not that of isolated beings, abandoned to the caprice of an individual destiny, but of creatures who, in spite of all that divides or obstructs them, know that they are close to one another, men-among-men, united in the same condition. One may feel that one is alone, but one never is.

From the sun that rises each morning and sets each evening we – and all plants and animals with us – draw our *life-force,* our physical and biological existence, governed by physical and biological laws that we may not, on pain of death, transgress . . . But there is another sun from which we draw, not our life-force, but our *raison d'être:* and this other luminary is dependent upon ourselves, for we are able to make it shine brighter or to extinguish it.

54. Japanese art. Figurine in baked clay. Jômon era, 2nd millennium B.C. Tokyo, National Museum. Photo Agraci.

It is through its power that civilizations which have
54 been buried under a load of centuries, engulfed by
55 the Asian jungle or covered by the lava of volcanoes,
are able to come to life again in brotherhood with us.
The archaeologist does not brave the difficulties of
excavation and the rigours of climate simply to lay
his hands on a hoard of 'treasure', but to revive the
memory of our ancestors. If he is to succeed, they must
have left some memorials of themselves – forms that
can make their presence felt. A people of whom we
possess no relics is dead to us, and if its name survives,
like that of Atlantis, it is because we still hope we
may one day discover some trace of it. Nothing could
be more stirring than the zeal of a Champollion in
deciphering the Egyptian hieroglyphs, which before
his time were incomprehensible patterns, and after-
wards were open books of pity, suffering and love.
Do we not feel the same emotion in poring over a
tablet from Ur or a stone from Akkad? The cunei-
form characters are powerless to dismay us; 'decoded'
by the orientalist, they have revealed the annals of
56 Sumeria and Assyria. So it is with art, which constructs – work by work, and symbol by symbol – the
complex physiognomy of vanished civilizations. And
if it is more difficult to 'get inside' a polynesian mask
than a painting of the 17th or 18th century, that is
because some forms are less familiar than others;
none are 'closed' to us altogether.

Whatever they may be, *all* works of art have this in
common – that man is their creator (the very expression '*work* of art' conveys this meaning). Not only
does man conceive them, he 'realizes' them also,
making of them classes of objects which are added to
those of nature without being confused with them.
The *making* is as essential as the conception. Through
it we have access to the work, not to the subject
it contains, but to the human presence which it
radiates.

If we need to be convinced of this, let us watch the
potter at his work. Having kneaded his clay, a grey
lump with greenish high-lights due to the moisture in
it, he places it on his wheel, which he sets in motion.
Then, plunging his hands into the mass, he opens it
out like a calyx, raises it and draws out the rim into
57 a thin corolla. Thus, little by little, the vase takes
shape, moulded from within, with rounded sides and
narrowed neck, while on its flesh of clay we see the
slight furrows impressed by the potter's fingers . . .
Two hands – that is all that is needed – craftman's
hands, mysterious hands! At what precise moment, as
the moist mass rises, can one say: '*that* is still clay –
this now is a vase?' And yet, though the moment of

55. Khmer art. *Head of Buddha,* Cambodia, 12th century. Paris,
Musée Guimet. Photo Musée Guimet.

56. Assyrian art. *Foreigner bringing Tribute,* fragment of bas-relief, 9th century B.C. London, British Museum. Photo Viollet.

transformation eludes us, no-one disputes the change when it is accomplished.

Colours, packed in tubes or boxes, are articles of commerce. But now the painter squeezes the tube or opens the box; can we say that they are still the same products while he arranges and mixes the colours on his palette? Now he loads his brush. Held at arm's length, the colour approaches the canvas – and no sooner is it applied than from being anonymous matter it becomes 'painting'.

I must repeat that the mystery of artistic creation is in no way to be confused with divine creation. While there is mystery in both, it is of different kinds. Michelangelo and Rodin cannot deceive us: the hand of God is a metaphor, and it is only in a spirit of anthropomorphism that we visualize it. For God, if one may speak of Him in these terms, there is no *manner* in Creation. It is.

Art is not created from nothingness, but it allows us human beings to *alter our relationships with the world of things*. God creates, the machine produces – or reproduces; the hand alone can *fashion*. Every single gesture is linked to the artist's body, to his mind

57. *Thus the vase takes shape, moulded from within.* Photo Bernard Juillerat.

and to his heart, and appears to other people as a message – as style.

The other great mystery is that we are conscious of it in this way! The work of art, neither a natural object nor an abstract idea, invites us in some sort to a 'gesture of sympathy', which has nothing to do with superficial emotion or sentiment, but is felt at the heart of human experience and of art.

It might seem rash to assert that the spectators in a theatre 're-enact' the movements of a dancer on the stage. However, it is clear that the dance is something more than a succession of juxtaposed and blended figures, making a spectacle for the eye alone; if it was only a matter of admiring a succession of co-ordinated movements, we should do better to visit a factory! An engine or a generator would have more to offer . . . But nor is the dance a superior sort of algebra addressed to the mind. Without the movements being actually performed in front of us it would be non-existent. So, if the dance is neither mere visual pleasure nor mental exercise, yet still has such power to enchant us, there must obviously be something else in it which neither the eye nor the mind alone can account for. Surely it is that the spectator, though he remains seated, perceives the dancer's movements *in his own body and through his own body*, follows and 'enters into' the dance, beyond the reach of eyes and mind. It is a 'sympathy of body' that allows us to share intimately in the dancer's measured movements. In the same way a work of art invites us to share in the artist's activity through a 'sympathy of hand'.

If we divest it of its sentimental associations, sympathy is the faculty of feeling, if not identically with other people, at least in a similar way. To become aware of the artist's hand is not to become an artist oneself, but to penetrate to the artist's consciousness; and one does so not by reason, but by the power of the work alone – a sort of living groove, which we enter like a needle in the groove of a gramophone record; and the music which another has composed begins to play in us as if it were our own.

Though the gulf between Greek sculpture and that of the Romanesque churches is a great one, the fact remains that the trace of the human hand in both of them is enough for neither to seem strange.

There are still some savages whose language is so rudimentary that when night falls they have to light great fires – not for warmth, but so as to see the gestures with which they accompany their words, and without which they would not be able to understand one another. Civilized language has outgrown this

58. *Held at arm's length, the colour approaches the canvas.*

Braque in his studio. Photo Held.

59

59. Michelangelo (1475-1564). *The Creation of Man,* fresco on the ceiling of the Sistine Chapel (detail). Rome, Vatican. Photo Anderson. Giraudon.

expedient, but still comes up against the 'inexpressible'. Though marvellously shaped for social intercourse, it finds great difficulty in expressing what is most deeply human in us. It is then that we too light fires – the fires of art – to make our meaning clear in gestures that are beyond the scope of words.

Of course, I do not wish to pretend that the artist does everything with his hands. Nevertheless, whatever tools he makes use of, he never leaves to them the *execution* of the work, as to machines that need only to be set in motion once and for all. *Handling* is distinct from *execution* in the sense that it always bears witness to the active presence of man. Burins, chisels, hammers, trowels, brushes and pencils are so many prolongations of the hand, and the artist keeps them under strict control.

But the arts also employ more formidable servants than these – servants that will not be docilely led by the nose, but presume to interfere and dictate their own requirements – subterranean sorcerers whom man has been endeavouring to subjugate more thoroughly since the dawn of time.

'. . . And from that time, notwithstanding that I had no knowledge of clay-bearing earths, I set myself to search for enamels, like a man who gropes in dark-

60. Auguste Rodin (1840-1917). *The Hand of God,* marble.

61. Greek art. *Assembly of the Gods,* frieze of the Parthenon (detail) 5th century B.C. Athens, Acropolis Museum. Photo Alinari.

62. Romanesque art. *Apostles* (detail), 11th century. Civate (Como), basilica of San Pietro al Monte. Ed. Bencini and Sansoni.

63. Bernard Palissy (1510-1589). Large rustic dish, faïence. Paris, Louvre. Photo Giraudon.

64. *Despite the hand of time.* Selinunte. Photo J.-M. Pilet.

ness. In those days, without having learnt of what substances such enamels were made, I crushed all manner of materials that I could think might make something, and having crushed and ground them, I bought a quantity of earthenware pots, upon which, when I had broken them in pieces, I placed the materials which I had ground, and marked them, and wrote down for reference the materials which I had placed on each piece; then having made a furnace to my fancy, I set to work to bake the said pieces to see if my substances might make white colours: for I sought no other enamel than white: because I had heard tell that white is the foundation of all the other colours ... Being thus many times deceived, with great cost and labour, I was every day crushing and grinding new materials, and constructing new furnaces, with great expense of money and consumption of fire-wood and of time ...' So Bernard Palissy 63 continues the legendary recital of his exploits.

One might suppose that technical progress would erase such chapters as these. Today it is well known that earthenware bakes at 800° C., stoneware at 1200° C., and that porcelain is vitrified at 1400° C. Even the mineralogical formulae for composing the three principal ceramic products are known. Electric kilns have been devised, which, precisely regulated by engineers, reduce the chances of error to nil. One might believe that science was ready to supplant the artist. But not at all. Theoretical knowledge is a meagre aid. Though it is no longer necessary to search for enamels as in the days of Palissy, it is still by dint of ceaseless experiments and fresh beginnings that the modern ceramists practise their craft. Fire is never more than an auxiliary, whether it is allowed its wild-animal whims or is harnessed to domesticity by science, and all that matters in the last resort is the use which the artist makes of it.

It is *in the fashioning of the work that the hand binds form to material, material to form*, signing and sealing its unique, meaningful and lasting character.

Whether one wanders among the ruins of Selinunte, 64 whose crumbled and weathered columns have slept for so long among the dry grasses, or whether one contemplates the sculptured race of vanished gods – some that have lost arms, others legs, with torsos that have wasted through the centuries – the *fragments* which survive, battered though they may be, and despite the hand of time and cataclysms, still attest in the smallest of their details to the permanent and visible presence of man. This is indeed a marvel – that a mark traced on a piece of stone is enough to preserve a sentiment of humanity!

The present state
of aesthetic experience

You may ask why it is, in appearance at least, that *aesthetic evidence* should be so far from evident that it requires all this effort to define it. The answer lies in our present-day way of life, which makes aesthetic experience more difficult than it used to be. Not only have the conditions of existence changed, but they have profoundly modified our relationships with the most familiar objects – *utensils,* by which I mean (using the broadest sense of the word) all objects made by man to answer his needs, and which are always around him – glass, furniture, houses, and so on.

The big stores are a symbol of our age. Their organization is so highly developed that they can (indeed do) claim to have everything for everybody. 'The best article at the best price' – this is the universal slogan of producer and consumer alike.

The second of these 'bests' is unequivocal. Nothing is plainer than a difference in price. As for the first, it is no less clear; it refers to the quality of the article, by which we understand its *practical quality,* its suitability for its destined purpose. The industrial production characteristic of modern times operates under the twin banners of *utility* and *economy*.

Yet, oddly enough, our age has developed at the same time a thirst for antiques! There are numerous antique-shops in all large towns, while certain streets in Paris can boast dozens of them. Junk-markets, formerly the resort of the indigent, are nowadays much in vogue.

An ephemeral, passing fashion? Definitely not. One cannot help smiling, though, when one notices shop-owners and manufacturers of mass-produced goods among the keenest collectors. Thus it is that a humble and ill-varnished earthenware dish is given pride of place in a display-cabinet, set off to advantage by special indirect lighting, and provided with a translucent label that is the envy of the owner's guests... Now, before it took its place in a collection, this dish was nothing more than a household utensil, such as was made by the Persians, the Chinese and other peoples before them; made not for display, but to be eaten out of. And it *was* eaten out of, because that was what it was for; and it would have seemed ridiculous to contemplate it instead of using it.

If we add these two circumstances together, we arrive at a curious conclusion: on the one hand we consider the modern utensil, apart from its practical

65. *Humble dish promoted to the status of work of art.*
Syrian or Egyptian art. Dish, glazed earthenware, 11th/12th centuries. Paris, Doucet coll. Photo Viollet.

66. Egyptian art. Tutankhamon's chair, XVIIIth dynasty, 14th century B.C. Cairo, Museum of Antiquities. Photo Viollet.

67. Mycenaean art. Gold vessel, 16th/15th centuries B.C. Paris, Louvre. Photo Giraudon.

and economical qualities, to be *neutral*. We make a god of nylon because it lends itself to any purpose, from a table to a pair of socks, but we do not find anything remarkable in its universal application, except to rejoice when prices come down.

On the other hand, we consider the ancient utensil – or so we are persuaded by the vogue for antiques – to be an *object of value*; but not on account of its usefulness, since we withdraw it from use, nor on account of its economic attractions, since it is usually very expensive.

Note that in both cases we are dealing with similar, though not identical objects. No matter how precious Tutankhamon's furniture may be, it is still 66 only furniture – chairs, tables, couches and beds, corresponding piece for piece with the furniture in our own houses.

The consequence is that present conditions of living anchor us gradually to the conviction that *what is useful has nothing to do with art, and even less with beauty; and conversely, that beauty in general and the objet-d'art in particular have nothing to do with utility.*

Yet it seems that the ancients, though they thought of utensils only from a practical standpoint, made art as it were without realizing it, and that we find aesthetic quality in most of the objects they have left us, not through any arbitrary decision of our own, but because this quality was, and still is, in them.

The ancients did not need to think about beauty in order to produce it; the conditions under which they worked seem to have made it unnecessary. While thinking only of utility, craftsmen made 67 utensils in which were present the three-fold essentials of art – an appropriate material, a form, and a man. It is wrong to suppose that beauty and usefulness are incompatible. The truth is that they *can* be incompatible – as we see in so many mass-produced objects, which have at best a small degree of charm – and that they can also be entirely compatible, as we see in most of the utensils that have come down to us from our ancestors.

Industrial production, in modifying our relationship to the objects around us, has also affected our conception and experience of art. One might shut one's eyes to this, were it not that our very homes are threatened by it. When workers' accommodation is to be built, the first essential is that the rents should be moderate. Therefore the apartments are multiplied in an identical pattern and in a small space. Thus the blocks of flats go up, twin brothers

68. *Modern uniformity, 'zero-point' of art?* Photo Robert Doisneau.

of the multiple stores. Everything is once more subordinated to the two imperatives of *utility and economy.*

Since utensils nowadays are enveloped in similar uniformity, and since they are always with us, we have allowed ourselves in time to suppose that there is a sort of *zero-point art* (as someone has said of literature) – a *neutral art,* of which they are characteristic samples. An absurd belief, since the notion of art implies the notion of *style,* which puts neutrality out of the question. But just as one ignores certain facts, so one makes the best of certain contradictions, without appearing to bother much in either case. Thus the assortment of objects that constitute our surroundings ends up by reconciling us to the *monstrous idea of an art without style.*

The mind may be rescued from this fallacy only to fall victim to another. Believing 'zero-point art' to be the normal state of utensils, one imagines that anything which rises above it can aspire to the higher degrees of art, as if it were enough to add any sort of artifice or ornament for the standard article to be endowed with *style.* Needless to say, a work of art has nothing in common with such expedients. It does not look 'better' or 'out of the ordinary' for the good reason that it never has been ordinary. Its nature is of a different order.

But, alas! The prodigious publicity-machine of industry is continually obscuring the question, and

it becomes harder and harder to resist its all-embracing influence. In the newspapers, on television and in the cinema the big furnishing-houses compete in ingenuity (and in generosity, they would say), offering to the (quite legitimate) covetousness of engaged and newly-wed couples their 'dream bedroom'. By a subtle shift of emphasis, quality becomes no longer a question of worth, but of *price.* The more expensive a piece of furniture is, the more (supposedly) beautiful it is also. So art is brought down to the universal criterion of our day, money! Nothing could be more convenient for both producer and consumer. For the former it is doubly useful: permitting him to make use of a *costly material* (so that the price may be beyond discussion), and to add to the standard article an *effect* which might influence the customer's decision. As for the latter, the feeling that he has got 'value for money', and possessed himself of 'something you won't see every day', is good enough. Thus trickery is aided by the complicity of the dupe.

I am not simply indulging a taste for sarcastic humour; far from it! I have paused to draw attention to these things because they are of very real importance in the problem that concerns us. Ideas about art are *formed,* and can be *deformed* just as easily. It is all too true that in the eyes of the general public the object worth acquiring is the one which flatters their self-esteem – the 'fancy' article; and the only reason (or rather, the only excuse!) for acquiring it is to feel 'one up' on one's fellows – a sophism which is all the more redoubtable for the sly spirit in which it is entertained. Beauty not only seems to be incompatible with usefulness; it tends imperceptibly to be associated with non-utility – or, in the terminology of the age, with luxury.

Most of our domestic objects, all that go to make up the familiar décor of our rooms, from which we each derive our daily store of images, suffer painfully from this misconception. How often in the countryside, in one of those rooms where the ceiling is formed of good carpentry, we are pained to see the pitch-pine bed, glossy and lacquered like a bier, and, on the white-washed wall, the inevitable funeral knell of a sunset at Capri!

When industrial production was unknown, or rare, the conditions of aesthetic experience merged more or less with those of ordinary experience. Though the ancients did not consciously make every utensil a work of art, the works of craftmanship which they produced disposed them to be aware of beauty and utility, together. In our age machinery has completely transformed that state of affairs. Daily life brings us continually into contact with machine-made objects, and, far from being of no consequence, this profoundly influences our attitude to works of art. Whether we like it or not, our habitual ways of seeing, feeling and thinking produce a sort of diffuse contamination which is difficult to eliminate. For this reason we need today to be particularly watchful in our approach to art.

Temptations of the mind

Biography

One could know nothing of art without experiencing works of art. But, when adequate experience is not to be had, can one not turn to the explanatory methods in which the mind is so fertile? Yes, but only with caution, for although the mind can illuminate, it is also capable of leading one astray...

As, for example, in one of our more inveterate habits – to believe that by knowing an author's life one can, by analogy, reach an understanding of his work. In this instance, instead of applying ourselves to the study of the works, *we let ourselves be tempted to look for an explanation in the man alone,* and we are encouraged to do so by an abundance of biographies, collected letters and reports of every kind.

But what sort of life is an artist's? In most cases quite banal – anxieties, sufferings, hopes and happiness – the common lot of us all! In this respect it is the same as any other perfectly normal existence. Life and art are two quite different things.

If you doubt this, the art of Egypt, of Chaldaea, and all (or almost all) of medieval art will help to put things in a proper perspective. The greater part of our artistic heritage consists of *anonymous* monuments. Romanesque capitals are no less beautiful for the lack of a signature! And who, examining a Limoges enamel, would think of inquiring whether 69 the artist was unhappy, whether he was married, or whether his life was long or short? Certainly, a work of art could not exist but for the artist, but it only becomes a *work* when the artist's creation is detached from him to enter the world of forms, which is also the spectator's world.

Even so, all would be well if biographers confined themselves to the role of historian! Few of them, however, can resist the temptation to represent an artist in the image which fame or rumour has foisted on him, instead of in his own; and there is a corresponding temptation for the public to believe in the traditional image, and even to demand it. A smiling Beethoven would be as disconcerting as an angelic Rimbaud; as for Van Gogh, we should scarcely recognize him without the flame of madness in his eyes, waiting to consume him!

Public opinion needs type images. Thus, whatever the biographer's talent, and however honest his intentions, it is seldom that he does not yield to complaisance or to a formula. Great man that he is, the artist is exempted from the petty details of existence. If anyone makes so bold as to represent him as mean or jealous (let us suppose that in fact he was), the reader takes no notice, his admiration for the man cancelling such passages as he proceeds.

In short, biography is a tricky genre, that is nearly always to some extent polluted. Either the author limits himself to relating the known facts, in which case one usually has the feeling that he has fallen short of his task, or else he is only too willing to gratify the public's desires, and colours his account to make his subject a *hero*: 'He, more than anyone... Alone among his contemporaries...'

Now, explanations are valueless unless they are based on solid reasoning that bears on the subject in an appropriate way. On the whole it is more advisable to avoid biographies than to risk misusing them. For what can we expect of them, except information about the *conditions* under which the artist created his work? Knowing the man is a matter of evidence and information; knowing the work is a matter of experience and judgment.

One can expect little more from artists' *letters,* which have been made so copiously available by the zeal (sometimes also the indiscretion) of certain publishers. What could be more touching than Van Gogh's letters to his brother Theo? Such struggles and such sufferings, described with so sharp an accent of truth that one cannot read the recital of them without being deeply moved. 'It is a bible', one critic [1] said of them, a critic whose habitual moderation lends an even brighter glow to his tribute. In contrast to these, the surviving correspondence of Rimbaud with his family offers a no less significant example, for there is not a line of it, not a word, that does not concern his business, his health or his profits – nothing that could lead one to suppose a poet might wield the same pen!

A particular danger arises when an artist risks expressing himself on the subject of his art in a letter, for then isolated phrases or formulae get taken from their context and are passed on to the public just as they stand. Thus, since Cézanne chanced to write to Bernard: 'Right! Treat nature in terms of the cylinder, the sphere and the cone, the whole set in perspective; let each side of an object or plane be directed towards a central point...', some people have felt justified in lopping off the latter part of the phrase and pronouncing that Cézanne based his art upon the primacy of those three geometrical figures – as if any one of his landscapes had ever been composed of cylinders, spheres and cones! Proceeding from interpretation to interpretation, they have even gone so far as to see in this truncated formula the foundation-stone of cubism!

Letters are not to be despised, far from it; but it does seem that one should accord them this much of justice, of deference even, – not to search them for things the artist never intended to put in them. Moving they may be, full (some of them) of the anguish of creation, of the struggles the man endured in the accomplishing of his task, or a-quiver with intentions which we can see taking shape there and gaining strength; yet we should remember this: these letters are not addressed to us, even though we are privileged to read them over the shoulders of the original recipients. Does the signature at the bottom of a letter mean the same as that in the corner of a picture? The name is the same, and so perhaps is the hand, but in one it is the *man* who addresses a private individual, while in the other it is the *artist* who addresses himself to the notice of the public. Let us not be unfair to either of them! What we are offered – offered expressly by the artist – is acquaintance with the work of art; all else belongs to the man and to his privacy. Biographies, letters, the accounts of personal friends and the anecdotes of contemporaries should all urge prudence upon us.

We need also to beware of the deliberate utterances of artists. Their statements, precepts and theories – in fact, all they say, think they say or mean to say – are very seldom enlightening, especially when their own works are in question. Of course, they have every right to express themselves as they think fit; I do not begrudge them that. If one of them says that 'Art is love', another that 'Art is life', and a third that 'Art is nature' – well and good. That is how they feel about it. But we must always bear in mind what such formulae as these really amount to. That they explain the artist's *conception* of art cannot be denied; but a conception and a work are not the same thing!

Listen to Leonardo da Vinci: 'If you wish to see if the general effect of the painting corresponds to the object copied from nature, take a mirror and place it in such a way as to reflect the real object, then compare the reflection with your picture, and consider carefully whether the subject of the two images corresponds to both of them, especially to the mirror: one should take the mirror for one's master – I mean a flat mirror – for on its surface

[1] Marcel Arland, responsible for the only complete edition of Van Gogh's letters, which appeared in 1955. (N.R.F.).

69. Romanesque art. *Sepulchral plaque of Geoffroy Plantagenet,* ▶ Limoges enamel, 12th century. Le Mans, museum. Photo Held.

things have much in common with a painting...'
(Note-books).

Take the mirror for one's master! Why, the very thing we all admire in Leonardo's art is precisely the transposition from nature, the distillation of reality through poetry. Similarly, when Van Gogh writes: 'But truth is so dear to me, the effort to render truth also ... that I would much rather be a cobbler with colours than a musician.' [1] Yet, what distinguishes his work in our eyes is that it does so much more than 'render truth'.

Therefore, while it is true that the work of art always presents a certain air of mystery, it does not follow that all explanations are valid. If we concede that a work is autonomous, at least that it belongs to its *own* order of existence, then any investigation based on the analogy of life involves a contradiction in terms, for that which gives us information about the *man* does not in fact enlighten us concerning the *work*. Indeed, more often it tends to obscure it.

'Literature', said Sainte-Beuve, 'is not for me distinct or separable from the rest of the man or his being... One finds oneself trying in numberless ways and for numberless ends to get to understand a man, as distinct from a mind. All those times that one has asked oneself various questions about an author, and found no answer, were they not because, in one's secret self, one is not sure that one has grasped him entire, even when the questions might seem to have no bearing on his writings: What did he think about religion? What were his feelings on the subject of women? On the subject of money? Was he rich, or poor? How did he work? How did he live? What was his vice or weakness? No answer to these questions is irrelevant in judging the author of a book or the book itself, unless it be a treatise of pure geometry, above all if it be a work of literature, that is to say, into which his whole self enters.'

Proust answered this passage, which illustrates to perfection all that I have condemned in this chapter, with an opinion which, in conclusion, I am happy to adopt as my own:

'Sainte-Beuve's work is *not* profound ... making him the supreme master of 19th century criticism, as Taine, Paul Bourget and so many others have contended. His method, which is to avoid separating the man from his work, to consider it relevant, in judging the author of a book (unless it be a 'treatise on pure geometry'), to know first the answers to a number of questions that have no obvious bearing on his work ('What were his feelings...'), to gather every possible piece of information on a writer, to collate his correspondence, to make enquiries of the people who knew him, talking with them if they are still alive, reading anything they may have written if they are dead – this method ignores something that can be learnt from a slight acquaintance with ourselves: that a book is the product of a different *self* from the one we exhibit in society, in our habits and vices.' [1] *It is what this other self produces that concerns us.* It is the work, then, the point of contact between artist and spectator, through the medium of a created form.

---

[1] Letter to his brother Theo, February 1890.

[1] *Contre Sainte-Beuve*, N.R.F., 1954.

Temptations of the mind

Theories

There is no getting away from it; knowledge of art is not to be gained from revelations about artists' lives. However, the mind does not accept this fact with resignation; *it wants to understand*. And if one explanation will not do, it looks for another.

Here is one which, by its very simplicity, seems to be definitive: 'One might say', writes Taine, 'that man is a superior species of animal, which produces poems and philosophies in much the same way as the silk-worm weaves its cocoon or the honey-bee constructs its hive.' [1] Taken as it stands, this phrase of Taine's gets us no further forward, but it hints at something which he says categorically elsewhere – that the conditions in which we live *determine* what we are. 'Air and nutriment in time form the body; the character and the contrasts of climate produce its normal sensations and, in the long run, its particular sensibility also; the whole man is there, mind and body, in as much as the whole man receives and retains the imprint of earth and sky.' [2] Here indeed we have an explanation. Man is the *product* of climate, environment and the moment, from which it follows that the condition which produces man stems itself from the same original causes, since all is but a chain of causes and effects, 'Here, as elsewhere, the only problem is a problem of mechanics: the total effect is a compound determined entirely by the power and direction of the forces which produce it.' [3]

I do not intend to discuss the implications of Taine's philosophy point by point, but its influence is still too widespread for us to be able to ignore the premises on which it is built.

We may observe that, in effect, what this theory aims at explaining is the *production* of the work of art. Without even trying to find out if the theory holds good or not, we can see clearly enough that understanding the *production* of the work and understanding the *work itself* are not the same thing. Thus Taine's adherence to the idea of determinism of race, environment and period is of little importance; the true problem lies elsewhere. Yet such is the seductive power of reputedly philosophical or scientific theories, that we readily let ourselves be carried away by them, even while realizing their comparative irrelevance. [4]

---

[1] Taine, *La Fontaine et ses Fables.*
[2] Ibid.
[3] Taine, *Introduction à l'Histoire de la Littérature anglaise.*
[4] In justice to Taine, it should be pointed out that he was himself well aware that his theory went too far. To avoid inconsistency he had to conclude that one has not to judge a work of art, but simply to *understand* it, that is to say, to grasp the mechanism of its production. However, in his *Philosophie de l'Art,* he attempts on the contrary to discover the necessary conditions for aesthetic judgment.

Can we hope for a better explanation in *theories of concordance*? The work of art, it is said, is linked to an epoch, to a society, and this is a fact that no-one would dream of disputing. But, from an ill-considered attitude of mind, it has been deduced that art should be in the image of this society, expressing it, and to be explained in terms of it. An attractive idea, but alas! a specious one!

Obviously it cannot be denied that art and society are related, but it is quite absurd to see the relationship as one of direct resemblance.

It is true there is a strong temptation to do so. Is not this what so many people are doing when they envy the ancient Greeks for having been so beautiful, imagining with all the simplicity in the world that they must all have been on the model of their statues? According to historians, the celebrated 'Greek type' was in fact very different: 'One has only to visit a museum, and *not* be an archaeologist,' writes Ferrero, 'to understand that Greek sculpture is a sensual art, which flourished in an era when beautiful women and handsome men were as rare as albino blackbirds.' [1]

Modern painting offers a still more striking example. Who could recognize the features of his contemporaries in the figures of Braque, Picasso, Léger, Rouault or Miró?...

Thus our theory of concordance is already in serious trouble, and the conclusions to be drawn from it are definitely suspect.

It certainly helps to know something of the society in which an art took root; it throws light on its milieu and explains its conditions, but – whether we like it or not – a work of art is not produced like an apple on a tree; it springs from a world whose existence will always elude the framework of determinism.

Yet, before it will subscribe to this view, the mind resorts to other stratagems. If concordance will not answer, why not try the opposite? There would be no art, some say, but for a *deviation* – of the artist, of society, or of life. Psychoanalysis has made a great reputation for itself in this line. According to Freud, as everyone knows, the *libido* is the funda-

[1] Quoted by Lalo, *L'Expression de la Vie dans l'Art* (Alcan).

◄ 70. Fernand Léger (1881-1955). *Woman in blue*. Basle, Musée des beaux-arts. Photo Held.

72. Leonardo da Vinci (1452-1519). *Virgin and Child with Saint Anne*. Paris, Louvre. Photo Held.

71. Jean-Baptiste Greuze (1725-1805). *The Broken Pitcher*. Paris, Louvre. Photo Bulloz.

73. Georges Braque (b. 1882). *The Musician's Table*. Basle, Kunstmuseum. Photo Held.

mental constituent of man's personality. When repressed, it produces that luxuriant vegetation of 'complexes', in which every single one of us has his own patch marked out, and a visiting-card for label. Luckily, the phenomenon of 'sublimation' provides a way of avoiding suffocation in the miasma of this internal jungle, and of raising ourselves instantly to the purest empyrean. In this it would appear that art, among several other activities, is the one that can help us the most; but, whatever beauties it offers us, it cannot help preserving the marks of its origin. Thus the famous *Broken Pitcher* is seen to be, not an agreeable genre picture as one too naïvely supposes, but a symbol of Greuze's unfortunate obsession with the idea of defloration!... The shape of the fracture and the details of the fountain prove it, it seems, beyond the slightest doubt. *The Virgin and Child with Saint Anne* is no less revealing: it provides, we are told, direct evidence of the obsession which haunted Leonardo: being a natural son, he could not escape the image of the vulture. If you outline the form of Mary on her mother's knee, the vulture duly appears in the triple guise of bird of prey, idée fixe and symbol! The Freudian school has multiplied this kind of interpretation to the point where one does not know which to admire the most – the psychoanalyst's ingenuity or the painter's talent... By looking on art as an expression of the individual or the collective subconscious, the psychoanalytical method no doubt explains a number of things, but the one thing that matters to us – how to know the quality of a work – it leaves in the dark. However, it is not psychoanalysis that is to blame (after all, every branch of research is legitimate), but rather its attempted application to the domain of aesthetic understanding.

A work of art of any kind presents itself with a certain air of mystery, and we are reluctant to give up trying to penetrate that mystery. So, we attack the problem from every likely angle, employing every likely means. How is it that man, alone among sentient beings, adds forms to nature which originate

74. Vieira da Silva (b. 1908). *The Town*. Lausanne, private collection. Photo Held.

solely in himself? How is it that some men succeed in creating a work which impregnates humanity for centuries? How is it that certain works at once exert a power which to others comes only gradually or not at all? There is no end to such questions, no end to their answers, but still the mystery we are tracking down grows more obscure instead of clearer. What one ultimately – and forcibly – demands is to *understand*. It remains for us to examine what we mean by that.

The elementary mechanism of the act of understanding consists in bringing the unknown to the known. In the problem which occupies us, it is the work of art (its mystery) which constitutes the unknown factor. Comprehension operates by *reduction,* and is expressed in terms of a relationship. The term to which the unknown is reduced is therefore necessarily considered as the known factor. Thus, to take Taine's phrase again: 'Air and nutriment...' (p. 71), it is clear, in the relationship he establishes, that *man* is the 'unknown' term, and *climate* is the 'known' term, and that the reduction of the one to the other implies that in knowing the climate one knows the man.

Where works of art are concerned, the most frequent type of explanation is based on the principle of *identity*. [1] Many theories draw their justification from it, including the one we discussed in the last chapter under the heading of biography.

Explanations of this order are open to every sort of compromise and ingenious twist; all you need is a formula beginning: 'Art is...' – and you replace the dotted line with whatever term you fancy. There is certainly no shortage of them! Beauty, intuition, instinct, the subconscious, love, religion, mathematics, life, society, history, are among the more popular.

But, one is tempted to remark, why not simply affirm that Art is... works of art? Well, obviously! Nevertheless, one ought to bear in mind this fact, upon which all are agreed, that art contains something of *its own,* which it alone contains, and that consequently one cannot reduce it to anything else without falling into contradictions. We are bound to conclude that any application drawn from the principle of identity, or from any sort of concordance, either has no bearing on the understanding of art, or, if it is claimed to have some bearing, misses

the true question, which is to know the work of art *for what it is* – not for *what it is not.*

Does the *principle of causality* promise any better result? As we have seen, it was probably Taine who employed it to the greatest effect, and, though his theory is now largely rejected, the fact remains that this sort of explanation is still much in favour. One of our commonest habits is precisely that of explaining phenomena by their causes. Scientific thought, no less than popular thinking, continually makes use of this method of comprehension, and it is equally in evidence among the moral sciences. No historian would wish to treat of an important event without first devoting a preliminary chapter to its causes.

Now, granted that a work of art is a human product, is one justified in considering it as an effect? Undoubtedly events predispose art towards one direction or another, but one should be rather cautious in affirming this. Is there any event which has a greater effect on men than war? Between one day and the next, all 'normal' conditions and habits are turned upside down; the state changes its face and its needs, and so do its citizens; according to the law of probability, art should do the same. In truth, there is a copious output to suggest that it does, as one can see by glancing through the publications of two world wars. They are crammed with portraits in full-length; Joffre, King Albert of the Belgians, Winston Churchill, Eisenhower – these are the figures which engaged the zeal of painters and sculptors alike. But everything that is subordinate to the event, that is directly 'caused' by it, is doomed to disappear, like the event itself when it is put out to grass in the fields of history. And what were the styles of painting which really asserted themselves in a world given over to the disorders and cataclysms of two wars without parallel? In the first, cubism; 73 in the second, non-figurative art. What do they show 74 in common? The desire for an order and discipline that one would seek in vain in the lives of men and of nations during the first half of this century!

One can, then, explain *conditions* and *circumstances*; one can even establish their causes; but the fact that there is a connection between such-and-such conditions or circumstances and such-and-such a form of art does not entitle one to assume a relationship of cause and effect; at all events, it is of no avail in assessing the quality of works.

The *principle of finality* offers yet another prescription for 'understanding': according to this, the work of art is the more beautiful the closer it approaches to a specific end. Thus Christianity and

---

[1] The word is not used in its strict logical acceptation. It means here the tendency, through some connection, to identify art with something else.

all religions that came before or after it have always considered it the duty of artists to be loyal servants of a faith. Now, although the Christian faith has inspired a host of masterpieces, it by no means follows that anything which aims to glorify Christ can claim the status of a work of art! One has occasion to realize this all too often at exhibitions of so-called *sacred art,* and more frequently still, I fear, when one sets foot inside certain churches...

The principle of finality may well explain the usage of a crucifix, the usage of a ceremonial mask or a prophylactic figurine, but in apprising us of their purpose it does not help us to know them as works.

If people want to go about proclaiming that art is life, or the ideal, the product of an environment, a climate or a race, that it ought to exalt the love of God or of humanity, the grandeur of a régime or the misery of a social class – they are at liberty to do so; but we must still recognize that all explanations drawn from principles of identity, causality or finality help us to understand, not the work, but what is *around* it: conditions, circumstances, influences, or ideas about art in general.

We must go still farther, and not be afraid to declare that, strictly speaking, a work of art *cannot be 'understood'* in the sense in which we normally use the word. Does this mean we must renounce the aid of our intellect? Not at all. Aesthetic knowledge has need of the intellect, provided we revise the customary methods of explanation. Rather than a means of understanding, it is a *means of getting to know* that we need, for one has to learn

75. Saint-Sulpice painting: *Infant Jesus appearing from the Tabernacle.* Photo Braun.

how to gain access to aesthetic quality. The human mind is quite capable of grasping this distinction. Let it do so, then, adopting a critical attitude of mind to avoid the tempting bypaths which too often lead it into error.

First outline of a system of aesthetic knowledge

How is one to *know* the work of art? Let us remember first of all that failure to agree on what is meant by this fundamental question is responsible for nearly all the misunderstandings, prejudices and differences of opinion that afflict us. Let it be quite clear in our minds that the branches of knowledge which take an interest in art – in its origin, its production, its nature and its function – touch also upon our problem, but *touch upon it* only, since philosophy, metaphysics, sociology, psychology and psychoanalysis are each concerned with demonstrating some theory of their own.

When scientific thought (in the widest sense of the term) investigates the nature of an object, it considers it as a *phenomenon,* that is to say as an assemblage of facts or characteristics perceived by the senses or by the intellect. Even when, in the guise of philosophy, metaphysics or sociology, it takes art as its object, it still regards art as a phenomenon to be accounted for. In other words, art is treated as an assemblage of facts or characteristics that have been perceived *already*; art has *already* been produced, therefore it is already a *fact*. But scientific thought does not begin to explain how it has been decided, or is to be decided, that *this* particular painting or *that* particular sculpture is a work of art. Now, though we all agree that the phenomenon of art is a fact, we agree also that not *every* painting or *every* piece of sculpture is entitled to the description of 'work of art'; on the contrary, it is held unanimously that only *certain* pictures and *certain* sculptures deserve it. In scientific thinking, then, knowledge of art consists of speculation about an *established* phenomenon. For us, knowledge of the work of art consists in asking ourselves, how do our senses and our intellect *accredit* this painting or that sculpture as an artistic fact, and what does the work yield to us from its own world and from ours, when the two worlds meet and are revealed in aesthetic experience.

We are concerned, not with the result of our awareness of a work, but with *the process itself of becoming aware of the work,* and what we need to establish is not so much a science (a corpus of knowledge) as a way of knowing.

One might expect art history to supply this; but what, in fact, does it do? As its name suggests, it is a branch of history, in the same way as scientific, economic or diplomatic history. What art history

76. Juan Gris (1887-1927). *Portrait of Picasso*. Paris, Bignou coll. Photo Galerie Louise Leiris, Paris.

sets out to investigate is the development of humanity as reflected in artistic activity. Like science, of which it partakes, it establishes facts, describes and classifies them, and displays them in their proper sequence. It is true that the art historian, unlike the pure scientist, is called upon to pass judgments of value. Instead of studying all objects of an epoch, as does the archaeologist, he takes a certain number only – those which he considers to be art. But how does he go about it?

Suppose we open a book on Greek sculpture. Beside the usual discussion of the age as a whole, the principal sites, the material and spiritual conditions of society, origins, influences, etc., we are informed about the themes of Greek art, and the two main ones – the male nude, and drapery – are specially mentioned; the place of gods and heroes in art is explained, and so is the symbolic, religious or esoteric significance of the statues. We are shown the works, grouped in chronological order, and the principal differences or similarities between one epoch and another are pointed out. This insures some sort of continuity, of which the stages, customarily called *development*, are most usually compared to the ages of man: infancy (the archaic, the primitive, origins); maturity (classicism, the golden age); decline (decadence, mannerism).

The labours of the historians are eminently useful, and without them we should be deprived of the object itself of our devotion. They hold the keys to this domain; they are its watchful and enlightened guardians, and it is they who unlock the door to admit us. Nevertheless, though they open the door for us, they do not seem much concerned to help us to an intimate acquaintance with their treasures.

Have you noticed, by the way, that most historians confine themselves to the past, and seldom venture into the present, arguing that 'time has not yet done its work' or that one 'needs a longer view' before being able to judge correctly? What can this mean, if not that they are waiting for a *measure of agreement* to come into being before they will tackle this task? But who is responsible for this agreement? How does it come about? Why in one direction rather than another? Why in favour of certain works rather than others?

Around 1913 the paintings of the Cubists were a subject of polemical controversy. Had they any quality whatever? The one quality that was recognized in them was that they were all equally mystifying. In fact, only a few rare spirits believed *at that time* in the quality of a Braque, a Picasso, a Gleizes,

76

a Léger or a Gris. Here it is proper to pay homage to Guillaume Apollinaire, for his book *Les Peintres Cubistes,* which appeared in that same year 1913, displays a lucidity that borders on clairvoyance. Today, of course, Cubism is a historical phenomenon that nobody argues about.

What has happened between 1913 and now? This. More and more minds have come to discover in Cubist works a quality that has finally gained general acceptance, which goes to prove that aesthetic truth is the result of a *progressive awareness,* and can only be arrived at in this way.

Thus, the history of art and aesthetic knowledge are two distinct, though complementary, disciplines. The starting point of the one is in an established phenomenon, of which it studies the development in time; the other sets out to establish the conditions under which man gains insight into works of art.

AN OBJECTIVE

What we must do is to lay down *methodical principles,* which on the one hand will save us from following all the false trails, and on the other will guide us onto that one which leads to true knowledge. There is still the difficulty that aesthetic awareness is *at one and the same time* an experience and a judgment, and that its object eludes *definition*; but that is no reason to despair of attaining it.

Here are three paintings: a still-life by Zurbarán, 77 Grünewald's *Crucifixion,* and the *Miracle of the* 78 *Slave* by Tintoretto. 79

In the first of these, I distinguish three groups of objects: to the left, a pewter plate containing four lemons; in the centre, a basket in which are five oranges, with a sixth that is barely indicated; to the right, another plate on which are placed a beaker, three-quarters filled, and a rose. That is certainly one sort of awareness, consisting in *identifying* the objects and *enumerating* them. *In this 'objective and quantitative' view* the picture appears as a representation intended to inform me about the nature of the objects and their number.

Grünewald's altarpiece likewise offers an opportunity to count and identify human figures. Three groups: to the left, Mary Magdalene, St. John the Evangelist and the fainting Virgin; in the centre, Christ on the Cross; to the right, St. John the Baptist and the Lamb.

But would I really take stock of this picture in this way? No indeed, for my eyes are drawn instantly to the centre, to the savagely lacerated body of the Saviour. What matters is the emotion produced in me by the sight of the objects, rather than their quantity or identity. Has one ever seen the body of

77. Francisco de Zurbarán (1598-1664). *Lemons, Oranges and Rose.* Florence, Conte Alessandro Contini-Bonacossi coll. Photo Held.

Christ so cruelly maltreated? What atrocious wounds! And this crown of thorns – an instrument of torture! Reacting thus, I behave before the picture as if I were present at the scene itself, an indignant witness of Christ's treatment by mankind. My view of the picture stems from the emotion which the objects represented arouse in me, a view which may therefore be described as *pathetic*.

In Tintoretto's picture, what intrigues me first of all is the crowd of figures and – even more – the strange creature that dives head-first from the sky. What is happening? The *Golden Legend* supplies the answer to this question: 'A Christian slave in the service of a provençal noblemen persisted, in disobedience to his master, in worshipping the relics of St. Mark. On his return to the house, his enraged master ordered that his eyes should be put out, but the instruments of torture were miraculously blunted. The executioners then tried to cut off his legs, but the sword broke in pieces.' Here, then, I am concerned with an *action*. Looking into the picture, I can distinguish the protagonists: here in the centre is the naked slave, stretched on the ground; the executioners look at their broken instruments in astonishment, while their master, even more dumbfounded, leans forward to reassure himself that he is not the victim of an illusion. The crowd look on with varied emotions. As for St. Mark, swooping like an eagle from the heavens, he extends an arm as succouring as it is robust to the humble slave who has adored him.

This again is a kind of awareness, but it differs from the previous one in that it takes shape within a *dramatic* view of the painting.

Before going any further, we can state that *there is no such thing as 'absolute' awareness, but only such as is gained from one mental view or another,* that is, from the position our consciousness adopts in relation to an object and to a predisposition of the mind. Thus my awareness of the three pictures reproduced took shape as follows: for the first, within an 'objective and quantitative' view (taking account of the picture in terms of the identity and number of the objects represented); for the second, within a 'pathetic' or 'affective' view (taking account of the picture in terms of the emotion produced by the objects represented); for the third, within a 'dramatic' view (taking account of the picture in terms of the action performed by the figures). A few nuances might be added to these definitions, but they would serve no useful purpose, since we see clearly enough without them that in each case I have

IMPORTANT

78. Matthias Grünewald (c. 1460-1528). *Crucifixion,* central panel of the Isenheim altarpiece. Colmar, Musée d'Unterlinden. Photo Bruckmann-Giraudon.
79. Tintoretto (1518-1594). *The Miracle of the Slave.* Venice, Accademia. Photo Held.

taken account of the picture in terms of *something extraneous* to what it is (objects, effect, action) – in other words, in terms of the *subject alone,* as if the painting did not also have its existence *as a painting.*

This is the moment to formulate my first principle, a negative one:

In order to know a work of art, one must reach awareness of it through an attitude of mind that is distinct from the attitudes dictated by the subject.

Let us be sure we understand what that means.

It means, *not* that the painter ought to ignore subject (that is a matter for the individual artist to decide for himself), but that the spectator has no right to look no further than the subject.

Not that the spectator should not try to *recognize the objects represented* (the lemons, the oranges and the rose in Zurbarán's still-life), but that he ought to look further than that.

Not that the spectator should not be *moved* by the sight of Christ's lacerated body in Grünewald's altarpiece, but that he ought to look further than that.

Not that the spectator should not *ask what is happening* in Tintoretto's composition, but that he ought to look further than that.

And so with all other possible views and attitudes, except for one, which forms the matter of my second, and positive, principle:

In order to know a work of art, one must reach awareness[1] of it through an aesthetic view, that is, an attitude dictated by the existence of the work of art as a work of art, and by the capacity of one's mind to apprehend it as such.

What is meant by an 'aesthetic view'? Let us go back to the still-life by Zurbarán. When I look at it more attentively I notice a particular sort of pleasure growing within me, composed of quite simple sensations to begin with: first of all I find myself relishing the *material qualities* of pigments and light, savouring the pitted surface of the yellow-painted lemons, the smoother and warmer-toned texture of the oranges; the neatly woven basket also has a texture pleasing to the eye, and so do the plates, with their metallic sheen, the petals of the rose and the sides of the beaker. But now, in their turn, *the forms* assert themselves: the orange spheres in the centre, piled above the basket, which supports them like a pedestal; the four lemons on the left,

[1] 'Awareness' is here intended to include all the activities of seeing, feeling, appreciating and judging. Since one can neither see nor judge for someone else, the best hope of discovering (and helping others to discover) the basis of aesthetic knowledge is to describe one's own experiences in the light of generally accepted observations.

80. Prehistoric art. Aurignacian Venus, Laussel. Paris, Musée de l'Homme. Photo Archives photographiques, **Paris.**

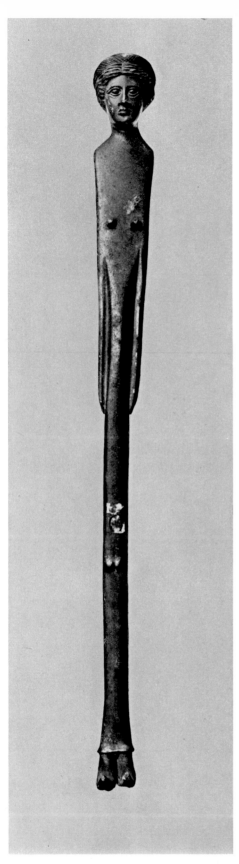

81. Etruscan art. Bronze votive figure, 4th century
B.C. Paris, Louvre. Photo Archives photographiques, Paris.

82. Alberto Giacometti (b. 1901). *The Chariot,* bronze. Private collection. Photo Galerie Maeght, Paris.

83. Martin Hole, 20th century. *The Flagellation.* (Illustrated Bible.)

each seen from a different viewpoint, adding up in sum to a sort of ideal image of this fruit; the ellipse of the plate on the right, and within it, echoing its shape, the bottom of the beaker; and echoing these again, delicately poised at the level of the rose, the twin ellipses formed by the rim of the beaker and the surface of the liquid it contains. Almost without my noticing it, a feeling of harmony grows in me. As if in obedience to some imperative 'Let there be light', the three groups of objects stand out from the uniformly sombre background, against which the table appears as an only slightly less sombre rectangle. Though the groups are placed in a row, I sense that they are linked together by bonds which, though tenuous, are firm. For instance, there is the orange branch, a graceful parenthesis, which includes at its extremities the group with the lemons and the group with the rose, gathering them into the common presence. But this 'presence' owes its unity even more to the play of light. Against the banked-up shadows of the background the fruits are bathed in the light of a primordial dawn, softened here and there by delicate shadows. Various impressions succeed each other and are repeated in my mind, more or less confusedly, according to whether I try to rationalize them, or simply abandon myself to the pleasures they give me. But they all have this in common – they belong to an order of experience which precludes their being reduced to any other sort of impression, as if their roots were in a spiritual clime, where things take on an existence other than their everyday guise as objects. I feel the presence of an invisible architecture, surpassing the sensations received from contemplating the objects themselves, and, slowly but irresistibly, the spiritual grandeur of this still-life expands within me.

Aesthetic knowledge, therefore, is founded on the following premise:

The work of art confers on persons and on things an existence which stems from an order of which they are both the symbol and the manifestation, without necessarily depriving them of their familiar aspects.

Naturally enough, aesthetic forms vary enormously in different ages and environments. The female figure has undergone many remarkable metamorphoses between the Aurignacian Venus, the Etruscan statuette and Giacometti's *Chariot*. Indeed, every civilization has had its own idea of the beautiful and it is useless to fix upon the 'Greek type' in opposition to the 'Negro type', or vice versa.

If taste and appreciation can vary to this extent, are we not bound to accept *en bloc* everything that belongs

80-81

82

to the same aesthetic system? This is the place to put forward the most essential axiom, which, like other self-evident truths, is usually overlooked or ignored:

A work of art can exist only within a certain formal order, i.e., a deliberately constructed system of relationships; and the quality of the work depends upon the degree of accomplishment of these relationships within the formal order to which they belong.

Whether we are dealing with an African idol or a Christian sculpture, what characterizes them both on the aesthetic plane is not the contrasting religious content that each expresses, but the fact that the artist, black or white, is faced with the same formal problem to resolve: the organisation of a mass in terms of solid and empty space, so as to awaken in the spectator's consciousness a sense of beauty as well as a revelation of meaning.

The vexed question of 'sacred' gives us the opportunity to apply this maxim and verify it on the spot. During the Middle Ages an iconography was evolved which in course of time became established for the principal themes of Christian art. Now, since these paintings represent sacred scenes, people have thoughtlessly come to believe that *any* picture of a religious subject is entitled to respect. Hence the industry which goes by the name of 'Saint-Sulpice'. Without looking for an example of this extreme variety, let us content with examining this water-
83 colour by Hole, entitled *The Flagellation,* which refers expressly to the text which it is intended to illustrate: 'Then Pilate therefore took Jesus and scourged him.' I hope I may be forgiven for com-
84 paring Piero della Francesca's sublime picture with this coloured illustration, which, like the frog in the fable, blows itself out, but (alas) does not 'burst'. (plenty of people still fall for this sort of thing! . . .) Note first of all how the grouping of the figures in the illustration is quite haphazard. The forms are related neither to each other nor to the composition as a whole. Indeed, one can scarcely speak of forms: they are more like coloured parcels. Only the subject counts: Jesus scourged by the soldiers. We feel pity for this tortured body, and our indignation is roused against the torturers . . . But we must take note that *this pathos is due solely to the subject, and not to the picture itself*; its source is the *anecdotal,* not the *formal* content of the work. There is plenty for the eye to take in – objects and figures, a scene. We can observe that the stone blocks of the wall are represented with minute precision – a minuteness for which the only apparent motive is a liking for picturesque detail. The vaulted passage-way to the right

adds diversity – it attracts one's attention and stirs one's curiosity – but all it does for the surface composition is to knock a hole in it. The lighting is indeterminate, with highlights scattered about indiscriminately, the only excuse being, perhaps, a taste for local colour. The soldier on the right lays on his strokes to no avail, for his gesture is lifeless, and the lash he wields is no less inert than his arm. It is a magazine illustration, nothing more – *meaningless except in the context of the scene it portrays.*

In complete contrast to this, the grandeur of Piero's picture derives from its formal accomplishment. His scene is divided into two parts; let us consider the left-hand sector. In an architectural space of mathematical purity are five figures, among them Christ, bound to a column. We can feel immediately that the architecture plays a part in the drama: instead of being an accessory item of décor, as in Hole's water-colour, it integrates the action within its enclosed space. The columns on either side seem to form a solid partition. There is no opening at the far end, no outlet. On the low ceiling, which presses down as if the better to crush the Saviour in the weakness of his mortal shape, the black band of the cross-beam seems even more explicitly to mark him as one doomed to die. Shunning every sort of facile allusion, the painter has refrained from giving psychological expression to his figures (two of them are seen from behind, and the faces of the other three betray no particular emotion). Hole's water-colour, on the contrary, uses facial expression as its spiciest ingredient: the grimace of the soldier in the centre, the sneering spectators in the doorway! As for the pavement, Piero does not use it in the least to evoke the appearance of a courtyard: for him these triangles and rectangles have a significance of their own, and the geometrical precision with which they interlock gives us a sensation of ineluctable fate, as if the jaws of a trap had snapped shut on Christ's feet. Observe, too, the treatment of shadows. With Hole they are incidental, serving only to indicate which side the light comes from, a simple matter of physical necessity. Note the one which makes a little patch under the raised foot of the figure on the left, the one which connect's the child's legs, or the one in the right-hand corner which provides a refuge for the artist's signature. In Piero's picture there is not a trace of anecdotal lighting. The figures stand out from the ground with a clarity that sets them in a light as of destiny. [1]

[1] Not that all shadows are suppressed; they are preserved in the folds of the drapery.

In the figure of the man holding the scourge it is the force of the gesture that is portrayed, rather than the gesture itself. Solidly planted on the axis of the right leg, the left leg forming an acute angle with the upright poise of the body, he lifts an arm which seems not so much brutal as implacable.

Piero della Francesca's painting makes us conscious not simply of a spectacle, but of the grand significance of the drama taking place before our eyes. The whole scene is translated into a dimension where divinity is felt as a tangible presence. The pathos is no longer a matter of superficial concern (pity for the victim, indignation at the mocking spectators), but acquires a *symbolic significance –* the involvement of humanity in the tragedy of the Son of Man. It is no longer a report of an incident, but a symbol of our human condition and the divine will.

This metamorphosis has been achieved by means of form. Hole's water-colour has no meaning beyond the incident it is meant to re-enact; Piero's work, on the other hand, only takes on meaning in conjunction with formal resources which create their own context. Thus one is justified in saying, with Focillon, that *the meaning of a work of art is the work itself.*

Since a work of art can exist only within some formal order, *one must necessarily seek to grasp its meaning within the framework of this order, and nowhere else.* There is, therefore, no universal criterion of beauty. Each formal order offers us different experiences and discoveries, which can only be reached through the patient, yet ardent, study of actual works. Thus aesthetic understanding is a process of methodical consideration, which in no way diminishes one's pleasure; on the contrary, pleasure is increased when it also has one's considered approval, and enjoyment is doubled by the participation of one's whole being. It should be unnecessary to point out that this discipline is not constraint. Essentially it is a deliberate method of directing one's attention. If cultivated, it becomes eventually second nature – and that is what one should aim at. A word of warning, though! There is no 'recipe'. This discipline is *the activity itself of feeling and judging from an aesthetic viewpoint.*

Finally, let me enumerate the conditions which appear to be most essential for its proper exercise.[1]

---

[1] This outline, forming the conclusion of the first part of the book, is also in the nature of an introduction to the other three, which respectively develop, extend and illustrate it. These three parts deal only with painting.

Approach the work of art without any kind of prejudice or preconception.
Look at it carefully and attentively.
Contrary to the popular belief, masterpieces seldom make an instant impression; more often they are baffling or intriguing at first.

Remember that aesthetic experience demands a changed attitude of mind, but that it takes time to shed one's habits and accustom oneself to new conditions – apart from one's not always feeling 'in the mood'.

Concentrate your attention on the aesthetic content of the work, to the exclusion of any other content, i.e.:

a) *consider the objects not as objects but as forms, and the forms not as representations of objects but as a series of relationships.*

Thus, in the three paintings we have studied, one observes that the objects, while having their representational function (here are some lemons – here is Christ – here is the slave . . .), also have relationships one with another (the lemons and oranges – Christ and St. John – the slave and St. Mark . . .) by virtue of which they become forms.

b) *consider the colours not as representing the impressions made on the eye by the reflection of light from natural bodies, but as media of formal expression.*

Seen from this point of view, colours are no longer subordinate to objects, and no longer serve only to distinguish them; they begin to exist on the plane of relationships with one another, a level of existence comparable to that of notes in music.

This is how the colours are harmonized in Zurbarán's still-life: the warmest tint – the reddish-orange of the fruit in the basket – is in the centre, like the flame in the middle of a hearth, while to either side the tonality grows cooler: to the left, the sharp yellow of the lemons and the bluish shadow of the plate; and to the right, the green of the beaker, 'balanced' by the pink of the rose. One notices that these colours are not only in harmony with each other, but also respect the sensibility of the spectator, who, appreciating their accord, savours them all the more fully.

c) *consider the surface of the picture not merely as a support, as a neutral ground destined to contain some representation or other, but as formal space, in the same way as the scale constitutes 'musical space'.*

If one were to move one of the three groups in Zurbarán's picture – the group with the lemons, let us say – and place it on the very edge of the table, we

84. Piero della Francesca (c. 1410/20-1492). *The Flagellation*. Urbino gallery. Photo Held.

can sense that the composition would not just be altered, but would be thrown completely out of joint. The displacement of one element in a work of art is never an isolated phenomenon, but a transformation of the network of relationships which constitutes the work. Thus the apparently insignificant areas on each side of the basket (seemingly the more insignificant for being merely shadowy parts of the table, and not particular objects) are as important, in terms of form, as the basket itself.[1]

Bear in mind all the time that aesthetic quality is the product of formal accomplishment, and of that alone. This axiom cannot be too often repeated. Aesthetic quality exists neither in the abstract nor in the absolute, but is inseparable from the works through which it is manifested.

This is not a superfluous precaution. One may

[1] These ideas are developed more fully in the second part of the book, in the chapter entitled *Colour*.

begin by looking at a work in the requisite manner, and then, for one reason or another, allow extraneous considerations to creep in. One can only succeed in maintaining the aesthetic point of view by keeping continual watch on one's sensibility as well as on one's mind.

Aesthetic knowledge cannot be boiled down to any particular idea or criterion of beauty, nor to any special kind of explanation or interpretation; it is the *activity* of judging beauty, and one needs to develop an *active capacity* of judgment. Though each one of us must be responsible for his own experience and judgment, it is nevertheless important to be fair both to the work of art and to oneself. I do not pretend that this outline of method will be of use to everybody, but I hope it may help those who have made the effort to recognize the circumstances of aesthetic experience, and who wish to go on to establish the *conditions of aesthetic knowledge.*

Agents of form

Painting and us

The astonishing development of the cinema has produced in our times a characteristic state of mind, which cannot be said to throw much light on the problems of art.

When film-producers – with a blare of publicity – announce the victory of the talkies over silent films, the triumph of technicolor over black-and-white, or the advent of 3-D and Cinemascope, they are suggesting that the quality of a film depends on its power of illusion, and that the glorious destiny of the film industry is to perfect this power still further. Experiments have already been made in recording smells, which – cunningly projected into the auditorium – will at last give the public the sensation of *total realism*.

But what charm will the cinema have when it exactly reproduces our actions, when the street, from which it is so often a haven of refuge, follows us in with its whiffs of dust and grime, and when the camera, instead of transporting us to a land of enchantment, drags us back into the everyday world outside?

One cannot too often repeat that *art is not imitation*. Technical progress has nothing whatever to do with artistic progress. Art never takes the form of

85. Rembrandt (1606-1669). *Landscape,* brush drawing. Paris, Louvre. Photo Giraudon.

consummate illusion, but is dependent on whether or not the artist is able to express a *new* truth.

Masterpieces are not necessarily elaborate *tours de force,* as the humblest drawing from Rembrandt's hand can abundantly prove. The strokes of his brush fan out in transparent washes, or curl like whipcord, and instantly the landscape or scene takes shape before our eyes, like the memory of someone seen once by chance, whose features stick in our mind. It is odd indeed that a scrap of paper can put all the fabulous resources of Hollywood to shame – its money, its stars, its scenes of living action! Time is *not* money; in art, time is quality.

However, rather than continue in this vein of recrimination, let us try to clear up a few points – first, the question of how, and in what part of us, we are affected by a work of art. A so-called 'spectacular' film produces violent impressions, exciting us in rather the same way as a fairground stimulates and jars our nerves with its noisy loudspeakers, its flashing lights and neon-signs, its jostling crowds and feverish activity – but with this difference, that the film probably adds a story and, perhaps, a moral for our edification. This kind of film, like this kind of fair, makes hardly any lasting impression. The moral of the one is forgotten as quickly as the tawdry glamour of the other. Too violently and too hurriedly assaulted, bludgeoned from all sides, our senses are blunted and take refuge in a sort of apathy to avoid being overwhelmed.

This bodily tumult is neither profound nor durable, and the effect disappears with the cause. It is a physical agitation that goes no deeper than the epidermis or, at most, the viscera; and *unless it is prolonged it has no place in the memory.* That, incidentally, is why those who wish (as they put it) to 'forget' crave the stupor it produces, and provoke it at need. And that is precisely why art rejects it – so that man shall *not* forget, but, on the contrary, shall *remember.* But since art cannot by-pass the senses, it makes use of them so that they help, instead of hindering each other, so that they rouse us instead of stupefying us, and so that, instead of being limited to physical sensation, they raise their perceptions in unison to a pitch where the soul itself is gradually involved.

And this is done with *economy,* each separate art touching only one of the senses at a time, or, if it touches several, reserving the primary role for one of them. Ballet would be nothing without music; but even so, it is primarily a pleasure for the eye, and the ear takes second place. Orchestral music, on the other hand, is solely for the ear, as the visual arts are solely for the eye. According to the organ of sense *which it addresses, each art disposes us towards an appropriate kind of attention and expectation.*

Yet there are so many varied approaches to our senses, and to the sense of sight in particular, that each of the visual arts tends to make use of a different one. Architecture and sculpture appeal to what we might call 'space-vision' (which sees in terms of volume), ballet to 'movement-vision', painting and the graphic arts to 'surface-vision'. Each art, then, chooses some *specialized sensation,* like a kind of gang-plank to our bodies, which develops a scale of sensibility capable of infinite nuances. (What are the hum-drum sounds of nature in comparison with the marvellous resources of music?)

Not only does one's 'reception' improve in quality, it changes in kind. Looking at a picture is not just a question of registering an image. The eye traverses and explores it, dwells in it. Free of all extraneous thoughts, voluntarily confined to one particular mode of attention, the retina no longer limits its activity to registering, but even anticipates the work with demands of its own. I think it was Democritus who said that our eyes put forth tentacles, as it were to seize the image. This explanation has caused amusement to scientists, who have substituted for it the theory (so much more serious!) of light waves; but the philosopher-poet, in his simplicity, gives expression to an intuition that we have all experienced; to us, seeing is not a mere physical phenomenon, fully accounted for by science. Our eye acts; it justifies or condemns ('this blue doesn't go with that yellow!'). With practice its enquiries can be multiplied and refined – not without reason does one speak of a 'practised' or 'experienced' eye – and in contact with art they soon become methodical, guided as they are by a quality that has grown to be a second nature. Thus – and here is already a precious gain – not only does art permit us to see more, and to see more clearly, but that which I have called the 'specialized sensation' permits us to *participate.*

Our senses, therefore, have two modes of operating: either they simply experience and register, or else they intervene to take an active part in the business. Only in the second case does art become a living reality, for it is only then that we ourselves contribute something to it.

Perhaps you wonder what I mean by that. It is surely true to say that a spectator at the theatre becomes in some measure an actor as soon as the curtain rises, even though he does not mount the

86. Pisanello (c. 1397-after 1450). *Profile head,* pen drawing. Paris, Louvre. Photo Held.

stage. When Rodrigue, in Corneille's *Le Cid,* faces the count and flings down his celebrated line: 'A quatre pas d'ici je te le fais savoir...', I know very well, in the comfort of my seat, that I am only an impotent witness of this mortal challenge, but still, a part of me leaps to Rodrigue's side as if to lend him support. I recall in a flash that he wishes to marry Chimène, that they are in love, and that the death of either Rodrigue or the count will be the end of all their happiness. I am aware of all these things at once, and the fear of imminent disaster fills me with apprehension. My heart beats faster, I suffer an anguish that takes my breath away, and I strive to intervene, to ward off the catastrophe, to grapple with destiny itself – a silent role, but what an active one, prompted by the poetic genius of Corneille! In this manner the action of the play is matched by a corresponding drama – imaginary, but of gripping power – in the spectator. When this fails to happen, the performance descends to mere empty mummery. The play which does not 'come across' is still-born.

Painting invites us to an equally active participation, though naturally of a different kind. Dramatic action is replaced by what may be called *formal action.* In their own way, lines, colours and shapes are characters, whose fortunes are enacted before our eyes – and we play our part in the *dénouement.* If I run my eye over the *Woman's Head* by Pisanello, and 86 see it only as the delineation of a human profile, I miss the point of the formal action, which, rather than the model herself, is the real subject of these lines – as if I contented myself with reading a résumé of *Le Cid* instead of going to see it in the theatre; the résumé gives me the plot, but the play can only come to life in a performance. If, on the other hand, I let my eye follow the three-fold curves of the head – enclosing the head-dress in the arc of a circle, containing the forward thrust of the forehead, and clamping tightly around the chin – then follow the contrary curve of the nose, and trace in turn the heavy plaits which form a monumental framework for the hair, the drawing becomes something different: I see each line as part of the sum of action which makes up the work as a whole.

The comparison of a painting to a play must not be taken too far – nor too literally, for there is nothing more horrible than 'theatrical' art! All I wish to do is to point out that each in its own appropriate way involves an action, in which the spectator plays his part. As Rodrigue is the personification of heroism, or Oedipus of sorrow, so can intimacy, vivacity or gentleness be personified in lines, in colours or in light. Considered alone, Rodrigue is no more than a half-historical, half-legendary personage; it is in *Le Cid* that he acquires his heroic stature, and it is through Corneille that he acquires a meaning. Considered alone, line is nothing – but what vigour it acquires in Pisanello's drawing!

Every art, then, is based on some 'action', and each one has its *particular locale in which the action takes place:* for the theatre, this is the stage. Have you noticed how fraught with expectancy it seems when the curtain goes up? Empty? Far from it! It is peopled by all the eyes that are fixed on it, filling it with a network as of living fibres. If the actor misses his cue or muffs his lines, then the spell is broken, acting falls to grimacing, the scenery sinks to the vulgarity of carpentry and painted canvas, while the audience relapses into a discomfiture from which it tries to find release in laughter. If the actor rises to his role, his power electrifies the stage, enriching it with every line: a few wooden planks are the stone stairway of Macbeth's castle – it is the audience that achieves the metamorphosis. It is the audience which finally empties the stage, when it withdraws its rapt attention from it.

One may say, by analogy, that the surface is to the picture what the stage is to the theatre, and it demands no less of the spectator. Have we not all at some time or other watched an artist set up his easel, open his box of paints and lay on the first touches of his sketch? We feel a lively curiosity. How will he set about it? What has he chosen to paint? But it is not only curiosity. Deeper within us there rises a feeling of anticipation, of expectancy: what is going to happen? It is as if, in the presence of a blank or as yet almost untouched canvas, one expects *something to happen.*

Here first is line, delicate and subtle – line, which runs its course from Egyptian wall paintings to Greek vases, from China to Japan. In short, brisk strokes it builds a nude of Dürer or a *landsknecht* of Urs Graf.

More softly, yet not limply, from the hand of Clouet it rounds the forehead of a queen, the bosom of a princess. Austerely curvaceous, it makes a luscious fruit of a torso by Matisse. Here now comes colour: flat, it gives the miniature a precious glaze; but then, like sun-ripe honey, it puts on translucent flesh with Giorgione, is full and juicy with Rubens, or turns ascetic with the earlier cubists.

Fascinated by space, man invents perspective, and into it the figures rush, no longer enclosed in an outline, but weighted with a body that is expressed as volume. With volume new beings are born, half aerial, half subterranean – the people of the shadows, who aspire eventually to autonomy. Painting struggles with the invading dark of Caravaggio, before reaching the tragic conflict to which Rembrandt carries it. Light, tamed into obedience by Corot, regains its liberty as a shower of sparks on the anvil of the impressionists. Now Seurat disciplines it once more, and now Rouault brings it to a new degree of incandescence . . .

For painting is *language.* One can no more make art out of tracings from reality than one can make a love-poem out of sighs, kisses and caresses. Poetry exists through the medium of words, painting through the medium of forms. By means of the specialized sensation of lines and colours, it is manifested – on the 'stage' which is the surface – in a formal action, in which we are invited to take part. But that is not all it offers. Though Oedipus mutilates himself and inflicts on himself the most terrible sufferings, the tragedy of Sophocles, for all its horror, still enraptures us. Though Hieronymus Bosch may terrify us with his monsters, his works arouse our admiration. Beyond the emotions which poetry and painting provoke in us, the beauty which is common to them both turns all to light. Art alone is able to attain this pinnacle where emotion – *first passed through, then transcended* – changes to an ideal vision, of which the symbol is fulfilment.

Preliminary observations

'Away with the subject!' This battle cry from the early years of the century still echoes oddly in our ears. The very fact that academic art rejoiced in splendid warriors in Roman attire, or odalisques reclining insouciantly on leopard-skins, has led too easily to the belief that all that is needed, for art to recapture its primordial innocence, is to do away with the helmets and embroidered tunics of the former, the too languid poses, the bangles and trinkets of the latter.

Painting first and foremost, pure Painting – as it was before the Fall! If we are to believe the new dogmatists, one has only to bring pencil and paper into contact with one another, and leave the initiative to them, for the work of art to 'happen' by some miracle of inspiration, without the trouble of taking thought; and the result will be judged (the proof is as simple as it is infallible) by the degree in which this encounter of pencil and paper convinces the spectator that 'this is like nothing one has ever seen', or even – 'this is like nothing one ever *could* see'.

The alibi of 'subject' has given way to the new and equally dangerous alibi of 'non-subject'. That is to say, the academic mentality is just as great a menace among those who shrewdly sense which way the wind is blowing, and proliferate their random dots and triangles.

To define 'subject' as that which the artist represents, is to suggest that art has as its aim the imitation of a model, and one concludes by implication (but how wrongly!) that the value of a work of art lies in its power of imitation. To define 'non-subject' as that which refuses to be restricted by any degree of imitation, is to suggest that the aim of art is to repudiate the copying of nature, and one concludes by implication (but how wrongly, once again!) that the value of a work lies in its total rejection of natural appearances. Of course, both conclusions are equally absurd. Instead of encumbering ourselves with false propositions, we should seek to know *if that which has taken shape on the paper, canvas or wall has quality; and to what extent we can recognize and judge such quality.*

There are no basic differences between the portrait of a girl by Auberjonois, Geertgen's *Christ* and the Etruscan frieze with the little horses at Tarquinia; they meet on equal terms in the domain which essentially concerns us – that of painting. Beyond any sacred or profane purpose they may have, these three works are related by the use which each makes of the language of form. Of course, they are different – in technique, in what they represent, in composition, in treatment of form, colour, lighting, and so on; but

87
88
89

87. René Auberjonois (1872-1957). *Simone*. Switzerland, private collection. Photo Emile Gos.

88. Geertgen tot Sint Jans (1460/65-1490/95). *The Man of Sorrows*. Utrecht, Archiepiscopal Museum. Photo Archiepiscopal Museum.

89. Etruscan art. *Figures and horses,* about 510 B.C. Tarquinia, tomb of the Baron. Photo Büchergilde, Zürich.

in each is manifested that common factor, which, even while it distinguishes them one from another, *raises them to a common plane of value. The language of form is nothing else than the painter's use of formal resources, the existence of which is revealed to the spectator through style.*

Before we attempt its analysis, there are one or two observations to be made.

A distinction is normally drawn between 'painting' proper, which consists of line and colour, and 'drawing',[1] which either dispenses with colour or gives it only a subsidiary role. Thus far the distinction is valid. Often, however, judgments of value are founded on it, the commonest being the idea that a painting is worth more than a drawing because it makes use of greater resources, pen-and-ink or pencil being regarded as poor relations. But let us compare the few square inches of a drawing by Callot with the square yards of a canvas by Detaille or Horace Vernet! What are all the stuffed uniforms and frozen gestures worth beside these allusive beings, these tattered silhouettes against the apocalyptic dawn of the *Arquebusade*? Just as military advantage depends not merely upon power and quantity of armaments, but also upon the energy and intelligence of the combatants, so does aesthetic worth take into account not only the resources employed, but the intelligence with which they are employed.

It is true to say that drawings were made use of by the artists of former ages mainly as preparatory studies, and that they were therefore regarded as of

90
91

91. Edouard Detaille (1848-1912). *The Czar at Pasteur's Funeral.* Versailles, Museum. Photo Giraudon.

[1] I am stretching the meaning of the word 'drawing' here to include all that is not strictly painting – to include engraving techniques in particular.

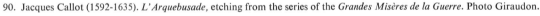

90. Jacques Callot (1592-1635). *L'Arquebusade,* etching from the series of the *Grandes Misères de la Guerre.* Photo Giraudon.

92. Paul Cézanne (1839-1906). *Fruit-dish and Apples*. Winterthur, Reinhart coll. Photo Held.

only relative importance. However, many painters preserved their studies, and they have come down to us in fair numbers, which shows that they were far from being despised. Indeed, their value was appreciated from the first: Dürer's drawings did not have to wait for today's connoisseurs to compete for them; they were collected already in his lifetime.

Whatever the original purpose of a drawing – whether it was a study for a picture or not – the qualities it can dispose of are the same as for a painting. We must ask ourselves the same question: *'Does this something which has been drawn have quality: and to what extent can we recognize and judge it?'*

The second point to be made concerns the distinction between different *genres*. Not so very long ago history painting was considered the noble genre par excellence. When Delaroche, having painted his

Death of Queen Elizabeth and his *Cromwell opening* 93 *the coffin of Charles I,* produced *Richelieu ascending the Rhône,* the doors of the Académie were opened wide to receive him. The painter was aged thirty-four, and the year was 1831. Half a century later a few apples of Cézanne's bowled them all over – Crom- 92 well, Richelieu, the fame of Delaroche, *and* the imaginary hierarchy of genres!...

Let us examine this notion of genre. Obviously, it is based on the nature of the subject. Thus, in addition to history painting, we have portraiture, still-life, landscape, etc., all deriving more or less directly from religious art. Until the end of the Middle Ages portraiture does not exist in Christian art as an independent genre. The early portraits of donors invade the realm of sacred art only with the utmost discretion, kneeling piously in one corner of the picture

100

and hardly venturing to raise their eyes. Besides, they are carefully represented on a smaller scale, in recognition of the gulf which separates them from the divine personages. But humility wears thin with time, and, towards the dawn of the Renaissance, donors no longer hesitate to vie with the saints, the Virgin or Christ Himself – at least in point of stature. During the Renaissance their audacity knows no bounds, and it occasions no surprise when Gozzoli or Ghirlandaio cast their patrons in the roles of the three magi or of female saints!

Despite this emancipation, the feeling was long to persist that secular painting was of less merit than religious, and until the end of the 19th century it occurred to no-one to apply the same standard of judgment to a basket of plums as to a *Crucifixion* – even if the former were by Chardin himself.

Is the man-in-the-street today any more ready to agree with the proposition that a bowl of fruit or a guitar can be more important than a human face? While trying honestly to accept it, he feels an insidious and stubborn resistance to the idea. 'Surely there's more in the human form than there is in a bowl and a few fish!'

One of the discoveries of our time (though prepared by all that has gone before) is that in art no object is worth more than another. Let us take good note of this truth, for it has taken (and is still taking) a long time to penetrate men's minds.

We may conclude that it is useful and legitimate to preserve the idea of separate genres, but only if we are careful to use it as a term of convenience, *with no qualitative overtones whatsoever*. Landscape, still-life, portraiture and the rest have no value as such, but only in what the artist is able to make of them.

We may extend this line of argument to the distinctions between different techniques – fresco, mosaic, stained glass, miniature or easel-painting. These terms, too, answer a need for classification, yet it is often supposed that one technique is, of its nature, better or less good than another; and from here mistaken ideas multiply in chain reaction... How many of us are left cold by the Ravenna mosaics, in spite of the sincerest efforts to kindle a glow of appreciation! Certainly, such people feel unbounded admiration for the nameless artists whose enthusiasm could go to the length of covering the walls of S. Apollinare Nuovo with tiny cubes, but it is the performance they applaud, not the work. Beyond that, mosaic seems to them an art which savours tiresomely of the age in which it flourished. 'After all, Europe was pretty barbarous in the 5th and 6th centuries!'

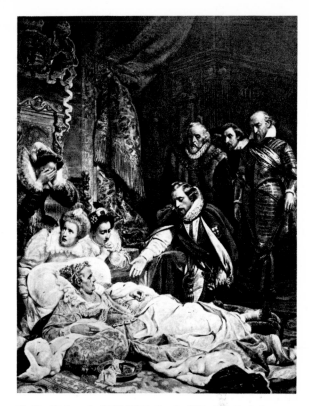

93. Paul Delaroche (1797-1856). *Death of Elizabeth*. Paris, Louvre. Photo Archives photographiques, Paris.

94. Benozzo Gozzoli (1420-1495). *John VII Palaeologus as one of the Magi*, detail of fresco. Florence. Palazzo Medici-Riccardi, chapel. Ed. Brogi.

It is the same with stained glass, which arouses in so many a similar prejudice. However smart it may 98 be to praise medieval glass, in general the layman 99 prefers that of later periods, the technical skill of which can rouse his spontaneous admiration.

Different techniques, we must conclude, *have no intrinsic value; only style – that is, the artist's use of the language of form under the conditions that each technique imposes – can give them any.*

A final point: the word 'style', like many others in the vocabulary of aesthetics, is loaded with ambiguities; or rather it is we who, through lack of discernment, use it loosely to describe different things.

If I place several of Raphael's religious pictures side by side, I become aware of certain characteristics common to them all: purity of drawing and figure-grouping, elegance of design, a predominantly light tonality, delicacy of handling, and so on. The same holds good for any painter. Each has his style, by which one means his way of painting, of treating subjects, forms, surface, lines and colours – in short, all that goes to distinguish his manner from that of any other artist.

If I now compare the works of Raphael and Michelangelo with those of the primitives who preceded them, I perceive that the two Renaissance artists, in spite of obvious differences, have certain traits in common. In this case the word 'style' alludes to features peculiar to the art of a particular period. In comparison with our previous definition, it concerns characteristics of a more general kind, which still relate, however, to the treatment of subject, surface, colour and line.

Now, as we have seen, the human mind is seldom content to leave well alone, but is tempted by notions of a hierarchy. The idea which prevailed until the end of the 19th century, and which a sizeable section of the public would defend to this day, is that Renaissance art is the summit of perfection in painting. Accordingly, all works prior to the 16th century are uniformly held to be 'primitive', i.e. to be lacking in something – the something being precisely this 'perfection' of the great period.

Fortunately, this sort of fallacy is becoming less common. Thanks to the spread of art books, the realisation is growing everywhere that different styles are not degrees on a single immutable scale of values, with Renaissance art at the top, but that each style contains within itself *its own* scale of values. Thus, as with genres and techniques, *styles have no exclusive merits of their own; each has the merit conferred on it*

95. Rembrandt (1606-1669). *Self-portrait.* Vienna, Kunsthistorisches Museum. Photo Held.

96. Chaim Soutine (1894-1943). *Herrings.* Paris, Katia Granoff coll. Photo Held.

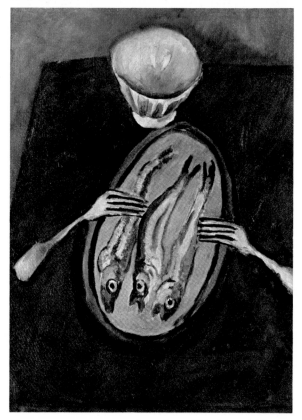

97. Byzantine art. *Last Supper,* mosaic, 6th century. Ravenna, S. Apollinare Nuovo. Photo Bulloz.

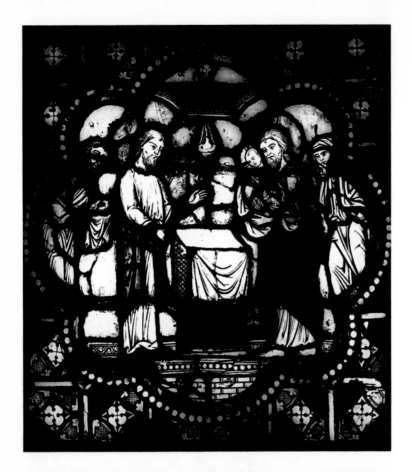

98. Gothic art. *Presentation in the Temple,* stained glass, 13th century. Paris, Charnoz coll. Photo Giraudon.

99. Renaissance art. *Death of the Virgin,* stained glass, late 16th or early 17th century. Church of Montfort-L'Amaury (France). Photo Viollet.

by the use which was made of the language of form during a given period of history.

As in any literature there are a number of genres (poetry, the novel, drama), each characterized by a different technique, but all sharing a common quality *as literature,* so in painting there are various techniques (mosaic, stained glass, fresco, miniature, easel-painting), each with its own methods, but all sharing a common quality – that of *form.* As poetry, drama and the novel include narratives, descriptions and studies of character, so do mosaic, easel-painting and stained glass embrace the 'genres' of portraiture, landscape or still-life. Now the novel – for all its universal vogue at present – does not put an end to poetry, and no more does easel-painting (equally universal in our time) condemn stained glass to desuetude. One can only say that certain genres flourish in certain periods, as techniques do also, but that all are one in enriching the human spirit by expressing it anew in different formal terms.

Can we define 'style'? The answer is 'no', if we attempt to imprison it in a formula; 'yes', if we limit ourselves to the statement that it is *different* from ordinary language.

Speech (or writing) is a vehicle for transmitting thought as conveniently as possible; its aim is communication; its function, social intercourse [1]. The language of art, on the other hand, is never confined to simple communication. It seeks not only to 'penetrate' but also to *affect the mind, stimulating emotion by its very manner of operation.* Its function is not social intercourse, but the transmission of a lasting experience.

[1] 'The act of communication is the act whereby a person, having knowledge of a perceptible fact associated with a certain state of consciousness, i.e. a desire for collaboration, expresses this fact in such a way that another person grasps his intention and reconstitutes the first person's desire in his own consciousness.' (Eric Buyssens, *Les Langages et le Discours.*) I shall return elsewhere to these fundamental questions, which it is my intention to approach by stages.

Steps towards an art of seeing

The observations made in the last chapter may help us to realize that reading a poem or looking at a picture are both fairly exacting exercises. Taste and inclination are not enough; we also need some sort of preparation, in which intelligence and sensibility are allied, and a certain amount of experience too.

Does this mean one may legitimately speak of an 'art of seeing'? I think so, as long as we remember that the word 'art' is being used here for want of a more precise term; it is not describing an activity that is intended to produce something, but one that is rather synonymous with ability. Thus the art of the helmsman (an example dear to Socrates) is not a corpus of theoretical knowledge, but the faculty which makes the helmsman able to pilot his ship. In the same way, the art of seeing is that which fosters the spectator's *aptitude* to understand and appreciate a work of art.

Fortified by this definition, let us now examine the two works here reproduced – the *Virgin of the Rocks* 100 (Louvre version) by Leonardo, and Matisse's *La* 101 *Lecture* – beginning with the former, which is a universally celebrated masterpiece.

To begin with, what do I *see*? As the picture's title suggests, a particular subject: in front of a rocky grotto, which opens onto the distant background, are four figures – the Virgin; the infant St. John the Baptist, sheltered beneath her arm; the angel with the pointing finger; and the infant Jesus with his hand raised in benediction. This is what Michel Florisoone says about it in his guide for visitors to the Louvre: 'The picture most probably illustrates an episode that occurs in some apocryphal gospels, which relate the miracle of the mountain splitting open to give refuge to St. Elizabeth, fleeing with the infant St. John from Herod's persecution; then the visit to her, while she was in the grotto, of the infant Jesus, who was borne there from Egypt by an angel; and finally the adoption of the orphan St. John by Mary.' Does this help us to see the picture any better? Not a bit. At most, it helps to identify the figures and to explain the reasons for their presence.

Now this type of information, though I would not deny its relevance in this instance, is by no means always needed: when one looks at an *Annunciation,* one expects as a matter of course to find the Virgin on one side and the archangel Gabriel on the other. Matisse's picture is called *La Lecture.* It is quite unnecessary to identify the two women; the title is sufficiently justified by the open book which one of them holds. As often as not a picture manages per-

101. Henri Matisse (1869-1954). *La Lecture*. Washington, Phillips Gallery. Photo Held.

◄   100. Leonardo da Vinci (1452-1519). *The Virgin of the Rocks*. Paris, Louvre. Photo Held.

102. Bernardino Luini (c. 1475-1532). *Holy Family*. Milan, Biblioteca Ambrogiana. Photo Alinari.

fectly well without a title; 'landscape', 'still-life' or 'portrait' are adequate enough descriptions.

Seeing paintings must never be confused with the *act* of understanding what they represent. The art of the spectator is to *appreciate works in respect of their formal quality*.

We need to be careful here, for one is usually tempted to say 'beauty' instead of 'formal quality' – and 'beauty' is the vaguest and most ambiguous of words. Most people suppose that beauty conforms to a certain type or standard, from which there is no deviation. If we were to take a vote on the 'beauty' of the *Virgin of the Rocks* and *La Lecture*, the former would undoubtedly get the majority (whether or not Leonardo's picture is actually superior to Matisse's does not enter into the question), and if we were to ask the voters why they chose Leonardo, we might expect their comments to boil down to this: 'Everything is better drawn and much better done in the *Virgin of the Rocks* . . . *La Lecture* looks like a sketch – the women might have been done with a stencil. Their faces are quite flat, and look how careless the hands are.' (Ah! the hands – that infallible criterion of art!)

Reasoning thus, they are almost unaware of the injustice they commit. It would take a very bold man to claim that he had actually *seen* 'beauty' itself! So our art of seeing includes this warning: do not judge the beauty of a work of art in accordance with your own mental idea of the beautiful, but accept the evidence which art and nature both provide on this point – *beauty can take many different forms*.

Our more irritable and impatient brethren may ask if it would not be simpler to declare, once and for all, that everything is beautiful – or else that everything is ugly! Rather than enter into useless argument, I would invite them to compare the *Virgin of the Rocks* with Luini's *Holy Family*, and this *Odalisque* by Matisse with a painting by one of his all-too-numerous imitators, and ask them if they can still maintain in good faith that the absence of a fixed type of beauty means that all works are of equal worth! Even without a fixed type, they will surely agree that works of art, while expressing beauty in different forms, can be distinguished by *variation of quality* within the formal language employed.

Let us look more closely at the *Virgin of the Rocks* and compare it directly with *La Lecture*. We are struck at once by the atmospheric unity of Leonardo's picture. Figures and objects are bathed in an atmosphere replete with shadows, from which only certain parts of the figures and certain parts of the landscape

102
103
104

103. Henri Matisse (1869-1954). *Odalisque*. Paris, Musée d'art moderne. Photo Giraudon.

104. Hermann Geiseler. *Reclining Woman*. Munich.

emerge. Colour is not absent – there is red, green, blue and yellowish-brown – but it is as if the artist had put a mute or damper on it.

To turn from Leonardo to Matisse is to step straight from twilight into the midday sun. The colours are the same: red, green and blue, while yellowish-brown has separated into yellow and brown. But we are witnessing much more than a simple switch from dark to light. For Matisse the colours are the controlling element, as tonal values were for Leonardo (i.e. Leonardo uses colours not for their own sakes, but in degrees of luminous intensity). Between the two, painting has undergone a complete transformation.

The children's flesh is treated by Leonardo as an opportunity for infinite modulation, producing a delicate contour, the modelling being tempered by *sfumato*, which avoids too pronounced a relief. With Matisse the light is of equal intensity throughout, and the colours are laid on in blobs and patches without any of the shapes developing at all in depth. The demands of pure colour are incompatible with modelling, because modelling (as we shall see in detail later on) involves alteration of colour. For this reason the bodies of the girls with the book are necessarily flattened, while Leonardo's figures are given the appearance of roundness and volume. Now this predominance of tonal values in Leonardo's picture, harmonizing with the requirements of modelling, has also the effect of organizing the picture space in depth. The infant Jesus is in the foremost plane, St. John the Baptist and the angel in the next, and the Virgin in the third, while in the background is the rocky wall with its opening that looks out onto the distance beyond.

In Matisse's case, depth and modelling are both precluded. In fact he is obliged to bring the background forward into the surface plane, so that the tapestry, the rectangle of green and the door are virtually in alignment with the two women.

Is it enough just to put colours side by side? Well, it can clearly be seen that Matisse's spatial organization is as elaborate as Leonardo's, though it is achieved by different means. In relation to the green of the background (a cool colour), the yellow of the dress (a warm colour [1]) gives the impression of being 'in front', but to stop it 'coming forward' too much the painter has dressed the second woman in blue (a cool colour), which serves to hold back the yellow. Thus space may be constructed of tonal values, as in Leonardo, or of colours, as in Matisse. The latter

[1] See the chapter on *Colour*, which is to follow.

artist adds to the cohesion of his space by using complementary colours: the red in the tapestry and in the dress on the right, and the green of the background and the two plants on each side, reinforce and complement each other, as do the yellow and blue of the dresses.

No part of the surface of the *Virgin of the Rocks* is left unpainted. Even the minutest 'blank' would seem to puncture and destroy the tissue of continuous gradations. Matisse, on the contrary, is obliged to leave margins of white so as to preserve the maximum intensity of his colours; they are not gaps, not the result of carelessness, but necessary intervals between the strong accents of the colours.

And now for facial expression; let us see how that is treated. Despite all the literature concerning Leonardo's famous smiles, none of his faces, when examined closely, express any precise emotion; we see no more trace of it in the Virgin than we do in the infant Christ. This is because the use of sfumato and tone-values is unsuited to the portrayal of marked psychological expression. But when Leonardo undertakes to paint a dramatic subject, he is not content simply to tone down the expressions of his figures accordingly. Instead he *changes both his technique* 105 *and his style*, as we see in the famous *Last Supper* in Milan. Fresco calls for composition in terms of mass, in contrast to the modulations of form that are possible in oil painting. The atmospheric qualities of the *Virgin of the Rocks* give way in the *Last Supper* to an emphatic method of design, which 'blocks in' the figures boldly. Dark and light colours tend to be placed in opposition, instead of being adjusted to one another by means of subtly graduated tones, and these oppositions help in establishing an appropriately dramatic atmosphere. Not only are the facial 106 expressions different, but the technique of treating the heads is also changed. In comparison with the 107 angel's features, those of the apostle are deliberately simplified. Indeed, everything is different – even to the manner in which the paint is applied. The brushstrokes in the *Virgin of the Rocks* are of extreme delicacy, while in the *Last Supper* they are executed with great boldness. Leonardo in fact makes the most of the potentialities of oil or fresco in accordance with the subject he is treating, and he takes good care not to make a fresco of the *Virgin of the Rocks* or an easel-picture of the *Last Supper*.

Matisse, subordinating all to colour, is faced with formal necessities of a no less exacting kind. His chosen course of emphasizing the surface is inimical to any degree of psychological expression that would involve suggestions of volume, so he gives the merest indication of features on the flat colour of the faces, features which have a decorative role comparable with that of the pattern on the tapestry, or of the blue lines which represent the door behind the green plant.

Look again at the composition of the two paintings; both are constructed with equal firmness and, indeed, present curious similarities. The *Virgin of the Rocks* is organized as a pyramid, its summit the Virgin's head, its sides St. John the Baptist and the angel. In Matisse's picture, where the style repudiates depth, the pyramid becomes a triangle, its summit occupied by the girl in yellow, its right side by the girl in blue, and its left side by the plant on the pedestal table (this plant performs the same function in the composition as St. John the Baptist, just as the figure in blue performs the same function as the group of the angel and the infant Jesus).

There are points of resemblance even in the backgrounds. The gaping rocks, which open onto blue distances, correspond to Matisse's tapestry with its blue motifs ringed in red. The dark mass behind the Virgin becomes the green rectangle, against which the head of the girl in yellow stands out. Highlights on the rocks, relieving the opacity of the shadows, become the pale margin surrounding the girl's black hair. Finally, we can observe a like solicitude in the right background of both paintings, where the rock silhouetted against the sky in Leonardo's work corresponds to the green plant against the door in the other.

Of course such analogies must not be pushed to extremes, but since they suggested themselves here it would have been ungracious to ignore them, and they can be of assistance in illuminating the everneglected truth that beauty depends not on imitating a standard type, but on *achieving expression through the language of form.*

At this level one can say that the *Virgin of the Rocks* and *La Lecture* are works of equal accomplishment. Whereas Leonardo subordinates everything to the luminous atmosphere resulting from the interplay of

105. Leonardo da Vinci (1452-1519). *The Last Supper,* fresco ▶ (detail). Milan, S. Maria delle Grazie. Photo Anderson-Giraudon.

106. Leonardo da Vinci (1452-1519). *The Last Supper,* fresco ▶ (detail).

107. Leonardo da Vinci (1452-1519). *The Virgin of the Rocks* ▶ (detail). Paris, Louvre.

105

106

107

tone-values and sfumato, Matisse subordinates everything to colour, with light of unvaried intensity. Each of these methods gives the work an appropriate and individual character, transforming figures, objects, shapes, colours, surface organization, draughtsmanship and brushwork. To sum up in simple terms, one may say that Leonardo deploys his forms in depth by means of interpenetrating tonal values, while Matisse deploys his in a single plane by means of juxtaposed colours, so that the pyramidal composition of the *Virgin of the Rocks* becomes triangular in *La Lecture*. One is expressed in the picture-space, the other on the picture-surface.

Seeing pictures, therefore, consists in *looking for their meaning and quality in terms of the coherent, though differing, use which they make of the language of form.*

As the helmsman steers his vessel, so the spectator steers his judgment. In both cases there is one course to be followed, others to be avoided; but, while the helmsman is menaced by reefs and storms, the spectator is exposed – though one might not think so – to even graver perils! To perish from the rigours of the elements is excusable, but there can be no excuse for falling through one's own fault into prejudice and self-deception.

I feel bound to state, in this connection, that the art of seeing calls for certain moral qualities, of which the first is to be *sympathetically disposed*, adopting towards the work an attitude not of refusal but, on the contrary, of openness – both of heart and mind. Whatever initial shock or surprise we may feel, let us be patient and say to ourselves: 'There may be something in this that I am not accustomed to, and perhaps that something has quality; let's try to find it, even if it means changing some of my ideas . . .' The preposterous opinions which critics formerly held on the subject of Cézanne should recommend sympathy to us not only as a moral quality but also as a matter of common prudence!

The second quality may make you smile, for it is – quite simply – honesty! However, in an undertaking like ours it is not a case of making up one's mind that one *is* honest, but of *learning the practice of honesty.* We shall have ample opportunity to recognize that this is no easy matter!

In conclusion, I shall attempt to define the right way to approach a work of art. First of all it is a question of seeing something (but this time we need not concern ourselves with the subject!). Reverting to the comparison between the pictures by Leonardo and Matisse, I note that my starting-point in the *Virgin of the Rocks* was the sensation of a luminous atmosphere governing variations of tone, while in *La Lecture* it was the sensation of a harmony of colours brought to an equal degree of saturation. The starting-point is a matter of intuition, which we may define in Poincaré's words as '*the faculty which teaches us to see*';[1] 'without it', he adds, 'the geometrician would be in the position of a writer who knows all about grammar but has no ideas to express.' In fact intuition alone can take a direct and immediate view of things. But still, it needs to be *controlled.* 'Invention is achieved by intuition' says Poincaré, meaning that *on finds what there is to be found,* that one discovers it.

Control is achieved through reflection, which, unlike intuition, is an indirect route to knowledge. Thus it is by intuition that I sense the decisive importance of the colours and the even tonality in Matisse's picture, and sense that luminous atmosphere is the basis of the *Virgin of the Rocks.* Intuition operates as a total sensation, seizing all one's faculties at once, whereas reflection proceeds by stages and with the aid of intermediaries. For instance, when I consider the composition of *La Lecture,* I am starting from the *notion* of composition, knowing it to mean the manner in which various parts of the picture are arranged, and by applying this notion I recognize the central triangle formed by the plant on the left, the girl in yellow and the girl in blue. Reflection works by successive *abstractions* (while I am concentrating on the composition I deliberately ignore the picture's other elements – colour, line and light), and each abstraction gives me a partial view of the work, crystallizing into a partial judgment.

At this point we meet an objection that never fails to be raised – that one cannot hope to analyse a work of art because by definition it is one and indivisible, and is not an amalgam of separate components. Now is the time, therefore, to put forward this basic principle – the cornerstone of aesthetic knowledge: *While it is true that a work of art is a homogeneous, indivisible and (strictly speaking) unanalysable whole, it is false to pretend that it can be grasped instantaneously in all its complexity. Intuition allows us to understand it in part, or more exactly, brings us into contact with it, but it is reflection orientated by intuition, and intuition guided by reflection, that lead gradually to knowledge.*

Knowing a work of art does not mean dissecting it, but means considering it from as many different

[1] *Science et méthode.* The italics are mine.

angles and points of view as may be necessary, provided that all of these are related to one's original intuition. The points of reference which knowledge, defined in this way, has need of are precisely the constituent elements of the language of form – surface, line, colour, composition, proportion and rhythm. We must remember that none of these elements exists in isolation, and it would be useless as well as wrong-headed to suppose that a work is the result of adding them together. On the other hand, it is useful for the spectator to consider them separately, since each of them provides him with a different perspective of appreciation, by which he can focus his attention first upon one point, then on another. If he does not do so, then either the work eludes him, or else it never goes beyond the inevitably summary impression of his intuition. In short, the art of seeing consists in starting with a true intuition, which should then be deepened and extended by properly conducted reflection. The part which *savoir-faire* plays in this process is the real subject of this book.

Space

What matters in a painting is not the fact that its limits define a space of a particular extent, but the fact that this is *space of another nature,* requiring *another kind of attention.*

In purely material terms the cinema screen is a blank canvas, like that of the painter; but as soon as the images of the film are projected onto it, it becomes the seat of 'cinematographic reality': heroes live, love and die on it, without any protesting voice saying: 'what's the use of watching these pictures – they are only a make-believe trick of light and shadow!' On the contrary, the spectator shares in the life of the characters, feels their joys and sorrows.

Pictorial space is likewise ambiguous. Like the cinema screen, it is a portion of space defined by its dimensions, and, like the screen when the film is being projected, *it is the seat of a reality* in which things that we know to be fictional are felt to be true. Every painting confronts us as *a space both real and imaginary,* defined in the one case by its geometrical dimensions and its material character, and in the other by the imaginary forms which occupy it. I should point out, however, that the imaginary space does not nullify real space, but only transforms it. Thus the painted forms are neither entirely imaginary, since they inhabit the geometrical and material space of the wall or canvas, nor entirely 'real' (in the empirical sense), since they inhabit the fictional space as well.

Now this real-and-imaginary space, the native element of painting, is only revealed under certain conditions. Darkness in the cinema has the same function as silence in the concert-hall. As the lights are dimmed, the audience stop looking about them at their neighbours or at the decorations on the walls; darkness isolates the eye and concentrates it on a single spot, blotting out all around it, in the same way that silence isolates the ear and concentrates the sense of hearing. This is a factor that people too often forget where painting is concerned. In this case it is the frame of the picture, like the beam of light which traces the limits of the screen, that marks out in the surrounding space the precise arena in which 'something is going to happen', and which assumes its 'other' reality as soon as the spectator, concentrating upon it, alters the nature of his attention.

It is not easy to convey a just idea of the kind of space which painting creates. Suppose I am standing at a window, watching the street outside: the houses 108 recede in depth, drawing closer together until they meet. I can distinguish the shapes and details of the nearer vehicles, while the more distant ones are only indistinct patches of colour.

Suppose I shut the window, without moving from my vantage-point; the scene, beyond the glass, is still the same; if I pick up a crayon and draw the houses and the church on the window-pane, then I have a tracing of the street; and if, instead of drawing it on the pane, I transcribe it onto a sheet of paper, then I have a *perspective rendering* of the street.

Now a perspective diagram like this is not linked to my being as a whole, but only to my perceptions. When I stood at the window to watch the street, I was acting as an observer, confining myself to taking it in as a spectacle, leaving all to my eye, and not letting any other consideration intrude upon it.

Imagine now that I return to the window, but no longer with the tranquillity of an observer. I am waiting anxiously for my small son, who has not yet come home. I keep glancing at the time, and continuously watch the corner of the street. My anxiety grows – you can get lost so easily at the age of five! The street scarcely exists, apart from that corner where he ought to appear. But there is no-one there. In fact, there are plenty of people there, but I hardly notice them; in my state of gnawing apprehension they are no more than passing shadows. But now a diminutive figure comes in sight! My heart beats faster, and I lean from the window. Nothing exists apart from this one small body, which gradually grows larger, just as an approaching figure on the screen increases in size from the distant shot to the close-up. Whereas a moment ago the street seemed desperately empty, with buildings and people reduced to phantoms, now it is warm and full to bursting – filled only with the presence of this slip of a child, who loiters on his way, quite unaware of all my fears.

Thus we see that a feeling of space is linked not only with objective perception, but (and this needs emphasizing) with all interior states. As everyone knows, one's sense of time is changed by states of mind or emotion, and in the same way the sense of space, and its representation also, are subject to metamorphosis. Our senses are not alone in making us aware of space; emotions, sentiments or ideas can do the same. Therefore there is not only *one* kind of space, as is commonly believed, but a great many different kinds.

In so far as painting is concerned, we see that methods of perspective vary in different ages and civilizations, and with different artistic mentalities and environments. But though these systems have distinct and individual characteristics, they have this in common: *they all reject documentary vision* – the neutral, every-day kind.

108. *The houses recede in depth, drawing closer together.* Morges (Switzerland). Photo Held.

109. The street in perspective.

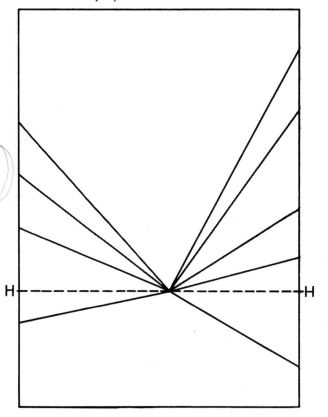

109

118

Italian Renaissance perspective is still unquestionably the most acceptable to the majority of people. Inaugurated by Giotto in the 14th century, and raised to a mathematical science by Brunelleschi, it was codified by Alberti in his two books on painting, which appeared towards the middle of the 15th century. How does it work? In essence it converts space to a two-dimensional surface, representing things on a wall or canvas as they appear in depth to the eye in reality. This involves the use of a dual perspective system: *linear perspective,* which foreshortens objects to give an illusion of depth, and *aerial perspective,* which 'foreshortens' colours – i.e. graduates them proportionately to their 'distance' from the eye. Thus the illusion is achieved by means of *calculated distortions.*

This method of painting has prevailed for about four hundred years – from the 15th century to the end of the 19th – and people find it hard to believe that it is not final and definitive, even though modern art has raised the whole question anew. The more accustomed one is to a thing, the less one is inclined to examine it. Yet, when one really thinks about it, one sees that Renaissance perspective also relies on certain conventions. To begin with, it implies a *fixed viewpoint* for the spectator, since the method of representation is governed by a *vanishing-point* that corresponds to the axis of sight. In fact the picture space is a sort of cube or parallelepiped – 'the world's great cupboard', as Paulhan amusingly wrote, 'in which figures and objects, Gods and haloes, were arranged as on the spokes of a wheel.'

How different from this is our normal way of looking at things! When we survey a stretch of country we do not confine ourselves to a single viewpoint, but adopt as many as we please. Our gaze can wander – scale a mountain, rest on a peak, swoop down to the valley, settle on a roof-top, skim over a rock or a passer-by; or, if we lie down, it can be enthralled by a blade of grass, behind which the mountains are but vapour. Far from any intellectual synthesis governed by a vanishing-point at infinity on the horizon line, we juxtapose images that are related to *different viewpoints* (we do not stay still, and even if we do our eyes are always on the move), so that in fact the vanishing-point is continually changing, and the landscape is made up of a number of variously disposed elements, rather as we have been taught in Cézanne's extraordinary still-lifes!

As soon as one rids oneself of vague and ready-made ideas, one realizes what an arbitrary thing space is in painting. Arbitrary – that is the word which gets left out, for it offends against the notion of an established order of things! Furthermore it is a word most often used in a pejorative sense. One of the main reasons why the public at large continues to say 'no' to modern art is the inescapable feeling that the painters of today treat the established order too casually, whereas the old masters . . .!

When I say that Renaissance perspective is arbitrary, that it is based on conventions and that Brunelleschi's 'machine for seeing' *is* a mechanical device, I mean to say that it has no basis in the real nature of things, but I do not mean that it has no basis at all. On the contrary, it is the product of a reasoned *choice,* and the works of such men as Uccello, Piero della Francesca and Leonardo have imbued it with imperishable worth. This shows us:

a) that in art one cannot reject conventions in favour of any return to 'natural laws';

b) that the validity of such conventions rests purely in the quality of actual works; and consequently that, however great the Renaissance artists may have been, other works and other artists can express an equally valid truth through other conventions and other renderings of space; and finally

c) that no system of conventions is ever arbitrary if its principles are justified by works of art.

Therefore the bases of aesthetic conventions, their truth and their meaning, are to be found in human consciousness.

Look at Mantegna's *Crucifixion.* Viewed from a fixed point, the scene is organized around a central axis, which defines a certain extent of space, and this arrangement understandably determines a particular mode of observation. Consciously or not, the eye is drawn perforce to the cross which stands in the centre of the picture; if it strays to the left, the foreshortened group of St. John and the holy women directs it back towards the figure of Christ, who incidentally is the only person depicted full-face; if it strays to the right, the foreshortened horse and rider have the same effect, and so do the foreshortened figures of the thieves in the upper zone of the picture.

This demonstrates an important fact: *painted forms influence the eye, inducing it to move, behave and perceive in a particular manner, according to the kind of space they constitute.*

Now compare Mantegna's *Crucifixion* with the fresco painted a century earlier by Andrea da Firenze. Here the scene is organized in an arc, which the eye traverses in a wheel-like movement, starting at the bottom left. Carrying the cross, Jesus emerges

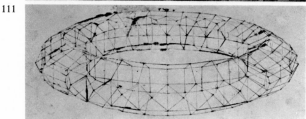

110. Paolo Uccello (1397-1475). *The Rout of San Romano* (detail). Paris, Louvre. Photo Giraudon.

111. Paolo Uccello (1397-1475). *Study of a 'mazzocchio'*. Florence, Uffizi. Photo Soprintendenza alle Gallerie di Firenze.

from Jerusalem, preceded by mounted soldiers; behind him follow the Virgin and the holy women. The procession ascends the hill in a sort of gully, and at the top Jesus appears again, crucified and surrounded by angels, while a great crowd is assembled at the foot of the cross. To the right the soldiers dice for his garments, while below we see his descent into Limbo, where, having cast down the gates and struck terror into the demons, he extends a succouring hand to Adam and – through him – to all of fallen humanity.

Instead of being developed in depth, Andrea da Firenze's space is a flat semicircle, which the eye takes in by a circular progression from left to right. This confirms the fact we noted above, and adds another quite as important:

In influencing the eye, painted forms influence the mind as well, persuading it to accept and 'enter' the type of space which they create, and in which they reveal their particular significance.

This is what is really meant by the term 'arbitrary'. Neither Mantegna's space nor that of Andrea da Firenze has a basis in what we call the nature of things, but, as we have seen, in the nature of man, or

rather in human consciousness striving to express itself. Expression is achieved through formal relationships which, though they differ from age to age, have a quality that is attested and preserved by the works of art they engender.

Renaissance perspective is not only a technical invention; it expresses a particular view of existence. It envisages space as a *definite area,* in which objects are marshalled submissively before the fixed, serenely god-like gaze of a privileged spectator. For the 'primitive' Andrea da Firenze space is like the page of a manuscript, on which the synoptic table of Christianity is unrolled for the faithful to read as they glorify God.

A third fact emerges from the other two. In influencing the body (when conditioning the eye's behaviour), and in influencing the mind (when conditioning the conduct of our thought), *every plastic expression of space is associated in our consciousness with a certain conception of the world and a certain sentiment of our place in it, which it evokes or creates in us.*

Thus contact, both physical and mental, is established between artist and spectator, enabling them to understand each other and to share the same processes of feeling and of thought[1].

No form in art is 'objective', or founded upon 'the nature of things'; it takes shape only in minds that adopt an attitude in common, and it eventually seems 'natural' purely because it is familiar.

The spatial system of the primitives (the Romanesque painters especially) is analogous in several ways to that of children. The visible symbols of the Christian faith are presented against a background devoid of depth – for example, the figure of Jesus in this fresco at Tavant, two or three times as large as the others. The narrative is unfolded in bands of decoration running one above the other, each comprising a number of separate compartments in which normally several moments of the same scene are represented simultaneously (as in Andrea da Firenze's fresco, although he is not a Romanesque artist), while the images are not organized in relation to any fixed point. The spectator is expected to move, his eye

116

---

[1] At least, this used to be so. It has not been quite the same since the beginning of the 20th century: space has been the subject of so much experiment on the part of contemporary artists that the understanding with the public is in danger of being broken. For any spatial system to become accepted and incorporated in the group-consciousness takes time. Only after twenty or thirty years did Braque's, Picasso's or Matisse's approach to space gain acceptance. Classical perspective has lasted for three or four centuries, while that of the Egyptians survived for three or four millennia . . .

112. Paolo Uccello (1397-1475). *Story of the Profaned Host*, predella panel. Urbino gallery. Photo Held.

113. School of Piero della Francesca (15th century). *Perspective study* or *Ideal City*. Urbino gallery. Photo Held.

roaming as it were, through a space enriched by the multiplicity of viewpoints, instead of occupying an imaginary balcony, before which the action takes place.

Thus the primitives appeal to a quite different mode of seeing and thinking, a point of view far removed from that of the Renaissance, but no less valid and rewarding. At the risk of over-simplification one might say they make us aware of the world, partly by juxtaposing separate images (each related to a different viewpoint), and partly by setting our minds in motion so that the sensation of continuous space is effected by a mental synthesis.

117-118   One type of perspective employed by the Indians and Chinese approaches that of the Renaissance in that it is tied to a horizon line, but, instead of a single horizon there are several. As for the objects, they are foreshortened not in depth but the other way about; it is the background that grows wider, so that the

114. Andrea Mantegna (1431-1506). *Crucifixion,* predella panel from the San Zeno altarpiece, Verona. Paris, Louvre. Photo Held.

115. Andrea di Bonaiuto, called Andrea da Firenze (op. 1343-1377). *Crucifixion.* Florence, church of Santa Maria Novella, Spanish Chapel. Photo Anderson.

116. Romanesque art. *Christ's Descent into Limbo,* fresco (detail), 12th century. Church of Tavant (France). Photo Held.

spectator's eye no longer has the impression of passing along a colonnade, as in Italian perspective, but of penetrating it and – because of the plurality of viewpoints – of being situated *at the centre* of the objects represented, *between* the buildings instead of opposite them. It is this *insertion* of himself among objects that counts for the Chinese or Indian spectator, whereas for the European, brought up in the school of Italian perspective, the *confrontation* of the objects is what matters more.

117. Ajanta: two buildings in 'Indian perspective'.

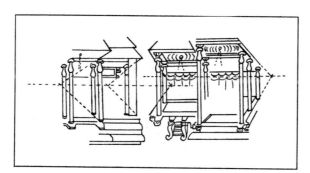

118. The same buildings seen in 'classical perspective'. Drawings by J. Auboyer.

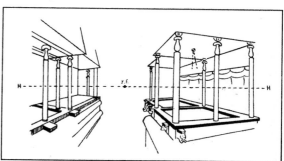

123

119. Egyptian art. *Agricultural scene,* Theban age, c. 16th-14th centuries B.C. Paris, Louvre. Photo Bulloz-Viollet.

As for the Egyptians, who represent their figures in a single plane, they are equally far removed from 'classical' perspective. The crowd of slaves about the body of a deceased dignitary is shown as a procession in which each element is isolated to be seen in full view and entire. Depth, which threatens the integrity of objects by foreshortening them and modifying their colour, is replaced by a strict system of conventions whose purpose is to preserve that integrity in line and colour.

120 Consequently the human body is treated in a manner which resists the modifying influences both of time and of natural space. The most characteristic features are emphasized at the expense of the rest. The head is shown in profile, in conformity with the picture-plane, but the eye is drawn back to appear complete, as in a full-face view. Similarly, by means of a 90-degree twist that could never be seen in classical perspective, the shoulders are shown in full view. The pelvis serves as a transition, and appears in threequarter view, while arms and legs are drawn in profile like the head. The colours also obey strict rules, being laid on flat without any gradation. The Egyptians' perspective, like the others, influences us through forms which enable us both to decipher and experience their attitude to life.

The cubist painters, whose efforts provoked such an outcry, were only doing the same sort of thing. They felt that the resources of Impressionist perspective were exhausted, and sought to replace it with a spatial system that could embrace their works in the spirit of the dawning century. As Paulhan repeated, paper *collages* are new 'machines for seeing'. Let us

121 examine this one, in which Picasso has mischievously included a tobacco packet lying on the folded, yellow-

ing newspaper. But can we actually say it is 'lying'? No, for the way it rests on the paper appears to defy the laws of gravity. Is it stuck or suspended in some way? Looking at the top right-hand corner one might think so, but the bottom left-hand corner contradicts the idea. In fact it is neither lying nor hung on the paper. An odd kind of space indeed! Is the packet drawn on the canvas, then? At one edge it is, but at the other it is not, for it appears to present its right side in relief. What are we to make of so ambiguous an object? Let us look at it more closely still. If in imagination you suppress the dark line which makes an obtuse angle across it, you have almost the image of a packet of tobacco in perspective – thanks to the break in direction of the label and the shaded area on the right. But instead of being foreshortened in recession it is foreshortened in projection, as in Indian perspective; hence the impression that it 'sticks out'. If you restore the dark line, the perspective is reversed, jumping back into depth, but even now you do not see it as in classical perspective, for it is now as if you were seeing the *inside* of the packet. An optical illusion? Well, Picasso *is* making use here of that kind of phenomenon, but he transforms it. In some places, and especially at the left side of the tobacco packet, he arranges his lines and planes in a different manner, deliberately relating them to the surface to prevent confusion. This is the hinge by which 'projection' and 'recession' are integrated with the rest of the composition and are made to conform to the picture-plane. As it appears in this detail, cubist space can offer us objects which, while losing nothing of their exterior aspects, are enriched with interior aspects too, as if the eye were able not only to move around an object, but also to get inside it – as

124

120. Egyptian art. Papyrus with a text from the *Book of the Dead* (detail) New Kingdom, c. 16th-11th centuries B.C. Cairo, Museum of Antiquities. Photo Held.

121. Pablo Picasso (b. 1881). *Le Journal,* collage. Paris, Dr. Dalsace coll. Photo Held.

if, in fact, we had two sorts of eye that both see simultaneously.

Cubist space, then, has its justification, like that of Egypt or China, each being applied to the discovery of some fundamental aspect of human truth. In other words, artists envisage their art – and themselves also – *in terms of the kind of space that gives them the most acute sensation of reality.* All painters in their turn take up the triumphant cry of Alberti: 'At last perspective [he was of course referring to his own brand] permits me to see the world as God saw it.' To attempt to discredit Renaissance perspective is as absurd as to pretend it is the only valid kind. Perspectives change as men change their ideas of existence. To each different expression of space there corresponds a different idea of reality.

But if the various types of perspective are only so many conventional systems, how is one to draw any distinction between two works that belong to the same system? Will they not be of equal quality, since they both obey the same rules? This objection can be cut short: whatever the convention adopted, it has no intrinsic aesthetic merit. It is a body of *conditions,* not of laws, and it cannot dictate a work to the artist; it offers him a form of language, but it is up to him to create his own 'speech'.

This is where many artists are at fault, including some who are highly regarded. There is an incoherence in Sodoma's decoration, due to the fact that the saint and the architecture are not treated in the same plastic spirit. The three-dimensional architecture puts the emphasis on linear perspective, while the treatment of the figure puts it on modelling, which implies depth of a different nature. The resulting impression is of a painfully amorphous and theatrical figure.

Piero della Francesca solves the problem thus: his figures are placed in an almost identical setting, characterized by a strictly linear space construction,

122. Sodoma (1477-1544). *Saint Victor*. Siena, Palazzo Pubblico. Photo Anderson.

123. Piero della Francesca (c. 1410/20-1492). *Madonna and Child with Saints*, Milan, Brera. Photo Held.

124. Gothic art. *Alexander the Great in Single Combat,* miniature, 13th century. Hanover, Kestner Museum.

125. *A photograph suspends the action; a work of art prolongs and enlivens it.* Photo Lipnitzki.

but they are not just reasonably well modelled figures and no more. They obey the logic of the chosen type of space, and their modelling is adjusted to geometrically defined volumes; their poses and gestures seem almost to stem from the character of the architecture, which in Sodoma's case is mere décor, unable to contain the swaying of the figure.

124 Here is a further demonstration, from a different approach. In the marvellous *Alexander the Great in Single Combat,* space is reduced to the two dimensions of the surface. The fury of the combatants is not diminished by this, but this kind of perspective necessitates a different employment of formal resources. Deprived of volume, the knights seem weightless, floating in a sort of savage dance, to which the lines give force and discipline. Blood streams in fiery filaments, and the bodies writhe like flames. Now let us imagine that some ass were to add even the smallest hint of modelling to this conflict of sinewy lines; the
125 thing would shrivel into a mere theatrical photograph where the most spirited gestures are nothing but actors' miming.

Space in painting is never to be confused with natural space. It is always composed of conventions which influence the spectators' senses on the one hand and their minds on the other. For the creator it corresponds to his most vivid sentiment of reality. Broadly speaking, *perspective conditions the formal language through which is expressed a common attitude of mankind to life and to the world.*

Just as in music the key conditions the character of notes in accordance with their place in the scale – *an arrangement governed by internal logic, but at the same time providing material for innumerable different combinations* – so in painting space conditions the character of forms and the manner in which they are arranged with a similar internal logic, and likewise providing material for innumerable different combinations.

In examining any work of art it is *essential to accept the kind of space it offers and adopt the attitude it requires, for only then does it assume a form and acquire a meaning.* It is reasonable to refer to Renaissance perspective in order to appreciate Raphael, and it is no less reasonable to refer to primitive perspective in order to appreciate a primitive painting, for otherwise one falls into prejudice and error. 'The dumb picture speaks from the wall' wrote Gregory of Nyssa. Still, to understand what it says, one must know the spatial system of the wall.

Line

With one swift silhouette a clever draughtsman can catch the likeness of a person and even his gestures; though it is only a rough abstraction, the outline is enough for recognition. A dress-designer does not bother with lengthy explanations, but shows the cut of a dress or coat in a brisk line drawing, which 126 serves just as well as a costly fashion show. The schematic drawing of an architect or engineer tells 127 his client far more than columns of calculations could!

Watch a child applying himself to the task of drawing a dog – pencil in hand and tongue thrust out. Tracing paper would save him the trouble, but – once the surprise of discovery was past – it is doubtful if he would want to use it. (A singular manifestation of the child's proverbial laziness!) Obviously the effort means something to him. Bent over his work, he repeats the actions of our ancestors tracing the likeness of bison and aurochs in their 128 caves with the aid of a little earth and powdered, calcined bone. Line here is a snare, trapping the fleeing reindeer or hemming in the tiger on the page of a painting-book. Our forefathers hunted animals and our children tame them . . . line as magic maybe? Perhaps in the background there is also the urge to appropriate, to make a thing one's own. To touch is to assess and (even more) to know a thing and know oneself. Line provides a hold on objects, and gives to the draughtsman in the exercise of this power a sense of his own existence.

Informing, identifying, explaining, describing and remembering are among the many ends that line can serve, but one should add that *in so for as it serves ends like these it is outside the domain of art; and it only enters that domain when it takes its own nature – its graphic quality – into account, regardless of the end it serves.*

126

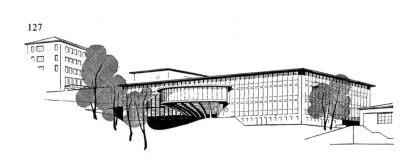

127

128. Prehistoric art. *Reindeer* (detail). Cave of Lascaux, circa 40 000 B.C. Photo Archives photographiques, Paris.

129. Honoré Daumier (1808-1879). *La Parade*, drawing (detail). Private collection. Photo Durand-Ruel.

130. Dubout (1906). Humorous drawing.

Comparison of a drawing by Daumier and a humorous cartoon will demonstrate this better than any explanation. The cartoon does not go beyond its satirical intention. We laugh, and that is all there is to it. In contrast, the pitiable clown who stands to attention beside the exuberant bulk of the fat lady, and the ravaged features of the mountebank in the foreground, make a lasting impression, in which the dominant sentiment is of human distress. Cartoon and drawing are both simply combinations of lines, but Daumier is not just doing the same thing better; he is doing something else, and does it *through the formal quality of his drawing*. But we must begin at the beginning.

On the sensual level, art is enjoyment. So far as line is concerned, this statement means that it makes either an agreeable or a disagreeable impression, or that it leaves us unmoved. A straight line is 'easy' to look at, and gives a feeling of ease; but such effects are of short duration, and if the straight line is too long we tire of it at once, and the feeling is lost. It is the same with a curve or any other sort of line. Thus, when a sketch pleases us, experience shows that our pleasure is born of something that is neither too disconcerting nor too predictable. It is a pleasure that needs to be kept alive by continual variety. This is not an arbitrary or tyrannical demand, but one that derives from the very nature of our sensibility, for which *things exist only in so far as we interest ourselves in them. Hence the rule that nothing in art should leave us indifferent.*

How threadbare in expression line must be, considering that it disposes only of the straight line or the curve! To argue thus is to take a superficial view, for art consists not of isolated elements but of their relationships. Even if it is a question only of straight lines and curves, these relationships can be of infinite variety, as ornamental art – one of the richest and most ancient of human arts – can amply demonstrate. Similarly a few notes are enough to make a piece of music, since intervals and duration modify their quality and character, giving them each time a new existence. 131

Take, for example, this collage by Picasso: *Bottle and Glass on a Table,* which dates from the Cubist period. When the initial surprise is past, one has no difficulty in recognizing the objects, despite the allusive and discontinuous style in which they are drawn. The bottle's angular top, its mouth shown as a disc, rests on a straight neck, which in turn springs from the shoulders. On one side the shoulder appears as a quadrant, on the other as a curtailed quadrant – and there the bottle ends! The lines break through each other almost as if the bottle had been broken into separate pieces – yet does it give any impression of mutilation? No, not at all, for here an unforseen and unforseeable phenomenon comes into play: *lines do not need to be drawn entire for us to receive the sensation of continuity; when suitably stimulated, the eye will supply what is lacking.* 132

In Picasso's collage the unity of the bottle is conveyed by a grouping of angles, curves and spaces which build it up as an assemblage, not of different 'parts', but – by virtue of the discontinuous line – of different tensions. The corroboration of memory is no longer required for the object to be recognized.

Every element in the language of form, even an element apparently so insubstantial as line, can thus constitute a space in which the eye, behaving in a manner different from that of normal vision, helps to establish the forms.

One might suppose that the interrupted outline was a Cubist invention, but a glance at this landscape study will show that Poussin also used it. The left hand side of the foliage is indicated by a complex of pen and brush strokes, while the right hand side is suggested by a few brisk squiggles on the sky. The trunks of two of the trees are interrupted at the point where they branch, without affecting their apparent robustness. Nearly all artists make use of the hiatus, almost as if line has need of pauses in order to deploy its full vigour within the spatial context of the design. 133

131. Etruscan art. Askos, 8th century B.C. Bologna, Museum. Photo Walter Dräyer, Zürich.

132. Pablo Picasso (b. 1881). *Bottle and Glass on a Table*, collage and drawing. Alfred Stieglitz collection, New York. Photo Held.

133. Nicolas Poussin (1594-1665). *Study of Trees*, pen and wash. Paris, Louvre. Photo Held.

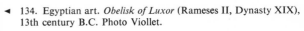
134. Egyptian art. *Obelisk of Luxor* (Rameses II, Dynasty XIX), 13th century B.C. Photo Viollet.

135. Primitive art. Pictograph. Cuna Indian, San Blas Coast, Panama. Photo Musée de l'Homme, Paris.

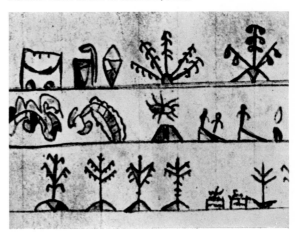

135

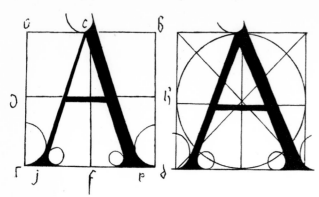

136. Letters by Dürer (1471-1528) and Luca Pacioli (1450 - after 1510).

The expressive power of line was appreciated by man from the earliest times. At the dawn of history it helped him to institute his very first 'ark of the covenant': writing. Its chosen symbols, more potent than the stammerings of speech, established communication in time and space, beginning the most stupendous of all adventures, for those silent voices that reach us from our remotest forbears are part of the living fabric of humanity. To communicate is to break free from isolation. To transmit is to deny the finality of death. Thanks to writing, time for us has ceased to be fate's executioner, and has become a tutelary genius, preserving what each one of us commits into its care. 134

Nor did our ancestors value line only for its power of representation. We know that in ancient times the virtue of a magic formula resided not only in the words, but also in a certain intonation, and it is not unreasonable to suppose that the magic virtue of writing lay likewise in a certain graphic

137. Moslem art. Granada, Alhambra, detail of façade. Photo Viollet.

138. Gothic art. Illuminated page, missal of the Abbey of Corbie, 13th century. Amiens, Library. Photo Archives photographiques, Paris.

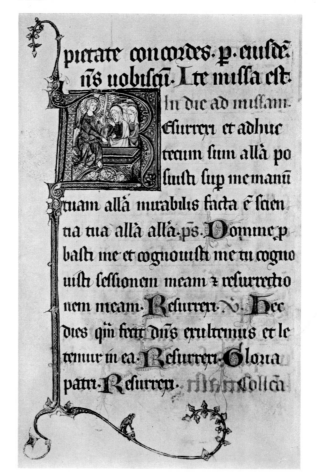

quality. To preserve their power, priests and scribes doubtless had to be able to invest the written characters with an excellence that made them hard to imitate. They did not set out to create art, but became artists by the accident of necessity! Thus, whether the characters are pictographic, ideogrammatic, syllabic or phonetic, one notices that in every case their quality owes at least as much to graphic excellence as to the import of the text.

This subtle affinity was strongly sensed by several of the great men of the Renaissance, who felt the need to create model alphabets that would bring writing into harmony with the new spirit that was abroad in the world. Amongst others, Alberti, Dürer and Luca Pacioli applied their genius to this idea. Even today, in spite of the prodigious development of printing, and although the magical aspect has disappeared, the families of letters each have their affinities and repulsions. A striking and familiar example of this is provided by the typography of advertising. The need to catch the attention of the passer-by – a reader in a hurry – results in the letters on a poster being given a more 'gripping' form. In this way the force of 'meaning' in writing is accompanied by a material, sensuous force in the shape of particular graphic qualities. Abstraction of the meaning does not annul the claims and needs of form. *Thus the plastic quality of linear symbols ceases to belong to writing, and becomes an autonomous expression of form, at precisely the moment when it is able to detach itself from the verbal content which it conveys, and to create a content of its own by its own means.* And thus it is that art as a whole invents the language of forms, parallel to the language of words.

Let us try to see this decisive transmutation of line actually happening. In the decoration of Moslem buildings cufic[1] inscriptions play a strange and important part. Inasmuch as it is writing, each inscription is *a group of words conveying a meaning* (usually a verse of the Koran): on the other hand, when its semantic content is abstracted, *it becomes ornament,* serving no purpose but its own. This proves clearly enough that line can lead a dual existence: as writing, it is subordinate to the verbal content; as ornament, it creates a world of form in which it is itself one of the constituent elements.

[1] A form of Moslem script, with thick and angular characters. The name is derived from Kufa, a town that was founded by the Caliph Omar, and was for long a capital. The cursive, or *Nesji* script, with its rounded characters, lends itself equally well to decoration. These scripts are found throughout the Moslem world in the form of friezes and ornamental inscriptions.

We can also see this process of transition in medieval manuscripts. The large initials at the chapter-headings are decorated with illuminations, in which variety of design and charm of colour are combined. There too, formal quality is subordinated to a text, but such is its vigour of expression that it sometimes breaks out and gives free reign to fantasy.

The Story of the Thief Punished[1] relates, in the manner of an old fable, the adventure of a malefactor who gets caught. We see him first at the extreme left, running away with his booty; unluckily for him, he trips head over heels, is belaboured with blows by the person wielding a stick, and finally, at the extreme right – the end (and the moral) of the tale – is apprehended by two bailiffs who put a rope round his neck. This is a perfect example of drawing which is still subject to narrative, yet is just beginning to be emancipated. One 'reads' it from left to right, and the action is divided into 'episodes', but – and this is of capital importance – *it transcends the verbal content. Its substance, its tone and style are derived from intrinsic, graphic resources.* The supple continuity of line (equivalent to the brevity and economy of a fable) is self-sufficient. Narrative, ruled by the power of words, is transposed into a kind of dance, ruled by the power of lines.

[1] This example is borrowed from André Lhote.

139. French School: *The Story of the Thief Punished,* drawing, 12th century. (From *Traité de la Figure,* by André Lhote. Ed. Floury).

It is in this sense that art is to be thought of as a language. Like verbal language, it serves to express and communicate our thoughts and feelings, and – different though they are – the languages of words and of forms have this in common: to translate the inner reality of our being, they both must resort to *equivalencies*.

If further proof is required, here – descending 140 now towards the ridiculous – it is: a fashion drawing, which should serve our purpose admirably. One can see its limitations at once. What matters here is the emphasis on hat, jacket and skirt . . . and beyond that? Nothing at all! The costume is everything – or rather, the idea of it one gets from the sketch. You may look at it for as long as you like, but it will still be no more than the pretext for

presenting a fashion. Line is subjected and reduced to its demonstrational purpose.

Now consider this drawing by Constantin Guys, 141 which conveys so well the girl's provocative yet indolent sensuality. This impression comes not from the idea one forms about the subject, but essentially from the graphic expression for which it is the occasion. Beneath the lavishly plumed hat, treated with broad strokes, the little face is no more than an outline and the dark blob of an eye – an anonymous creature. In contrast, her personal charms are most frankly displayed by the plunging décolleté of her dress: triangular as a dart to the left, long and rounded as a fruit to the right. The provocative venality of the courtesan emerges from the use of contrasted angles and curves, light and

140. *Line is here only a pretext.*

141. Constantin Guys (1805-1892). *Créature.* Nadar collection, Paris. Photo Archives photographiques, Paris.

142. Greek art. Attic amphora, *Achilles and Ajax*, 6th century B.C. Rome, Vatican Museum. Photo Anderson-Viollet.

dark patches, broad strokes and thin, which create their own content and achieve the status of forms. They are no longer a pretext, as in the fashion plate, but the text itself.

With this in mind, let us now consider some of the ways in which line is used.[1]

[1] It should be remembered that a means of expression cannot be precisely defined, since it does not exist in isolation, but that it can be studied and understood in its active relationships. The distinctions which follow are not intended to describe lines of different species (like zoological species). Rather than invent an elaborate terminology or proceed to generalizations, I have preferred to examine a few characteristic functions of line in order to show, if possible, the principle upon which it acts in painting. Needless to say, there are many other instances which I have not gone into.

143. Georges Braque (b. 1882). Drawing from the artist's sketchbooks. Photo *Verve*.

144. Child's painting. *Zebras in the Park*. Milan, Scuola Mazzon.

Silhouette line

I use this term to describe line in its function as the boundary between a form and the field which surrounds it, as in this 6th-century amphora, on which **142** the figures stand out from their background by means of a simple outline. Even when the outline is not expressly marked, and this is often the case in painting, it still exists as the meeting-place of two fields of **143** differing tonality, as in the drawing by Braque.

At first sight, the line with which a map-maker demarcates the indentation of a coast hardly differs from the sort of line we are here concerned with; both result from a mental abstraction, and both are unaffected by air, atmosphere and light. But, though they have a similar intellectual origin, they are in fact essentially different. The map-maker's line is intended only to respect topographical accuracy; the artist's, while also respecting 'topography', is guided by graphic qualities of its own. The map-maker's line is abstract, systematic and static – a straightforward intellectual equivalent; the artist's is abstract, but neither systematic nor static, for it is constantly elaborated and modulated, constantly in movement. The elements it is composed of are not a sum of straight lines and curves, intended to *describe* a form; instead they engender proportions and relationships which *signify* a form, and introduce it to the realm of art.

One can readily appreciate that, the more silhouette line is emphasized, the more it demands that the space which it contains should conform to the picture plane (is not line the very expression of two-dimensional space?) The artist who decorated the amphora set his figures on its sides without the least allusion to depth; similarly in Braque's drawing there is no shadow or relief to disturb the unity of the surface plane. *There is, therefore, a formal correlation between silhouette line and two-dimensional space, since every formal device implies a world of form, an order in which it takes its own place and plays its own part.* The principle of the coherence of a work of art is founded on this fundamental law.

It seems that children understand this instinctively. The kind of line they use to represent people and objects marks out areas of surface without shadow. When they turn to colour, they do so spontaneously – to do a bit of colouring. These zebras are silhouettes **144** of white, barred with black, against the uniform green of the background; the little girl is simply four flat shapes one above the other – black, red, pink and yellow.

Silhouette line, then, is not just one 'variety' of line, it signifies a certain attitude on the part of the painter, an attitude which determines his style and method of working. The primitives, the Egyptians, the Etruscans – all those for whom the *surface* is the paramount element of painting – use silhouette line to demarcate the fields of flat colour with which alone it is compatible. *Thus a tendency towards the hegemony of a particular formal element is equivalent to the birth of an order.* Such an order is characterized by the fact that one cannot make simultaneous use of two conflicting formal systems.

How many text-books abound in gross errors due **145** to ignorance of this truth! Pretending to instruct, they begin by fixing the outline of a head in one continuous line; and then, to show that modelling has no secrets for them, they add shading within the area defined by this outline, with complete disregard for the consequences – or inconsequences!... When extended to colour, this method results in those lamentable art-school works, indistinguishable in their mediocrity. Even some 'artists' do little better. Here is a dry-point etching by William Strang, symboli- **146**

145. Pretending to instruct . . .

146. William Strang (1859-1921). *The Fisherman*, dry-point etching.

147. Chinese art. Stencil.

cally entitled *The Fisherman*. The conventionality of this neo-classical subject is dreary enough, but its formal incoherence is worse. On the one hand, the 'artist' has employed silhouette line to emphasize the outlines of his figures; on the other, he has painstakingly modelled the bodies with meticulous light and shade, so that the softness of the flesh clashes uncomfortably with the wiry hardness of the outlines.

Silhouette line, therefore, is predisposed towards the *surface plane*. As soon as it penetrates three-dimensional space, it tends to be modified or to disappear. It is compatible with the surface, incompatible with depth and modelling. Popular art, in the East and the West alike, has drawn infinite resources from 147 it. Whether one thinks of Chinese stencils or the images of Epinal, the principle is the same: line dividing contrasted fields, of black and white or of different flat colours, which always respect the integrity of the surface plane.

Contour line

This term, as distinct from the preceding one, is meant here to describe line that implies a certain depth in space, instead of the autonomous outline of a shape cut out with scissors. You have probably noticed how children like to draw a nice, round sun in the 148 middle of a picture; but have you noticed that this sun, though amply provided with rays, produces no light, and that the objects around it are quite unaffected by it? The child represents space by an abstraction that owes nothing to the senses; and light, 'indicated' by a yellow round, is also an abstraction, likewise owing nothing to the senses. For the child everything is reduced to its intellectual essence, and that is why silhouette line is familiar to him, since it defines his *symbolic view* of the world.

The primitives have this in common with children – that they also represent *ideas* rather than things seen, but, unlike children, they do so with deliberate intent. It is not the awkwardness of children that they share (though this is stated all too frequently), but a particular manner of 'indicating' the world. For instance, the use of a gold background answers the need for an ideal light suitable for the symbolic presentation of the Christian drama.

As soon as these intellectual conditions are modified, and the sun, no longer an abstract symbol or a gold background, becomes what it is for our senses – i.e. a source of light – those forms which once were controlled by the picture surface tend to dilate and to develop in space. The surface breaks up,[1] and the forms acquire modelling. They put on a new flesh and muscle (superfluous fat, too, if the artist is at fault), are filled out as volumes, tempered, enlivened, or blurred sometimes, by shadows.

Examining the *Mona Lisa,* one soon realizes that 149 much of her charm derives from the supple line that envelops but does not confine her – much more than derives from the too legendary smile. The forms are no longer expressed on the surface, but penetrate the picture space with the aid of the light which opens the way for them. One is not aware of the silhouette of the Mona Lisa, since line no longer divides two equally flat areas, but develops in depth – line meta-

[1] We shall see later how this happens; here I am only touching on this point.

148. *For the child, space and light are abstractions which serve to 'indicate' the world.* Exhibition of childrens' art, Lausanne, 1957. Photo Held.

149. *The supple line that envelops but does not confine her.* Leonardo da Vinci (1452-1519). *Mona Lisa.* Paris, Louvre. Photo Held.

150. Master of St. Matthew. *Lamentation over the Dead Christ.* Fragment of a Crucifix, c. 1220. Pisa, Museum. Photo Alinari.

151. Giotto (1267-1337). *Lamentation,* fresco. Padua, Arena Chapel. Photo Anderson.

morphosed through contact with the space it has itself created.[1]

Whereas silhouette line tends to appeal to the mind, contour line tends more to inform our senses. Combined with light and volume, it provides a relationship nearer to ordinary experience.

So it is that with Giotto the ideal world of the Middle Ages makes way for a more human world, which, while not ignoring God, establishes a more 'fleshly' contact with him. We should remind ourselves that this is not a question of 'progress', but of a change in attitude. Giotto's figures do not break with Christian tradition, they present a humanized version of divine events.

This transformation is effected essentially by means of a new spatial plasticity. Instead of the silhouette line of the primitives, he uses contour line, developed in depth, though depth is suggested only with great restraint. Here we are witnessing a kind of incarnation. 150-151 Scarcely a century separates these two *Lamentations,*

[1] In this connection it is worth noting that silhouette line is particularly suited to profile portraits, while contour line prefers a three-quarter view, which is more adapted to deployment of volumes.

but what a world of difference there is between them! In the work of the St. Matthew Master everything is presented in terms of surface and line, which make their appeal to the mind, while in Giotto's picture the emphasis on contour and volume appeals more directly to the senses. These two important aspects of ourselves – mind and senses – correspond to different formal systems, each of which produces its appropriate order.

Nevertheless, it seems there is no such thing as *purely* intellectual art (one touches geometry at its extremity), and that there is no such thing as *purely* sensuous art (which would be equivalent to total realism). It is between these two extremities that the vast field of art opens out fanwise, its every expression appealing in some measure both to the mind and to the senses.

In this portrait, attributed to Hans Maler, silhou- 152 ette line gives the face a diagrammatic clarity, while the patterns of the head-dress and bodice add a

152. Attributed to Hans Maler (early 16th century). *Posthumous* ▶ *portrait of Mary of Burgundy.* Lehman collection, New York. Photo Held.

note of decorative richness. In contrast to this, the
153 portrait by Floris demands an almost exclusively
sensuous approach – as if one could actually touch
and press this buxom female form. The two pictures
are expressed in different formal languages, addressed
154 to different aspects of our sensibility. Van Eyck shows
us the point of equilibrium between these two tend-
encies. In the portrait of his wife one can observe that
its clarity of form is due almost entirely to the use of
silhouette line on the left side of the head-dress and
the left side of the face (light tone against the dark
background, flesh-pink against the creamy colour of
the linen), but that the right side of both face and
head-dress are purposely deprived of linear clarity,
and lightly modelled in shadow. If, in imagination,
one 'folds over' the left side of the face onto the right
side, one obtains – besides the anatomical peculiarity resulting from such an operation – a formal
peculiarity that is no less significant: the features
seem excessively cold and sterile in execution. If, on the
contrary, one imagines the right side folded over on
the left, the effect is equally disagreeable: the features now have the insipidity of excessive realism. In
what, then, does the art of this portrait lie? Essentially in the way the artist has contrived to relate one
half of the face to the surface plane, and, from there,
to set back the other half in an unobtrusively suggested
space. Thus pictorial space is not inescapably committed to either the second or the third dimension,
but can combine them both, as long as it does not
thereby lose its coherence. Van Eyck's portrait, contained in clear, emphatic lines (not hard, continuous
outlines, as in Strang's etching), allies graciousness
with vigour. It is not without reason that he is held to
be one of the greatest masters of painting. Nor is it
without reason that Manet is considered as the regen-
erator of modern art. At a moment when painting
was sinking into pettiness, he understood the long
neglected qualities of silhouette line, and the howls of
155 abuse which greeted his *Olympia* are today merely evidence of the depths to which public taste had fallen.

Line, therefore, is one of the most important means
of expression in painting. Once it has broken free from
writing, it creates its own content and its own space.
Silhouette line suits two-dimensional space, contour
line suits three-dimensional space, but, as we have
seen, this does not mean the artist has to choose one
to the exclusion of the other. Every pictorial space is
complex; none is incoherent. What matters in the long
run is that the artist should adopt an attitude which,
though it may be carefully concealed 'comes across'
in his arrangement of formal devices and resources.

153. Frans Floris (1518-1570). *Portrait of a Woman*. Dr. **D.**
Hannema collection, Goor, Netherlands. Photo Zeijlmaker,
Zutphen.

154. Jan van Eyck (1385/90-1444). *Portrait of the Artist's Wife.* ▶
Bruges, Palais Communal.

146

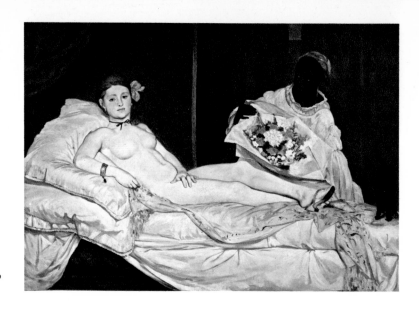

155. Edouard Manet (1832-1883). *Olympia*. Paris, Louvre. Photo Held.

Colour

We enter the marvellous world of colour in infancy. How eagerly the toddler presses his nose to the window; what rapture when by chance the door is opened! The rainbow glows everywhere. The rainbow! – Was it ever so bright as on the nursery shelves, where dolls and giraffes, camels and puppets, paraded side by side? The most beautiful hours of childhood are 'painted hours', quartered in red, green, blue and orange, like one's first rubber ball.

Then the excitement of the box of crayons among the presents at Christmas-time, with which one could 'recreate the world'. With a few strokes, trees spring from the earth, the roofs of houses are tiled in red. Green fields appear in a twinkling, sprinkled all over with dots to represent every sort of flower. And the sun, of brilliant yellow, has the air of a genial spider in his web of rays! Sometimes the trees become red, the houses blue, the fields violet and the sky yellow – but does it matter? Rather than the colour of things, it is colour itself that is important, for colour to the child is the very symbol of festivity. Grown-ups may smile, but they remember this in their carnivals, processions and military parades.

Alas! One has to return to everyday existence, and the festival is forgotten. No more dressing-up! And colours – like people – resume their workaday garb. The red of the bunting returns to the street crossing, to halt the impatient motorist, while green repeats its monotonous 'Go . . . Go . . .' They even go back to the office – red tape, white collars, blue files and yellow desks. Forgetting the past, colours too behave like model employees!

Do they lose all their power? No, fortunately. What would a bar be like if it was lit like a schoolroom? It needs a subdued light, yellowish or pinkish, so that its customers may be conscious of 'atmosphere'. Whatever uses colours are put to, they retain their affinities with our inward moods and states of mind. One would never choose the same colour for every room in the house! This colour suits the kitchen and that suits the living-room, while another is right for the bathroom. We speak quite naturally of 'gay' or 'austere' colours, of a 'cold' blue, a 'warm' or an 'astringent' yellow, an 'acid' green.

Is there such a thing as pure colour-perception? To answer 'yes' – on the grounds that if you stand two people in front of the sea, they will both say it is blue – is to take too simple a view. Not only does the appearance of an object change with the light (a wall that is dazzlingly white in the mid-day sun turns to ash-grey towards evening), but the mechanism of sight is also subject to all sorts of phenomena and disturbances which we take too little into account.

If, in the height of summer, one looks away from a brightly lit object – a placard, say, or a piece of metal – one sees it 'in negative', dancing before one's eyes like a butterfly. A thousand and one such tricks are played upon the retina, and they do not make matters any easier.

What do physicists[1] have to say on the subject of colour? In substance, two things:

1. All colour theories that have come down to us, from Aristotle to Goethe (with the partial exception of Newton), are fairy-tales, as are also the accepted ideas on the subject that are held by the public at large: the pseudo-problem of primary colours, the anthropomorphic division of the solar spectrum into seven colours, the inadequate description of tints in terms of their qualities (blue, red, yellow)!

2. Having made this clean sweep of the past and of most current ideas, they define light as 'a radiation of energy . . . that is nevertheless only a limited part of the vast field of radiated energy.' The colours of the spectrum are measured in optical wavelengths, expressed in millimicrons. All the colours are situated between 380 mμ (violet) and 800 mμ (red). Above and below these limits we see nothing (below 380 mμ the waves represent electrical phenomena, and above 800 mμ they represent phenomena of heat). The number of distinguishable grades of colour in the spectrum, as estimated by various authorities, is somewhere between 130 and 200.

According to the researches of Bohr and, above all, of Einstein, it seems that 'each simple radiation contains certain corpuscles or photons which travel at something like 185,860 miles per second, and whose individual energy is greater, the shorter the wavelength.'

Finally, as expressed in a remark of Langevin recorded by Maurice Boll, it follows 'that a red photon and a violet photon differ only as do a fast-moving atom and a slow one.' Thus the universe contains 'only a single type of photon: two photons, one red and the other violet, are *the same photon,* but with different degrees of energy.'

What do we gain from this information? Doubtless very little that concerns our understanding of colours

[1] Marcel Boll and Jean Dourgnon, *Le Secret des Couleurs,* P. U. F.

in painting, but a good deal that concerns the attitude we adopt towards them.

Let me make my meaning clear. When the physicist turns his attention to colour, he seeks (in his own words) to 'objectify' its phenomena. This means that he chooses to consider these phenomena as far as possible in their pure state. Furthermore, he imposes on his research certain conditions which are necessary to scientific method. He tries first of all to eliminate what he calls the 'parasitic intervention of the observer.' 'Charm of colour' is a mere phrase; what matters is to measure and record. The 'parasitic intervention of matter' is also to be eliminated; the scientist is interested, not in the particular blue of a particular fabric, but in the blue produced by the immaterial rays of the spectrum. Finally, he progresses by a series of analyses, eliminating the 'parasitic intervention of other colours', and endeavouring to study each colour separately.

Thus when the scientist investigates the properties of colour, he does so from a standpoint which consists essentially of the elimination of the so-called parasitic interventions of the observer, of matter and of the relationships of colours with each other. A perfectly legitimate standpoint, of course, but one that should be recognized as possessing no sort of finality. Like any other human activity, science cannot fasten upon reality itself, but offers *a particular view of reality.* So colours are not the same thing *for the scientist* as they are *for us.* Each viewpoint implies a different kind of knowledge and a different method of acquiring it. Colour is a question of degree to the scientist; to us it is a question of *quality.*

Let us see if we can define our position more precisely.

In the first place, painting has no use for immaterial colours. Up to now no picture has been made from the breaking-down of light through a prism. All the colours used in painting are, without exception, *material.* Some pigments are of animal or vegetable origin (though these are becoming increasingly rare), while others are mineral (either natural or artificial). And this is not the only distinction that can be made. The appearance of colours is no less dependent upon technique; the red of stained glass, with the daylight blazing through it, is very different from that of tapestry, and colours appear quite differently in fresco and in oil. The nature of the medium, and of the surface on which it is laid, can also be important; water-colour is transparent and allows the support to show through, while oil-paint usually hides it. Even the manner of applying the paint can make a difference.

156. Romanesque art. The *Assumption*, stained glass (detail), c. 1145. Le Mans, cathedral. Photo Giraudon.

Thus, in painting, *colours have no existence independent of matter,*[1] and it is through matter that we are made aware of them; the green of a piece of linen cannot be made the same as the green of a piece of lacquer-work. *Far from being a question of degree, colours for us are defined primarily by a sensuous quality which is a major part of their reality.*

Here is a second point. In ordinary life the retina does not experience colours in isolation. If one goes out-of-doors, one is greeted by the multicoloured profusion of nature. In this respect the way we look at pictures is near to our normal, everyday vision, for in painting *we are never conscious of isolated colours, but always of colours in association with one another.*

How do they associate? Red is defined by the physicist as a wavelength (800 mμ), and green as another (550 mμ); but to our eyes this numerical relationship means nothing. What we notice – transcending any order based on measurement – is that red and green are enhanced, seeming both to gain in intensity, when they are placed side by side. This behaviour of colours, while not in the least invalidating scientific theory, shows that our senses do not react with indifference to their relationships, and that in fact *we take notice of colours through certain selective relationships, conditioned by our own sensibility.* That is to say, the intervention of the spectator is anything but parasitic; in painting it is quite essential.

One more point remains to be cleared up. In ordinary life colours are nearly always associated with the identity of objects. The mechanism of memory works by such automatic associations, without our needing to open our eyes: fields, leaves, trees and bottles are green; dawn, the sun and dead leaves are yellow; the sky, the sea and the horizon are blue . . . It is as if each object had been allotted its own livery once and for all. This need for identification is so strongly ingrained in our consciousness that we are indignant when an artist paints red trees or violet-coloured leaves; and indignation knows no bounds when he has the effrontery to paint a man's face green! And this brings me to the last and most important point:

In painting, colours are not the distinctive recognition-marks of objects, but belong to an autonomous order, which the artist may use freely to express himself.

To sum up:

a) in painting colours are not confined to the representation of objects.

[1] This point was developed in the chapter: *Materials.*

b) in painting colours do not exist independently; thus no colour is intrinsically beautiful or ugly.

c) in painting colours exist only in relation to each other: 'Give me mud,' Delacroix exclaimed, 'let me surround it as I think fit, and it shall be the radiant flesh of Venus.'

Can these relationships – or rather, the principle by which they operate – be specified? Consider these two landscapes, one by Gauguin, the other by Ruisdael. 157-158 Both subjects contain approximately the same main elements: land, water, sky – and a mill. Apart from these similarities, they are totally different. In the *Mill in Brittany* the colours occupy circumscribed areas: the green meadow in the foreground is 'cut out' like a patch of material, on which are pinned the shapes of the women and the dog. The tawny trees, the buildings and the clouds are stitched together, with the 'seams' left showing. Moreover, the colours are not those of reality. Of almost equal intensity throughout (perhaps rather more brilliant in the middle distance), they deliberately contradict the impression of depth so as to spread out the landscape like a tapestry. The horizon is brought forward, and lies flat against the poplars. One can scarcely describe it as landscape, for instead of penetrating space in depth, the eye finds that its gaze also 'spreads out' to take in the orchestration of colours laid flat on the canvas.

In comparison to this, Ruisdael's picture seems to belong to a different world, and to be addressed to a different part of our being. Melting into the distance by almost imperceptible gradations, the landscape narrows to a fragile band, broken by the splendid movement of the clouds piled up behind the mill. The vast expanse of the sky is moderated by the sudden, lively patch of light at the edge of the water. Here are no juxtapositions of pure colour! Colour is no more than a light mist in the windy air. Instead of spreading out, one's gaze sharpens to penetrate the moving immensity of space, which is weighted only with the ballast of a few roofs and boats and figures, and which the solitary tower of the mill alone attempts to hold in check. It would be difficult to imagine a more striking contrast than that which these two works present.

By and large, one can say that colour-relationships in painting are governed by two principles – one of them chromatic, the other tonal.[1] Tonal values

[1] Of course, these are not absolute distinctions; the terms 'chromatic' and 'tonal' are not meant to represent a difference of nature, but a dominant characteristic. This is the justification of such distinctions: by concentrating our attention, they help us to see these complex phenomena more clearly.

are a question of greater or lesser degree of luminous intensity; chromatic values concern colours of an equal degree of saturation.[1] These principles are borne out by what scientists teach us concerning the retina, since, in the light of biological studies, it seems fairly certain that our vision is of two kinds.

In *diurnal vision* the eye is especially sensitive to colour, and sees the details of objects distinctly. This is the way one looks at a view in the noonday light – a hill planted with olive trees, for example, the trees standing out clearly as a mosaic against the red earth.

In *crepuscular vision* the eye loses its sensitivity to colour, but becomes particularly sensitive to tone – i.e. to variations of light and dark. Though it no longer distinguishes objects in detail, it is able to 'place' them with accuracy up to a considerable distance.

Thus diurnal vision tends to 'bring things forward' as clearly defined patches of colour, while crepuscular vision 'sets them back' according to their degree of lightness or darkness. And it is not only the appearance of things that changes; our sense of distance is also modified. In diurnal vision, where colour is dominant, distances tend to 'shrink', and in the other they tend to 'grow'.

A great deal more could be said on this subject,[2] but this much is enough to show that chromatic and tonal values are not gratuitous inventions, but that both have roots in the changing behaviour of our sight, and give rise to different states of consciousness; in either case, our perceptions, feelings and thoughts are different. The important thing is not that artists produce images which conform to these two modes of seeing (if that were all, they would merely be a superior sort of optician), but that they exploit them both. Each mode offers a means of elaborating a pictorial space in which the forms will take on a particular character, gaining in effectiveness and energy of expression. Without pressing this idea too far (it is developed more fully in the studies of individual works in Part 4), one may say that Gauguin's choice of the 'chromatic principle' permits him to stress the 'structure' aspect of landscape, while with Ruisdael it is the 'light-and-atmosphere' aspect that is emphasized. Two different artistic temperaments are revealed, both of them lyrical, the former putting the accent on impassioned mastery, the latter on contemplative

tranquillity. Thus each approach is a mode of expression with qualities peculiar to itself. In attempting to examine these qualities more closely I shall, for the sake of clarity, deal here with the 'chromatic' approach, and leave the 'tonal' approach to the next chapter.

On this skyphos (a kind of bowl) the vase-painter 159 Hieron has represented the return of Briseis. The red figures stand out superbly against the black ground, presenting a simple two-colour harmony with this peculiarity – that the black is a glaze, while the red is the natural terracotta of the bowl. Thus the material qualities of the two colours are different – the black giving an impression of glossy smoothness, whereas the red suggests a coarser, rougher texture. In addition to these material qualities, which provide a distinctive tactile pleasure, we find that the red and the black mutually 'stimulate' each other – their juxtaposition makes both of them seem more intense. This effect is due to the phenomenon of *irradiation* by 160 which colours (light colours in particular) gain in strength when they are set against a dark background. Thus areas of different colours, even if there are two only, act upon one another so as to modify their effect on us.

Stained glass is especially susceptible to this phe- 156 nomenon, not only because the light of the window as a whole is set in the darkness of the wall, but also because each small luminous area is surrounded by a band of lead. It has been observed that the masters of this craft quickly learned to exploit this by deliberately reducing the size of the transparent areas, and the astonishing vigour of Romanesque stained glass is largely due to this practice. When seen from close to, 161 the hands of the figures often seem atrophied or skeletal; but seen from a proper distance, in the full brilliance of the window, they expand by irradiation.

In the frescoes at Tavant, where the figures are 162 painted on a light background, one notices the same principle applied in reverse – the hands are made bigger. Since they are of the same tone as the wall, the eye tends to neglect the smaller area in favour of the larger; therefore the artist purposely increases the size of the hands so that they will not be 'lost' in the effect of light on light.

The same phenomenon has been widely exploited in popular art, where figures are made larger or smaller not only as a matter of physical stature, but in virtue of their colour relationships.

One could not hope to examine *all* the applications of colour relationship. Apart from those which are sufficiently general to appear in the majority of works,

[1] Obviously, in each case the colours are an effect of light; but they act differently according to whether the light is a fixed source of equal intensity, or a variable source implying differences of intensity.

[2] Thus, as we are taught by Boll, 'in a weak light we are more sensitive to blue than to other colours; . . . in full daylight we are more sensitive to red and green.'

157. Paul Gauguin (1848-1903). *Mill in Brittany*. Paris, Louvre. Photo Held.

158. Jacob van Ruisdael (1628/29-1682). *Mill at Wijk, near Duurstede*. Amsterdam, Rijksmuseum. Photo Rijksmuseum.

it goes without saying that each artist invents his own for his own ends. But it is important to underline what all of them have in common: *in painting, colours affect spatial structure and forms, regulating and modifying them in accordance with the relationships they establish.* This circumstance is due not to the intrinsic nature of the colours, but to the effect they have on us, which means that our consciousness is always involved with the work.

It is generally felt that the majority of colour-photographs have no artistic interest beyond their documentary appeal, which is perhaps surprising when one considers that they contain the same elements as painting – space, figures, colours, and so on . . . But this is precisely where the basic difference lies: colours in photography are meant only to *reinvest* objects with the appearance of nature, whereas in painting they create a space of their own in which the forms of objects acquire significance. In a photograph the objects are merely 'there', but in a painting they are *incorporated*. The photo may delight us, but the picture attracts and holds our attention by virtue of the human presence expressed in it.

Furthermore, photography has no control over the number of colours or their intensity, but reproduces everything with indifference. This offends another side of our sensibility, one which derives from the actual constitution of our sense of sight. Scientists tell us that, apart from the dual mechanism of vision, we probably perceive colour (according to the work of Jung) through 'three types of receiver, which are not equally sensitive to various radiations, and which are linked to the brain by different fibres.' This explanation takes into account an experience that can be readily verified: however hard one tries, it is virtually impossible to look with equal attention at more than three colours *at the same time.* The world of advertising knows this well, and seldom makes use of more. In painting the rule is equally valid, though not formulated in the same terms; paintings are not restricted to three colours, but, if there are more, they tend to be organized in 'chords' of two colours or of three, so that the over-all harmony and unity of colour can be grasped without confusion. The extreme

163 case, perhaps, is Dufy's *Violin,* in which, apart from the two light patches, the same sonorous red extends over the whole surface; but more often they are 'two-note chords', such as the association of red and black in the skyphos by Hieron, or, more often still, 'three-note chords'.

164 In *Les Diligences de Tarascon* Van Gogh builds his harmony on the chord of red-blue-yellow. As Che-

159. Greek art. Skyphos by Hieron. *Return of Briseis*, 5th century B.C. Paris, Louvre. Photo Held.

160

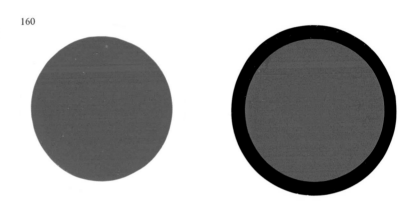

vreul has observed, 'juxtaposed colours of the same tone value appear with their maximum difference as colours.' One notices in this picture that the yellow of the wall, the red of the vehicle and the blue of the shadow are in fact differentiated with the greatest clarity, but that the red is dominant, thanks to its natural intensity. Van Gogh, therefore, is careful to assign the red to areas that are proportionally smaller, reserving it for the window frames and the band on the side of the *diligence*. He is equally careful in his choice of complementary colours: reducing the quantity of violet (red + blue), the complementary of yellow, he increases that of green (blue + yellow). Thus, in relation to the yellow of the wall and the blue of the shadow, sky and ground, the red is 'balanced' by the presence of the green areas, which reaffirm the blue and yellow in muted tones.

Even so, there is a danger here. As we know, two complementary colours, when juxtaposed, stimulate each other to a point which can be distracting and disagreeable; thus red and green are scarcely tolerable when placed side by side or one above the other. To avoid this effect, which would have destroyed his subtle balance, Van Gogh has broken up the green areas, leaving fairly wide intervals between them, whereas the blue, yellow and red form continuous localities. But for this kind of forethought, the picture would collapse into confusion. Thus the use of colour in painting is subject to a natural logic which has its basis in human sensibility, and which serves our need for expression.

Is it possible to formulate the rules imposed by this logic? One, at least, has been observed by all great artists: *colours must be integrated with the picture plane, because painting can no more escape the surface on which it is revealed than dispense with the processes by which it is revealed.* However subtle the emotions it provokes, the most beautiful of easel-paintings or frescoes is still the organisation of a space in terms of lines and colours.

165 Transferred to the wall-surface, the figures of the *Offering of the Cup* become flat silhouettes, and the colours become flat areas. Far from being the result of primitive incompetence, these flat colours are the necessary consequence of the transference of objects from the three-dimensional world of ordinary reality to the two-dimensional world of the wall.

This, you may say, is reducing painting to the level of decoration, a word which somehow rings disagreeably on the ear. This objection misunderstands both the term and the thing itself. All peoples at 166 all times have applied themselves to *decoration*. And

161. Romanesque art. *Vision of St. Ambrose*, stained glass, 12th century. Le Mans, cathedral. Photo Giraudon.

162. Romanesque art. *Man carrying a Beam*, fresco at Tavant (detail), 12th century. Ed. du Chêne, Paris.

of what does it consist? Of *forms* which, whether coloured or not (in either case the problem is basically the same), are arranged in relation to the *surface,* in accordance with a certain *rhythm* and with certain *proportions.* Of those four factors, one – the surface – is invariable; the other three can be of infinite variety. That is true enough; yet, when the eye traverses the surface under the triple guidance of the forms which seize its attention, the rhythm which regulates its progress and the proportions which determine the length of its stride, it seems to the spectator that the surface itself is in motion and engenders movement.[1]

Consequently one can understand why pure colours are incompatible with modelling and depth; they can only achieve congruity in the kind of space that their nature implies. This is why most amateur painters, obsessed with the idea of rendering depth, perpetrate works which, for all their diversity, are alike in their inertness and incoherence. Even some artists of renown slip up occasionally. Signorelli may be an admirable artist (particularly as a draughtsman), yet his Orvieto frescoes are almost unendurable; modelled relentlessly, the colours clearly show how much they suffer!

A distinction can be drawn between the *surface space,* appropriate to decoration, and the *picture space*[2] which, without need of modelling, gives colours another level of existence. This may sound mysterious, but let us reconsider certain data. Of the six colours comprising the three primary colours (red, blue and yellow), and those which result from mixing any two of them (orange, green and violet), some are regarded as *warm* colours, and others as *cool* colours – as if perceiving them involved some sensation of heat and cold. They form a double progression in opposite directions, the 'warm' colours going from yellow through orange to red, the 'cool' colours from green through blue to violet.[3]

---

[1] This aspect is considered especially in the chapter: *Movement.*

[2] These are terms of convenience. Painting in the first place is always manifested on a *surface*; but, as the work takes shape, the artist creates a *space* – the space he needs to place his forms in and express what he has to say. This new space inclines sometimes towards the surface plane and sometimes towards the illusion of depth; the former tendency corresponds to the term *surface space,* and the latter to the term *picture space.*

[3] Some authors believe this to be a physical or biological phenomenon; others believe it is a psychological phenomenon – i.e. that the thermal effect is the result of association of ideas, red being habitually associated with fire, green with trees and grass, etc. For our purpose it is less important to seek its cause than to note how closely it is bound in with our consciousness (most languages contain this distinction between warm and cool colours).

163. Raoul Dufy (1877-1953). *The Red Violin*. Paris, private collection. Photo Skira.

164. Vincent Van Gogh (1853-1890). *Les Diligences de Tarascon*. New York, Henry Pearlman collection. Photo Skira.

165. Etruscan art. *Offering of the Cup* (detail), end of 6th century B.C. Tarquinia, tomb of the baron. Photo Büchergilde, Zürich. ►

Now this 'thermal' effect of colours is usually accompanied by an equally noticeable spatial effect: warm tints give the impression of 'coming forward', cool tints of 'going back'. This phenomenon is so general that it is at the basis of international road signs. Thanks to its property of 'coming forward', red serves as the signal of warning and prohibition, while green, which 'goes back', opens the way ahead. This elementary example is enough to convey an idea of the ways in which art can exploit the spatial effect of colours.

As regards the respective positions of the women in Dufy's *Baigneuses,* one sees that the seated figure on the right is *in front of* the standing figure on the left; but their respective colours tend to bring them into the same plane, conforming to the nature of the space chosen by the artist. In effect, the red brings the bather on the left 'forward', while the blue takes the other one 'back'. This spatial compensation of the colours firmly establishes the surface balance which was threatened by the respective positions of the figures, transforming static extent into dynamic space without recourse to depth on modelling. This is an aspect of *modulation,* of which Cézanne was – for modern times – the inspired originator.

To sum up, we perceive colour sometimes by diurnal vision and sometimes by crepuscular vision, which correspond to what I have called the chromatic and tonal principles in painting. In this chapter we have been concerned only with the former. We have established that in this chromatic context colours are preferably employed in flat areas; but it would be wrong to suppose that it is enough simply to place them on the surface, for, when colours are integrated upon it, the surface ceases to be a simple geometrical area, and is transformed into a *surface space,* in which, thanks to the forms controlled by rhythm and proportion, a presence comes to life. In the widest sense of the term, decoration is the art of employing colours in such a way as to bring about this metamorphosis. Modulation – also in the widest sense – is the art of transforming the geometrical area into a *picture space,* exclusive of relief and depth, principally by means of the thermal and spatial effects of colours. Decoration and modulation, then, are both methods of expression within the chromatic approach.

Colours exist in accordance with a logic of their own, and themselves create the space in which they may find expression. We cannot therefore demand that they should reproduce reality, and even less that they should respect our prejudices. It is for the spectator to grasp and enter into that logic by which they attain the quality of language.

166. Mesopotamian art. Elamite vase in terracotta, end of 4th millennium B.C. Paris, Louvre. Photo Giraudon.

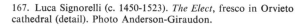

168. Raoul Dufy (1877-1953). *Baigneuses,* water-colour. Paris, ▶ Musée du Petit Palais. Photo Skira.

167. Luca Signorelli (c. 1450-1523). *The Elect,* fresco in Orvieto cathedral (detail). Photo Anderson-Giraudon.

Light

Although two-dimensional space was commonly used from the very earliest times until the Renaissance, although it has been restored to favour by painters since the end of the 19th century, although it is endowed by the optical phenomenon of 'diurnal vision', and although in the hands of an artist it is a perfectly coherent system of formal expression, the fact remains that most people still feel there is something bogus or queer about it. No doubt this is because it is quite unlike the familiar space we know – the space in which we perform our actions and make our gestures.

But what sort of space do we inhabit? If I walk down the street, I see buildings and vehicles, step round a fruit-seller's barrow, push my way through the crowd... That is the essence of it: we move in a world of volumes, continuously aware of relief – the fruit-seller's apples, the edge of the pavement, the staircase at home. Sensations of relief, sensations of depth and distance too, are an integral part of our consciousness.

The world about us reaches its peak of perceptible reality when it is neither too light nor too dark; dazzled by too much light, we shut our eyes; deprived of light altogether, we are blind. In the average light of an average day we know where we are, can move around objects, follow their contours with our hand, traverse the space they occupy. Metaphysics apart, we may truly say relief and depth are, with light, the normal companions of our earthly existence.

Examining this photograph, taken on the shore 169 of Lake Garda, let us briefly recall how the eye perceives depth. First, by the relative dimensions of objects, which diminish in proportion to their distance: the road narrows like a spear-point towards the horizon, and the sections of the parapet (all of the same size, and equally spaced) melt away from us like a row of sugar lumps. Second, by *progressively diminishing clarity of detail:* whereas the nearer water is broken into wavelets, the middle of the lake seems only a faintly rippled surface, and the farthest part seems quite flat. Only the nearest section of parapet shows the grain of the stone, while the others are polished smooth by distance. Close to, the rocks form a series of clearly defined planes; in the distance they melt into the hazy sky. It so happens, then, that for the eye differences of light and dark are strongly marked in the fore-

169. *How does the eye perceive depth?* Lake Garda.

ground, and are diminished by distance until at the limits of sight they almost completely disappear, and objects are fused in a single neutral tone. Thus a change in the form of objects, and a change in the degree of lighting, both resulting from our physical make-up, are basic to our perception both of distance and of relief. Our psychological make-up is also involved. Supposing I were a Martian – newly arrived on this planet, and knowing nothing of roads, rocks and lakes – I should be unable to see anything in this photograph but an arrangement of variegated patches: but as a citizen of this world I am able, from experience, to interpret the patches and *reconstitute* roads, rocks and lake. Each time that I translate patches into objects, my mind is intervening – an intervention that ultimately becomes unconscious [1], so that by force of habit relief and distance seem to be self-apparent.

It is understandable that the painters of the Renaissance should have made a positive cult of perspective: 'It is the most beautiful and delightful of all things that mathematics has brought to light!... This science may boast that it is the life and soul of painting... One should begin with it and end with it, for it should be everywhere!' It is also understandable that the works which foreshadowed it should have aroused such enthusiasm as is witnessed by the legend which so soon grew round the name of Giotto:

'The art of painting began to revive in Tuscany, in a hamlet near Florence named Vespignano. Here was born a child of marvellous genius, *who knew how to draw a sheep from nature.*' [2]

In actual fact, perspective did not cause art to reproduce nature (as is ceaselessly and erroneously stated), but to *draw nearer* to nature. This is precisely what astonished the generations that followed: 'In truth,' writes Vasari of Giotto's frescoes at Assisi, 'there is great variety to be seen in this work, not only in the gestures and attitudes of the different figures, but in the composition of each scene; besides which he represents very well the various costumes of those times, and also *certain observations and imitations of nature.* One of the finest is a scene in which a thirsty man, *whose craving for water is*

vividly suggested, leans forward on the ground to drink from a spring, with such great and truly marvellous animation *that it seems almost to be a living man who drinks!'* [1]

Now, though Giotto may indeed have brought art closer to nature, he never copied nature, nor tried to copy it. The genius he displayed – the genius to which Vasari paid tribute – has unfortunately been responsible (in careless minds) for a misconception that lies at the root of one of our most stubborn prejudices.

Hailed in the Renaissance as the lawful wife of painting, the third dimension has been rudely turned out of doors by the artists of our own time. Today she is maligned as 'the root of all evil', but the trouble is really a case of misunderstanding. It is all very well to be against the third dimension in painting, and to declare that modelling is a custom that has fallen into decay, but no-one with a grain of honesty can dispute the merit of the great Renaissance artists. It is as well not to judge hastily, and not to condemn perspective and illusionism in the same breath.

We have observed that colours change with variations in the strength of light.[2] Corresponding to the change of intensity in the source of light, there are modifications of colour which are called in painting tone-values – or simply *values.* Thus a red tint passing through every degree between black and white (considered here not as colours but as the extremes of illumination) proceeds through an infinite number of shades. But the red tint is constant; what changes is its relation to the scale of light and dark. As may be seen from this example, values always indicate a relationship. A single colour is susceptible to a great many degrees.

We saw in the case of the photograph of Lake Garda that values are connected with two of our basic perceptions – perception of relief and perception of distance. How, then, do we escape the obviously absurd conclusion that, in making use of them, the painter is merely emulating the coloured photograph?

For one thing, it has appeared so far that two-dimensional space is the natural condition of painting; that is to say, the representation of relief and depth seems incompatible with the surface, and this incompatibility has every appearance of finality. On

171

170

[2] If one doubts this, one need only refer to the impressions of people who go mountaineering for the first time. Though the peaks may seem near to their eyes, the true distance is revealed to their legs! It is by actually traversing ridges and slopes, by actually measuring it in oneself, that the sense of scale reaches some sort of accuracy. And here is a photograph which illustrates the phenomenon equally well!

[2] As related by Vasari. The italics are mine.

[1] My italics.

[2] The reader will recall the distinction between 'chromatic' and 'tonal' perspective. The former was considered in the preceding chapter; it is the latter that concerns us here.

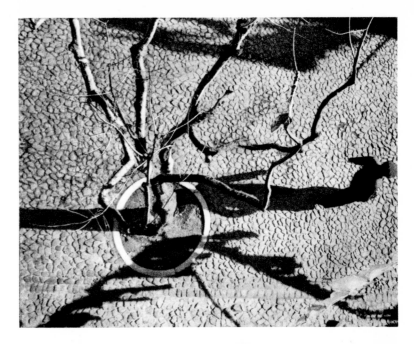

170. *When shadows become unusual sources of information.*

171. Giotto (1267-1337). *St. Francis causing Water to gush from a Rock*, fresco. Assisi, upper church of St. Francis. Photo Anderson.

172. Giorgio Vasari (1511-1574). *Defeat of the French at Marciano,* fresco. Florence, Palazzo Vecchio. Ed. Brogi.

173. Paolo Uccello (1397-1475). *The Rout of San Romano.* Florence, Uffizi. Photo Held.

the other hand, artists who have made use of values have left us works which rank among the proudest achievements of humanity – Giotto, Piero della Francesca, Leonardo and Rembrandt, to name but a few! Let us not be discouraged by this, but face the difficulty squarely.

And to begin with, where exactly does the contradiction lie? Hearken to the all too numerous visitors who linger in front of the frescoes in the Palazzo Vecchio at Florence, Vasari's crowning achievement. '*There* are men that really *are* men, and horses that really *are* horses', exclaims the tourist, and his admiration is increasingly aroused until he decides that this is better than painting: 'It's like sculpture', he declares of his own accord – if the guide has not said so already! 'These horses – it's as if you could put your hand on their backs, or touch the far side of the stirrup...'

Here now is what meets the gaze of the astonished tourist in the Uffizi: more armed men, more horses – but what a difference! A disappointment? Yes, if by that one means that there is no illusion of reality in Uccello's picture; the white chest of the horse at the left is modelled, but would anyone have the idea of putting a hand on its back or touching the far side of the stirrup?... a strange sort of relief which invites contemplation but in no way encourages the fingers to touch. So much for 'sculpture' in *this* work!

How, then, does it come about that the second of these two pictures is held to be a masterpiece, while the first passes merely as an exercise in virtuosity? *Why?* The question is all the more irritating since both pictures present approximately the same subject, and both make equal use of tone-values in their treatment of it.

To avoid all possibility of our taking the wrong turn at this critical point, let me recapitulate what has emerged so far. In ordinary life tone-values are an aid to perception, providing the dual sensation of relief and depth; but painting cannot deny the imperative claims of the surface plane without destroying one of the essential conditions of its existence. Thus it is faced by the following alternative: either values are used in defiance of this condition (witness the countless legion of trompe-l'œil paintings); or else they are used with due respect for it, in which case the result *can* be art. The inescapable conclusion is that *values are only compatible with painting if they constitute a formal space (i.e., respecting the surface); failing this, they can produce a fair imitation of natural space, but are devoid of expressive power*. This is what was perfectly understood by Uccello, and totally ignored by Vasari.

Let us see if we can observe this metamorphosis taking place. Here we have on one side a detail from Fouquet's *Virgin and Child,* on the other a photographic portrait. [1]

Both heads have the form of a sphere – or rather, an ovoid – and both are illuminated in a way that brings out their modelling; so much for the features they have in common. Considering the Virgin's head first, one notices that it is divided longitudinally into two parts, the axis running approximately from the corner of the left [2] eye to the nostril and the left corner of the mouth. The smaller of these two parts contains a predominance of modelling, the other a predominance of plain surface. In the former the arch of the eyebrow is accentuated by a shadow, in the latter it is not. The veil casts no shadow at all – not even upon the ear, which stands out on the left side with the same surprising clarity as the line of the cheek, neck and shoulder. In spite of appearances, Fouquet's modelling does not really give any illusion of reality. While the right side of the face forms a series of protuberances and hollows, the left side tends more to conform to the surface plane. Thus the modelling is not treated in the same way throughout: accentuated on the right side, it gradually diminishes towards the left, and disappears altogether at the edge of the face. Any volume subjected to natural lighting behaves, no doubt, in a manner analogous to this, *but not in exactly this manner*.

This can be verified by examining the photograph. Without concerning ourselves with the iridescent highlights on the eyelids and lips (softened and subdued by Fouquet), we see that both sides of the face are treated in the same way, with no thought of formal 'compensation'. The brow is underlined with shadow on both sides; the nose is blurred in outline, but is emphasized by the blot of shadow beneath it; the dark upper lip contrasts crudely with the lower lip, which (by reason of all the little wrinkles of light upon it) has rather the appearance of a caterpillar on the 'twig' of shadow below it; finally the veil, which almost dissolves into a greyish vapour flecked with white, cuts across the left cheek in a black band of shadow that follows every

[1] I should perhaps remark that the former, reproduced in black and white, contains only tonal relationships, and that the latter has clearly been touched up to give it an 'artistic' look.

[2] It should be remembered that all such descriptions 'left' and 'right' refer to the *spectator's* left and right.

contour of cheek and chin, constricting and reducing this side of the face.

What precisely is happening? For normal vision, and for photography, shadows are first and foremost *points of reference* which help us to identify objects by their volume. As reference points (and fairly crude ones at that – a face seen against the light is only an indistinct mask) they derive from optical phenomena which we are accustomed to interpret, *but which are indifferent to the space in which they appear*. In painting, on the contrary, shadows (and, therefore, modelling too), while still giving information about volumes, still partaking of the same optical phenomena, and still helping to identify objects, *are an integral element of the picture space and become forms that can convey a meaning*.

As we have just seen, Fouquet does not model the two sides of the face equally, but transmutes them; his shadows are not mere *adjuncts* of form, as in reality or in a photograph. In reality and photography, shadows change with alterations of lighting or of the object's position, but the object itself remains the same. *In painting, shadows influence forms.* Not only does Fouquet suppress certain features, such as the cheek-bone on the left side, the eyelashes or the shadow one would expect beneath the veil, but he alters the relationship of the facial surfaces, increasing that on the left side and reducing that on the right. More subtly still, he alters the relative roles of his formal resources, giving, for example, an importance to line which it does not possess in reality; instead of abandoning it to the play of light, he isolates and strengthens it, and even (with infinite delicacy, it is true) 'distorts' it. Comparing the picture and the photograph, one can see in what manner he does so: on the left side, line suppresses the detailed conformation of cheek and chin; on the other, it is bent to a more than natural degree so that the modelling of the right side of the face may be contained within its tension. Note also the angle formed on the right by the cheek and neck (cheek and shoulder in the photograph): in the photograph it is amorphous, weakened by the projecting cheek-bone and the blurred shadows of the clothes; in the Fouquet it is a deliberate passage, marking both the difference between the cheek and the neck (emphasized by the horizontal of the throne) and the formal continuity from one to the other (the vertical of the neck 'taking up' the oblique line of the cheek). In the photograph, lines are fortuitously juxtaposed; in the painting, they are articulated.

174. Jean Fouquet (c. 1420-c. 1480). *Virgin and Child*, detail. Antwerp, Musée royal des beaux-arts. Photo Giraudon.

175. *In a photograph, modelling is informative; in a work of art it is expressive.*

When an artist simply makes colours paler to represent light, and darker to represent shadow, he produces a kind of modelling that is not compatible with art, in so much as he fails to integrate them with the surface by means of formal compensations and equivalences. In reality and photography the object dictates its own shadows, but in painting it is controlled by them.

In fact, there are two sorts of modelling. 'Imitative modelling', connected with our ordinary perceptions or with photographic representation, makes us aware of relief by seeming to place us in natural space, as if we were actually in the presence of the object; this is purely an exercise of technical virtuosity, with trompe-l'œil illusion as the summit of its achievement. With 'formal modelling', tone values still give the impression of relief, but instead of situating us in natural space, as if in the presence of the object, *it situates us in another order of space – that of art*. Only on these terms can the artist formulate a language of which the thing he represents is the occasion, not the object, and make contact with us through a style that is manifested in the work of art.

One may now realize how ridiculous it is to condemn the use of modelling out of hand. There are too many great masterpieces which prove it to be legitimate. What *is* true is that most contemporary artists have given up using it, which does not mean it is bad in itself, but simply that this particular means of expression is not in harmony with the sensibility of our age.

It follows that, when confronted by a work in which modelling is used, one should neither be carried away with admiration for its miraculous power of imitation, nor adopt a rigidly contemptuous attitude; instead, one should try to appreciate the degree in which the artist has integrated modelling with the other formal agents to make a coherent space. On these conditions the employment of tone values is as legitimate as the employment of flat colours; it reaches the status of language.

Now what about depth? As photography demonstrates, it is perceived through alterations of form and lighting. Bearing that in mind, let us examine this view of Passau. There are four principal planes 178 – the river, the town, the country beyond, and the sky. Though they are placed *one above the other* on the photograph, they appear to be ranged *one behind the other* in depth. One's attention is immediately drawn to the dark zone of the town, which stands out between the lighter zones of the river and the distant landscape. Thus differences of light and dark serve the eye as points of reference which we interpret as if we were actually standing on the hill from which the photograph was taken.

176   Here now is a sketch by Claude Lorrain, which also gives us a 'view', of the Roman campagna this time. Broadly speaking, it contains the same number of planes – bare earth in the foreground, flanked by a spur of rock; a sheet of water; a hilly landscape;

and, finally, the sky. Just as in the photograph, these zones are superimposed vertically, but appear to extend in depth, one behind the other. Why is it then, that beyond these common data we feel something altogether different? Looking at the view of Passau, we realize that tone values here have the effect of situating us in the spot where the photograph was taken, as if we were really there. Claude's drawing, on the other hand, rather than placing us

176. Claude Lorrain (1600-1682). *Landscape in the Campagna,* pen and wash. Vienna, Albertina. Photo Mermod.

topographically in the campagna, gives us above all the feeling that we are looking at a work of art. *Our situation is different, and so is our attitude.* Might this be because the details are fewer and less precise in the sketch? A glance at another photograph, taken against the light, enables us to answer 'no' to this question, for although in this view of the Volga the planes are simplified in the extreme, one would never mistake it for a painting. The true answer lies elsewhere. As we have seen à propos of volume, the artist uses values to construct a different kind of space, in which we are placed in a different way from that of nature, but which is every bit as real as is our particular relationship to it.

Certainly this sketch gives us the sensation of depth, but equally certainly that is not *all* it gives us. Claude's planes, while indeed suggesting distance, at the same time draw the eye back to the surface. It is in observing this dual condition that forms acquire their plastic validity.

The painter's problem is to control his values so that they may convey the sense of depth without destroying our sense of the surface plane. That is how Claude has gone about it, substituting a methodical organization, in which the planes provide

178. *As if we were really there.* View of Passau.

a mutual framework[1], for the mechanical graduations of the photograph. The surface stands upright – as well as stretching backward to suggest distance; sensitive as a membrane, it obeys the commands of space without ever the least sense of strain or rupture.

Let us examine the drawing in detail, to see if we can get to the heart of this metamorphosis: here, *right in front,* is the earth and the spur of rock; *further off,* the expanse of water; *still further off,* the hills, crowned by two castles; finally, *beyond the horizon,* the sky. If you half close your eyes, it is easy to see that this succession of planes is due to one's perception of dark and light zones lying adjacent to one another. But how does Claude use tone values? The strongest contrast is at the meeting-point of the sky and the spur of rock on the left. The effect of such a contrast in reality is to make the darker part 'jump out' violently, to the detriment of the lighter part, as can be seen in this photograph where the group of piles stands out against the light in much the same way as Claude's rock, but in such

177. View of the Volga.

[1] These ideas owe much to the judicious views propounded by André Lhote.

179. View of a seaport.

brutal contrast that it disturbs the rest of the land-scape. To avoid this impression of dislocation, Claude modifies his contrast. He puts patches of lighter tone on the rock and in front of it, thus bringing it more into line with the sky; with equally light tones all round it, the spur neither 'jumps out' nor 'falls back' into the distance. But if you cover 180 the light patches with your hand, the drawing is as 179 dislocated as the photograph.

Now concentrate on the central part of the drawing; that is where the intermediate values are ranged in the greatest number and variety, and where the impression of depth is conveyed most vividly to the eye. If one isolates them from the rest of the drawing, one sees clearly enough that the double-181 crested hill is further away than the left-hand castle, but, when one looks at them again as parts of the 182 whole, one notices that the hill is 'pushed forward' by the dark tone of the cloud above it, and that it is likewise 'pulled forward' by the shadow of similar 183 tone on the central part of the water. As for the two castles, which 'push back' the horizon into the light background, they are themselves 'pushed' into the third plane by the light stretch of water, and 'pulled' forward at the same time by the dark tone of the foreground. Compare with this the 179 central part of the photograph of a seaport! Here is no compensation produced by the interplay of different planes. As one's gaze progresses onward from the foreshore, the contrasts diminish automat-ically, and all we get is the impression of increasing distance.

Examine now, if you will, the right-hand part of 184 the drawing. At the point where the most distant mountain stands out against the sky, Claude takes care to frame it by darkening the sky and by making the belts of trees below the castle darker still; in doing so, he 'compensates' the effect of distance. A similar phenomenon can be observed at the extreme right edge. There again, a comparison with the photograph is enough to demonstrate the artist's 179 intervention. The darkest zone in the drawing is in the middle of the trees, while the foreground plane is made deliberately lighter.

Depth, therefore, like modelling, is not at all incompatible with art, but we must know just what we mean by this. In reality tone values are graded in accordance with optical laws, providing points of reference for the eye and pinpointing our situation in natural space. In painting, however, tone values become valid agents of expression only when this natural effect is modified by an interplay of various planes, organizing the scene in depth while still respecting the surface.

Objects take shape in this plastic space, which is imaginary (since it does not exist in nature) and at the same time real (since it exists for us), and from it they derive their form and their expressive qual-ities. To convey the spacious serenity of the cam-pagna, Claude intensifies some of the light accents at the horizon, and invents others – rocks, clouds, castles, rivers and sky all being incorporated in the language of form, just as Claudel verbally inserts a pine tree to intensify the hieratic grandeur of Japan-ese landscape: 'And this evening, where I saw Fuji like a colossus and like a Madonna enthroned in the glory of the infinite, the dark tuft of a pine rears up beside the dove-coloured mountain.' Neither Claude nor Claudel is reproducing nature; but in expressing it they express themselves.

We can see the collaboration of colours and values once again in Ruisdael's picture known as *After Rain*. Without embarking upon another demon- 185 stration in detail, I would point out how the land-scape maintains its formal equilibrium, in spite of the yawning gulf of the sky. Right in the middle of this picture stands a double row of trees, like a little avenue in perspective. If you cover the light accents of the browsing sheep, you will observe that this perspective effect is emphasized, as in natural space; but when you move your finger the light patches of the sheep pull the trees forward, as it were. The brilliance of the meadow where the lighting is con-centrated threatens to break out of its bounds, and

180. A uniform mass of shadow would produce an effect of ▶
dislocation.

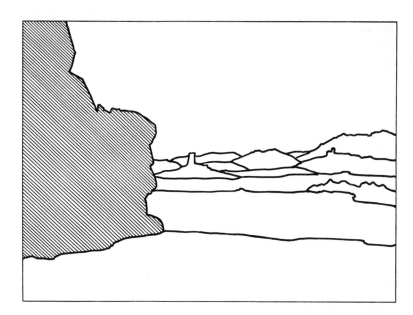

182. Reciprocal thrusts produced by tone values. ▶

181. If one isolates them, one sees that the double-crested hill is
further away than the left-hand castle.

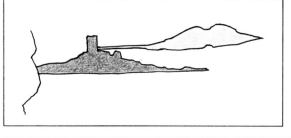

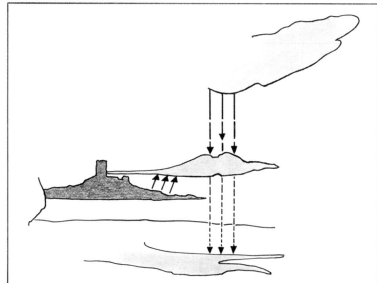

◀ 183. As for the two castles, which
'push back' the horizon... they are
themselves 'pushed' into the third
plane by the light stretch of water, and
'pulled' forward by the dark foreground.

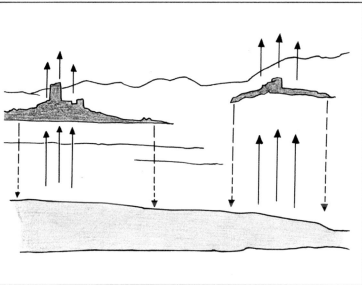

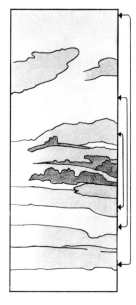

184. Compensations of tone values ▶
organising the formal space.

so the artist pins it back in place by means of the dark accent of the shepherd and his dog. 'We need not take any notice of the shepherds on the right who watch over the flocks;' says one commentator[1] 'they are not true Ruisdael, but trivial accessories added to please his patron. It is in the austere beauty of the landscape that the essence of the picture lies, and that is where the eye is instantly drawn...' And this author goes on to imagine that Ruisdael must have been 'prey to I know not what secret anxiety...' Certainly it is very desirable to try to explain a work of art, but only on condition that one sticks to the work, and the work alone! To pretend that the shepherds are 'trivial accessories', and that they could well be dispensed with, is to misunderstand their formal function and to describe the work in terms of what it represents, instead of in terms of the language it constitutes.

Naturally, Rembrandt must be cited among the artists who have given the highest degree of ex-186 pression to tone values. His etching of the *Three Trees* will verify what I have said about the suggestion of depth in painting. There are few landscapes that evoke such a feeling of the vastness of space as this one does, with its striking contrast between the three huge trees in their solitude and the minute buildings of the distant town. Yet, though the eye seems to leap into this space, it covers no actual distance. The tone values are arranged with such simple yet consummate art (for example, conceal the dark clouds to the left – and the town immediately seems to slip much farther away) that the distance is fully 'contained'; let me stress, however, that the *idea* of distance that we form is not abstract; it is produced by *sensations*. We *see* the etching; but our sensations respond to formal language, and instead of remaining linked to our normal perceptions, instead of referring us to the world of objects in which we ourselves move, they link up with our feelings and refer us to our interior world. In both cases we *perceive* something, but *our awareness of what we perceive is on two different levels.* One of the basic conditions of painting is that the surface lets the artist convert objects into elements of language, and lets the spectator convert his perceptions into feeling and significance.

187 Beside the *Three Trees,* this etching by the Dutchman Anton Derkzen van Angeren cuts a poor figure (though not altogether devoid of merit) because the tone values are inadequately organized.

185. Jacob van Ruisdael (1628/29-1682). *After Rain.* Florence, Uffizi. Photo Held.

The dark fence dislocates the landscape,[1] while the pale tones at the right weaken its consistency; and between these loosely articulated extremities the clouds are scattered about for no better reason than to 'furnish' the sky.

Look now at this other etching by Rembrandt, the *Woman by a Stove.* Thanks to his instinct for 188 tone values, the artist manages to balance the forms so that the modelling neither projects nor recedes excessively. The recess of the niche is 'compensated' by the relief of the stove and the woman's bust. However, one must not run away with the idea that values are a question of mathematics (add a bit on one side, and subtract it on the other); though the principle is one of compensation, obviously it is only the manner of its application that can give it any quality. Notice how in this etching the niche is not evenly concave. The strokes representing the shadow in the left-hand part of it are dense and oblique at the top, and then are gradually spaced out and tilted towards the horizontal as they descend. Similarly, the woman is not modelled uniformly; the dress is flat in comparison with the bust, and the right arm is flat in comparison with the left. Without going into all the details, one can

[1] Armand Dayot, *Les Offices* (The Uffizi), Ed. Lafitte.

[1] An effect analogous to that noted in the photograph of a seaport (fig. 179).

186. Rembrandt (1606-1669). *The Three Trees*, etching. Photo Giraudon.

187. Anton Derkzen van Angeren (20th century). *Dutch Landscape*, etching.

188. Rembrandt (1606-1669). *Woman by a Stove,* etching. Photo Bulloz.

189. Whistler (1834-1903). *La Vieille aux Loques,* etching. Photo Seinet.

see that formal compensation cannot be mathematically applied. It should be apparent enough for us to sense it; but when it is too apparent we at once reject it. A work of art commands attention through the coherence of its unseen organization.

Whistler's etching pales into insignificance beside 189 Rembrandt's; this kitchen remains a far less satisfactory formal space than that in the *Woman by a Stove,* for all that its recession is compensated by the volumes of the utensils – and in particular by the two dishes in the bottom right-hand corner. The compensation is less assured (for instance, the perspective of the ceiling, and the background shadows, are feebly managed), and the tools it employs are not so judiciously integrated in the scheme. (Is not the role of the two dishes on the right a little too obvious?)

Rembrandt is one of the artists who have best understood how a discriminating use of values can transform a painting. We see this in his landscapes, in his portraits and in his religious subjects. In the *Stormy Landscape,* the picture is not, as in the case 190 of Ruisdael, constructed of successive 'screens' which, in spite of their plastic function, remain more or less true to the natural motif. The values no longer originate in a greater or lesser intensity of daylight, but are raised to the limits of elaboration, ringing sonorously from the pigment itself. One colour, vibrating between warm and cool, suffices to create the drama, in which the forms are the silent protagonists.

In reality, then, the appearance of objects is associated with their relief and their position in space, and this basic and continuous experience tends to make us demand of the painter that he should depict things as we see them. But, if he yields to this demand, he is depriving us, since only in formal terms can a true understanding be created between artist and spectator.

By virtue of the compensation of light and dark tones in different planes, and of the infinitely delicate graduation of light, pictures based on values admit us to a consistent space in which forms, although they are modelled, do not encourage us to take hold of the objects, and, although they are ranged in depth, do not encourage us to traverse the intervals between them. Thus tone values, which by reason of modelling and depth run the greatest risk of misleading us into illusionism, are – paradoxically – our protection against it. But it is true that they have this power only in the hands of the greatest artists.

190. Rembrandt (1606-1669). *Stormy Landscape*. Brunswick, Herzog Anton-Ulrich Museum. Photo Held.

Light and Colour

'Two-dimensional painting' and 'three-dimensional painting': it is time we took our bearings to see what is meant by these two expressions, which so constantly recur – usually in direct opposition to each other. First, what *is* a dimension? Geometricians tell us that it is 'each of the extensions required in order to calculate the area of a flat figure or the volume of a solid one.' Thus 'plane geometry concerns the measurement of figures contained *in a single plane* (rectangle, circle, square, etc.), while solid geometry concerns the measurement of figures whose volume is defined *by extensions that are not contained in a single plane* (cone, sphere, cylinder, etc.).' [1] In both cases it is a question of *abstract* dimensions, in which geometric bodies of an abstract nature are constructed for the sole purpose of being *measured*.

In the light of these definitions it can be said that the expressions 'two-dimensional painting' and 'three-dimensional painting' are doubly inappropriate: firstly, because there are no abstract bodies in painting, but only material forms; secondly, because our attitude to pictures is not the fixed and definite attitude of a geometrician who measures something, but a complex reaction, compounded of the direct influence of the formal elements upon us, the promptings of our own sensibility, and the effort of understanding one another through the medium of forms. Geometrical problems end with a *solution*; the end of painting is to produce a *work of art*. No work of art is ever, or could ever be, mistaken for geometry – not even the most abstract of abstract paintings, since the organization of its figures, their colours and their material presence calls not for calculation but for appreciation.

Thus, though the same terms are used, the dimensions of geometry and those of painting belong to two different orders. But, since language does not possess a separate word for each of the expressions of space in art, and since the terms 'second dimension' and 'third dimension' correspond to a familiar experience, it is reasonable to use them by analogy *simply as terms of reference.*

We have seen how, in this sense, the Primitives show a preference for two-dimensional painting, in which the picture space tends to conform to the surface plane. The figures in manuscript illuminations are made up of lines, which tirelessly trace the silhouette of man or beast, bird or monster. As a means of expression, it seizes on the object not

191

---

[1] My italics.

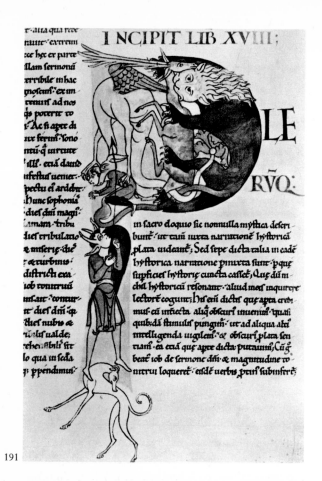

191

so as to represent it, but so as to convert it into a form that is in keeping with its pictorial space.

If you turn from parchment to mosaic – from the manuscript page to the gigantic *Christ Pantocrator* of Monreale – the spatial system of the Primitives is still the same. Gold backgrounds, which were used so frequently, reinforce it; unrelated to nature, yet by no means abstract, they are the very emblem of this formal language, which expresses a view of the world founded on man's reverence for the divine.

Considered from this angle, Giotto's achievement appears even more audacious. He breaks with the tradition of the gold background, replacing it with the unchallenged blue of the sky. Admittedly, stained glass and mosaic had used a blue background long before this; but in Giotto's case the innovation brings with it a *change of style,* corresponding to a change in religious sentiment. Objects are detached from the surface plane, and set in a space which establishes depth and relief of the kind we have studied already. Joachim and the shepherds, standing beside rocks that are deployed in volume, are no longer abstract symbols. Though still distinct from it, the sacred drama draws closer to the world of appearances, becoming an *action* in which the faithful play their parts. In this process, whereby sacred values give place to religious, and religious values to human, the language of form is also changed.

In truth, human values cannot be accommodated to any and every mode of expression, for each has need of its own mode if it is to be made communicable. The sacred, for centuries organized in terms of the picture plane, quickly declined in three-dimensional space, where it was too much exposed to the charm of appearances and the spectacle of life.

192

193

191. Romanesque art. Decorated initial, St. Gregory, *Moralia,* 12th century. Dijon, Library. Photo Archives Photographiques, Paris.

192

192. Byzantine art. *Christ Pantocrator,* mosaic, 12th century. Monreale, Cathedral. Photo Alinari.

193. Giotto (1267-1337). *St. Joachim Returns to the Sheep-fold,* fresco. Padua, Arena Chapel. Photo Anderson-Giraudon.

In the chapter on colour I discussed the principal applications of two-dimensional space, and in the chapter on light those of three-dimensional space. Between these extremes there are spaces of many intermediate kinds. Let us look at an example midway between the two. Between Rembrandt on one hand and the Primitives on the other, it is surely Vermeer who provides the most perfect example, for his art is a miracle of equilibrium, based (paradoxically) as much upon colour as upon values. Here is one of his most beautiful works, the [194] *Artist in his Studio*. What is the secret of its mysterious power? Largely, I think, the impression of plenitude which it conveys, the unexpected blend of clarity and softness.

We can trace the source of the clarity easily enough. The Primitives have shown us how clarity is obtained by using lines to enclose forms and define the limits of surfaces, and by using flat colours to make each area a distinct zone. Thus Vermeer's outlines do not melt into the contours of the figures, but silhouette them – both the painter, who is seen from behind, and the model, seen in profile. Surfaces are marked decisively – the painter's canvas, the easel, the cover of the book, the back of the chair, the diamond shapes of the tiled floor, the background wall. So long as we confine ourselves to this kind of observation, it is as if Vermeer's art were two-dimensional.

But what is the source of that impression of *softness* which we experience at the same time? Notice how, at the mention of this word, one's attention is transferred from the tiles or the wall to the hanging curtain, the materials on the table, and especially to the girl's face. These are the areas where values are more actively in evidence; volumes are apparent in the folds of the curtain, in the materials, in the girl's drapery and even in the map that hangs on the wall; the curtain is like some great organ with brocaded pipes, whose notes range from bass to treble through the gradations from dark to light; a feeling of depth, intimate and restrained, breaks through.

Two apparently hostile worlds are here reconciled, with the happiest results for the picture. Vermeer has fearlessly chosen the boldest possible course, based simultaneously on modelling and on the surface plane. But, in making this decision, he foresees the dangers incurred by his audacity, and contrives a whole series of cunning transitions from one to the other. In fact, modelling is not confined to certain objects, as it seemed just now, but is developed in obedience to a subtle discipline throughout the picture. It is allowed a certain amplitude in the folds of the curtain, is reduced in the fabrics on the table, takes on a sort of mineral rigidity in the model's blue robe, and is finally resolved in the crinkled surface of the map. As the eye progresses along the rising diagonal from left to right, one sees the modelling gradually diminish and harden until it is absorbed into the plane of the wall. One sees the same thing if one follows the descending diagonal from left to right: the curtain is modelled more strongly than the girl, and the girl more strongly than the painter. Thanks to these transitions, two-dimensional and three-dimensional space interpenetrate and interlock from plane to plane. Finally, the colours tend to be cooler in the brightly lit areas, and warmer in the shadows: reddish-brown is dominant in the hollows of the folds of the curtain, blue-green is dominant where they swell outward; the model is draped in blue, while the painter wears dark brown, with two patches of red for his stockings. Instead of conflicting, colours and values unite, and – without losing any of their individual qualities – cement their union with reciprocal contributions to the total effect. This is indeed a strange sort of pictorial space, and probably Vermeer alone has ever brought it to such a degree of complexity under the guise of simplicity! It is pervaded by an exquisite sense of perfection, to which the artist no doubt alludes discreetly in the little spheres he is so fond of – the pearls at the model's ears, the nail-heads on the chair, the knobs on the maulstick and the map.

Between the two-dimensional art of primitives and moderns, and the three-dimensional art of the Renaissance, the works of Vermeer form an intermediate world which fits our sense of poetic reality, that which we feel when we see commonplace events exalted by the powers of the human heart.

To appreciate the gulf which separates the artist of genius from the utterly pedestrian, one need only compare the *Artist in his Studio* with this 'work of [195] art' by the Hon. J. Collier (Vice-President of the Royal Society of Portrait Painters), which was exhibited in 1931 and was reproduced in the *Illustrated London News* with the caption: 'An old master as seen by a contemporary master: the romance of Fra Filippo Lippi.' [1] Apart from its title, this painting presents approximately the same subject, the

---

[1] One recalls that the painter Filippo Lippi, having fallen deeply in love with the young nun who acted as his model, carried her off and married her.

194. Jan Vermeer (1632-1675). *The Artist in his Studio*. Vienna, Kunsthistorisches Museum. Photo Erwin Meyer.

same characters and accessories: the artist, his model, the picture he has begun, the tiled floor, the background wall... But, whereas in the Vermeer these objects are assimilated into the language of form, and become art, in the hapless Collier's case they are merely the excuse for a display of romanticism. Lines and colours ignore the picture space, servilely submitting to the sentimental and documentary character of the subject.

Let us examine yet another aspect of the use of tone-values – chiaroscuro, a procedure which permits the rendering not only of differences of luminous intensity in relation to depth and relief, but of variations in the lighting itself. Technically, chiaroscuro is obtained by carrying a tint in one direction towards the strongest light, and in the other towards the deepest shadow.[1] By reason of the contrast implied in this procedure, it is particularly suited to subjects of a dramatic kind. It enjoyed an almost

[1] Contrary to the general belief, 'chiaroscuro' does not apply only to shadow.

195. *The studio is only an excuse for a display of romanticism.* The Hon. J. Collier, 20th century.

universal vogue from the 16th century to the 19th, though today it has been virtually abandoned.

Here, then, we have a mode of formal expression which was one of the great innovations of the latter part of the Renaissance, and which was for a time so much in favour that painting was even supposed to consist in expressing it. Out of respect for it, the accumulated dirt on old paintings was for long thought to be an effect of art! (It is hard to imagine what efforts were needed to prove that cleaning is not mutilation; one remembers the violent controversies over Rembrandt's *Night Watch*.)

Now, even the best mode of formal expression is valueless in itself; only the artist's use of it can give it value. Perhaps we should examine this point more closely.

How about Caravaggio's use of chiaroscuro? The 196 darkness is abruptly pierced to reveal David with his gory trophy, and the spectator experiences a *frisson* of horror... Its pictorial qualities are undeniable, but the chiaroscuro, it seems, plays rather too much the role of a spotlight; the light picks out the principal objects from the gloom which pervades the canvas: David's torso, the sword and Goliath's head. Yet, strictly speaking, neither the design nor the colours are affected by it; the chiaroscuro is *added* to the scene to emphasize its effect, making no contribution to the spatial structure of the work. This is why it eventually becomes boring.

Look now at another picture, with a subject even less prepossessing, if that be possible. What a pathetic creature she is, this *Bather* by Rembrandt, 197 pitiably holding up her shift as she enters the water. And yet we feel immediately that here is a masterpiece! Like Caravaggio, Rembrandt uses chiaroscuro; but while with Caravaggio it is only an oratorical device, with Rembrandt it becomes an accomplished means of plastic expression. The reason is that with Rembrandt light and shadow do not simply play on the picture like the effect of a searchlight directed from outside, but are part and parcel of its substance. Instead of picking out pre-existent forms and colours, the chiaroscuro and the forms are closely integrated with one another. We see this in the draughtsmanship: lines do not just follow the contours of objects, as with Caravaggio, but melt into passages of paint that are governed by the values themselves. Modelling is also affected: instead of being simply revealed by the lighting, the bather's flesh diffuses its own light, producing volumes which do not 'go round' as in classical perspective, but which are in accord with the

196. Caravaggio (1573-1610). *David with the Head of Goliath*. Rome, Borghese Gallery. Photo Alinari.

chiaroscuro. Ostensibly, nothing could be more trivial than a tucked-up shift, but Rembrandt makes it an admirable passage of painting. This is because light and shadow not only penetrate it, but constitute its form from within. The colours, transformed in their turn, are reduced in number to harmonize with a dominant tint.

When chiaroscuro is confined to the role of a spotlight, it can produce a sort of magic-lantern effect, or, if the 'projectionist' is clever, a theatrical one; and who has a better claim to the title of 'master-projectionist' than Caravaggio? Rembrandt does not need the projector: the light which he creates within his paint surface is an integral part of the work, animating the figure *from within*. With him, chiaroscuro ceases to be an accessory and becomes a *structure*. If any additional proof is

desired, note how, in the *David*, the dark background has the effect of throwing forward the light area of the hero's body; and how, in the *Bather*, it belongs to the picture, at one with the woman's flesh, which is engendered of light and shadow. The space of the *Bather* is homogeneous, while in that of the *David*, despite all the artist's talent, there is something of a composite nature. Once again this basic law of art is confirmed: modes of plastic expression cannot be *added* to each other; they become language through *integration* with each other.

It would be wrong to suppose that Rembrandt achieved the only possible expression of chiaroscuro. Georges de La Tour succeeded in creating his own, 198 which is no less remarkable. In his case, line does not melt into shadow, but sharply defines the lighted sides of objects. His planes, modelled only in part, are constructed like an edifice. Although he suppresses the realistic details of folds, wrinkles, muscles etc., this is not so as to give 'distinction' to his paintings, but to emphasize the monumentality he aims at. For the same reason he modifies the colour scale.

Neither with Rembrandt nor La Tour is chiaroscuro something added to the picture; with both, it is part of its very substance.

Before either of these painters, before Caravaggio even, El Greco had made chiaroscuro the particular vehicle of his lyricism. What an overwhelming picture his *Resurrection of Christ* is! Not because 199 Jesus soars into the sky while the soldiers fall prostrate at the miracle (this is a question of subject), but because the picture achieves an expression which has the virtues of style. Whereas the fall of St. Paul in Caravaggio's painting seems contrived, 200 that of the soldier in the foreground of the *Resurrection* seems true, in spite of the improbable attitude of his body. Here chiaroscuro is not a dramatic accessory; in combination with colours and lines, it is the drama itself. With Rembrandt chiaroscuro throbs with life; with La Tour it attains a controlled exaltation; with El Greco it expresses a passionate lyricism. His figures are elongated, their modelling is perfunctory, space is diminished, drawing goes by the board, proportions are altered, and colours are split into flames that crackle in the wind. Do you see how, in this explosion of almost audible violence, one hand alone, that of Christ, remains unscathed? The contrast between the Saviour's serenity and the terror of the soldiers is not a matter of stage-craft, but the outward ex-

198. Georges de La Tour (1593-1652). *The Newborn.* Rennes, Museum. Photo Giraudon.

pression of an interior truth that has found its proper language. This is what has never been understood by the Guido Renis of this world, for whom the summit of ambition is to draw a beautiful face 201 and a beautiful body, to paint the folds of a loincloth to perfection, and then to achieve a sort of trumpery mysticism by seasoning it all with a dash of chiaroscuro!

Whatever its period, a picture is not a work of art by virtue of what it represents, nor by virtue of any conventional notion of the beautiful. This truth, which the general public is always tempted to forget, was undoubtedly brought out more into the light of day by Impressionism, and the salutary reappraisal which dates from Impressionism is bearing fruit in our own day. What actually happened? Leaving aside theoretical and historical

189

199. El Greco (1541-1614). *The Resurrection of Christ*. Madrid, Prado. Photo Held.

considerations, one may answer: *the advent of a new vision,* by which one means that towards the end of the 19th century colours and lines were used by the Impressionists to create a pictorial space of a kind previously unknown, an expression of human truth corresponding to the modern age, an expression which humanity has gradually accepted by a process of self-recognition.

In formal terms, the problem boils down to this: when light falls on a rounded object, such as a teapot, it determines three zones: at the two extremes are the most brilliantly lit and the darkest parts; between the two is the half-tone which makes the transition. As we have seen, this behaviour of light is linked in everyday experience with our sensations of relief and depth. Much of ancient, medieval and modern art is in general hostile to it. It was at the time of the Renaissance in particular that the use of tone-values came to be associated with pictorial space, and forms became volumes, ranged in depth. But, as I have insisted all along, although this manner of seeing is nearer to our normal image of things, it differs from it in this essential – that the old masters respected the integrity of the surface plane, and did not descend to illusionism. For that reason it was aesthetically valid.

In the light of these facts, the achievement of the Impressionists becomes clear. What concerned them was, on the one hand, to preserve values while renouncing the depth and modelling with which the Renaissance had associated them, and on the other to exploit pure colours while renouncing the flat tints, calligraphy and decoration with which they had no less generally been associated outside the Renaissance tradition. The resolution of these apparently contradictory requirements is precisely the origin of the new vision and mode of expression.

Here are Titian's *Concert* and Renoir's *Les Confidences*. In the former, the few colours are subjected to varying degrees of luminous intensity, producing a subtle, skilful modelling, full of charm. The colour tends towards orange-yellow in the light passages, and orange-brown in the dark ones, the transition being made through a cool half-tone. 202-203

Renoir is not more arbitrary than Titian, but he employs a different formal language, of which the guiding principle is to *convert values into colours.* His shadows, instead of enveloping and modelling the light areas, *themselves take on different tints.* The result is a complete metamorphosis. No longer prompted by shadows, the eye loses its sense of relief and depth. However, when one looks more

200. Caravaggio (1573-1610). *The Conversion of St. Paul.* Rome, S. Maria del Popolo. Photo Anderson.

the ears) almost corresponds to the blue of the nearer dress. In their concern to preserve the light in colours, while freeing them from relief and depth, the Impressionists multiply the brush strokes on the canvas. Space is no longer constituted by the modelling of forms, but by their innumerable vibrations. Depth has disappeared, volume is repudiated and the contours of objects are broken, yet the painting does not dissolve into chaos. On the contrary, it discovers a new reality; light is made queen, the fresh morning light of an endless festival. It is not my intention to discuss Impressionism in all its phases, but simply to demonstrate its principle and show how it has helped us to look anew at the problems of art. [1]

While Primitive painting inclined towards two-dimensional space, and that of the Renaissance towards three dimensions, the spatial structures of Vermeer and of the Impressionists remind us that the eye is capable of as many different points of view as there are valid works of art. Every human verity in art is the achievement of a mode of formal expression.

[1] In the fourth section of the book the reader will find a detailed study of an Impressionist work, Renoir's *Moulin de la Galette.*

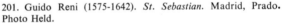

201. Guido Reni (1575-1642). *St. Sebastian.* Madrid, Prado. Photo Held.

closely, one sees that this does not result in the two-dimensional space of the Primitives. Even though chiaroscuro is banished, something of its presence survives. Let me explain. In Titian's *Concert*, modelling is conveyed by the controlled combination of light parts and dark. As we have noted, the former tend towards orange-yellow and the latter towards orange-brown – to warm tints, that is – while the transition is effected through a cool half-tone. The sequence is as follows: warm light, cool half-tone, warm shadow. The Impressionists modify this order of succession so as to eliminate the effect of modelling which results from the passage from light to dark. With them, the shadows tend towards blue, of a value approximately equal to that of the light tints. In *Les Confidences*, the light blue on the heads (at the temples, under the chin and behind

191

202. Titian (1480/90-1576). *The Concert*. Florence, Pitti Palace. Photo Held.

203. Auguste Renoir (1841-1919). *Les Confidences*. Winterthur, Reinhart collection. Photo Held.

Form, Distortion, Decoration

It should now be clear that we must regard painting as another world; but not an alien world, since we have free access to it. I look at a picture, and pleasurable sensations are aroused in me; as I stand motionless in front of it, a part of my consciousness is awakened. One speaks of a 'citizen of the world', so why not of a 'citizen of art'? For art also is a city, or rather, a country.

But what are the inhabitants of this pictorial space which we value so highly? Who are the natives? Men, women and children, one is tempted immediately to reply, but there are the trees also, the sky, the earth, the sun, the scintillations of light... I had better stop there, or I shall need to cite the whole of the visible universe. But even that would not be all, for the invisible universe is not excluded. Here are angels, archangels, God himself 204 – beings that have never been seen, but whose likeness has been made familiar by generations of painters. Here are devils and monsters too. One can only conclude that everything which has, or can be given, a shape belongs by right to painting. Yet we still have to reckon with the teeming populace of decorative motifs, the countless combinations of 205 lines and shapes with which mankind has adorned utensils, walls and houses: traceries, garlands, spirals – and every sort of hybrid form!

In the apse of S. Apollinare in Classe, the cen- 206 tral image of the saint is figurative; but can one say the same for the trees, the rocks and the sheep? Are they not more truly decorative, in the same spirit as this fragment of a Coptic textile, where 207 branches, leaves and birds, though recognizable, have renounced their own nature in order to conform to the rhythm of the whole? There are whole tribes of the semi-figurative and the semi-decorative...

Modern artists, too, have discovered new worlds and new beings. In the works of Klee and the 208 Surrealists, the inhabitants of the dream world 209 appear before our eyes on the canvas. Lastly, newest of all, comes the generation of Mondrian and Kandinsky – non-figurative art, with all its fertile 210 and imperious progeny...

How can one take it all in? So many categories – so many pitfalls! Figurative painting, semi-figurative painting, non-figurative, decorative, abstract – the very fragility of such terms is sufficient proof that they refer to something inessential, and for good reason! Based on subject matter, they all lend themselves to the same errors and misunderstandings as did the old classification by genres.

204. Pieter Bruegel (1525/30-1569). *Fall of the Rebel Angels*. Brussels, Musées royaux des beaux-arts. Photo Bulloz.

205. Art of Asia Minor. Small jug, earthenware, c. 2000 B C. Prague, National Gallery. Ed. Artia.

206. Byzantine art. *Saint Apollinaris,* mosaic, 6th century. Ravenna, basilica of S. Apollinare in Classe. Photo Held.

196

207. Coptic art. *Branches, leaves and birds,* tapestry, 4th century. Paris, Musée de Cluny. Photo Viollet.

209. Joan Miró (b. 1893). *Woman, Bird and Stars.* Lausanne, private collection. Photo Held.

◄ 208. Paul Klee (1879-1940). *Timider Brutaler.* New York, Mr. and Mrs. Arnold collection. Photo Held.

210. Piet Mondrian (1872-1944). *Broadway Boogie-Woogie.* New York, Museum of Modern Art. Photo Museum of Modern Art.

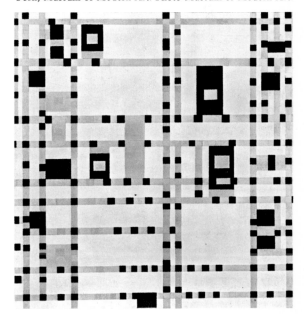

Let us therefore get things into perspective, and this first of all: that the 'Imaginary Museum' (as Malraux calls it), in which we assemble all the masterpieces of humanity, has its counterpart in an 'Antimuseum', which is often the more flourishing of the two! Look through a magazine of about twenty years ago, or stroll through certain rooms in provincial art galleries, and you will see all too clearly what the 'Antimuseum' is. It comprises all that, under the pretext of art, merely apes the taste of an age, a society, or a moment, and all that, for lack of genius or power, does not pass beyond mediocrity – the pastiches and the failures.

Fortunately, some mysterious and implacable justice, like the angel of the Last Judgment, puts its scales to the service of the truth. For every one of the elect, how many there are of the damned! Not damned, even: the damned at least shriek and struggle, and (if not devoured by the Devil) *exist*; whereas these unfortunates, whose heaped-up canvases, frescoes and mosaics make no impression on the scales whatsoever, are cast out into nothingness. One can appeal against the sentence of a judge, or one can appeal to the divine mercy, but there is no appeal against the pitiless verdict of time. True, it allows an occasional respite or reprieve, which does nothing to lessen the confusion.

What do we find among the art which time rejects? The same: figurative and non-figurative, semi-decorative and abstract – in short, everything which has the air of being art, but is not so in the eyes of the angel. But if a Rembrandt draws near, one little Vermeer or a miniature by Corneille de Lyon, then the upraised scourge is arrested for a moment.

Everything or anything *can* be painted: that which exists or that which does not, that which has shape or that which has none, flowers or women, cones or children, monsters or triangles, trees or goats, *on condition that they become 'naturalized' in painting*. That is the basic and essential condition. In so far as they fail to take this into account, categories and classifications are as factitious as they are invalid.

Juridically speaking, naturalization means giving to a foreigner the rights enjoyed by the natives of a country. But it is not merely an administrative formality. The country of adoption requires certain information, and inquires in particular as to whether the alien can be said to be 'assimilated'. It is the same in the land of art. Before receiving the rights of citizenship, objects must renounce their alien qualities – those they possess in nature – and assume those of the country of adoption. *This is how objects attain the status of art – through being naturalized as forms.* With no aboriginal population, the world of painting consists entirely of such assimilated objects, transferred from reality by the artist's genius, and adjusted to the needs of form.

While on this subject, it might be as well to consider one of the problems which bother the general public most – the question of *distortion*. The most frequent complaint is that artists have taken liberties with the human form. This attitude, as we have seen, is the result of two prejudices and one error. The first prejudice is that the human figure is immutable, the second is that it is essentially more dignified than other objects, and the pernicious consequence is the formation of fixed notions by which people claim to judge works of art. Now painting (and here lies the error) does not aim to show us our own flattering idea of ourselves, but to *express a human truth,* which is something quite different.

One realizes that every expression of truth demands its own appropriate formal language, leading

211. *A 'masterpiece' of the Antimuseum!* E. de Bonnencontre, 19th century. *The Three Graces.* Photo Braun.

212. Rembrandt (1606-1669). *Jesus (or St. John the Baptist) Preaching,* pen drawing. Paris, Louvre. Photo Bulloz.

to a different treatment of forms, and that this treatment can often pass for 'distortion' in the eyes of the uninitiated spectator. 'Even while the artist is engrossed in the struggle to group the formal elements in as pure and logical a manner as possible, so that each will be indispensable in its place and none will clash with the rest', observes Paul Klee amusingly, 'he hears some profane voice over his shoulder, pronouncing the fatal words – But it's not at all like Uncle!'

213 Is the *St. Gregory* of the Abbey of Saint-Amand a 'likeness'? Is it not somewhat disrespectful to represent so great a saint with a body so flat and a head so small, with a blue beard, with his knees so low and his legs turned out? And the arms! And these atrophied, frog-like or lobster-like hands! Here is distortion that borders on deformity. And

it is true, the saint's figure *is* deformed, *so long as one compares it with one's general idea of mankind.* But when one considers it from the standpoint of art, it is quite a different matter.

What is the artist trying to do? Obviously to 'portray' Pope Gregory. But what kind of a portrayal? Perhaps this question seems preposterous: does not portrayal – or portrait – mean the reproduction of the model's appearance? No; that is an altogether specious notion. No doubt, the external aspect of a person makes him recognizable, but how could it begin to convey the formidable presence of this man, who was one of the Church's greatest popes; who – in a period of incessant troubles – managed to save Rome from famine and to force the Lombards to raise their siege; who – battling victoriously against the perils from without – suc-

199

ceeded in stamping out heresy, while at the same time pursuing the propagation of the faith; and who – to crown this intensely active existence – completely renovated western liturgy and church music? Six centuries later the artist takes up his brush. It is no use for him to think of reproducing the appearance of the model (the fact that there *is* no model is beside the point). What he wants to do is to express the truth of this extraordinary being, and primarily the superhuman authority with which God has invested him. Yet intentions do not make a work of art. The painter knows that he must take formal requirements into account.

What does he have at his disposal? The manuscript page – *a surface, on which it is his task to create a pictorial space appropriate to express the truth incarnate in this man.*

Thus it is by deliberate intent that he chooses to represent St. Gregory alone, full-face, occupying the whole page. The expression of power necessitates a change of proportions, so the artist reduces the head, legs and arms, diminishes the extremities in favour of the central mass; but since he is working in a two-dimensional space, and cannot have recourse to volumes, he increases the trunk by developing it lengthways on the surface. There might be something shocking in this 'distortion' if the artist mechanically added to the body what he took away from the limbs. But see how carefully he transforms his space in consequence. For one thing, he introduces stabilizing elements, chiefly in the form of geometrical shapes: the rectangles of the ground, the seat and the book, the circle of the halo, the branched form of the pallium, the straight lines, and so on; for another, he links these with mobile elements: the waves of the hair, beard, neck and the border of the robe, the curling *rinceaux* of the ground, and especially the shadows of the folds, which cascade down the front of the vestments, pour off the arms and swirl around the knees. These two species of formal element give rise to relationships which 'naturalize' the distortion and 'assimilate' it plastically.

Notice how the pallium, with its rigid vertical band, stems the fall of the folds like a supporting stake. The same effect, produced by different means, can be seen in the sleeves, where the openings, built of straight lines, are as rigid as metal, while the rest of the garment seems to tumble in abandon.

Though linked to the surface of the page, the space in this illumination is not at all inert. The interplay of formal equivalences animates and enlivens it. This can be appreciated in the treatment of the lower part of the figure. On the right, the spreading, fanlike folds below the knee are stopped at the edge of the robe by a straight line which consolidates them. On the left, where the green folds flow like water at the edge of the garment, it is the motif of the embroidered hem that restores the balance by reason of its rigidity. There are still subtler relationships than these. Have you observed how the positions of the book and the saint's head would cause the picture to 'lean' to the right, if this were not counteracted for the eye by tilting the axis of the pallium ever so slightly to the left of the median line? The top of the bench also contributes to this adjustment; its right end-face is hidden, but the artist shows the left end-face so as to add a bit more 'ballast' on this side.

The features of the Pope have given way to the truth of the saint. Who could still doubt his authority? Yet this has been neither 'stated' nor 'described'. It is truth *expressed*; we feel its power and understand its import solely through the medium of form. Preoccupied with form, we are no longer distracted by anatomical disproportion, and we ignore the atrophy of the extremities to concentrate on the mobile interplay of surfaces, colours and lines. We no longer demand that the saint's power should be demonstrated by some ceremonious gesture in the manner of an orator or a Roman general (a convention which corresponds to our ideas of greatness), nor do we expect it to be demonstrated by the image of a figure with tensed muscles at the peak of physical effort (corresponding to the realism of a snapshot), but we accept that it should be, not demonstrated, but *translated* into the language of form. Thus, a truthful painting is not one which limits itself to copying the model, but one which finds an equivalent formal expression for the ultimate truths of humanity. All else is falsehood.

Now let us take up a final point, connected with the preceding one, and also subject to a great deal of misunderstanding: the question of decoration. In the widest sense this word comprises all that is ornament or embellishment, all that is *added* to something to produce a pleasing effect. It is an adornment of the principal object, and for that reason is regarded as an accessory and is soon forgotten. What could be more amusing than to

213. Romanesque art. St. *Gregory the Great,* illuminated manuscript, 12th century. Paris, Bibliothèque nationale. Photo Bibliothèque nationale. ►

214. Edouard Vuillard (1868-1940). *Portrait of Madame Sert*. Winterthur, private collection. Photo Held.

glance through a fashion magazine of the early years of the century?

All the more extraordinary, then, that a hat we would smile at can rouse our admiration when it adorns the head of *Madame Sert!* Needless to say, 214 the sitter herself has nothing to do with it. It is Vuillard, and he alone, who brings about this changed response, causing us to react in different ways to two similar hats. We have referred to the reason for this just now. When it is a matter of fashion, we look upon decoration as a symptom of the taste of a particular time, a taste both exclusive and ephemeral. Vuillard's hat is indubitably a hat, but, since we react to it differently, it must *also* be something else. Indeed, so it is: at the same time as he paints a hat, Vuillard also paints a *form,* which the photographed hat is not.

The hat in the photograph is a faithful image of 215 the real thing, an ornamental accessory. It has only a fortuitous relationship with the wearer, and an even more fortuitous relationship with the background (it is quite immaterial that the girl is shown in front of a niche; she would be the same, and so would her hat, if the photograph had been taken in the street).

Vuillard's hat, on the contrary, is a form *in the sense that all other elements in the picture are strictly related to it, and it is strictly related to them.* Note how the artist has integrated it in the picture space; suppressing any suggestion of depth, he sets it within a circumscribed field, of which the profile and bust of the sitter are also parts. He avoids the banal effect that might have resulted, by exploiting the interplay of varied areas of colour. Thus the brown background is pierced by a light rectangle (presumably suggested by a window), which is itself broken up by patches of green (presumably suggested by trees), and there are blue strokes, like claw-marks, on the dark cloak. But, of all these broken areas, it is the hat which presents the greatest complexity: its surface is split up as if it were cut into facets. Cover the light rectangle in the background, and the hat is a gaudy excrescence. Cover the hat, and the contrast between the dark background and the light rectangle is uncomfortably violent, hardening the profile by reducing it to a silhouette. On the other hand, the relationship between the hat and the light rectangle produces an unexpected result – *the appearance of light in a space without depth.* But instead of the light coming in through a window, and making the profile 'go round' as in reality, it is transformed in the flat

216. *The culpable truthfulness of military artists.* Photo Archives photographiques, Paris.

facets of the hat, and – thanks to the little rectangles of alternate white and blue – diffuses a radiance without shadow or reflection, and without volume either. Needless to say, this hat is not possessed of magical powers. Its power derives entirely from the relationships of lines and colours which constitute it and the rest of the picture.

That is the truth of the matter: either the decoration (clothes, headgear, trees, houses, furniture or anything else) becomes form, integrated in a coherent formal language – in which case it participates in the constitution and the significance of the work – or it is an accessory which, despite all its intrinsic beauty, remains an extraneous embellishment.

What a lot of military artists have displayed a culpable degree of truthfulness in representing their generals with caps on their heads, simply to leave no doubts as to their rank! In contrast to these gallant souls, who paint 'at the salute', Dürer shows us how to make the most brilliant use of a head-dress without stars or braid. He crowns the broad features in this *Portrait of a Man* with a hat of majestic virility, worthy of the head that wears it. Yet, while it has all the character of a great cornice above the face, one notices that it fulfils a particular plastic function, compensating by its breadth and mass for the modelling of the fur and the face. If you mask it with your finger, the face comes forward and projects excessively. In fact, it is the hat which welds the volumes to the background and ensures the picture's equilibrium. To counteract the contrast between the modelling of the man and the flat surface of his headgear, Dürer has rendered the hat in curved lines which recall the curves of volumes, [1] and so the transition is smoothly effected.

In brief, the terms 'form', 'distortion' and 'decoration' are not responsible for the confusion that arises from the varied meanings we attach to them. Meaning is never one given thing, but always the result of some relationship that we establish. So, if we insist that these terms should refer explicitly or implicity to the *idea* which we have of the objects they designate in reality, we are ourselves to blame for the confusion. If, on the other hand, we accept that they designate *objects belonging to the world of painting,* these same terms can reveal the light of truth. We should make the effort to do justice to art by using a vocabulary that is conformable with it, its sense guided by aesthetic experience alone.

[1] In Vuillard's portrait, where the plane is dominant, the hat is constructed of straight lines. And see to what purpose Raphael makes use of a biretta!

217. Albrecht Dürer (1471-1528). *Portrait of a Man*. Madrid, Prado. Photo Held.

218. Raphael (1483-1520). *Portrait of Cardinal Alidorio*. Madrid, Prado. Photo Held.

Medium and Technique

When we read a book, our senses are not deeply involved; except in luxury editions, typography and quality of paper make little impression. It is quite different when we look at a painting, for then the senses play an essential part, at least as important as that of the intellect or the imagination. In fact, *a change of medium entails a change of the 'pictorial text'*. These two portraits by Rembrandt, one engraved and the other painted, are different works, 219-220 in spite of their identity of subject. In the former, the features of Dr. Bonus, and the light which plays on them, are generated from the fine network of hatching woven by the etching-needle on the copper plate; in the latter they are generated from finely ground oil paint, which moulds them in colour and impasto. Forms change according to the medium (here, for example, the hands) because the reality of a picture depends as much on its material as on its 'text'. This is what makes it so difficult to describe

219. Rembrandt (1606-1669). *Ephraim Bonus,* etching. Photo Giraudon.

220. Rembrandt (1606-1669). *Ephraim Bonus,* oil. Amsterdam, Dr. F. Mannheimer coll. Photo Bruckmann-Giraudon.

219

221. Giorgione (c. 1478-1510). *Concert champêtre*. Paris, Louvre. Photo Held.

222. Romanesque art. *The Creation,* fresco (detail), 12th century. Church of Saint-Savin-sur-Gartempe (France). Photo Hurault-Viollet.

a painting to someone who has not seen it. At best, one may convey an idea of the subject, but it is virtually impossible to convey a true idea of material qualities. This difficulty besets all books on art, and, needless to say, it cannot be avoided in this one. The words 'line', 'colour', 'space', 'form', 'surface', 'depth' etc. are, in effect, abstract terms. The way we use them, influenced by our childhood lessons in geometry, confirms this abstract sense. Yet the things they describe are all *concrete phenomena,* blending with each other in the unity of the work of art. We are impelled to distinguish between them because we cannot grasp this unity at a single glance; we have to grasp it from *successive and complementary points of view,* in conformity with our own nature and that of the work. Abstract terms simply help to guide our thoughts and concentrate our attention. What do we find when we concentrate our thoughts on materials?

It is common knowledge that the Renaissance produced a copious flowering of nudes, those of Giorgione and Titian being unquestionably among 221 the most beautiful. Now, nudes like these had not existed before. They were unknown in the Middle Ages, when the nude was scarcely tolerated except, perforce, in the figures of Adam and Eve, or occasionally in the devils and the resurrected men and women of the Last Judgment. Compared with Renaissance works, the nudes of the crypt at Auxerre, or those of Saint-Savin, are shivering, 222 miserable beings, who only remind us of the curse of sinfulness. What Giorgione and Titian discovered was the voluptuous charm of flesh, which shows woman not as an outcast from Paradise, but as a choice fruit of the earth – an earth without sin (and perhaps without God), a garden of delights, untroubled by the memory of Eden.

It should be recognized that this metamorphosis is connected not only with a change of morality, a new feeling for life and a new conception of man (and woman), but also with the discovery of a new medium: that of oil painting.

Of course, it is not a question of the medium being determined by new circumstances, but rather (as we saw in the first section of this book) of it finding its 'vocation', as it were. This, incidentally, tends to show that the behaviour of materials and forms, though unpredictable, is not purely an effect of chance. Between the poles of chance, which is the absence of any known cause, and causality, which is the elimination of all chance factors, there is room for other types of relation, including that which I have described as 'vocation', and which finds expression in painting through affinitive relationships.

223 The example of mosaic provides proof of this. As everyone knows, mosaic is composed of small cubes of stone, marble or glass – fragments of *diverse origins,* of *unequal sizes,* making a surface that is *rough* in some places and *smooth* in others; fragments which are *juxtaposed,* and therefore cannot interpenetrate, each one forming a *separate locality, of which the edges remain visible where they adjoin.* These are not arbitrary conditions, but are part of the very nature of the medium. When one visits Ravenna, one comes to the conclusion that the art of the great mosaicists is founded on the fact that they respected these conditions in all that they did. Because the colours consist of sharply defined areas, they are predisposed towards a two-dimensional space, and one can see how spontaneously they adapt themselves to the flat surface of the wall; the human figures likewise obey the logic of this spatial system, and are set flat in the picture plane; there is little or no modelling; shadows become juxtaposed colours, which strengthen the design by encasing the forms in a sort of armature; instead of merging into each other, the objects preserve their individual integrity; and finally, the cubes of unequal richness, roughness or smoothness give the mosaic its characteristic surface texture and decorative grandeur. At the same time as our eye is appreciating these rhythmic surfaces, it is also taking pleasure in their material quality.

In comparison with the mosaics of Constantinople or Ravenna, even the cleverest of those in St. Peter's at Rome are paltry and insignificant. Executed at the command of the Popes, by artists who once were famous, their purpose was to reproduce the most celebrated paintings of the Renaissance, and this with such fidelity that in the end one cannot distinguish them from originals in oil! As many as ten thousand different shades have been counted in some of them. It would be hard to imagine a more unprofitable waste of labour than this aping of the properties of another medium, this painstaking endeavour to construct a space in depth, with volumes and shadows rendered by the employment of tone-values. The colours, multiplied to excess, become insipid. The surface texture, maltreated to the extent of being polished, also loses its interest. Indeed, all that constitutes the true character of mosaic has disappeared – and a murdered medium can only bring forth still-born objects. Could any

achievement be more barren than that of a Marcello Provenzale, who succeeds in having his mosaic 224 mistaken for a painting?

The only impression we retain from this vast performance is one of gratuitous virtuosity; and there is nothing paradoxical in this. Whereas the anonymous artists of Ravenna have proudly affirmed the indissoluble unity of form and medium, the post-Renaissance copyists have denied it. For them, mosaic is an industry, and its apparent prosperity is only a cloak for its artistic indigence. Thus the artist's materials make their presence felt by imposing limitations, but limitations that are also sources of strength, since it is they that give each medium its individuality. To this individuality every art-form owes some part of its complexion.

Techniques, like media, are also closely related to the world of forms. In its widest sense, technique is the sum of procedures entailed in the use of certain tools, conditioned by the nature of the materials on which they are used, and by the artist's intentions. Thus there are as many different techniques in painting as there are different kinds of material. It is still widely – and erroneously – supposed that technique is purely a matter of craftsmanship, and that the artist's work can be divided into two separate phases: *first* the conception of the work, which is (or is imagined to be) the creative phase, *and then* the execution, or technical phase. Now, though it is true that one can be a craftsman without being an artist, it is impossible to be an artist without being a craftsman, because the process of artistic creation is an indivisible whole: conception *plus* execution.

Technique is not simply a series of procedures for executing forms; *it plays its own part in the genesis of forms.* At the risk of pushing analogy too far, one might say that, while the artist procreates, it is technique that gives birth to the work, and that both artist and technique are as sterile without each other as they are fruitful in union with each other. Technique – and this is the point I want to make – is *equally* creative.

Indeed, the history of art is not far from being a history of techniques. Oil painting, beginning in the Renaissance, gives rise to a world of forms that the Middle Ages did not *and could not* know. Yet, contrary to the general belief, oil paint was used in the Middle Ages. That may sound somewhat contradictory, so I should hasten to add that it was used in a particular and limited way – mainly on wood sculpture, as a protection against humidity, and on

223. Byzantine art. *The Miraculous Draught of Fishes,* mosaic, 6th century. Ravenna, Church of S. Apollinare Nuovo. Photo Held.

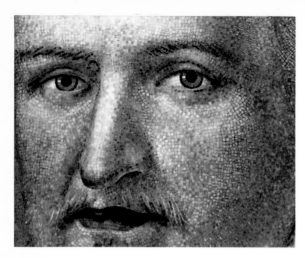

224. Marcello Provenzale, 17th century, *Pope Paul V,* mosaic (detail). Rome, Borghese Gallery. Photo Giraudon.

flags and banners that were exposed to the inclemencies of wind and rain. Oil painting was known, but it served a utilitarian purpose, largely unconnected with art. The brothers Van Eyck, therefore, did not invent oil painting, but what they *did* invent was much more important! *It was they who delivered oil painting from its utilitarian function and made of it a creative technique,* and it was in their altarpiece of the *Adoration of the Mystic Lamb* that this metamorphosis was gloriously accomplished, revitalizing the art of painting from top to bottom. Far from being mere processes of execution, techniques are creative forces, intimately associated with the life of the forms which they help to produce. Brought to life by the artist's genius, they retain their creative power so long as they are true to themselves, but lose it as soon as they seek to plunder one another in an imitative spirit, as we noted in the case of mosaic.

It is curious to observe how, in the course of history, techniques have appeared, have asserted themselves, have decayed or have been revived, as if they had common links with the life of man as well as with the life of forms, so that one can hardly tell whether it is new ideas that inspire changes of technique, or whether it is changed techniques that inspire men to express new thoughts. Oil painting only emerged from its utilitarian function at the moment when Renaissance naturalism was established and was extolling the poetry of earthly things; but one can equally well suppose that the thriving success of this naturalism was connected with the development of oil painting. It is as if, guided by mysterious affinities, man goes out to meet the technique, and the technique comes to meet him.

Setting aside this question, which belongs more to the realm of psychology or of the philosophy of art, let us see how technique makes its presence felt in a work of art. We might look back to the example of mosaic, or – better still – reinforce it with the example of stained glass (Fig. 156).

In essence, the technique of stained glass consisted in assembling pieces of glass of various colours within a network of lead strips. The pieces were of different sizes, and originally of different thickness; they were trimmed with a red-hot iron and with metal pincers; even so, their surface remained uneven, often indented, and the colour in the body of the glass was pitted with flaws and air-bubbles. Yet it was by paying due regard to these limitations that the Romanesque and Gothic masters of stained glass laid the foundations of their art, and created forms in harmony with a space composed of assorted fragments of coloured glass. Here again, modelling is excluded, or is only used with the utmost restraint; the forms scarcely emerge from the surface plane, and to this they owe their monumental, hieratic character. In contrast to mosaic, in which the development of line is difficult, stained glass gives full scope to it. Line is employed to represent faces, bodies, hands, and the folds of vestments, generally without suggesting contours, and, since it belongs wholly to the surface, tends naturally towards calligraphy, as in manuscript illumination. Since the light is distributed over a great many fragments of varying size, it is not suited to a large variety of colours, so the tints are deliberately few in number, the accent being placed on their brilliance. The leads, which might seem only to have a functional role, are in fact an essential feature of the work, partly because they enclose the forms, and partly because they enhance the colours by contrast. The more intense the light, the more emphatic the forms appear; yet they do not dissolve as the sun declines, though the contrast diminishes with the fading light. So far from being a matter of improvisation, technique – like medium – imposes certain limitations on the artist, but at the same time makes these limitations fruitful. [1]

[1] This is just what most people find it so hard to accept. For them, what counts in general is fidelity of reproduction, and techniques appear to be little more than the means to this end – sometimes crude and sometimes more refined. One can understand why oil painting, which of all techniques lends itself most readily to imitative effects, should be their idea of perfection!

225. (Hubert and) Jan van Eyck (1385/90-1444). *Ghent Altarpiece:* central panel, *Adoration of the Mystic Lamb*. Ghent, Cathedral of St. Bavo. Copyright A.C.L., Brussels.

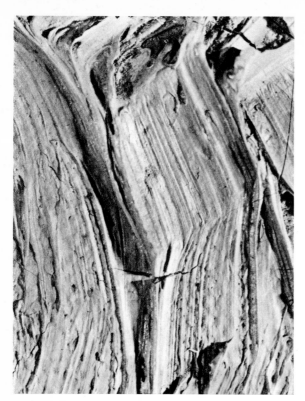

226. Vincent Van Gogh (1853-1890). *La Roulotte,* macrophotographic detail. Paris, Louvre. Photo Musée du Louvre.

227. Camille Pissarro (1830-1903). *Chemin Montant,* macrophotographic detail. Paris, Louvre. Photo Musée du Louvre.

Thus medium and technique are *constituent elements of the work of art.* Forms are not pre-existent to them, but take shape *with* them. A mosaicist and a fresco painter do not 'think' on the same lines. The concepts which each of them formulates are stimulated, guided, and elaborated in part by the material presence, in the one case, of the cubes of glass, and in the other, of the plaster wall and the pigments. Thought is inert if it has no framework to support it, and needs to submit to conditions of some sort if it is to be constructive.

Painting, then, can make contact with us in as many different ways as there are different media and techniques. Neither mind nor senses are touched in the same way by a water-colour as by an oil painting. The effect of the water medium is to give objects a comparatively fluid look, as if their power actually resided in their fluidity. By contrast, oil paint confers on them, if not always robustness of form, at least a more 'sensory' presence; whether they are solidly constructed, or broken up in the dazzle of impressionism, they remain more tactile than forms in water-colour. Just as we have no direct access to the souls of others, so we have no direct access to pure forms. Like souls, forms only exist for us as manifested in the 'body' of a technique or the 'flesh' of a material. That, no doubt, is why our contacts with works of art are so different from our contacts with ideas. Ideas transmit a conception of man, while art transmits his presence.

Now, if a work of art touches us in this way, it is because it is itself 'touched'. This is not just a play on words. Our being touched means that we are contacted through our sensibility, that we receive an impression, that something is *imprinted* in us. Medium and technique do not submit passively to the intervention of the artist, but neither does he submit passively to them. They impose certain limitations on him, and he *imprints* his personal mark on them, contacting them – if not in their sensibility (that would be rather too fanciful a suggestion!) – at least in their *temperament* – and one cannot deny that they have temperament. *Touch* is thus *the meeting-point between material and technique, on one side, and the artist's hand and his tools, on the other.* Inscribed in the flesh of the work, touch is perpetuated as a living, visible and enduring mark. Two passages of paint that are similar in tone and colour, one by Van Gogh and the other by Pissarro, 226-227 are revealed by macrophotography to be of quite different formal structure. Van Gogh's paint flows

214

228. Frans Hals (1580-1666). *Portrait of a Man,* detail. Paris, Musée Jacquemart-André. Photo Bulloz.

in wide bands, with the impetus of a stream of lava, while Pissarro's proceeds by a series of interlaced patches, like sprays of leaves stuck to the canvas.

But what about the medieval illuminators – does this apply to them? Certainly, their touch is very different from Van Gogh's; but it is nevertheless perceptible, and its plastic validity lies precisely in its restraint. Precision of draughtsmanship and purity of flat colour are the constituents of its decorative power, and to this end the handling is kept smooth and 'tight', thus contributing in its own fashion to the spiritual structure of the work.

One can see how absurd it is to expect all works of art to have the same degree of 'finish', since every work must have the sort of finish which suits it best. We must firmly reject the ridiculous (but still widely accepted) notion that a picture is the more beautiful in proportion to the degree of minuteness or the length of time that the artist has devoted to it. The greatness of Van Eyck has nothing to do with his minuteness of technique or with the time he took to complete his works; it lies in the fact that he knew how to exploit minuteness and time to create a world of new and authentic forms. Likewise, the greatness of Frans Hals lies not in 228 the fact that he scorned minuteness, but in the fact that his boldness of touch – especially in the late works – is in step with his visionary imagination.

Paint, in itself alone, is lifeless flesh. It is the touch of a hand that awakens it to life. Touch is that nervous trace which gives the personal accent to an artist's handling. It is the spark of life, and it is structure too, organizing the picture space, and itself organized in harmony with the forms. Thanks to its power, painting is a sphere in which the spirit not only breathes, but also leaves its mark.

The agents
of form in action

Composition

Photography is within everyone's reach nowadays, and there is no shortage of picturesque 'views'. Here, in fact, is a very inviting one, with all the charm of diffused half-lights. Beyond the nearest screen of trees is an ancient well, its cool freshness mingling with the smell of moss; the shadow patterns on the ground stop short at a group of stones on the left, of which one is round in shape and shines brightly in the sun. A glade opens out to the right, where the light breaks through the leaves, and one begins to think of walks one has had, or would like to have. Photography is an evocative instrument, a substitute image in the main, which one tires of sooner or later.

Look now at Cézanne's painting. At first glance we have the paradoxical sensation:

that it is the same scene;

that it is a quite different scene;

that we respond to it in the same way *and* differently.

On examining it, one is struck first by the resemblances. It is indeed the same spot; here are the trees, the well, the millstone, the foliage and sky. But one is quickly aware of the differences: surely there is an extra tree in the clump on the right – and fewer branches on the tree to the left! And how much less numerous the stones and leaves are! It becomes clear that the face of the landscape has been modified by additions and subtractions. Looking closer still, one sees that the trees are not placed in the same way, and that the well has come forward as if seen through a magnifying glass. Instead of the blur of sunlight to the right, there is an open network of leaves; the undergrowth in the foreground is reduced to a few stems; the big tree at the extreme right has become two trees; the two trees forming an X are set farther apart at their foot, while their vertical angle has been narrowed. Although the woodland is still there in its broad outlines, the artist has not left a single detail unchanged. Identity of subject and picture is never more than superficial.

229

230

229. Photograph of the motif. John Rewald.

230. Paul Cézanne (1839-1906). *Millstone and Cistern in the Woods of the Château Noir.* Merion (Pennsylvania), Barnes Foundation. Photo Held.

Nature, we know, is prodigality itself. We enjoy the profusion with which she surrounds us, yet sometimes we can tire of it. Our senses, assailed from all sides, receive only a confused impression – captivating, but lacking all restraint or control. When all is moving, how can one appreciate movement, and relish it? When all is varied, how can one appreciate variety, and enjoy it? When all is abundant, how can one appreciate abundance, and take delight in it? A work of art cannot compete with nature, and does not aim to do so, since in origin and principle it is *primarily a reflection on nature*. Nor is reflection simply a matter of taking thought; it is equally evident at the level of sensibility. The artist replaces nature's prodigal display with an *order* – i.e., an ensemble of linked relationships, which adequately express his reflection, and give the spectator controlled enjoyment in place of vague pleasure. Cézanne's woodland is not just a simplification of the motif; indeed, strictly speaking, the work of art and the photograph cannot be compared at all, though we may put them side by side for explanatory purposes. The work of art is derived from order, and that implies the intervention of man.

Composition is the application of formal resources, the establishing of the work's basic relationships – those which determine the division of the surface, the disposition of the forms, and their proportions. It supplies one of the mind's fundamental needs – coherence; and it is linked with one of the profoundest aspirations of our being – to build a reality of which man is the author. That is the essential difference between the photograph of the woodland and Cézanne's painting of it: one refers exclusively to nature, and the other *to nature and mankind inclusively*.

There is a simplistic view that seeks to equate pictorial composition with geometry. If we reduce Cézanne's painting to a diagram, it is still recognizable. The principal elements are undoubtedly indicated, but the work of art has vanished. And this is why: the object of a geometrical figure is to demonstrate, and that of geometry itself is to speculate, but demonstration and speculation are both equally foreign to art. Art cannot imitate geometry any more than it can imitate photography, and the artist cannot provide a substitute for ideas any more than he can provide a substitute for sensations. Thus, in painting, the composition of a picture is never entirely subordinated either to nature or to geometry. Forms may be combined in such a way that they are *almost* geometrical patterns – as with the cubists or the abstract painters – or in such a way that they are *almost* a transcript of natural appearances – as with Millet or Courbet, for example. However, the art of the past and that of the present are alike in respecting these limits and never going beyond them.

This is confirmation of the existence of an intermediate order between thought and feeling, an order whose nature transforms the elements it makes use of, the definitions we give to those elements, and even our perceptions of them – in short, an order which establishes a new kind of relationship.

We may judge the truth of this, on a single point, by comparing Cézanne's picture alternately with the photograph and the diagram. In both the latter, one notices that the objects – whether trees or geometrical shapes – *occupy* the surface, each having its portion of it. The dimensions of the diagram, in accordance with its geometrical nature, define an area suitable for *division* into equal or unequal parts, while those of the photograph are like a *container* in relation to its *contents*. In both, our attention is drawn principally to the positive shapes rather than to the spaces between them, the empty

231

231-232

231

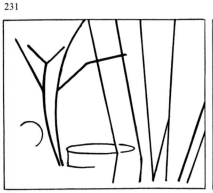

232

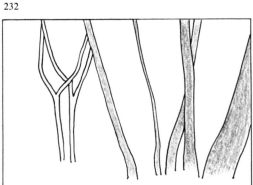

233

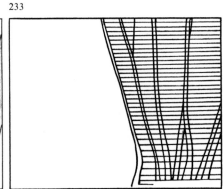

spaces seeming to be more or less neutral and irrelevant.

233 Pictorial composition, as revealed in Cézanne's painting, offers something altogether different: far from presenting a divisible surface, it presents a homogeneous whole, and it follows from this that the 'empty' spaces are no less important than the 'solid' shapes, or – more correctly – that the distinction between solid and void no longer has any meaning. The intervals between the trees have as much formal significance as the trees themselves. The relationship of container to contents is equally irrelevant, for it is no longer simply a question of locating objects in a neutral space. Space has been promoted to the same level of existence as the objects; it is space which stretches the sensitive net in which the forms are caught – and which the forms themselves constitute – and in this way it becomes as 'active', as effective, as they.

Far from being a matter of putting various elements 'in their place' (like a jig-saw puzzle), composition operates by metamorphosis. It is the prime essential of the language of form, through which trees, foliage, stones, spaces and colours become *forms,* equal in nature if not in importance, their texture sustained by an internal force.

The trees in Cézanne's picture still represent trees, but at the same time they produce an impression of measured solemnity. Whatever elements the artist employs – words (designations of objects) in the case of the poet, or images (likewise designations of objects) in the case of the painter – he cannot, whether he be poet or painter, employ them without *converting them into means of expression.* The feeling of measured solemnity which grows in us as we contemplate Cézanne's picture is produced by form. Thus composition in painting is not so much a matter of 'getting the parts into relationship with each other' (it is often so defined) as of *establishing relationships between a variety of elements which are converted into forms in order to transmit the artist's sensations or emotions to the spectator.*

Having clarified this point, let us see how it is revealed. First, by an *effect of wholeness.* Perhaps it is trite to remind the reader that nothing can be either added to or subtracted from a work of art, but behind the triteness lies an important truth. When one looks at the photograph of woodland, it is easy to imagine one's gaze continuing beyond its edges to right or left. The limits of a photograph are provisional and fortuitous; they are mainly dependent on the motif, and they have the effect of cutting up a landscape into separate sections. On the other hand, the limits of a picture are *definitive.* As we have seen, they determine a specific space in which a presence makes itself felt – a presence distinct from all around it, made wholly manifest in the picture, and in it alone. Of course, it is possible to enumerate parts and elements in Cézanne's painting – the millstone, the well, the trees, the sky and so on – but this is as meaningless as it would be to isolate the words of a poem according to the parts of speech – verb, article, complement, etc. Grammatical order is not the same as poetic or artistic order; in the latter the parts are *totally and organically interdependent.*

If one compares the Cézanne with one of the innumerable pictures of the innumerable amateur painters of woodland scenery, the meaning of this organic interdependence can be grasped easily enough. Martin-Kavel's trees are no fewer in num- 234 ber, and no less leafy; like the photograph of the Château Noir they provide a combination of branches, sky, dead leaves on the ground, and stones. Yet Cézanne's picture is essentially different both from Martin-Kavel's and from the photograph. In these the sum of the objects represented makes up a *total,* while in the Cézanne it makes a *totality.* Totals result from adding elements to each other in a quantitative sense; *totality is produced through each of the elements surrendering a part of its individuality to the whole, and changing in a qualitative sense.* Cézanne's woodland is not a product of simple addition, nor is it the result of a juxtaposition of objects. Trees, well, millstone and colours compose themselves to participate – each in its own way, but every one without exception – in the expression of measured grandeur which the canvas exhales.

We may elucidate this point by noting how the artist has arranged the trees on the right-hand side of the design, which are of varying size and thickness in the photograph, but all approximately equal in the painting. Tree 2 (in the photo) is overawed 235 by the presence of its neighbours, seeming all the more slender and insubstantial for the fact that tree 1 is comparatively robust and tree 3 (actually two separate trunks) is definitely large. Conscious of this danger, Cézanne modifies the subject by adding an extra tree between 1 and 3 – giving us the 236 sequence 1, 2, 2a, 3, 4 – and at the same time reduces all the trunks to more or less equal size. By virtue of this transformation – insignificant at first sight – he introduces elements which engender relation-

234. *A painting which tries to rival photography.* Martin-Kavel, 19th century. *The Viaduct.*

ships that are lacking in the natural trees of the photograph.

What *are* these relationships? Well, let us observe the trees closely. In the photo, the angles of their trunks and the intervals between them are a matter of purest chance; but in Cézanne's painting, trees 1 and 2 rise on parallel axes to the left, trees 2 and 2a form an acute angle, trees 2a and 3 provide further parallels and another acute angle (less acute than the preceding one), which is amplified once more between trees 3 and 4. This means, if we still concentrate on the one aspect only, that Cézanne, far from reproducing the elements of the landscape, has translated them, and has imposed a rhythm on them;[1] hence the reduction of the trunks to a common dimension, and their arrangement at studied angles. Following each other in a rhythmical sequence (the trunks corresponding to the downbeat, the intervals between them to the up-beat), Cézanne's trees do not cease to represent trees, *but they simultaneously give the spectator a feeling of harmonious order,* a means of expression that nature does not possess. Their existence derives in part from the image of the object represented, and in part from the rhythm they produce within (and by means of) the picture – a rhythm one would seek in vain either in nature or in Martin-Kavel's painting.

Perhaps we can familiarize ourselves with this phenomenon by considering it from another angle. It is well known that the prodigious influence of Italian art in the 17th century was due largely to the school founded by the brothers Agostino and Annibale Carracci, with the aid of their cousin Lodovico. Now, their *Accademia degli Incamminati* claimed to do no less than to teach the way to paint masterpieces by combining the best qualities

237

[1] This problem is studied at greater length in the chapter entitled *Rhythm.*

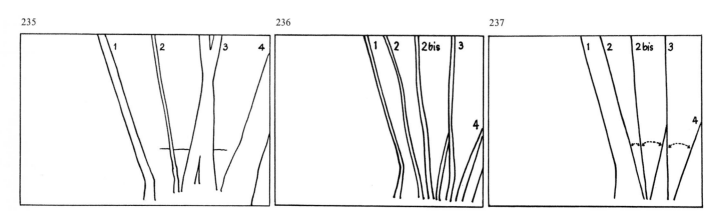

235   236   237

238. Annibale Carracci (1560-1609). Decoration of the Galleria Farnese, detail. Rome, Palazzo Farnese. Photo Alinari.

of the best masters. Borrowing from Florence the science of draughtsmanship, and from Venice that of colour and light, the Carracci believed – doubtless in all sincerity – that they could discover and communicate the secrets of a 'universally perfect' art. The result – their own works first, and then the works of their numerous followers – was a luxuriant growth which spread throughout Europe and even to the New World. This academicism, inspired by the best reasons, but ignoring reason itself, throws new light on the nature of composition. When one contemplates the key work of the Carracci – the 238 decoration of the Palazzo Farnese in Rome (principally the work of Annibale) – one is quickly aware that its charm derives from the decorator's cleverness in exploiting celebrated works and established formulae. Faithful in this to his ideal of eclecticism, he models his great herms, which seem to hold up the vault, on antique statuary; the recollection of the *Farnese Hercules,* one of the most famous of Greek marbles – and one which was in any case close at hand – is visible both in his *Hercules at the Feet of Omphale* and his *Polyphemus.* The presence of Michelangelo is even more obvious; there is not a figure or motif, even to the over-all scheme of decoration, that does not recall the Sistine Chapel, with this reservation – that on the ceiling of the Palazzo Farnese the empty spaces are filled with medallions or *ignudi*. And it is no mere matter of influences! The artist makes no attempt to disguise his borrowings, but openly proclaims them, just as he glories in perfecting modelling to the point of illusionism, and in imitating the colour and texture of bronze in the medallions. Certificate of culture? Diploma of virtuosity? An enthusiast

for the great Renaissance masters, Annibale Carracci spiritedly proves to what extent he can rival them, but his talent – and this is the inevitable limit – does not go beyond that of an imitator.

The decoration is a brilliant academic exercise, and has all the air of forming a whole. Each of its parts in isolation displays definite pictorial qualities; but over-all unity is lacking. Thus, while composition has the effect of organizing the various parts into a unity of impression, it should be added that it can achieve this only through *unity of expression,* of which only the creative artist is capable. The most beautiful anthology of selected fragments cannot ever replace a single true poem.

At this point it might be supposed that a work of art is a perfectly adjusted, but static, whole. This is not the case. In truth, all painting contains movement, and invites our *active* participation. It may be said now, in anticipation of views which I shall develop further on, that the artist depends chiefly on the interplay of lines and colours to produce this hidden energy which makes his work an animated whole. Could the way in which the Egyptian painter arranged his different patterns of 239 form and colour on the dresses of his figures be the result of chance – or of concern for vestimentary exactness? Following the motifs from one figure to the next, the eye is drawn into the very movement of the marching procession. And here is a modern example: in this composition by Kandinsky, *Le* 240 *Gros et le Mince,* one is instantly aware that the eye is invited to trace the triple trajectory at the end of which the three balls (yellow, blue and red) defend their ground inch by inch, like outpost sentinels, against the advance of the monster, which swells and contracts its pseudopodia. *Thus composition also has the effect of producing and controlling the interior movement of the picture, by which surface, lines and colours come alive.*

Is not, then, the unity of the work compromised? Is there not a risk of its elements disintegrating? What is the phenomenon that holds them together, like electrons gravitating round the nucleus of the atom? It is here that another quality of composition is displayed – *tension,* which forms the subject of the next chapter.

In its widest sense, therefore, composition means the sum of factors which control the relationships of a work so as to give it unity. This interior cohesion is due to the artist's unity of expression, and is revealed in the spectator's unity of impression. It is organic – matter, structure and movement all in

239. Egyptian art. *Jewish Women*, detail; dynasty XII, c. 20th century B.C. Beni Hasan, tomb of Khnum-hotep. Photo Held.

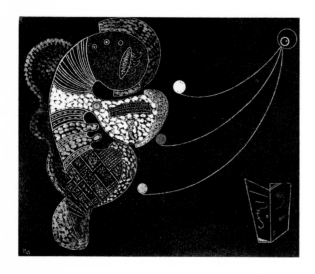

one; it is language – content, feeling and style all in one.

Metamorphosis is its principle; it adjusts all the elements of the work to a single meaning, and, by altering the nature of our approach to it, raises our minds and our sensibility to apprehend it.

240. Wassily Kandinsky (1866-1944). *Le Gros et le Mince*, gouache. Paris, Galerie Maeght. Photo Held.

Tension

Although it is a part of everyday experience, the phenomenon termed 'tension' is not easy to describe. Almost every morning the papers tell us that 'international tension' is increasing – or, occasionally, that it is decreasing, in which case they speak no less significantly of an 'easing' of the situation. One could almost suppose them to be referring to some dangerous and unpredictable current that flows through our planet. Indeed, every one of us contributes to that current, and what we call 'political sensitivity' is made up of thousands of discharges, produced by and flowing through ourselves. Without them, without those alternating fears and reassurances, the words 'peace' and 'war' would be mere concepts instead of states of mind we live through.

The theatre offers a similar phenomenon, except that it is the occasion of pleasure rather than trouble. Why does one go to a play? Certainly not simply to see how it ends. The fascination is in following the characters through their alternations of good and bad fortune, which produce alternations of hope and anxiety in the spectator, thus arousing and maintaining dramatic interest.

Here we touch upon a basic trait of human behaviour: total movement and total calm alike lead to apathy; if we are to be roused to a state of awareness, there must be some threat to our sense of equilibrium; it ought never to be quite upset, or – if it is – we should feel that it can be readily restored. It is known that sensation is not perception of a state, but perception of a change of state; even the sensation of balance is felt only in relation to a threat of that balance being disturbed. *Thus our sensibility only operates when stimulated by some sort of tension.* It is tension that produces the activity which we call attention – and this is not meant as a play on words.

Sensibility to form depends likewise upon tension, but in the arts the phenomenon is so complex that it is difficult to embrace all its aspects. Nevertheless, I shall try to demonstrate its principle in the following pages, starting with some elementary examples.

241 If you divide a rectangle in half, the resulting effect of symmetry is exhausted at the first glance.

242 If you divide the rectangle into two unequal parts, you have already the beginnings of tension. Instead of merely registering that the parts are unequal, as a machine would do, the eye perceives a threat to equilibrium, and tries to counter it by men-

241

242

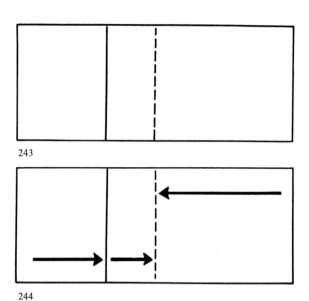

243

244

this surface through the kind of attention which it invites one to give it. [1]

Our first example was concerned with treatment of the surface. Here is another, just as simple, concerned with space. Have you noticed how in still-life paintings, besides the usual dishes of fruit or bowls of flowers, there is nearly always a knife in one corner – or else a pipe, a fork, the edge of a book, or some other straight form set at an angle? In the one reproduced here, Fantin-Latour has 246 put a plate of apples and pears in the foremost plane, flanked by some grapes and a knife set obliquely on the table, and in the second plane a vase with a bunch of flowers. One notices also that the background is a surface with its axis parallel to that of the picture plane. 247

The fruit and flowers are represented in space, but, owing to the short distance between them and the background, the painter cannot place much reliance on perspective to convey the sensation of depth. Therefore he strengthens the effect by means of shadows which model the objects, and – still more – by means of the knife. In this design, where

243 tally replacing the unequal parts with equal ones. Spontaneous though it is, this reaction marks the beginning of an activity; since the eye cannot alter the fact that the rectangle is divided into unequal parts, it begins to exert a 'pressure' on each of them, in whichever direction the mind demands for balance to be restored. It is a continuing and deliberate
244 activity, dictated as much by physical as by spiritual needs – a dual and reciprocal activity, since the vertical band between the black line and the dotted line – the meeting-ground of the two areas in the process of restoring equilibrium – becomes 'activated' too.

Any artist knows how to exploit this phenomenon,
245 and here is an example of striking simplicity: on one side is Jesus with a disciple, and on the other, Lazarus, upright in his tomb. The two parts of the scene are disposed in rectangles of unequal size. Remembering what has been said above, we can see that the dotted line marking the centre of the mosaic passes through Christ's wrist, isolating the reviving hand within the belt of 'high tension'. The power of the gesture, which gives the scene its meaning and its unity, derives largely from the *formal* significance of the area in which it is placed. The inequality of the two areas, and the impulse to redress the balance, lead the eye into a back-and-forth movement which gradually draws every part of the picture into a simultaneous play of mutual compensations. Thus tension has the effect of 'activating' the eye and 'sensitizing' the work. One is not now simply concerned with perceiving a group of objects disposed on a surface, but with animating

[1] This example proves once again how difficult it is to talk of painting. Here it is because forms have no objective reality, the spectator's consciousness being always a necessary condition of their existence, and it is almost impossible to find words which express this ambiguous state of affairs. If the language is too objective, one side of the truth is lost; if it is too subjective, the other side is lost. The best course is not to stick to one term to the exclusion of another, but steadfastly to examine each form in relation to the state of mind which it implies, without sacrificing one to the other.

245. Byzantine art. *The Raising of Lazarus*, mosaic, 6th century. Ravenna, church of S. Apollinare Nuovo. Photo Held.

226

246. Théodore Fantin-Latour (1836-1904). *Flowers and Fruit.* Paris, Musée des Nations. Photo Held.

247

248

249

two-dimensional space tends to predominate, the function of the knife is to introduce a salutary interruption in the form of an oblique plane contrasting 248 with that of the background.

Instead of alighting – and remaining – upon the surface, *the eye is drawn into the picture, and the* 249 *sensation of depth is obtained.*

While it is the role of composition to arrange the elements in such a way that no one of them is without formal significance, it is through tension that it achieves this end, producing a series of contrary impulses which rouse, sustain and renew our *sensibility to form.*

This interior vibration of the work of art, and this inner vibration of our own consciousness, only become apparent under certain conditions. The work must contain both 'areas of stability' and 'areas of instability', and the composition must present forms which interest us because of the relationships in which the artist has placed them, and not by reason of what they represent.

The *Last Supper* by Dirk Bouts is an example of 250 a picture based on a triangular 'area of stability'. 251 The central axis passes precisely through the parting of Christ's hair, his nose, his throat, his thumb, and then through the host, which he holds in his left hand. Christ's head forms the apex of the triangle, the heads of the two disciples in the foreground form its base, and its two halves balance each other exactly. This triangle is framed in a wider one, formed by the rows of apostles at each side; the table makes a third, intermediate triangle, which corresponds to the inverted triangle of the ceiling.

The primary effect of this arrangement is to establish *points of special tension.* In the central triangle our attention is immediately drawn to the angles formed by the heads of Christ and the two disciples, and, by its very position, this triangle establishes a hierarchy that owes nothing to the respective importance of the personages represented, but is due to the *geometrical situations* in which they are placed. When a triangle is drawn thus, angle A instantly holds the attention, while the others, perhaps because of their symmetry, go comparatively unnoticed. This is why Raphael reverses the triangle in his *Vision of a Knight* so that its apex coincides with the knight's 252 heart – the arena in which the contest of vice and virtue takes place.

To go back to Bouts' *Last Supper,* and in particular to the central part of the picture, we can observe how the stabilizing triangle holds the whole design

227

250. Dirk Bouts (c. 1415-1475). *The Last Supper,* detail of altarpiece. Louvain, church of Saint-Pierre. Photo Held.

together through being combined with some of the figures. We see Christ full-face, and the two disciples from behind. When one has contemplated them for a while, one begins to 'feel' the triangle in question, the three heads forming its angles. But what about its sides? Obviously, they are not actually traced; but, on looking more closely, one can follow the left side from the disciple's eye to the left eye of Jesus (passing through the hand of another disciple, whose fingers seem to point the way), and the right side from the other disciple's eye to the right eye of Jesus (passing through the joined hands of St. John), while the base links the eyes of the two disciples, almost on a level with the edge of the table, and just below the host.

Now this triangle – we must make this quite clear – *does not actually exist* in the picture; at most one can say it is *suggested,* and that it is our imagination which constructs it. None the less, it would be wrong to regard it as entirely imaginary, since we are encouraged to discern it by *deliberate indications* on the part of the painter, as is proved by the fact that it would be impossible to substitute a circle, an oval, or any other shape for the triangle. With this much established, let us try to analyse what takes place in our minds.

If the centre of the *Last Supper* were *actually* a triangle, it would merely *impose* its shape on me. On the other hand, if the figures were distributed haphazardly, I obviously would not and could not imagine a triangle. Under the actual conditions of perception contrived by the artist, triangle and figures are interrelated and provoke a dual reaction on my part: I tend to *reduce* the group of three figures to the geometrical figure of a triangle; and also, since I find that they cannot in fact be thus reduced, I tend to consider the figures independently of the triangle. It is the fertilizing power of tension, as manifested in this dual impulse, that gives life to *forms*. Forms are neither objects nor images of objects, but owe their existence to plastic contingencies created by the artist and recognized by the spectator.

Tension does not depend on the nature of the object represented. Of course, it is not a matter of indifference that Christ is represented in Bouts' *Last Supper,* or that he is surrounded by his disciples, but – pictorially speaking – it is *the way in which the figures are arranged* that matters, and not their respective degrees of sanctity. If we cut out the
253 figures and group them apart from their setting, we have three different portrayals, none of which *a*

251. Dirk Bouts. *The Last Supper.*

252. Raphael (1483-1520). *Vision of a Knight.* London, National Gallery. Photo Anderson-Giraudon.

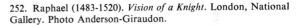

229

253. Dirk Bouts. *The Last Supper*, details.

priori attracts more attention than another. Replace them in the picture, and it is not easy to escape the almost hypnotic power of Jesus. Everything converges on him – not, it is true, all the faces (some, indeed, are turned away from him), but all the areas of tension established by the composition. Remove this figure, and it is extraordinary to see how the *empty space* retains the same power.

254   I propose to call this special locality, which attracts the greatest degree of attention, the picture's 'focus of tension'. Film makers, as well as painters, know its potentialities and how to exploit them; you will have noticed how difficult it is to take one's eyes from that part of the screen in which the action is unfolding and fix them on some other part, such as the background or décor. They are drawn willy-nilly to one particular point, as if the screen acted on us through a specially 'sensitized' zone, which – though it moves about – never becomes confused with the surface of the screen as a whole. It is true that, in comparison with painting, a film 'still' always seems to be somewhat stiffly or somewhat loosely composed, but this is because, in the cinema, tension has to organize images both on the screen – i.e., in space – and in succession – i.e., in time. Painting, which deals essentially with space and not with time, must naturally take greater pains with composition if it is to hold the spectator's attention, but, whether it be on canvas or on film, the focus of tension acts on us like a magnetic pole. We gravitate towards it, and the current which animates the work seems to flow from it.

One should not conclude from this that it coincides with a single point, in the geometrical sense

254. Dirk Bouts. *The Last Supper*, photo-montage.

255
256

230

255. Jan Vermeer. *The Love-letter*. Amsterdam, Rijksmuseum.
Photo Bulloz.

256. Still from the film *Le Diable au Corps*.

257. Tintoretto (1518-1594). *Adam and Eve*. Venice, Accademia. Photo Held.

258. Francisco Goya (1746-1828). Engraving from the series of *Caprichos*. Photo Held.

of the term. Rather, it is a *locality,* and may occupy a greater or lesser portion of the surface. Whereas in Bouts' *Last Supper* it corresponds to the head 257 of Christ, and in Tintoretto's *Adam and Eve* to the 258 apple, one can see that in Goya's engraving it embraces the whole head and the hat of the old woman.

Moreover, there need not be a multiplicity of objects in a picture for the focus of tension to make itself felt.

When one considers Jean Clouet's portrait of the 259 *Dauphin François,* one finds that one's gaze is brought back almost hypnotically to the child's face. Yet neither the hat nor the clothes have been neglected; on the contrary, the artist would appear to have devoted the best part of his attention to them – they so abound in details that the area occupied by the face looks quite denuded by com-

259. Jean Clouet (c. 1475-c. 1540). *The Dauphin François*. Antwerp, Museum. Photo Antwerp Museum.

260. Pablo Picasso (b. 1881). *Maia and her Doll*. In the artist's possession. Photo Held.

261. Pablo Picasso (b. 1881). *Portrait of Nush Eluard*. In the artist's possession. Photo Held.

parison. Where, then, does its power to fascinate come from? The answer is – from deliberate but disguised distortion: in the left[1] half of the face the eye is shown as if seen from directly in front – in the same plane as the picture surface – an impression that is reinforced by the fact that there are no other features or forms close to it. In contrast to this, the right[2] side is considerably foreshortened, and turned onto a plane which intersects the other. The two sides of the face are thus set in contrary planes, quite irreconcilable with reality, and the effect is emphasized on the right by the raising of the eye and brow, and on the left by the white extension of the head-dress, which suggests the outline of a face seen from the front. This effect is all the more remarkable in its audacity since it is not modified on either side by shadows, and since the background is devoid of depth. Wandering over the clothing and the hat, the spectator's gaze is quite literally *caught* by the face, whose two planes close on it like the jaws of an ingenious trap. Picasso is undoubtedly the 260-261

[1], [2] Spectator's left and right.

painter who has gone farthest with this kind of experiment – some of his heads run full-face and profile into one another so brutally that it is almost painful to look at them – but, though it is here pushed to its extreme, the principle is the same as Clouet's.

The focus of tension can equally well occupy an otherwise empty space, as we saw in Bouts' *Last Supper* when the figure of Christ was removed. Here is another example, where we need not resort to photo-montage. Pedro Berruguete's picture 262 shows St. Peter Martyr kneeling before the crucifix, lifting up his eyes to the Saviour's body. Between these poles the 'high voltage' area is established, and here the artist has inscribed the prayer which rises from the Saint's lips, and which – by virtue of its formal situation – is charged with a vibrant fervour that moves us, even if we cannot decipher the meaning of the words.

263. Antonello da Messina (1430-1479). *Crucifixion*. Antwerp, Museum. Photo Bruckmann, Munich.

264. Italian School, 13th century. *Crucifixion*. Birmingham, Barber Institute of Fine Arts. Photo Bulloz.

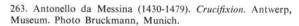

263 264

265. Paris Bordone (1500-1571). *The Ring Returned to the Doge.* Venice, Accademia. Photo Held.

This type of *binary* composition (consisting of *two* elements) is to be found in most pictures of the *Annunciation* – the angel on one side and the Virgin on the other, with between them the space traversed by the eye – the space through which the divine message is transmitted – illuminated sometimes by a shaft of light, and often containing a tiny image of the Child. *Ternary* composition (of *three* elements) is equally common, as in innumerable paintings of the *Crucifixion*. But we must remember 263-264 that the mere placing together of three forms is not in itself enough to produce an effect of tension. As we have seen, this must result from interaction between the forms and our consciousness, each stimulating the other.

In Bordone's famous picture the focus of tension 265 coincides with the body of the fisherman, stretched out between the Doge and the nobleman at the foot of the steps. This latter personage is of minor

266. Giotto (1267-1337). *Apotheosis of St. John the Evangelist,* fresco. Florence, church of Santa Croce. Photo Alinari.

importance in so far as the subject is concerned, but in formal terms his presence is of crucial importance. He establishes the line on which the fisherman is 'held up' to our gaze; if you remove him the picture 'goes limp', and the fisherman's gesture is no more than a commonplace image of an act of restitution. As it is, by reason of the tension between the two poles of the Doge on his throne and the nobleman at the foot of the steps, that gesture is instinct with life.

In addition to the focus of tension, there are what we may call *axes of tension*. The role of these is to persuade the eye to move in certain directions, and to articulate the work as a whole into perceptible compartments. Let us take a look at Giotto's fresco 266 of the *Apotheosis of St. John the Evangelist,* in which the pillars of the temple and the upright figures form a series of vertical axes. Consider the centre of the scene in particular. In themselves, the two central pillars are simply supports, but the situation is altered by the insertion of the diagonal line which runs through the body of St. John. This oblique line cuts across the compartment formed by the two columns, and thereby 'sensitizes' it. Without the diagonal it would have remained inert, but now a

270. Giotto. *Apotheosis of St. John the Evangelist.*

dual motive force is set going: the eye is stimulated on the one hand to a vertical motion, and on the 267 other to a diagonal motion, and the tension pro- 268 duced by this relationship causes one to picture the actual course of the saint's ascent.

Thus the axis of tension is likewise the result of a relationship. In our example the contrary direc- 269 tions, instead of conflicting with one another or cancelling each other out, act in concert on the eye, preventing us from feeling that St. John is either 'falling' or 'suspended' in the air. It is as if we ourselves bear up the Saint on the successive thrusts 270 of our gaze, and lift him to the waiting arms of Christ. We are helped in this by the horizontal accents which Giotto introduces here and there, like landings on a stairway.[1]

Finally, let us study the example offered by Rogier van der Weyden's beautiful and terrible *Pietà.* If we draw a diagonal line from the top left 271 corner to the bottom right, we find that it divides Christ's body into two unequal parts: the left half of the face, the left arm and half of the left foot are in the upper triangle; the rest of the body, lying along two axes which are intersected at their junction by the vertical axis of the cross, is in the lower triangle. The posture and colour of the body indicate clearly enough that this is a corpse; but it conveys more than an idea or image; it is the very presence of death that we feel, not from the dreadful sight of physical corruption, but from the sight of a body

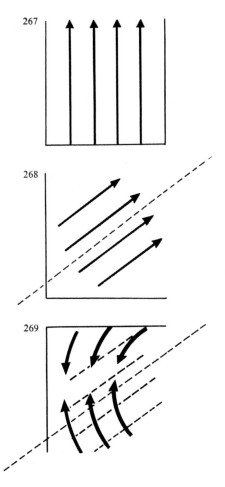

[1] In many pictures the trees, buildings and additional figures which the artist places in the background or at each side, do much more than compose landscapes or groups. They are there to reinforce the formal organization of the surface.

reduced to the inertia of its simple, physical mass. The poignant quality of this picture owes far more to composition than to Rogier's painted tears, which are so much admired. Without the imagined diagonal, and without its relationship to the broken body of Christ, we should see simply the representation of a sagging corpse, whereas in fact the effect of tension causes us to *feel* how it is broken and how it sags.

Thus the cohesion of a work of art is not a particular or definitive thing; it is an act of consciousness – consciousness in action.

To sum up, we are aware of tension through the perception of the particular nature of the work. In everyday experience perception is exhausted as soon as the thing perceived ceases to be novel – i.e.,

when it ceases to stimulate. In aesthetic experience, on the contrary, perception is maintained; it is as if the object were continually revealing itself and, by this continual revelation, renewing its power to stimulate.[1]

Tension, therefore, leads us to active perception. The artist achieves it by a particular treatment of the surface, which makes us aware of the forms in relationship to the plastic unity of the work, and not to the objects they represent.

---

[1] I have here only considered examples concerned with compositional structure. Needless to say, tension can equally well be conveyed by lines, colours, tone values or light, but I have not felt it practicable to consider each in detail. However, I shall be returning to this subject and developing it in the chapters which follow.

271. Rogier van der Weyden (c. 1400-1464). *Pietà*. Brussels, Musées Royaux des Beaux-Arts. Photo Bulloz.

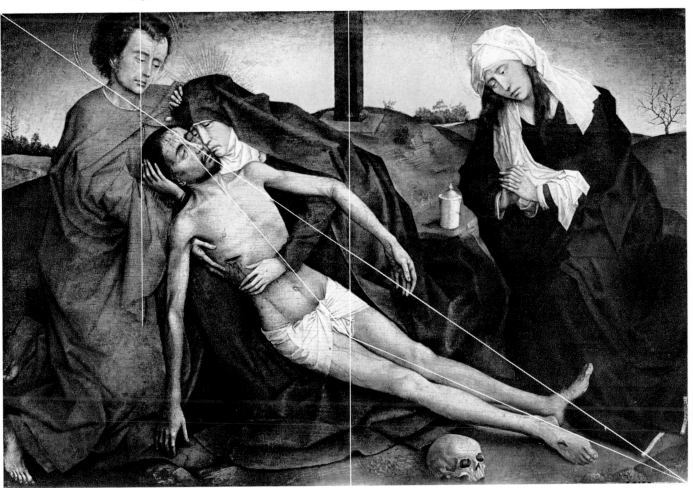

Construction

Nothing would seem easier than to write a novel: one need only take the first news item that comes to hand, and develop it. This was Stendhal's procedure in *Le Rouge et le Noir,* where he followed closely the accounts printed in the *Gazette des Tribunaux.* His plot can be summarized in a couple of lines: a young man, consumed by ambition, becomes the lover of two women in turn, and then, having wounded the first of them for motives of revenge, dies on the scaffold. At the level of this intrigue, construction consists of grouping characters and events in a common sequence of action.

At subject level it is the same in painting. In this sketch Poussin depicts an incident in the life of 272 Moses, as related in Exodus: how he took refuge in the land of Midian after killing an Egyptian, how he saw the daughters of Jethro insulted by shepherds at the well, and how – filled with righteous fury – he rushed to their defence.

However, what really matters is not that Stendhal followed the *Gazette des Tribunaux* or that Poussin followed the story in Exodus, but that they performed in one case the function of a novelist and in the other the function of a painter. At its highest level construction consists of elaborating the parts so that they attain the status of a work of art. The novelist develops his subject in time, the painter develops his in space [1].

---

[1] This is only a provisional distinction, as we shall see later, but I use it here as a useful approximation.

272. Nicolas Poussin (1594-1665). *Moses Defending the Daughters of Jethro,* wash drawing. Paris, Louvre. Photo Held.

273. Rogier van der Weyden (c. 1400-1464). *The Last Judgment*. Beaune, Hospice. Photo Bulloz.

When Rogier van der Weyden paints the *Last*
273 *Judgment,* his first concern is that we should comprehend the subject. His polyptych is divided hori-
274 zontally into three zones: in the uppermost is Christ,
flanked by angels bearing the instruments of the
Passion; in the central zone the Virgin and saints
witness this supreme office of Deity; and in the
lowest zone are the naked bodies of the resurrected.
Only the angel with the scales occupies two zones
at once.

275   In the vertical sense, the polyptych centres on the
great panel containing the figure of Christ in judgment, with three additional wings on each side. At
276 the bottom right are the damned, and at the bottom
277 left the elect. Paradise opens through a gothic gate-
way on the extreme left, while the flames of Hell
leap up on the extreme right. The distribution of
pictorial elements in space corresponds to that of
narrative elements in time.

First of all, then, construction consists of the
painter's assigning a *portion* of space and a definite
situation to each object and figure, or to each group
of objects and group of figures; this distribution
satisfies the primary requirement of the act of communication.

Let us take our examination further. I have
pointed out that Rogier's polyptych is *developed* in
both a horizontal and a vertical sense. That is to
say, the eye follows certain *directions* rather than
others – the picture's order is in fact conveyed by
an immediately comprehensible arrangement. If
this order is to be perceived, it must be related to
something self-evident, and in the case of painting

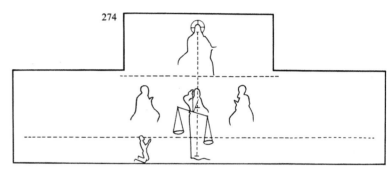

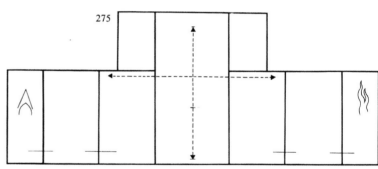

240

276. *Last Judgment*, detail. *The Elect.*   277. *Last Judgment*, detail. *The Damned.*

278. Pieter Bruegel (1525/30-1569). *Haymaking*. Raudnitz, Bohemia, collection of Prince Lobkowitz; at present deposited in the Museum, Prague. Reproduction Anton Schroll, Vienna.

it is the frame which supplies this need. As we saw in Chapter 4 of Part II, it determines at one and the same time a particular space and a particular kind of attention on the spectator's part, and it also influences the manner in which one makes contact with the picture by *suggesting* certain axes on which it may be 'read' [1]. The lines in the work which refer to it may actually be drawn or may have only a virtual existence. Poussin's sketch shows a combination of vertical and horizontal lines, with diagonals added in the groups to the left and right. In Rogier van der Weyden's picture there is no line that runs in an exactly horizontal or vertical direction, yet we feel the presence of both quite plainly. Thus there are lines in the picture which are determined not by the objects or by the artist, but simply by the fact of a surface confined within a frame.

278   Now we may go a stage further. Here is a painting by Bruegel which at first glance seems merely to recount an episode of rural life: peasants are busying themselves with baskets or rakes; in the middle distance is a village, with its houses grouped round the church, overshadowed by a great crag; far in the distance a river flows away to merge into the blue of the horizon. So much for the rustic muse! As soon as we begin to *look at* the picture, instead of indulging in day-dreams about it, we observe that there is a certain measure and rhythm in it. Of course, nothing forces the eye to rest on one spot rather than another, and we may well suppose that one spectator will begin by noticing the woman perched on her horse, another by contemplating the blue sky, and another, perhaps, by taking in the

haymakers in the field or the three women in the foreground. But, while it is true that the individual spectator can let his gaze wander as he likes, it is also true that the picture makes certain suggestions which are difficult for him to ignore. One does not proceed entirely haphazardly among the objects depicted; the eye is no vagrant, but a traveller who means to explore the country, savour its climate and get to know its customs. Therefore it does not neglect any suggestion or indication that is offered.

In Bruegel's painting there are two directions which   279 especially influence the eye: one makes it follow the line of peasants in the foreground, and the other makes it follow the slope of the village up to the crag. Note that neither of these lines is actually traced, but they exist – or so we feel. When a platoon of men falls in on parade, each man finds his own place by taking note of intervals and distances. Allowing for the obvious differences, it is the same thing in painting: *the objects are distributed along invisible lines which are sensed and traversed by the eye.*

These invisible lines are determined by the format of the picture as well as by pointers which the artist arranges like surveyors' rods across the canvas. They mark out *potential routes* for the eye. The mind enters into the spirit of the game and, stimulated from one point to the next, *rediscovers* them under the artist's guidance, enjoying both the pleasure of his company and the pleasure of discovery. Finally, the mere fact of following a path which is not traced, but is suggested allusively, leads to a fuller and more satisfying sense of participation.

Like signposts on the highway, these imaginary lines do not indicate a destination, but they do suggest an *itinerary*. At its second level, construction

---

[1] This is why rectangles – figures which assert the dual presence of vertical and horizontal – are the most useful format. Other shapes, such as the tondo (circular) or oval, are comparatively rare.

279
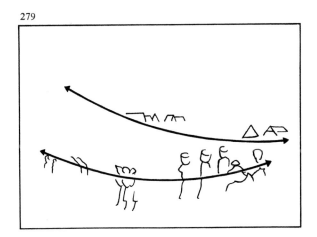

280
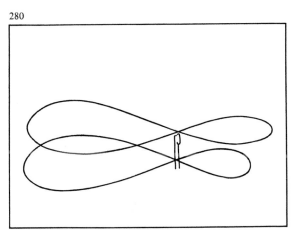

consists of a subtle network of tracks which lead us into the heart of the work – to its meaning and its quality.

But construction is also *structure,* and that is what we must now examine. Look again at Bruegel's picture. Following the lines of the peasants in the foreground and of those in the field, one finds that they fit into a pattern; similarly the crucifix at the side of the road, which might seem merely to be an anecdotal accessory, assumes major importance, forming the pivot of the great figure-of-eight in which the peasants are arranged, and which adjoins another figure-of-eight taking in the two parts of the hill.

As we have seen already, the basic factor in painting is always and of necessity the surface plane, but the artist is at liberty to create space of an intermediate kind between the second and the third dimension. This complex sort of space, in which objects take shape at the touch of the painter's brush, *needs to be perceived by the spectator in order to exist,* and the role of constructional figures is precisely to help us to perceive it. It is therefore not surprising that simple geometrical figures lend themselves most readily to this purpose: square, triangle, rectangle and circle on the picture surface; sphere, cone, pyramid and cube in the picture space. However, they can also be more complex – St. Andrew's cross, trapezium, ovoid or parallelepiped....

Nothing could be more instructive on this point than to note how spontaneously the so-called 'primitive' artists, or *'naïfs',* make use of it. Instead of giving way to the promptings of instinct (so often airily identified with the voice of nature), it is noticeable that they nearly all make it their rule to display the elements of construction as patently as

282. Henri Rousseau, called the Douanier (1844-1910). *The Toll-house.* London, Courtauld Institute. Photo Held.

281

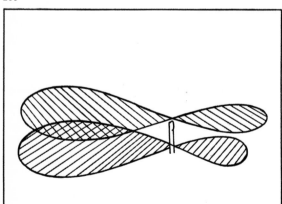

283. Pisanello (c. 1397-after 1450). *Portrait of a Lady of the d'Este Family*. Paris, Louvre. Photo Held.

possible. The Douanier Rousseau, Camille Bombois 282 and Louis Vivin all provide proof of this, and indeed it is what gives their pictures a schematic charm of character of a kind which most artists normally avoid, preferring a less obvious use of constructional figures. But, whether they are obvious or concealed, no artist can do without them, just as no artist can employ them to the exclusion of everything else.

At first glance Bruegel's picture appears to conform to the three dimensions of classical perspective – there is a foreground, a middle ground and a background; objects are reduced in size according to their distance from the eye; the colours become progressively cooler towards the blue of the horizon. But that is a superficial view. Examination of the painting shows that its space does not conform to this mechanical progression; it is organized in *planes which differ in their orientation and inclination.*[1]

Now these planes *are not perceived as separate pieces assembled together.* On the contrary, what is so striking about the picture is its perfect coherence. Here is a space invented and made real by the artist, a space which is neither flat plane nor perspective, a space which – though nameless – nevertheless exists, since the painter has created his forms and fixed his style within it. The reality of Bruegel's space is undeniable because its living structure asserts itself. Like tie-beams, the two great hori- 281 zontal figures-of-eight weld the planes together, so that their changes of orientation and inclination are felt not as breaks but as the appropriate structure of a work whose parts are organically interdependent.

When they are suggested to the spectator in this way, the elements of structure do not need to be more explicitly indicated. The arrangement of objects, colours and planes acts like a series of signposts, directing the eye and holding its interest. In this way the core of the work is constituted – that core which Claudel has splendidly described as creating 'a mutual gravitation, a common appeal that emanates from within and involves all the varied objects which the frame obliges to act in concert'. *(L'œil écoute.)* It is no longer a painted surface that we look at, but a living space, in which structural elements define the area, establish the economy of the work and govern our approach to it.

It is easy to understand why structural shapes are nearly always disguised. If they were not, their

[1] This system also counterbalances the impression of distance produced by perspective, and thus preserves the picture's formal integrity.

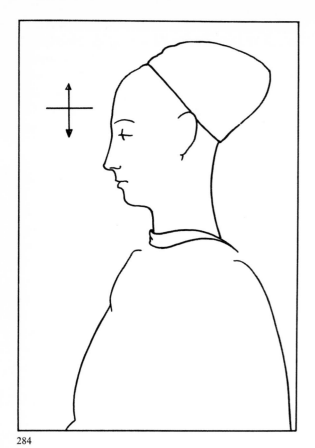

284

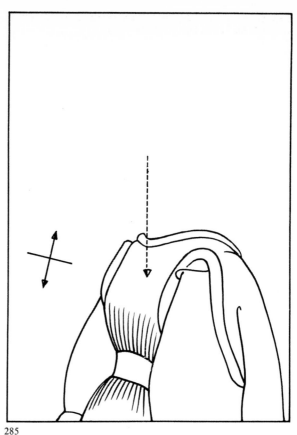

285

potency – and that of the objects – would soon be exhausted. Woven into the texture of the work, they act upon us indirectly.

One might suppose that construction requires a fair number of objects, but this is not so. It can be found in portraits, as for instance in Pisanello's 283 *Portrait of a Lady of the d'Este Family.* Here the painter charms us with the grace of his sitter, but it is his art that holds us; the charm derives from the art. The head is outlined against the background 284 like a two-dimensional figure; at most one can discern a faint shadow above the eye and along the cheek. The picture as a whole has a decorative quality, produced by linear rhythms and succulent 285 colour. Following the line of the neck and shoulders, one comes to the series of folds on the bust, which serve to model and to modulate the clothing. Here, in contrast to the face, we enter an area that is treated with some slight suggestion of volume. How does the artist pass from one to the other? By establishing the different planes of the picture on the basis of shapes which articulate them and serve as hinges: as we have seen, the head is set in a plane parallel to the background, but the shoulder intro- duces a second plane cutting diagonally into the

first. These two linked planes form a complex space which is able equally to receive the flatness of the profile and the restrained modelling of the bust and sleeves. To prevent the two planes from con- flicting, Pisanello effects the transition from one to the other by means of the obliquely curving cord at the neck-line of the dress; if you conceal that cord, the whole portrait seems flat.

I hope that the part played by construction can now be more clearly appreciated. We have noted how it is the artist's practice to create his space somewhere between the extreme limits of the second and third dimensions. Now this intermediate kind of space can be infinitely varied, so long as it does not become amorphous. Therefore the artist must give it form, and since he cannot invent something of which we have no experience (in that case com- munication would be impossible) he utilizes elements which remind us now of the surface and now of depth (both of which are perfectly familiar), *but assembles them in his own fashion.* Thus the purpose of constructional lines is to form links with one another and to guide us into the space which together they constitute. Constructional shapes, while establishing the structure of the work,

246

286. Pieter Bruegel. *Haymaking*, detail.

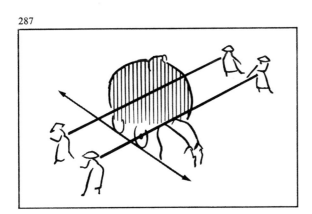

287

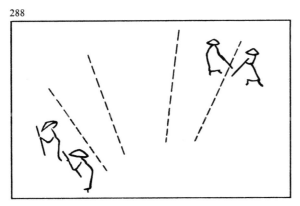

288

serve also to put us into the requisite state of mind.

Lines and shapes assist our progress. They guide us, and in guiding us they reassure us; in reassuring us they offer a peculiar pleasure. Hidden, but not dissembled, they reveal themselves to those who seek them. It is through them that one gains access to that space in which the forms exist, not in terms of their figurative content, but as language.

Let us take a final example to crystallize our ideas on this. In this detail of Bruegel's picture one notices immediately that the hay-cart is much too steeply tilted and that the ground also has an exaggerated slope. One is tempted to ask why the cart does not run down the hill or topple over. However, on closer inspection one realizes that the danger is quite illusory. The objects that are represented condition each other in such a way that they themselves construct the appropriate space to retain them. Two pairs of peasant women – one pair on each side – steady the heavy cart as if the lines that run between them were actually battening it down. Without even taking into account the two haymakers who prop up the load with their forks, let us note how the four women play their part. Bruegel has depicted each one of them in a loosely swinging pose, and this, combined with the angles at which they hold their rakes, provides an uphill thrust that counteracts the slope of the ground and holds the cart in place.

In a wider view, one sees that the rest of the landscape is also governed by devices of this kind. The triangular tongue of woodland, projecting downwards, is confronted by the triangle of the wooden gate. The field, too, pushes a broad triangle into the wood, while the cart and its team form another on a different plane. Every part of the picture is rigorously constructed, and this strict economy is what gives the work its power.

I would end on a note of warning. Because a work of art is based on structural lines and shapes, it does not follow that it consists of nothing else. It is a popular fallacy to suppose that in recognizing the structure one possesses the whole secret of the artist – a singularly gross misconception. What we must always remember is that structural lines and shapes have no power in themselves, but merely *within* the work of art which they innervate. To isolate them so that they are more obvious to the spectator is legitimate; to pretend they are the actual substance of the work is not.

One should also treat with caution all the meretricious definitions that are bandied about so freely:

that the vertical represents balance; that the horizontal represents stability, and the diagonal instability; that the circle symbolizes the perfection of the infinite, and so on. The value of constructional forms lies in the fact that they are suggestions, not explicitly stated; thus one can never be sure of unravelling all their varied aspects. Just as one cannot reduce a novel to its plan, one cannot reduce a picture to its canvas; but plan and canvas none the less exist.

In truth, they are only apparent on reflection – when we feel impelled to analyse. One no more thinks of the picture's construction *while* looking at Bruegel's *Haymaking* than one thinks of the novel's plan *while* reading *Le Rouge et Le Noir*. If we are nevertheless aware of them, it is because they satisfy certain needs of our minds and our sensibility, and because in recognizing them our pleasure is augmented. Just as the plan of Stendhal's novel places the characters and events within the space of time it covers, so construction places the forms in *pictorial space*. Only thus can the time element in a novel and the picture space in a painting become something we experience, and their significance be conveyed.

To sum up, every work of art is a complex whole, based on its own unique space. On one level, construction picks out the various parts of a work so that the subject can be understood. On another level, it provides signposts to help us read its meaning. On a third level it leads us into its actual structure. Suggested from within, constructional figures serve as stages by which we can pass from habitual space (that of geometry and of everyday experience) into *such-and-such* a formal space of *such-and-such* an artist. In helping us to *set foot there*, they make us share the aesthetic fulfilment in the very place where it is accomplished.

Proportion

In its widest sense proportion describes a relationship – the relationship *linking the parts of a thing to each other and to the whole.* This is a notion that concerns things in their *quantitative aspect,* and it is based on *measurement.*

Normally we modify this notion of relationship. Average human proportions are our standard of reality, and anyone who is much more than six feet tall – or less than five – seems out of the ordinary. Noses are said to be 'too' long or 'too' short, as if nature should model each organ in accordance with a set pattern (Cyrano de Bergerac is the unforgettable illustration of this). Thus the first thing to bear in mind is that for most people the term 'proportion' conveys not so much the idea of a relationship as that of a fixed dimension or norm [1].

How do artists see this question? From very early times they have studied proportions and

---

[1] *Proportion* describes the relationship of parts of a thing to each other and to the whole; in principle, the terms of the relationship are infinitely variable. The *norm* suspends this variable character by setting limits to the terms. It is in this sense that the expression 'proportions' – in the plural – has common currency. Normal proportions, so-called, are those which correspond to our every day experience of the world. In our present context, where we are concerned with the word in its sense of a relationship, I consider it more judicious to use it in the singular.

289. Average proportions of a man. (*Nouvelle Anatomie artistique,* Dr. Paul Richer.)

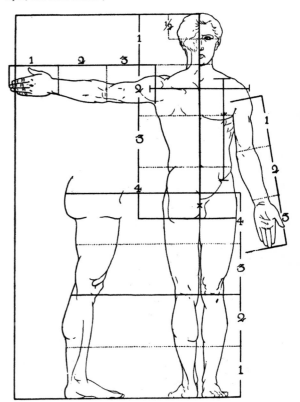

290. Polycletus (5th century B.C.). *The Doryphoros* (copy). Naples, Museum. Photo Alinari.

291. Lysippus (4th century B.C.). *Agias* (copy). Delphi, Museum. Photo Viollet.

290 codified them. We have all heard of the canon[1] ascribed to Polycletus (5th century B.C.), according to which the height of the figure is seven times that of the head, and we know that in the canon of 291 Lysippus (4th century B.C.) there are eight instead of seven heads in the total height. This problem has often been studied – even in the Middle Ages, 292 as is proved by the drawings of Villard de Honnecourt (13th century). Paul Richer has thus described the one here reproduced: 'The whole head, seen full-face, is inscribed in a square, the width of the face being half the total height. Horizontal lines divide the head into approximately equal zones, the

first of which is occupied by the hair, the second by the forehead, the third by the nose and the fourth by the mouth and chin.' Two centuries later, Albrecht Dürer was so passionately absorbed in this sort of research that he virtually gave up painting towards the end of his life, but left four books devoted to the study of proportions![1] The engraving of *Adam and Eve* (1504), on which, a few 293 years later, he based his celebrated diptych in the Prado, is composed of *constructed figures,* founded not on studies from the living model but on numerical relationships. The researches of Alberti and Leonardo are equally famous, and those of Jean 294

---

[1] According to Eugène Guillaume, the word canon (which means *rule*) assumes in the language of the visual arts, when applied to the human figure – or even to animals, the special meaning of 'rule of proportion'; it is a system of measurement by which one may determine the dimensions of one part from those of the whole, and the dimensions of the whole from those of the smallest part.'

[1] *The Four Books of Human Proportion,* which appeared only after the artist's death, were intended as the prelude to a much vaster work, *Die Speise der Malerknaben (Fare for Apprentice Painters),* a title which suggests the importance he attached to these studies.

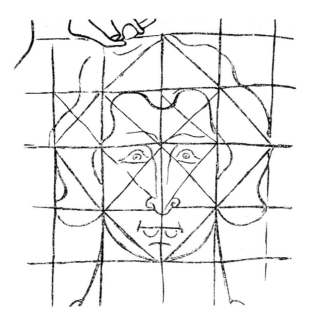

292. Villard de Honnecourt (13th century). *Head of a Man,* drawing. Paris, Bibliothèque Nationale. Photo Held.

Cousin (16th century), though less illustrious, have become a classic in this field [1].

The purpose of such studies has been summed up by Dürer in a formula which seems as obvious at first glance as it is mysterious on reflection: 'In truth', he writes, 'art lies hidden in nature: he who can extract it possesses it' *(denn wahrhaftig steckt die Kunst in der Natur: wer sie heraus kann reissen, der hat sie).* In the view of most commentators, these words are to be interpreted as follows: 'Convinced that one can arrive at a *mathematical formula of beauty* [2], which was known to the ancients, but the secret of which has since been lost, he [Dürer] sought the answer to this problem with all the passion of an alchemist in search of the philosopher's stone... He wished to rescue the teaching of art from the empiricism of the workshop system. *He dreamed of making beauty a scientific subject* [3] – that is, a question of measurement – thus putting an end to the tiresome disagreements between men's contradictory tastes.' (A. Michel, *Histoire de l'Art,* Vol. V.)

The popular interpretation of proportion tends to confuse it with the average or (so-called) normal, which is naïvely supposed to represent the natural order of things. The interpretation which I have just quoted, though more learned, is equally specious, since it tends to confuse the idea of proportion with that of a canon. The aim of this preamble has been to put the reader on his guard against them both.

Let me try to illustrate their dangers. According to the first interpretation – the popular one – this panel by Giovanni di Paolo undoubtedly raises a host of questions by reason of its oddity: just look at this St. John the Baptist marching off to the wildnerness, cleaving through the mountains like Moses dividing the waters of the Red Sea! The highest peaks are scarcely half as tall again as he

295

[1] They are, in essence, as follows. The head is contained eight times in the total height of the body, divided thus:

from the top of the head to the chin	1 head
from the chin to the nipples	1 head
from the nipples to the navel	1 head
from the navel to the pubis	1 head
from the pubis to the middle of the thigh	1 head
from the middle of the thigh to the knee	1 head
from the knee to the bottom of the calf	1 head
from the bottom of the calf to the heel	1 head

The head itself is similarly divided, and every part of the face is subject to minute calculations: 'the eye is divided into three parts, the central one being occupied by the pupil; the thickness of the upper lip equals one eighth of the width of the mouth, which equals one eye and a half...' etc. (*Académie plastique,* by E. Cuyer.)

[2] My italics

[3] My italics.

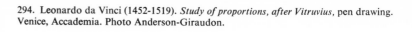

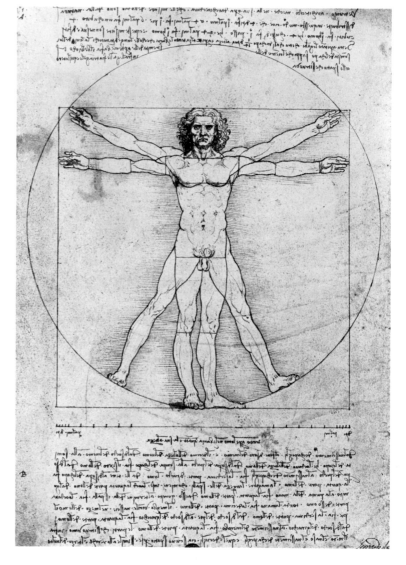

293. Albrecht Dürer (1471-1528). *Eve*, right wing of diptych. Madrid, Prado. Photo Held.

295. Giovanni di Paolo (c.1403-1483). *St. John the Baptist*. London, National Gallery. Reproduced by courtesy of the Trustees.

296. Romanesque art. *Christ of the Apocalypse,* detail of fresco, 12th century. Auxerre, Cathedral. Photo Hurault-Viollet.

is! The trees are like a sort of moss along the rocks, and the houses look like toys. Everything is 'out of proportion' – that is, *if one refers to normal experience alone.*

If one lets oneself be guided by the second interpretation, it soon appears that no painter apart from Dürer, Leonardo and Raphael knew how to construct a figure, and that Romanesque or oriental art, for example, is worthless.

That is where these two dangerous and widespread conceptions lead us: the one towards the misconception of supposititious 'reality', of which I have given many examples; and the other towards the equally pernicious misconception of 'ideal beauty' – mathematical beauty, which ends up unfailingly in academicism, and for which Leonardo, Raphael and Dürer are usually held responsible.

To do them justice, and to put the problem in its proper light, one need only read Dürer's words afresh: 'In truth, art lies hidden in nature: he who can extract it possesses it.' To perceptive critics,

297. Raphael (1483-1520). *The School of Athens,* fresco. Rome, Vatican (Stanza della Segnatura). Photo Anderson-Giraudon.

298

254

like Waetzoldt, they do not mean at all that Dürer is seeking a mathematical formula for beauty, like the alchemist and his philosopher's stone; Dürer's system of making 'ideal' figures is not taken to mean figures 'of perfect beauty', but figures constructed *according to certain relationships which can be variable*. Thus Dürer does not claim to reveal the prototype of beauty, but, as he writes, 'to grasp the secrets of nature'. Starting from his own observation, he discovered that organic bodies, like mineral ones, are *composed of parts which correspond to one another*. It is to this natural law that he pays homage, not to some fixed image, carefully and definitively worked out by a nature reduced to mathematics, to be revealed only to the privileged few.

Thanks to Dürer's intuition, which has so often been distorted or wrongly interpreted, the problem can be seen in a clear light, free from falsification. What is it actually concerned with? With coherence, the foundation of any work of art. But coherence is a complex phenomenon with many sides, and one of its aspects is proportion, *which concerns questions of size or scale in the work*.

If one compares the scale of dimensions in any photograph of a gathering of people – perhaps even a congress of philosophers – with Raphael's 297 *School of Athens,* one finds that the photograph shows a crowd of indeterminate beings in an equally indeterminate setting. Raphael's fresco, on the other hand, in spite of its great number of figures, at once gives the feeling of something constructed, and the longer one looks at it the stronger the feeling becomes. In the presence of this fresco, mind and sensibility are soon made aware that its dimensions are not a chance matter, as in the photograph, but that they are all related to some scale of magnitude.[1] Plato and Aristotle are of approximately the same height; but with what subtle care Raphael has varied the stature of the other figures, by placing them on a different plane or a different level, or by their different attitudes. Make no mistake about it, this is not simply a matter of adding together equal and unequal elements, but – in conformity with the very nature of proportion – of assembling them *in such a way that we become conscious of the relationships in scale that* 298 *control them.* Thus the dimensions of Plato and

Aristotle reappear in other figures, and vice versa.[1] And there is more to it than that. These relationships link the figures not only to each other but also to the architecture and its intervals. Take, for instance, the interval between the first and the second arch on the central axis, which is exactly the same height as Plato. This examination could be pursued at length in every part of the picture, and it shows that the elements of a painting, like those of a temple or cathedral, are linked by a rigorous system of relationships. These relations exist between objects of similar or dissimilar nature. Indeed, the nature of the objects has nothing to do with proportions: *the relative and respective dimensions of the forms within the work as a whole are what matter.*

Defined in this way, proportion in painting serves to convert figurative or non-figurative objects into plastic forms. On the one hand, forms are developed as figures, architectural elements or intervals, *and on the other – simultaneously – they are developed as relationships of scale within a given format.* This is exactly how a writer proceeds. Situations, characters and scenes in a novel exist on the one hand as elements of the action, and on the other as parts of the book as a whole – chapters in each part, paragraphs in each chapter and sentences in each paragraph – a system which, in a worthwhile work, is always the subject of careful thought.

It is therefore not surprising that proportion should profoundly affect the mind and sensibility of the spectator. As with other pictorial elements, it serves primarily *to arouse and hold one's interest.* Dimensions mean nothing in themselves; but when the artist translates them into relationships he gives them significance and claims our attention. The *School of Athens* presents equal and unequal elements which stimulate and refresh our interest through the interplay of an inequality perceived in similarity, and of a similarity perceived in inequality. As we have noted, merely seeing a painting does not constitute awareness of it. Contemplation must grow into experience, i.e. it must be active. Proportion helps in this, for the similarities in its relationships make it easier to acclimatize ourselves to the work, while the differences save our perception from becoming blunted.

[1] *It is therefore our receptivity to the phenomenon of quantitative relationship that constitutes the true nature of proportion.* This receptivity is not mathematical. It is based on a scale of estimation, on which the principal 'notes' are the simple fractions and multiples met with in ordinary life: half, third, quarter, three-quarters, whole, double, treble, etc.

[1] Dimension signifies an absolute measurement; proportion signifies a relative measurement resulting from the relationship of two dimensions.

299. Nicolas Poussin (1594-1655). *Saint Matthew*. Berlin, Kaiser-Friedrich-Museum. Photo Giraudon.

300. André Lhote (b. 1885). *Baigneuses*, fresco. Paris, Musée d'Art Moderne. 301. André Lhote. Preparatory study.

At the second level, proportion is concerned with the treatment of planes and forms within the picture space. Notice how the planes in Poussin's *St. Matthew* increase in height from the lower to the upper zone. This vertical proportion does far more than the traditional accessory of wings to stress the angel's presence beside the saint.

Structural shapes are also based on proportion, and – while the visible forms leave us on the surface – let us in 'on the inside' of the work. Comparing André Lhote's study for a fresco with the completed work, one can see that its structure, though concealed, shows up sufficiently through the forms for it to convey a sense of the rigorous relationships on which it is composed.

But where does the artist start out from to establish his relative proportions? It would seem at first sight that he has unlimited freedom to choose as he likes. In point of fact, it is usually the over-all format of the work which serves as his starting point, though it does not dictate to him categorically. The format provides a height and width which already constitute one definite relationship, and the painter seldom fails to make use of it.[1] Lhote's fresco is revealing in this respect. Having to paint a surface very much wider than it is high, the artist has organized it by adjusting the stature of his figures to it.

But proportion is also *an ingredient of style,* and it is at this third level that the spectator really feels its expressive power. Comparing Corot's *Chartres Cathedral* with Delaunay's *Eiffel Tower,* one notices that the former lays emphasis on a certain tranquillity in the forms, while the latter is the opposite of tranquil. The nature of the objects themselves undoubtedly has something to do with these impressions. Chartres cathedral is in fact more squat in outline than the Eiffel tower. But when we say that Corot's picture breathes a spirit of calm, and that Delaunay's is like the eruption of a vital force, we are not referring to actuality. We are not expressing what we feel in the presence of the cathedral or the tower themselves, but what we feel in contact with Corot's and Delaunay's paintings. Now these feelings result from the manner of treating forms in the two pictures. The choice of format is significant to begin with. Faced by the necessity of developing his forms vertically, Delaunay uses a narrow rectangle; Corot chooses a wider one, better suited to contain the mass of the building and the landscape.

In the *Chartres Cathedral,* the unequal height of the two towers threatens to introduce an uncomfortable element of disparity, yet – strangely enough – nothing could convey a more powerful impression of balance than this painting! This is because the relative dimensions of the forms have been faultlessly regulated. The left-hand tower with its spire is 'brought down to earth' by means of the mound in the foreground, which is of the same height at its centre. The right-hand spire is matched by the tree which perches on the summit of the mound, and the tree to the right, if extended down to the diagonal path, corresponds to the height of the left-hand spire. Taking the total height of the left-hand tower, one finds it is equal to the interval of sky between the left extremity of the cathedral and the upper edge of the picture, while the interval of sky above the shorter tree is again equal to the left-hand spire. The interval of ground between the left edge of the mound and the bottom of the picture equals the height of the right-hand spire. One could go on indefinitely exploring this painting, which most people would suppose to be 'copied' from the subject.

As can now be realized, the dimensions of forms are governed by relationships which the artist exploits for a particular effect. Thus Corot uses the inequality of the towers for two purposes: first, by accentuating it, he makes each element 'tell' by virtue of contrast; secondly, by contriving hints of similarity, he suggests to the eye a sense of regularity. The total effect is one of serenity, due less to the presence of the cathedral itself than to the management of relationships.

Delaunay takes an entirely different line in his *Eiffel Tower.* The whole picture seems to surge upwards under a single impulse. That, one might think, belongs to the nature of the subject; but, if one compares the picture with a photograph, the difference is instantly apparent. The photograph certainly conveys that general impression of height and slenderness which belongs to all upright, elongated objects, such as masts, fir-trees or pylons; but Delaunay's painting goes beyond the general impression and gives us the sensation of a mighty force propelling the mass of steel into the air. The edifice

---

[1] Apart from the particular question of proportion, one can see that the subject of the work may also have much to do with it. For example, an *Annunciation* and an *Ascension* would not be readily adaptable to the same format, since one is more naturally developed horizontally, and the other vertically. This applies also to abstract compositions. Whether they are geometric or otherwise, shapes respond to the suggestions of the format, and even when an abstract painting does not apparently suffer from being hung a different way up from the way it was painted, something within us usually makes us conscious of the mistake. Now, if it is agreed that there is a connection between the subject of a work and its format, it will be understood that there are even stronger reasons for a connection between the dimensions of the forms and those of the whole work.

302. Jean-Baptiste Camille Corot (1796-1875). *Chartres Cathedral*. Paris, Louvre. Photo Held.

303. Chartres Cathedral. Photo Guilde du Livre.

304. Proportion adjusts the elements of the picture in accordance with the artist's expressive aims.

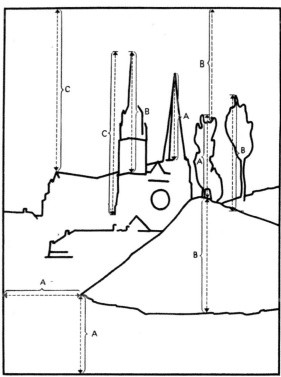

built by the engineer Eiffel is an inert mass of metal, while Delaunay's is a living force. Now this expression of power, which unfolds like a paean of victory, is partly an effect of proportion. Whereas Corot modified the relatively slight inequality between the two spires by contriving a number of compensatory suggestions of equality, Delaunay purposely emphasizes the inequalities in his subject. The structure of the tower rises in a straight line to the first articulation, which is deliberately placed *above* the lower storey. The remainder of the tower is divided into two elements which are each half as high as the lower part – a treatment which conveys the impression of projection upwards from the ground so powerfully that the whole building seems to shoot up like the jet from a fountain. The inequalities are just as apparent in a horizontal sense. Firmly spread out at its base, the Eiffel tower is planted on its feet like a boxer, but hardly has it flexed its muscles before it is borne up by its own strength and narrows like a lance towards its summit. Colour, of course, adds something to the effect of the forms, but proportion plays the major part. There can be no doubt that it contributes powerfully to the feeling of lyrical exaltation which this work expresses.

In short, proportion governs the existence of forms in so far as their dimensions are concerned. In concert with the format, of which the height and width constitute one fixed relationship, it acts on the spectator at various levels. At the first level, it makes him aware of the work's extent, holding his attention by means of unequal terms, whose inequality is nevertheless controlled. At the second level, it is an element of the language of art in that it relates the forms to each other and to the work as a whole. At the third level it contributes a certain expressive quality to the forms and the work as a whole. *In this way spatial structure is expressed in terms of dimensions, and – simultaneously – style extracts quality from quantity.*

307

306

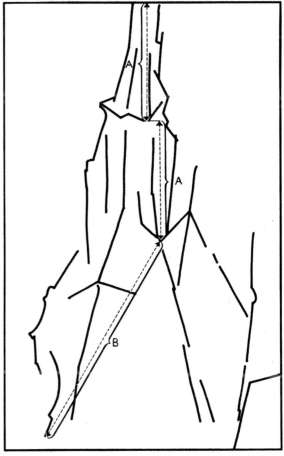

307

◄ 305. Robert Delaunay (1885-1941). *The Eiffel Tower.* Basle, Kunstmuseum. Photo Held.

306. The Eiffel Tower.

Movement

To judge from the preceding chapters, one might suppose the quality of a work of art to be almost entirely a question of construction. In fact, though construction is indispensable, it does not embrace every aspect of plastic reality. Pure form gives only partial satisfaction; we feel an inward need for it to fill out and come alive. This is because a work of art is not addressed to our minds or to our senses exclusively, but to the point where they meet, which is also the meeting-point of the two governing principles of *structure* and *movement*.

We have seen how the work of art is affected by the first of these principles, so let us now examine the second. Yet how can one talk of 'movement' in painting, when walls or canvases are by definition immobile? This is the paradox we must now investigate.

In his famous *Epsom Derby,* Géricault paints 308 horses such as have never been seen or recorded by eye or camera. In actuality a galloping horse is tense with exertion, its body swaying, its legs bun- 309 ched under its belly, its hindquarters flattened. In short, the photograph conveys the effort of the animal rather than the speed which the effort produces. Géricault, on the contrary, elongates the bodies of his horses; they fly along with necks and tails outstretched, like the fuselage of an aeroplane. More surprising still, their limbs are painted in defiance of observable truth, with the fore-legs stretched out in front and the hind legs out behind – suspended in air.

The horses in the painting are elements of language, going beyond mere representation to transmit that sensation of violent speed which every spectator at a horse race has experienced, but which no camera can capture. Thus, movement in painting is not simply the image of actual movement. In art, it is always something *expressed.* 310

In the example I have chosen, movement is still associated with objects really moving through space. To suggest real movement, the painter has resorted to a whole series of *distortions,* which – far from striking the spectator as such – render the expression of speed all the more convincing. But an artist can still suggest movement in the absence of any moving model – for instance, in a still life – by means of line, colour, light, brushwork, and form; for these purely pictorial elements, which are used for representational and constructional ends, *are also the vehicle of expression.* We must now consider this *interior movement,* through which 'life' circulates in a work of art.

308. Jean Louis Géricault (1791-1824). *Epsom Derby*. Paris, Louvre. Photo Giraudon.

309. *A photograph shows galloping horses tense with effort.* Photo Viollet.

310. Assyrian art. *Lion Hunt of King Assurbanipal*. 7th Cent. B.C. ▶ London, British Museum. Photo Viollet.

When Colette writes: '*Le silence, brodé à grands ramages par les abeilles et les rainettes, une tiédeur sur laquelle se refermaient les charmilles massives, un orage ballonné, tenu en respect derrière la colline, la lointaine pédale d'une batteuse de blé – tels sont encore aujourd'hui les matériaux qui me servent à reconstruire l'été...*'[1] we are delighted not only by the individual elements of notation – *silence, rainettes* – but also by the organic inflection of the sentence, the movement which runs right through it, and which conveys the very rhythm of the author's speech. So it is, too, in painting: we are delighted by line which has evocative power, as opposed to the line which merely describes and delimits the contour of an object.

311 In this feeble illustration of Achilles standing beside his friend Patroclus, the figures are rendered by a continuous outline which manages to suggest a couple of lads dressed up in antique costume, rather than a brace of heroes. We register their postures and their costume; we note how Achilles lets fall his lyre in surprise, since it is none other than Ulysses who is entering the tent. Why all this mythological information? Because it is the sole purpose of the illustration. Divorced from the text, it is nothing. The line which traces the contours of the figures is lifeless. From Achilles' mat of hair

---

[1] 'Silence, embroidered in bold patterns by bees and tree-frogs, warmth shut in between massive hedgerows, a bulging storm-cloud, keeping its respectful distance beyond the hill, the treadle of a distant threshing-machine – such even now are the materials from which I reconstruct the summer...' Colette, *Flore et Pomone*, in, *Gigi et autres nouvelles*, Guilde du Livre, Lausanne.

it proceeds to his shoulders, of which one is shown in three-quarter view and the other full-front, while the head is in profile. Without reference to changes of plane, the line cuts out the silhouette on the page as mechanically as a jig-saw.

Now compare Picasso's engraving of *The Sculptor's Workshop*. What vigour there is in this! It is 312 not that the line is more accentuated – it is actually of about the same thickness throughout – but it creates a series of planes and animates them with supple strength: the right shoulder – that of the arm that holds the dagger – is twisted to the rear, and the upper arm is also held back behind the body. To balance this, the other arm is flexed, the torsion of the fore-arm redoubling its power. The torso, developed in contrasting planes, radiates a splendid strength. What need is there of muscular or anatomical details? Picasso dispenses with them altogether, whereas the hapless Achilles and Patroclus are covered all over with tiny strokes – scratches? Or tattoo-marks?

The motive character of outline applies not only to lines which envelop a form, but also to those which link forms to each other. This is the characteristic of *arabesque*. Examining this photograph of 313 the Paris Bourse, one assumes that its impression of animated activity is the result of all the silhouettes which interrupt and overlap one another. But when one looks more closely, the impression of animation is nil; we invented it ourselves by association of ideas. It is no use the actors raising their arms, clenching their fists, opening their mouths or

312. Pablo Picasso (b. 1881). *The Sculptor's Workshop,* etching (Vollard series, 11 April 1933). Photo Yvan Bettex, Pully.

311. Scholarly application is no substitute for art!

311

313. The Paris *Bourse.* Photo Viollet.

314. Frans Hals (1580/81-1666). *The Regents of the Saint Elizabeth Hospital, Haarlem*. Haarlem, Frans Hals Museum. Photo Bulloz.

315. Jan de Bray (c. 1627-1697). *The Regents*. Haarlem, Frans Hals Museum. Photo Bulloz.

frowning; they are frozen in mid-gesture, as at the wave of a magic wand, and what finally strikes one is their corpse-like immobility.

314 Look now at Frans Hals' *Regents*. Five men are gathered round a table, and, though they neither move nor gesticulate, one seems to sense a secret tremor, as if life were circulating from one to the other. Beside this painting it is the snapshot that appears lifeless. Of course, construction has much to do with it. While the photograph portrays a confused, haphazard group, made even more confused by the depth of the space it occupies, the regents are distributed in an orderly way across the

316 canvas – a group of three on the left and a group of two on the right. Furthermore, the artist has deliberately inscribed each group within a triangle. Without going any deeper into an aspect that was dealt with in an earlier chapter, we may observe that this triangular construction contributes to the picture's 'legibility', and that it would be pointless to look for anything analogous in the photograph.

However, while we are on the subject of the photograph once again, we may note how confused, also, are the connecting lines between the figures! Continually chopped and checked – by a hand, a hat, or part of a face – they start off in a hundred contrary directions that end up by cancelling each other out. When, on the other hand, one follows from left to right the crestline formed by the *Regents'* shoulders and hats, one soon perceives that *this is*

319 *a continuous though variegated line, linking the key-points of the picture.* There we have, at one and the same time, a definition of arabesque and a new insight into the difference between photography and art. In photography objects are juxtaposed or superimposed, *but without being linked to one another as forms* – hence that danger of looseness in design which is so difficult for the photographer to combat. Objects may also be juxtaposed or superimposed in a work of art, *on condition that they are formally united within the space they constitute.* In painting, the lines *between* objects are every bit as important as those which indicate their contours.

This is a point worth looking into. If arabesque were no more than a sort of hyphen between forms, it would be difficult to accord it much importance. Let us judge of this by referring to the painting by

315 Jan de Bray. Here, too, the line of shoulders and hats is perfectly discernible. If you make a tracing

317 of it, you will produce a line which, in itself, would appear to be neither better nor worse than Hals'. Why is it, then, that the arabesque effect in the latter

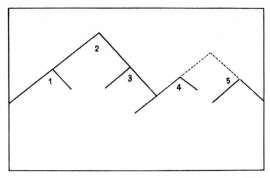

316

seems so different? This question throws light on the basic function of arabesque: *dynamism*. When reduced to a simple tracing, the line that links objects is arabesque only in name. To be truly so, it needs to be related to other formal elements which 'activate' and vitalize it. In de Bray's painting, the regents are grouped two by two, as if posing 318 for their picture. The outline of shoulders and hats serves the sole purpose of giving prominence to the worthies in the background – doubtless to satisfy their self-esteem. In Hals' work, on the contrary, the outline *continually interferes with that of the* 319 *constructional forms,* which project and curve inward like capes and inlets, giving rise to those 'incidents' from which tension is born. It is from such relationships, which stimulate an interplay both of contrast and of concert between the elements of form, that arabesque derives its interior movement, which in turn is communicated to the entire composition. *For the spectator, then, arabesque is not a static outline, but a path of dynamic progress.*

It goes without saying that arabesque lends itself equally well to direct evocation of movement. Thus in this work by Rubens, *The Rape of the Daughters* 320 *of Leucippus,* the general movement of the picture 321 is organized around the sinuous line which runs from the horseman on the left to the right arm of the girl on the ground. Articulated to this long curve, on either side, are *lines of stress,*[1] which curl in a series of spirals, and which, being adapted to the forms of the objects represented, animate them from within. But note that this is not just a matter of simple addition. The movement of the horses, the riders, and their victims, is quite different from what it would be in reality; the painter has modified it deliberately so that, combined with arabesque and lines of stress, it gives the scene its intensity.

[1] *Lines of stress develop out of arabesque, of which they are in part extensions, and in part tributaries. In other words, they mutually reinforce one another.*

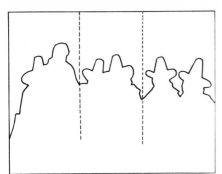

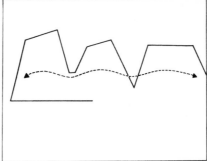

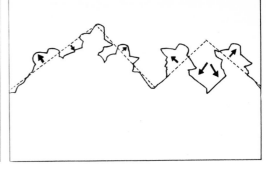

317   318   319

Whether lines directly evoke exterior movement, or whether they give dynamic shape to a figure or object, as in Picasso's *The Sculptor's Workshop,* their formal expression is manifested by an interior movement, such as runs through the sentence by Colette, which gives their content an immediate and vibrant presence.

It will be understood that any of the elements of form can play their part in this – colour, light, values, and so on – but it is always through *relationships* that dynamism is achieved.

320. Peter Paul Rubens (1577-1640). *Rape of the Daughters of Leucippus.* Munich, Alte Pinakothek. Photo Bulloz.

Has the drama of Christ carrying the Cross ever 322 been more forcibly expressed than in this wash drawing by Poussin? Indeed, we leap straight to the heart of the drama, even before we have recognized the personages concerned. Faces are missing, bodies unfinished; there is nothing that tells us immediately what is happening. Christ himself is virtually unrecognizable, reduced to a few blobs and dashes below the cross, and only the outlines of the horses are treated a little more clearly. Yet who would think of complaining? Who would think of reproaching the artist for haste or incompleteness? Can this great battle of light and dark be described as a 'rough sketch'? Here is the ascent to Calvary,

321

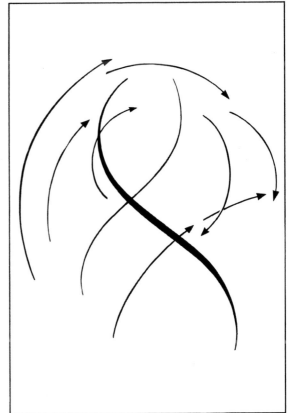

269

moving from right to left, broken abruptly by the collapse of Jesus. The infuriated soldiers turn in their saddles to lash him. Repudiating representational images, the artist purposely suppresses the left sides of his figures; the right sides, on the contrary, are weighted with extra-thick shadows, as if to show how the soldiers, vanquished by their own cruelty, give way without resistance to the dark side of their natures. The interior movement of the scene arises out of this treatment of forms in terms of light and dark. Broad ribbons of wash, gaping spaces – yet it is the savagery of the soldiers, the sufferings of Christ, and the compassionate indignation of the artist that take shape before us and within us through the communicative power of dynamic line and wash.

It is carried to the point of paroxysm in Poussin's drawing, but, when employed in a more relaxed mood, the opposition of light and shadow can produce a more measured movement, and convey less violent emotions. Such is the case with the *Christ in the Carpenter's Shop* of Georges de La Tour. Bent like a gentle giant over bis brace and bit, St Joseph is absorbed in his work, while the young Jesus holds the candle to give him light. From the shadows which model Joseph's body the spectator's glance approaches the lighted area, descends from the old man's forehead along his arms to the tool which he grasps in both hands, after which we find that we are attracted rather to the face of Jesus than to the remarkable translucency of his hands. Are we merely admiring an effect of light that renders the scene more touching? Not at all, for the light and shade, while evoking an atmosphere of tenderness, also guide our attention to the carpenter's work, and – more subtly still – lead us to relate the lighted areas to each other, and, by the interrelation of the faces, equally enveloped in light, make us feel that these two beings quite literally 'touch' one another. The link

322. Nicolas Poussin (1594-1665). *The Road to Calvary,* wash drawing. Dijon Museum. Photo Rémy.

323. Georges de La Tour (1593-1652). *Christ in the Carpenter's Shop.* Paris, Louvre. Photo Held.

between Joseph and Jesus thus becomes apparent to the senses, without its being expressly stated or demonstrated. Light and shadow act in unison to signify the humanity of Jesus, which, through the symbol of Joseph the craftsman, involves all men and their labours.

When limited to copying, painting is inert; when elevated by the suggestive power of movement, it can convey the ineffable. It is a marvellous power, which masters of chiaroscuro like El Greco, Titian, Tintoretto, Rembrandt or – nearer to our own day – Daumier have exploited with equal brilliance for a variety of ends.

In conclusion, it is important to realize that *movement* is as necessary as *structure* to the life of a work, that it is likewise one of its vital principles. 'Movement' applies normally to the displacement of an object in space, but in art, even when the artist paints a galloping horse or some other scene of real action, he never confines himself to copying the appearance of actual movement; at most one may say that in certain circumstances he will be guided by it. *Thus, movement in painting is of a special and particular nature, arising from the elements of form and their relationships.* Formal dynamism, which gives the structure of the work that secret animation without which it would perish, does not depend on the subject but purely on the manner in which the language of art is employed. That is why it is just as capable of breathing life into a fruit-bowl by Chardin, a jug by Braque or a vase by Zurbarán as into a battle-piece by Delacroix. It is the vehicle by which the sensations, emotions and thoughts of the artist are conveyed.

Rhythm

'The notion of rhythm', says L. Weber, 'is one of our most familiar concepts. The succession of nights and days, of warm and cold seasons, of periods when the vegetable world seems to be dead and when it burgeons with life, the alternation of work and rest, of waking and sleeping... are perpetual examples of rhythmic motion.'[1] As this author remarks, it is among the most familiar of all ideas; it is when one tries to define it that the trouble begins. So let us take it in easy stages.

Rhythm does indeed seem to be part of our existence – our organic existence for a start. At every heartbeat our blood supply is refreshed, nourished by the dual movement of our lungs, inhaling and exhaling. Our most habitual movements, spontaneous or acquired, also show rhythm – for instance, the action of walking. Watch labourers at their work; grouped in twos or threes, they adapt their actions to their alternating blows of pick or mallet. The 'heave-ho!' of the old-time boatmen had no other purpose; and, when a military band goes by, see how the soldiers put down their feet as one man, in time to the beat of the bass drum.

Certainly, there is music of a more complex kind than that of a brass band, but is there any that dispenses entirely with rhythm? Poetry, too. Can one imagine anyone, however philistine, reading a Shakespeare sonnet as if it were a page of the telephone directory?

What inner need does this demand for rhythm satisfy? In the case of organic movements, those of heart and lungs, we have to confess that we do not know; but the answer seems clearer where voluntary movements are concerned. At the level of the manual labourer, rhythm permits force to be concentrated in such a way as to obtain maximum efficacity with minimum exertion. It is an instrument of economy, and one finds it wherever muscular energy comes into play.

Even physical activities which have no utilitarian purpose are associated with rhythm. When the coxswain cries 'In!... Out! – In!... Out!', and the oars dip together into the water, is it not for the pleasure – as much as for anything else – of executing perfectly synchronized movements as a team? That is the sportsman's pleasure. And if I go to a concert or ballet... The orchestra unfolds its cadences, and the dancer her steps, and I perceive in the labyrinth of varied figures, some striking the

[1] L. Weber, *Le Rythme du Progrès,* quoted by Lalande in his *Vocabulaire de la Philosophie.*

eye and some the ear, an architecture of movement which grips me and carries me with it.

While not pretending that rhythm is identical in all cases, it is undeniably present in most of our activities – physiological, mental, mechanical, artistic, muscular, spontaneous, conscious or unconscious; and, since it expresses a fundamental aspect of our behaviour, it does have characteristics which are common to every case, and from which the basis of a definition can be drawn. Rhythm, beyond all doubt, is *movement*; but it is distinguished from movement in general, such as was studied in the last chapter, by a quality all its own: the repetition of 'up-beat' and 'down-beat' at fairly regular intervals. It is this *periodic* character, this *regular* succession of changes, that gives it the special quality to which we respond.

Why these observations? you may ask. They may be valid for poetry, and perhaps still more so for music – that is, *for the arts which have their existence in time* – but they cannot apply to painting or sculpture, *which have their existence in space.* But wait!... We have already established that this distinction is more apparent than real.

When one looks at a blank wall, the eye remains inactive once it has broadly taken in its extent. If the

324

wall is pierced with bays at regular intervals, one's attention is stimulated. 324

Now, this embryonic rhythm – window, wall, window, – not only has the effect of stimulating one's gaze, but also (and this is more important in our present context) *of organizing it in terms of duration.* Though the wall does not move, one's glance traverses it; it is engaged by the series of solids and voids, hovering from one element to the next, and the sum of such steps corresponds to the total time needed to traverse the intervals of wall and window. This is a schematic example, but one may deduce from it the following fact of capital importance: *that aesthetic contemplation, while having its origins in space, is linked also with a sense of duration that renders a work of plastic art amenable to movement and rhythm, to tempo in fact, in the same way as poetry.*

325. Domenico Veneziano (c. 1400-1461). *Annunciation.* Cambridge, Fitzwilliam Museum. Reproduced by permission of the Syndics of the Fitzwilliam Museum.

At first glance this abolition of the differences between the arts of time and the arts of space is surprising, but it is less so when one reflects that architecture, painting, sculpture, music and dancing, when experienced as art, are all experienced in the same area of our consciousness. Though their methods and the objects they deal with are different, they cannot disown their essential kinship, since they all appeal to the same aspect of our inward nature.

With that much said, and rather than pursue the matter in the abstract, let us examine this *Annunciation* by Domenico Veneziano. With colour suppressed, as in this photograph, we find we are confronted by a wall which the artist has articulated with a portico of equally spaced columns. In terms of the surface plane there are five main elements, with the columns as the 'down-beats' and the intervals between them as the 'up-beats'. To emphasize their link in time, the artist has crowned his portico with a continuous cornice, running across the full width of the picture. Then, to stimulate the spectator's interest, the uniformity of the structure is interrupted by projecting elements, of which the effect is all the more powerful since they alter the direction of the line of columns. The cornice is therefore composed of sections of unequal length, the central and most important section being saved from monotony by the ternary articulation of the wall beneath it. Note also how the cornice – far from seeming to weigh heavily on the wall – produces, on the contrary, an impression of lightness, thanks to the arched opening and the slight recession of the bays on either side. Similarly, the weight of the forward projections of the cornice is diminished to the eye by reason of the slenderness of the supporting columns.

The rhythm of the picture is also developed in depth. First we have the foreground architecture – vertically the twin groups of four columns, horizontally the dark squares of pavement in perspective. The second plane coincides with the passage that leads into the garden, and is articulated by the bases of the columns at the entrance, the wall, and the shadow which falls obliquely on the paving. Finally, the third plane is articulated by the lawn, the intersection of the paths, and the flowering plants by the closed door.

Looked at in this way, the picture is composed like a stanza of verse, or like a series of stanzas, for this is indeed a poem – Domenico Veneziano's poem on the theme of the Annunciation. Thus we

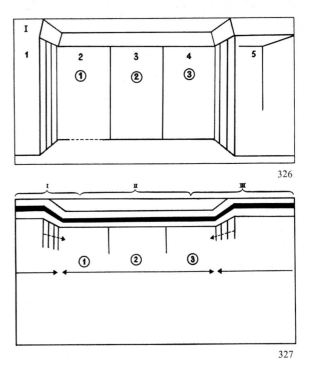

326

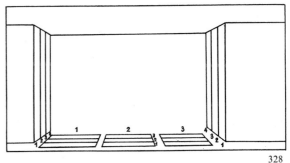

327

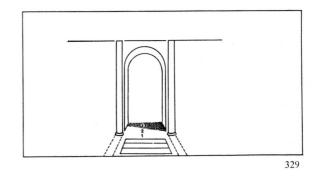

328

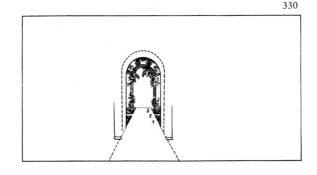

329

330

331

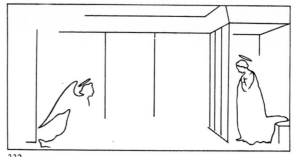

332

are enabled, through the qualities of rhythm, to enter into the artist's feelings – and into those of the angel and the Madonna – without need of psychological expression or touches of stage-craft.

331 On the left of the picture, but within the central area, is the angel, who kneels with one finger raised, imparting the divine message: 'And behold, thou shalt conceive in thy womb, and bring forth a son, and shalt call his name Jesus. He shall be great, and shall be called the Son of the Highest . . .' In actual fact, of course, not a word is spoken; the angel does not even open his mouth. Here we must be specially attentive: of the three central elements, only that on the left is occupied – by the angel; the other two are apparently empty. Now, in terms of form, this apparent void is precisely the area to which the transmission of the divine message is entrusted, starting from the slanting alignment of the lilies. By virtue of the three 'bars' (to return to our musical analogy), of which the first contains the angel and the other two are silent, the painter makes us simultaneously aware of the Word and of the distance which separates it from God's chosen vessel.

332 This dual effect is emphasized by the relative positions of the figures. Mary is placed *behind* one delicate screen of columns, while the angel is *in front of* the other. Furthermore, the Virgin is situated *among* the columns of the foreground, belonging in some sense to her surroundings, as, with lowered head, she makes her reply: 'Behold the handmaid of the Lord; be it unto me according to thy word'; the angel, on the contrary, is placed on a level with the nearest column, *as if he does not belong to the same order of existence*, but merely passes through it. Indeed, Saint Luke continues: 'And the angel departed from her.'

Thus, within a framework of contemporary architecture, with the resources of rhythm to help him, and without recourse to supernatural effects

(his Virgin has a matronly look, and his angel – but for the wings – is like a handsome kneeling youth), Domenico Veneziano succeeds in communicating a *sense of the supernatural* and his own mood of reverence. A poem; for – beyond what is stated or represented – it is the ineffable that strikes us by some mode of suggestion that is all the more com-pelling for the fact that the secret of its power remains hidden.

We may verify this point by comparing two *Annunciations* by Piero della Francesca and Fra 333-334 Angelico. One does not need to pore over them to discover that they are quite different in spirit, for all their identity of subject. The general arrangement is more or less the same, however, with the surface divided into two unequal parts, the angel in one and the Virgin in the other.

The binary division of the fresco at Arezzo, 335 strongly accentuated by the opposition of column and architrave, tends to make each 'bar' self-con-tained. This rhythm, so evident in the foreground plane, is taken up and repeated in the door and wall of the background. To give the fullest effect to it, the artist has modified the proportions of every element, heightening the part in which the Virgin stands. Thus, through rhythm, the significance of the fresco is revealed: for Piero della Francesca humanity has a nobility of its own, of which sin has not deprived it, and which it rediscovers in its moments of destiny.

How different is Fra Angelico's picture! Instead 336 of marking the rhythm by contrast (verticals inter-sected by horizontals), he makes it all a matter of smooth transition. The column between the Virgin and the angel is indeed a formal 'caesura', but it is not at all like Piero della Francesca's. While it divides the space in two, it does not invite one to 337 stop and consider each part separately, but rather it links them together. Let me illustrate this point with an example; here are two lines of verse by Agrippa d'Aubigné, both describing Cain:

276

333. Piero della Francesca (1410/20-1492). *Annunciation* (detail), fresco. Arezzo, Church of S. Francesco. Photo Anderson-Giraudon.

334. Fra Angelico (1387?-1455). *Annunciation*, fresco. Florence, Convent of S. Marco. Photo Anderson-Giraudon.

...Vif, il ne vécut point. Mort, il ne mourut pas...

...Il était seul partout, hors en sa conscience... [1]

In both, the caesura falls on the sixth foot – on 'point' in the first and on 'partout' in the second. But while it represents a pause, i.e. a stop, in the former, it is a simple accent in the latter. Consequently the first line reads rhythmically as the juxtaposition of two hemistichs, each with its own unity:

Vif, il ne vécut point.   *Mort, il ne mourut pas.*

The second, on the contrary, reads as a single sentence articulated in the middle:

Il était seul partout, hors en sa conscience.

In Fra Angelico's fresco, the linking rhythm is 338 emphasized by the two symmetrical arches in the foreground, and still more by the cadence of the interior arches. While these repeat the same motif in a rhythmic crescendo – as if the beating of the

[1] *...Alive, he did not live. Dead, he did not die...*
...He was alone everywhere, except in his conscience...

335

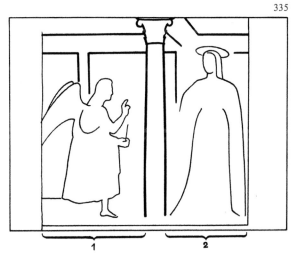

336

277

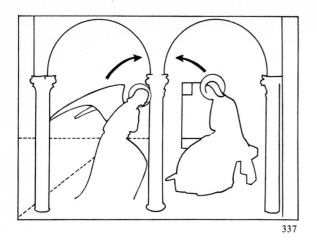

337

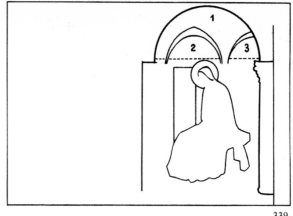

339

angel's wings still reverberated among them – they also indicate the direction of the divine messenger's movement towards the Virgin. In her part of the picture space the arches are arranged quite differently. Parallel to the background wall, they form three 'bars' which emphasize the Virgin's composure and also, by their inequality, suggest her inward perturbation. While the angel's head seems as if thrust forward by the impetus of the arches, the Virgin's is held slightly back. Fra Angelico humanizes the Annunciation. God surrounds with an aura of tenderness the one who shall be the mother of his son.

All three artists treat the same subject, but where Domenico Veneziano places the accent on the supernatural character of the celestial message, Piero places it on human dignity, and Fra Angelico on divine mercy. In each picture rhythm plays a role of secret revelation.

It goes without saying that any of the other pictorial elements may be the agent of rhythm – light, colour, tone-values etc. The use which the artist makes of chiaroscuro in Tintoretto's celebrated picture of *Susannah and the Elders* is particu-

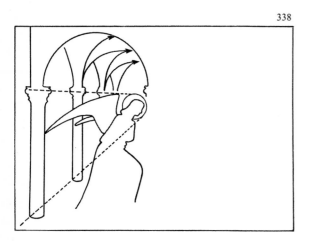

338

larly instructive. The rectangular surface is divided into two approximately equal parts: to the left is the screen of foliage, with the two old men at its extremities; to the right is Susannah, emerging from her bath. One's first thought might well be that the picture lacks unity, for the left-hand side suggests depth in the most unambiguous manner, while the right-hand side, except for the vista in the background, tends to conform to the surface plane. One can appreciate this clearly enough by masking the two sides alternately.

What sense is there in this 'anomaly'? When one looks more closely, one notices that the picture is composed of dark and light masses, the latter forming four areas of differing intensity: above and to the left, a vista of garden; below and to the left, the head of the nearer elder; above and in the centre, the other vista and the other elder; to the right, Susannah's body. The eye is stimulated by this pattern of contrasts and similarities, and moves in succession from the heads of the two old men to the nude and back again, these three light areas forming a kind of triangle with the sides converging upon Susannah. In this way the old men's lust is given visible expression. And there is more to it; since each of them is placed at one end of the screen of foliage, it is their actual concupiscence that we are made aware of.

But this is where the artist's sovereign skill produces what may be justly called a miracle. Although the dotards are already emerging from their cover, are already passing the barrier that separates them from Susannah, it all takes place *as if the woman is really beyond their reach* – as if chastity is a surer protection than the arbour and its shade!

But is she not naked, and her nakedness at the mercy of anyone who can get past the screen? Notice, though, how this nude is treated. The light

340. Tintoretto (1518-1594). *Susannah and the Elders*. Vienna, Gemäldegalerie. Photo Held.

341

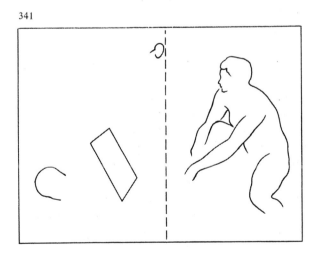

342

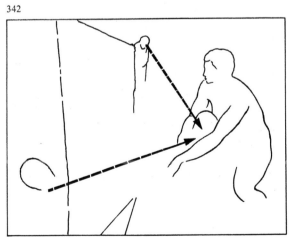

does not make its volumes 'go round', as in the old mens' heads, but undergoes a double metamorphosis, in the first place following the sinuous and imperious line of the back, in the second place repressing any very lively suggestion of modelling. This does not mean that flesh tones are abolished or become allusive. Their existence could scarcely be more powerfully affirmed, but they are transposed into a new key, *to become linear and luminous rhythm.* In Tintoretto's picture, chastity is not just an attribute of Susannah; it is something *tangibly present.* Susannah is visible, but she remains *unattainable.* The purity of the subject is suggested by the hidden power of formal structure, and by rhythm in particular.

Let us turn to an example based on the primacy 343 of colour. In this still life by Matisse one finds plenty of familiar things: a plate, some oysters, two lemons, a jug, a knife – but so allusively represented that it requires some effort to recognize them. And what exactly are these three concentric zones – the blue, the orange-pink and the vermilion? Where is the table? Or is the plate on the floor? What an odd carpet, then – and still odder napkin! Nevertheless, from out of this bizarre assemblage (bizarre, that is, for anyone who looks for the precise reconstitution of places and objects) there emanates an impression of irresistible necessity. That the picture makes a unified whole cannot reasonably be disputed – that is, if one allows that reason is not the slave of day-to-day reality, but can also lead us to realities of other kinds, for example to the reality of colour, which one has every reason to believe lies at the heart of Matisse's enchanted world.

He exploits complementary colours, surrounding the central rectangle of blue with a band of orange that intensifies it, and putting two stripes of vermilion across the green napkin. But not in a mechanical way. There is, indeed, the violet of the jug to echo the yellow of the lemons, but see how Matisse lightens and subdues it; if this colour were darker or more concentrated, it would conflict with the dominant blue and red of the picture.

The 'thermal' character of colours has been equally well managed, as can be appreciated if one masks all that lies outside the central rectangle: seen thus, the blue grows cold and hard, and the yellow of the lemons hardens with it into green. Thus the orange and vermilion act both upon the quality of the other colours and upon their 'temperature'.

Leaving that aspect of the question on one side, let us see what part rhythm plays here. In whatever direction one's eye traverses this still life, the colours are divided into bright and less bright tints, in a system of *alternation.* For instance, if one follows the diagonal that starts from the artist's signature, one encounters in succession vermilion, orange-pink, dark blue, the light blue of the plate, dark blue, the pale violet of the jug, and then the orange again, which – with the speck of vermilion right in the corner – forms a 'down-beat'.

This *rhythmic treatment of colour intensity* gives the composition a supple character that saves it from mere decorative effect. In whatever direction one explores it, the rhythm reappears just as happily. It is for the sake of this that Matisse arranges his objects with a tint of different intensity between them (the knife, the jug, the scattered oysters), or, when they touch (the plate, the napkin, the lemons), inserts a strip of greenery.

Rhythm also affects the *number* and *size* of the areas of colour, and their *disposition* in the picture space. Looking at the middle of the picture, one is ready to believe that the blue rectangle is a single, uniform block. But this is an illusion, due to bad habits of mind – or simply to laziness. Far from being uniform or continuous, the blue area is in fact broken into in the middle by the series of objects scattered across it, its corners are trimmed unequally, its sides are slightly curved, and the blue itself is made up of strokes of varying intensity. Thus divided or interrupted (it is the same with the rest of the picture), the colours incite one's eye to regard the painting in terms of a *binary rhythm,* which is 344 plainly accentuated by the two red stripes on the napkin, the arrangement of the oysters on the plate in pairs, and the two lemons. When one steps back a few paces, the alternations of colour and shape seem now to suggest a *ternary rhythm,* expressed in 345 the three green areas of the napkin, the three oysters on the blue cloth, the grouping of three pairs of oysters on the plate, and the three sprigs of greenery around it. A surprising effect, this, inviting us to take both a close look and a more distant look, so that we inwardly change position and feel our attitude to the picture changing. In this new sort of space, which the artist offers for our delectation, we are not tempted to touch or take hold of objects; but neither are we encouraged to look on them as silhouettes, as if the artist had simply flattened them out. We sense their presence and feel their charm. Matisse's secret is to have conferred upon humble objects – oysters-shells, jug and knife – all the enchantment of a fairy-tale, and to have rediscovered

343. Henri Matisse (1869-1954). *Still Life with Oysters*. Basle, Kunstmuseum. Photo Held.

344

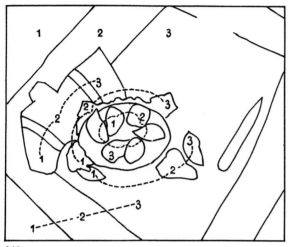

345

the ways of wonderment in the midst of the 20th century.

In the most general sense, then, rhythm is movement. It is endowed with specific properties, appearing on the one hand in the guise of *intensity* (of sensory origin, producing the effect of 'up-beat' and 'down-beat'), and on the other in the guise of *number* (of intellectual origin, controlling the intervals between beats). The most characteristic effect of rhythm in painting is to convert space into space-time. The introduction of the time element creates a new order of experience, in which aesthetic contemplation becomes a series of changes linked together in a given space of time.

We may use a familiar comparison to make this phenomenon clear. A film sequence is made up of successive images which show us (suppose it be a sequence of a man drinking) first, the man with his arm at his side and the glass on the table; last, the man with his arm bent and the glass to his lips; between these two, the succession of images that leads from one to the other. In isolation, each image represents a different *state* of the same gesture; but, as soon as the film is projected, the succession of separate states is transformed into a succession of *passages* from one to the next, and we see the movement itself.

Now the picture surface has more than one thing in common with the cinema screen. It, too, is a motionless panel that can become the scene of connected action. But its images are animated in a different way. The painter has neither film nor projector; *with the means at his disposal, he must create conditions through which our own consciousness, in its contact with the work, provides the motive power.* It is the movement of our own eyes, stimulated by the work itself, and prolonged by our mental activity, that adjusts our varied states of perception into a time-sequence, thus producing both the internal dynamism of the work and the sensation of its life that we experience.

This movement is never a replica of the sort of movement which the camera goes in for. Cézanne's *Card Players* will never put their cards on the table, 346 and Géricault's horses will never reach the winning-post. What art gives us is *not so much the action itself as the feeling it expresses.* Our experiences of heat, light or cold, our feelings of animation, joy or sorrow, even the ideas that we form, since they are a living experience, are all accompanied by some degree – great or small, long or short in duration – of excitement. Joy makes our hearts beat strongly,

346. Paul Cézanne (1839-1906). *Card Players*. Paris, Louvre. Photo Held.

fear takes the breath away; an inspiring idea, like that of liberty, exalts us. In short, every part of our experience literally 'moves' us – sets us in motion. Now, sensations, feelings and ideas are not directly communicable. Nevertheless, by means of rhythm, language is able to transmit the subtlest inflections of our inner life. With rhythm, a sentence is no longer just a sequence of words that add up to such-and-such a meaning, but can be the vehicle for expressing the very essence of a thought or feeling, making us share the original sensation. Thanks to rhythm, which we perceive in effects of regularity or irregularity, in changes of strength or in changes of speed, we are able to put our finger on the artist's pulse.

It is the vehicle of a special kind of communication between men, transforming the various formal agents into 'mediators' which allow us not only to understand one another, but to communicate, to attune our hearts in unison. Communication becomes true communion, an experience renewed at every contact with a work of art.

Harmony

I use the term 'harmony' with some hesitation, since it can lead to all sorts of misunderstanding. In current usage, anything passes for 'harmonious' which is associated in an agreeable or flattering way with the idea of perfection.

Can one explain the prestige which Greek sculpture has so long enjoyed purely on grounds of aesthetic merit? Does not man's wish to believe in a standard harmony that has been achieved once and for all have a lot to do with it?

It cannot be denied that this faith in an ideal standard has flourished in certain epochs, nor that it has produced masterpieces; but it has also produced the worst kind of academicism. Nowadays, fortunately, the tendency to judge art in terms of ideal beauty is on the wane. Our contemporary consciousness is gradually grasping the truth that, if beauty is one and indivisible, its manifestations are unlimited, and that the column-statues of Chartres yield nothing in point of 'beauty' to the masterpieces of antiquity. Harmony has ceased to mean a condition in which the elements of a work combine as best they can to imitate a 'perfect' model, and has come instead to mean a condition in which *all the elements of a work combine to produce a unified impression on the mind and senses, constituting and exhibiting a style.*

In actual fact, the terms 'composition' and 'harmony' are very nearly interchangeable, but whereas 'composition' signifies more the interior organization of the work, 'harmony' signifies the effect of such organization upon the spectator. I do not wish to engage in polemics upon this subject; but those who would deny the distinction will doubtless allow that a work, since it exists always in relation to our consciousness, may be considered in terms either of its intrinsic constitution or of what the spectator feels about it. I am simply using 'composition' and 'harmony' to indicate this difference.

With that point settled, let us take a look at Sophie Taeuber-Arp's picture, *Broken Cross,* in 347 which two types of element are present: elongated, band-like rectangles, and a disc. The bands are not strictly uniform, for they are all of different lengths,

347. Sophie Taeuber-Arp (1889-1943). *Broken Cross.* Photo Jean Arp.

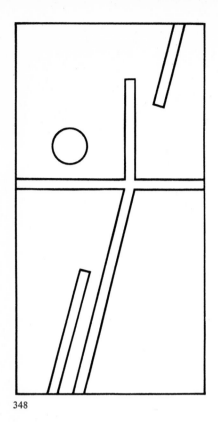 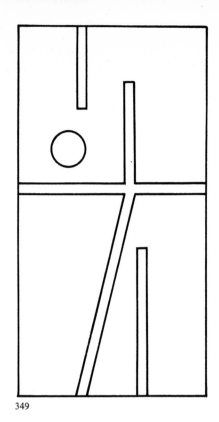 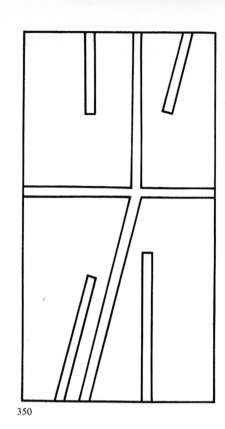

348   349   350

but nevertheless the composition conveys a sensation neither of instability nor of pure symmetry. [1] This is surely because the bands, though different, share a circumstance in common – that of direction. In actual fact, one of them is horizontal (the arms of the cross), three are diagonal and three are vertical. As one observes, on closer examination, the two isolated diagonal bands intensify the breaking movement of the cross, while the two isolated verticals restore its equilibrium. Finally, the disc, by its very rotundity, emphasizes the twisting movement of the lower branch of the cross. If you mask the isolated verticals, the picture seems more like a *shattered cross*. If you mask the isolated diagonals, the symmetrical effect of the verticals produces a sense of inertia. And if you mask the disc, diagonals and verticals lose their relationships, and the composition relapses into disorder.

348
349
350

The essential nature of harmony in art is revealed by this comparatively simple example: *it consists of various elements, presented in such a way that they are perceived in a common relationship.* This has nothing to do with identical forms or identical arrangement, but implies some measure of *resemblance, constituted by the relative situation of each element to the others, and of them all to the work as a whole.*

Obviously a picture can be based on a harmony of greater or lesser complexity, but, whether it be figurative or abstract, it cannot dispense with it altogether, since harmony satisfies the most basic requirements of our sensibility. The first of these, already referred to in other contexts, is *interest* or *attention*. Stimulated by the interplay of similar and dissimilar, one's consciousness is *activated*. As Valéry has rightly observed, it needs then to be kept active: 'Change becomes desirable in itself', he writes, '*variety* is needed as a complement to the duration of our feeling, and as an antidote to the satiety which results from the exhaustion of our organism's resources when its attention is focussed upon something of infinite, yet local and particular connotation.' *(L'Infini esthétique.)*

At the same time harmony has a direct bearing on our *pleasure*. Once it has been satisfied, pleasure is extinguished in satiety, no matter how intense it has been. Therefore harmony so regulates a work's relationships that we are offered various and suc-

[1] Symmetry implies the repetition of identical forms, or the identical arrangement of different forms; asymmetry is its opposite. The former leaves us indifferent because it keeps on repeating the same echo, the latter because it repeats none at all. They are the two outer limits of harmony, which is currently defined as *unity in variety*. In subscribing to this definition I do not wish to become involved in theory, but simply to pursue my inquiries into the knowing of works of art. For our purposes, a definition is not an end in itself, but only a point of departure or point of reference.

cessive pleasures. How are we to explain why we learn a poem by heart, unless it is because the delicate play of rhymes, rhythms and pauses gives an enjoyment that repetition is powerless to destroy? How otherwise explain why we want to listen to a symphony which we have heard so often that we know almost every note in advance? How otherwise explain why we may hang a picture on our walls, and find ourselves pausing to look at it every day?

The mind is no less sensitive to harmony. Almost as soon as it has taken in a group of forms it begins to spot resemblances. When it finds them, it immediately starts to probe and question them, and the information which they yield produces a gradual and growing impression of familiarity in a new environment. Colours and forms beckon and echo one another; flashes of insight illuminate the path. But things must not be made too easily reassuring, or the mind will sink to a state of torpor. It must meet obstacles here and there, which further resemblances enable it to surmount. Thanks to this dual process of surprise and recognition, a work of art is *a field of perpetual discovery* for the mind.

351 Let us examine Duccio's *Three Marys at the Tomb,* and see how the phenomenon of harmony manifests itself. This panel is a fragment of the famous polyptych (the '*Maestà*') at Siena, and it illustrates the following verses of the Gospel according to St Mark: 'And entering into the sepulchre, they saw a young man sitting on the right side, clothed in a long white garment; and they were affrighted. And he saith unto them, Be not affrighted: Ye seek Jesus of Nazareth, which was crucified: he is risen; he is not here: behold the place where they laid him.'

One's eye takes in the whole scene at a glance, the actors in the story and the décor: on the left are the three Marys; on the right, the angel, seated on the lid of the tomb; behind, the mountain, standing out on the gold background. The subject presents no difficulty. There are few different kinds of objects, and they are arranged in a highly intelligible manner: for instance, the group of women repeats the same motif three times, like a colonnade. There is no symmetry, though: each woman differs slightly from the other two in attitude and gesture, and still more in the colour and form of her dress. This triple motif, crowned by the three haloes which merge in a single radiance, is echoed in the three summits of the mountain, similarly crowned by the gold of the background. On the right, the front of the tomb is ornamented with apparently symmet-

rical elements. Apparently – since of the four panels only one is complete, the others being partially and unequally obscured.

But it is in the construction of the picture, through the forms which it suggests, that the mind is introduced to a more subtle scheme of things. The vertical rectangle which contains the Marys cor- 352 responds to the horizontal rectangle of the tomb. Similarly, the oblique parallelogram of the marble 353 slab echoes that of the woman in red (also oblique, but leaning the other way), while a third forms a pendant to them both – the slope of the tallest mountain. These shapes, on which the composition 354 is based, are reinforced by the triangle of mountain, itself linked to the tomb by the vertical axis of the angel. This latter complex of forms resembles a pair 355 of scales; the lid of the tomb forms the arm of the balance, and thus – in spite of its curious position – remains in equilibrium.

There is nothing mechanical about this. To effect the passage from tomb to mountain, the artist makes use of *transitional shapes*: first the oval 356 of the wings, then the circle of the halo. These also help, in some measure, to convert the contrast of vertical-versus-horizontal into movement.

In this way an observant mind keeps noticing elements which, while seeming to serve purely figurative ends, participate in the secret, emotive architecture of the work. The pleasure of spotting them brings a renewal of mental activity, and this in its turn leads to further perceptions.

There are still other potentialities which harmony can awaken in us; indeed, it has to do so, if the mind is to make the kind of discovery of which I have just been speaking.

How did we look at the picture to begin with? First of all, the eye wanders across its surface, encountering human figures and objects; but, as soon as the subject is identified, it starts off again, in a state of expectancy, as if something is still lacking. And 'something' suddenly appears: similarities in the three women and the three peaks of the mountain; similarities in the parallelograms. The source of these discoveries is *intuition,* the imaginative faculty of the mind. Now harmony does not appeal to intuition as to a concept, *but stimulates it into activity,* and it is the exercise of our intuition which makes us really 're-invent' the work, and participate in the creative act of the artist.

Harmony also brings our *sensibility* into play. It is, of course, very difficult to draw a precise line of

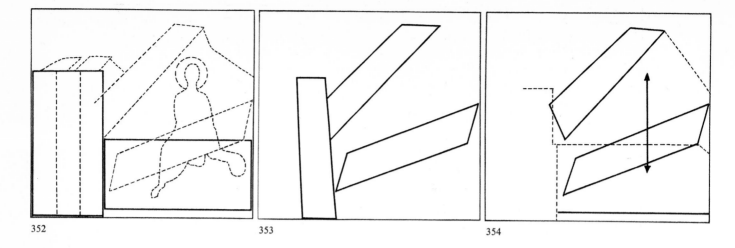

352   353   354

demarcation between mind and sensibility, especially in art, where that which is addressed to the mind is never purely intellectual. It is nevertheless true that the surface skin of colour, the networks of line, the shapes of colour-areas and the variations of light are all subject to a class of perception which first involves our senses and feelings.

Can one possibly follow the outline of this rocky background without feeling a sense of upheaval? When one contemplates these deep fissures in the mountainside, one comprehends the cataclysm that has just taken place, as if the earth has been violently rent asunder to throw up the tomb of Christ. Strong contrasts of light and dark, the dark areas made more sombre still by the thick, ink-dark runnels which score the face of the rock, give emphasis to this restless ground-bass, against which is set – in the right foreground – an altogether different theme. The geometrical forms of the tomb announce and prepare it: the eye emerges from the tumult into a region of orderly lines, where the colours, which are put on in broad and scarcely modulated zones,

have the effect of calm following the storm. The angel confirms this sense of peace that comes over us.

His attitude and outline to some extent echo the rocky mass behind him; but whereas the mountainside is constructed of straight lines, with nail-shaped fissures opening in its flank, the angel's figure – while not letting one forget the triangle in which it is described – is filled with a network of interlaced curves. From his head to his right foot, one's glance describes a long arc, subtly related to his sinuous outlines. In the interior of the figure, the curves of the folds of drapery, together with variations of colour and light, produce a restrained sort of counterpoint, governed by the master curves.

The angel's celestial nature is likewise conveyed by the artist's use of light. He spreads it somewhat parsimoniously on the womens' robes – only on some of the folds, especially near the bottom; on the tomb it is distributed in strips – on the framework around the decorative elements; on the mountain

355   356   357

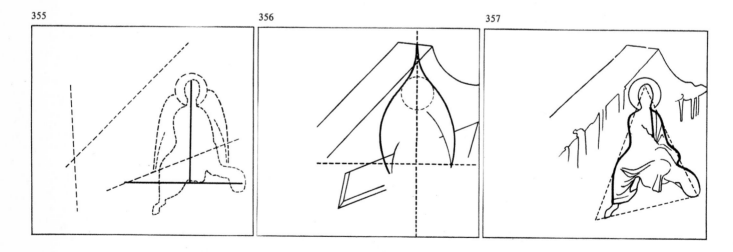

351. Duccio di Buoninsegna (1260-1318). *Maestà* (detail): *The Three Marys at the Tomb*. Siena, Opera del Duomo. Skira reproduction.

it is scattered about in small accents here and there. The great concentration of light is upon the figure of the angel, who blooms like some luminous flower between heaven and earth, the traces of celestial glory still clinging to him in the common air of here-below. One understands why, in contrast, the artist has painted the three women (apart from their haloes) as more 'opaque' than the angel; despite their sainthood, they are as yet creatures of this world, and not entitled to the luminosity which radiates from him.

Colour, too, helps to express the essence of the forms: the human nature of the three Marys is conveyed not only by this relative opacity, but also by the choice of colours, their intensity and their disposition: red, blue and violet, with green effecting the transition. But the contrast between the women and the angel is not a radical one; they also have a close degree of interrelation. Lighting and colours are combined in couples which act as intermediaries between them: a dark green and a light green, a dark blue and a light blue, a sonorous red and a violet-pink, a golden yellow and a warm brown. This pairing of light and dark tones links the angel and the holy women in a mutual pulsation of life, in contrast to which the alternations of light and dark on the mountain reverberate like a mournful, solitary echo.

To take stock of the observations made so far, we have noted that the effect of harmony is to stir our interest, our notice and our thoughts, i.e. different aspects of the mind, which do not come into play successively or systematically – as my analysis might seem to suggest – but by a series of complementary and simultaneous steps. Harmony is therefore the stimulus of a specific activity, which – in contact with works of art – is manifested in sensations, thoughts and feelings. And these are not expressed in action (as is the case in normal experience) or in reflection; *they join forces to proceed in a single direction, and carry us in that direction with all our powers of concentration.*

Let us examine this last point with reference to Duccio's picture. As we have seen, it illustrates an episode in the life of Christ, relating to the Resurrection, an iconographic theme which goes back as far as the 4th century.[1]

The painting's subject – in the narrower sense of the word – corresponds very closely to the text of the Evangelist: here are the three women, and the

angel seated on the sepulchre; behind is the mountain, sundered by the earthquake. In forms instead of words, this is the same event being described.

But, beyond the subject and what it tells us, we feel the pull of something else. Our attention is already being attracted by forms which signal to one another. Pleasure is already being roused by colours whose significance we perceive. Our mind, penetrating beyond the objects represented, is already grasping the structure which the figures form part of; and we begin to experience a complex emotion, compounded of fear and serenity. The more we look, the more clearly and surely the meaning of the work comes across to us, the more clearly and surely we apprehend it.

First, there are the three Marys, whose alarm is shown by their gestures and by their slight movement of recoil; then, the angel, who points with his finger to 'the place where they laid him' – gestures which the artist takes care not to stress too heavily. In fact, *we get to the heart of the work through the harmony of its formal constituents* rather than by the dumb show of the figures. Christ the Son of Man, whose tomb testifies to his burial by the hands of men; Christ the Son of God, whose empty tomb testifies that he is risen; Christ in all the mystery of his dual nature – the foundation-stone of Christianity – becomes a tangible presence for the spectator.

The painter proceeds deliberately by masses – of the women, of the mountain, of the tomb – in order to emphasize that the scene takes place on earth, where everything has its weight and its destiny. This terrestrial reference is stressed remarkably in the main part of the tomb, which is confined to the horizontal in every respect, and which opens towards the group of women on the left – an extension, in some sort, of their humanity.

Now consider the main axes: the group of women 358 is traversed by a diagonal, and the mountains by a diagonal in the opposite direction – the same direction as the lid of the tomb. Only the tomb itself and the angel are unaffected by this play of diagonals, the former lying in the horizontal plane and the latter in the vertical. In relation to these co-ordinates, the diagonal axes introduce an element of instability matching the startled movement of the Marys, within whose group, moreover, lie the points of intersection of these three axes. The impression of instability is heightened by the rugged surface of the highest peak and by the folds of the draperies. But, at the same time, the two diagonal axes which 359 converge on the group of women lead also in the

[1] It was only from about the 12th century onwards that painters began to represent Christ himself with a banner in his hand.

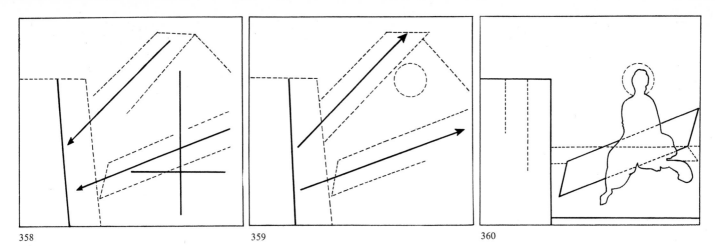

358   359   360

other direction – like the arms of a pair of compasses – towards the focus of the picture, the area illuminated by the angel's presence. The vertical axis is surrounded by curves, which – contrasting with the straight lines that enclose them – give a feeling of lightness and movement. The attitude of 360 the angel is in this respect even more suggestive: he appears to be sitting, and yet he also seems to be weightless, to be hovering 'seated' on thin air, whereas the women standing by him have their feet firmly planted on the ground. Now the posture of 356 the angel, though it is unreal, does not seem unnatural, by reason of the tension the artist has created between the triangle of mountain and the horizontal mass of the tomb – a tension which has its articulation in the oval of the wings and the circle of the aureole, and without which the lid of the tomb would lack all semblance of equilibrium. It should be 361 noted that the two parallelograms occupied by the grey slope of the mountainside and by the woman in red act also upon the lid of the tomb, firstly by echoing its shape, and secondly by establishing two oblique axes which 'redress' its balance. Thus the actual material obstacle, the slab which sealed the tomb, grows light and immaterial, and – linked with the angel's immaterial presence – becomes the visible symbol of the opening through which Christ rose from his mortal state. The metamorphosis is also powerfully alluded to by the angel's hand and wing, but even more powerful is the arc of the wing which cuts across the slab and adds to its upward thrust by introducing a suggestion of rotary movement.

Thus, despite the absence of Christ himself, the mystery of the Resurrection is accomplished before our eyes. The painter makes us share the reactions of the three holy women – fearful at first, but reassured by the angel's voice. Nature alone,

confounded by the event, is unable to bear the strain of so sublime a spectacle. Above the crannied rocks stretches the plain gold ground, which isolates the scene and establishes a proper distance between the figures and their setting, and between the spectator and the picture.

Finally, thanks to rhythm, the recognition of resemblances is no longer purely a visual matter: if one may put it this way, the eye 'imitates' the shapes which it discovers. The background plane is 362 dominated by the ternary motif of the mountains, whose rhythm gives a sense of instability due to the unequal height and spacing of the peaks. This irregularity is accentuated by differences in mass and by the unevenness of the crest-line and the various sections of rock. The counterpart to this is the rhythm (ternary also) of the holy women – but how much gentler now! The intervals are reduced; the three bodies differ only slightly in axis and mass; the colours are spread over more or less equal areas, with red and violet predominating. The womens' fear evaporates at the sound of the angel's voice. On the right-hand side the rhythmic organization is more complicated: first there is the tomb, its

361

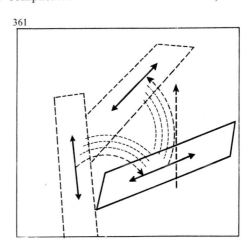

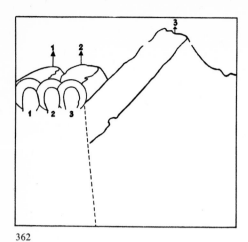

362

geometric forms reinforced by the regular and near-symmetrical rhythm of the ornamental panels. In opposition to this orderliness, which emphasizes the material weight of the tomb, is the rhythm of the angel, developing in a spiral motion about the axis of his body. The lid of the tomb, by reason of the angle at which it is tilted, shares equally in the rhythm of the tomb and in that of the angel. Thus, as the eye takes in the picture, it does so not only in the abstract but also by the measured movements which lead it from the upheaval of nature to the mingled emotions of the holy women, and from there to the miraculous poise and balance of the celestial apparition. The mystery of the Resurrection is no more an enigma, no more a problem. Though hidden still, *its reality is made accessible through the experience to which the artist invites and guides us.*

To summarize, harmony is the concord of the artist's formal relationships as experienced by the spectator. In any work of art it tends towards an intimate combination of unity and variety. It acts on us by stimulating interest and pleasure, by activating mind, intuition and sensibility, and it reveals resemblances that give us guidance. Yet this is not knowledge of an intellectual order, and cannot be reduced to ideas. Through the medium of rhythm, the mind's activity is transformed into a kind of 'imitation', by virtue of which one participates in the inner life of the work instead of simply apprising oneself of its contents. Though less precise than the intellectual kind, this kind of knowing is no less valuable. It conforms with all that is deepest in our nature, and is concerned not with reason but with direct experience.

Form and content

I embark on this chapter with certain misgivings. Under the necessity of concentrating in it the essence of all we have seen so far, I run the risk of seeming to summarize too drastically. I would ask the reader to believe that my aim is not to simplify, but to fulfil the need for a final re-orientation.

Art adopts an attitude very different from that of ordinary common sense or science. It does not look for ready-made answers like the one, or for problems in need of solution like the other. For art, man's situation in the world, the world itself and man himself, are mysteries. A work of art does not discuss or explain; it asks no questions and holds no opinions. The artist does not reduce life to formulae, nor does he apply his particular kind of knowledge to practical uses. On the contrary, he accepts the fact that existence cannot be explained, but only *revealed*, which implies *a different order of knowledge*.

A work of art is the fruit of two inventive processes, one relating to the conception – to the mystery expressed by the artist (himself a mystery, part of the wider mystery of existence), and the other relating to language – to the resources which enable him to communicate with the spectator. Thus the work addresses itself to the spectator more in the way of a poem than of a message or piece of information.

Imagine some untried actress attempting to sustain the role of Hermione in Racine's tragedy. She will scarcely have spoken the first lines of the famous soliloquy in act V:

Où suis-je? Qu'ai-je fait? Que dois-je faire encore?
Quel transport me saisit? Quel chagrin me dévore?
Errante et sans dessein, je cours dans ce palais.
Ah! ne puis-je savoir si j'aime ou si je hais?[1]

before the audience, amused by her pompous style of utterance and exaggerated gestures, bursts into laughter or hisses. But when one reproaches the poor lady for not knowing what she is saying, even though she is speaking the exact words of Racine in their correct order, one is admitting by implication that the words *do not only have the meaning that derives from their actual order in the sentence, but also a meaning that derives from something deeper, the presence of which is hidden but decisive.*

[1] *Where am I? What have I done? What should I do now? What rapture is this that fills me? What grief is this that devours me? Lost and aimless, I wander through this palace. Ah! Can I not know whether I love or hate?*

363. Ambrogio Lorenzetti (d. 1348). *A Castle by the Sea*. Siena, Pinacoteca. Photo Held.

Whether painting or poetry is in question, aesthetic revelation does not come by an act of faith or by intellectual assent, but by *an intimate response of our consciousness to the inner meaning of the work*. Unlike other branches of knowledge, art depends above all upon our ability to participate. When an actress of true calibre replaces the inadequate one, those same words and lines – which seemed so funny before – suddenly lay bare to us the tumult in Hermione's tortured heart. We are moved, we share her anguish, carried away on the conflicting waves of love and hate that struggle within her. Aesthetic emotion transforms the actress, the stage and the audience. In fact, *during the performance, I am* Hermione, though I do not cease to be myself. I suffer her torments – until the curtain falls and separates each one again in his own identity.

It is just the same with painting. Perhaps the mystery is of a different sort, and is revealed by a different route, but it is still the phenomenon of participation that gets us there. Can one imagine a more delightful landscape than this *Castle by the Sea* by Ambrogio Lorenzetti? Its charm is of a complex kind. The castle, toy-like with its tower

and its two gay splashes of red, peeps out from behind a mountain of almost lunar pallor. The trees march off like a procession of monks, each minutely characterized in its homespun habit. The dark lagoon is contrasted with the peaceful curve of the sea. The beach? There scarcely is one – just a wire-thin line. And the exquisite, almond-shaped boat that joins the land to the sea... is it hanging in air? No, but it too is imponderable. Nothing here seems to obey the law of gravity. There are no roots to these trees, no foundations to this castle. As for the pathway, there is nothing to anchor it to the ground, not even the fields – spread out like pieces of cloth – through which it passes. Yet it does not give the impression of floating loose, any more than the mountains do.

One is tempted to call it freakish, but one soon changes one's mind. Deliberately and with precision, Ambrogio Lorenzetti constructs a landscape which, though free of the effects of gravity, is subject to a rigorous inner logic. In a space where the planes tend to be superimposed, but where there is also a mild effect of depth, the objects are grouped as delicately as birds – so dematerialized that one could almost expect them to take wing. *The truth is that their centre of gravity lies elsewhere.* And that is how the painter's mystic vision becomes a *reality* to the spectator. Stripped of their material aspect, and leaving behind all such mundane attributes as distinctive planes, sunlight or atmosphere, the objects are depicted in a new world. This landscape – in which trees have no shadows, in which land and sea meet but do not mingle, in which the colours are sombre and neutral on the low ground but brighten upon the heights in a supernatural light that seeks only the hill-tops – surely it is addressed rather to the soul than to the eye.

How inadequate the term 'content' is, to describe what we have just seen; the image it evokes is quite inappropriate, for a work of art is not a receptacle. Furthermore, it falsifies the relationships of the work both to its own meaning and to the spectator. If one discards this image, the term is still unsatisfactory: the content of a decree is the sum of its provisions, which leaves us once more with a quantitative concept. *In art, content* (we must continue to use the word, for want of another) *means something quite different, and implies a quite different attitude on the part of the spectator.*

It is not something tangible, but a sign – or rather, a whole series of signs which direct colours and forms towards a reality that the spectator becomes progressively aware of as he is led to feel the existence of something beyond his immediate perceptions. Thus in painting (and in the other arts, for that matter) the word 'content' has a special meaning. It signifies what is *represented* in the picture, *and* what the picture means; that which one sees, the outward appearance, *and* that which is invisible; the two *together* constituting the essential reality of the work.

According to Kant, reality lies beyond all possible experience. *In art it exists only by virtue of a possible experience – aesthetic experience, that is to say, which has as its material the work of art, its mode of expression and its inward character.* Beware of the false idea that the reality of a work consists of what we see when we look at it simply as an object. The reality dwells in a borderline area where fact and imagination, the visible and the invisible, are united. This is the area of human expression – of language. Reality in art belongs both to the tangible world and to the world of the consciousness, and it is revealed through 'symbol-images'. Its 'exterior' face refers to common reality, in which objects are to be perceived and distinguished from one another;

its 'interior' face refers to that deeper reality in which objects can point towards some particular and perceptible significance.

Separate objects, when merely added together, are never anything more than a sum of separate objects. When abstracted by intellectual processes, they are no more than concepts or categories. Only when raised to the condition of a work of art can they be joined in a *superior unity*.

Art is not to be included among the marginal or supplementary activities of man. Fundamentally it represents his effort to convert the diverse materials of nature into language, a heroic and awe-inspiring enterprise which translates the image of things into expression, helps us towards the heart of the mystery of what and where we are, and – without altogether solving that mystery – discovers a meaning in it that we can accept.

Bruegel's *Hunters in the Snow* depicts a winter scene, which at first glance appears to contain nothing out of the ordinary. But let us now carefully note the successive stages in our contemplation of it. In the first stage we are only concerned with seeing what it represents: three hunters, followed by their dogs; to the left, some people busy round a fire; in the distance, a landscape spread out beneath a group of rocky peaks, under a cold and lowering sky; to the right, tiny figures – walking, sliding and skating on some frozen ponds. Scattered trees and snow-mantled roofs remind us that this is a countryside of peasant villages. On this preliminary level, our pleasure consists of taking note of the subject. 364

But – and this is the second stage – another feeling comes over us gradually as we look at the picture. These hunters, trees and houses, this sky and the snow, are not presented merely as objects. We ourselves are linked with them in some way that we do not immediately understand; the scene is no longer just something to look at from outside; we begin to penetrate into it, as if we are able not only to identify the various objects but also, in some sort, *to identify ourselves with them.* We discover that this world is our world also, that we are one with the huntsmen, with the trees and the snowy peaks. The picture changes in our consciousness: the objects in it are transmuted into symbols which cause us to share in the destiny of these weary men and their exhausted dogs, to breathe with them this air so rarefied by cold.

Finally, in the third stage, this participation crystallizes in a sense of significance. In this landscape, where we see life adapting itself to the season (people skate, carry wood, return from hunting, attend to their work), one's glance cannot help following the dominant direction which is indicated by the hunters' line of march, and emphasized by the orientation of the row of trees. The cold now ceases to be merely a seasonal phenomenon, and gradually assumes the magnitude of an elemental force. It is pointless for life to go on, for it is stricken with sterility; men skate, but they are like puny insects on the ice; the huntsmen return to their homes, yet they are but shadows struggling step by step; even the famished-looking dogs have the air of a funeral escort. Here we are at the heart of the mystery that runs all through the picture, and we must attempt to formulate it: winter forces man and nature into a pitiless isolation, of which the black bird in full flight seems like a mocking emblem. At the end of this stage, revelation has come; our souls unite with the artist's in the same insight of frozen desolation.

We owe this penetration of the mystery to the efficacy of the language which is produced when the artist succeeds in making his plastic resources work together in unison. In the presence of Bruegel's picture one cannot but recognize, firstly that the impression of frozen desolation is felt as *true*, and secondly that it is not due to actual contact with nature. Thus the reality of this desolation, which is not actually present, entails *the transformation of image into symbol, and of symbol into a tangible presence*. In fact, the artist directs his efforts not to perfecting an image of winter, but to expressing his feelings about such a landscape under snow. Thus, the analogy in every work of art does not refer to something outside the work, but always to the language in which it is couched.

Bruegel, a master of pictorial equivalence, employs a uniformly cold range of colours, dominated by white, which seems here to suggest the smooth hardness of a metal carapace rather than the softness of snow. Against this white, the blackish tints of the trees, the skaters and the birds form a contrast which intensifies the brilliancy of the carapace and also its inhuman quality. The greenish-grey steel of sky and ponds completes the transformation of the landscape into a kind of desert, in which men – and birds, too – are prisoners of the cold. The warmer browns of the houses, and the flames of the fire, remind us that there is still a remnant left of life; but, in face of the immensity of the frozen wilderness, this remnant seems pitifully feeble. The trees, in their rigidity, emulate the mountain peaks, while the bushes – like balls of cotton-wool – struggle in vain against the petrifaction of winter. Finally, the silence which here reigns supreme does not moderate the isolation of the forms, but emphasizes it.

Now, in spite of the feelings of sadness and desolation which the picture evokes, it is a pleasure to contemplate it. However paradoxical this may seem, we require a picture to move us – to tears, if need be – if we are to admire it. *To a great extent, aesthetic pleasure is due to the fact that the language of art is felt as an agent of communion and fulfilment.*

This is where the ultimate aspect of this strange pleasure emerges, though we can only glance at it briefly. Not only are objects transformed into symbol-images, but, in the course of this metamorphosis, the artist arranges them in regular relationships. A picture, like a poem, obeys laws – not fixed laws, but laws that are *inwardly and reciprocally imperative*. It must be understood that this does not mean that it submits to external rules; it means that a discipline is observed in the creative process, linking its elements analogously to the same hidden reality, so that they all combine to express it. They are rules of appropriateness more than anything else.

We have seen, for instance, how the frame plays a decisive part in relation to the work's construction. The *Hunters in the Snow* gives us a horizontal rectangle in which the ratio of the shorter sides to the longer is roughly 1.0:1.4.

In the vertical sense, it forms two more rectangles, 365 the right-hand one with sides roughly in the ratio 1.0:1.3, and the left-hand one with sides in the ratio 1.0:1.5.

Horizontally, the surface is divided into four 366 rectangles. In the lower pair we find again the ratios of 1.0:1.3 (for the left-hand one) and 1.0:1.5 (for the right-hand one). In the upper pair of rectangles the ratios are 1.0:1.3 (the right-hand one) and 1.0:1.2 (the left-hand one).

Two diagonals pass through the lower rectangles, 367 one indicating the direction of the hunters' progress, the other forming the edge of the snow-covered slope in the foreground.

By their proportions, these rectangles contribute to the articulation of the surface according to the degree of depth that the artist wishes to suggest, and not according to the mechanical requirements of perspective. The lower right-hand rectangle, with its accent on horizontality, strengthens the impres-

364. Pieter Bruegel the Elder (1525/30-1569). *Hunters in the Snow*. Vienna, Kunsthistorisches Museum. Photo Meyer K.G.

sion of emptiness which is evoked by the frozen ponds. The one above it, based on the less elongated ratio of 1.0:1.3, is adapted to the stabilizing motif of the peaks on the horizon. The pendant to this area is the lower left-hand rectangle, in which the huntsmen stumble onwards. To balance the impression of emptiness in the right-hand part of the landscape, the upper left-hand rectangle is almost square in proportion (1.0: 1.2), thus stressing the vertical thrust of the three large trees. This partitioning of the surface, in agreement with the distribution of space in depth, obeys the inner logic by which each element conditions all the rest.

Where rhythm is concerned, one can hardly fail to be struck by the rhythms – ternary in each instance – of the skeletal trees and the hunters. Every element in these rhythmic combinations is strongly accentuated, first by the respective positions of the 'downbeats', and then by their contrast with the rest of the picture. Thanks to this treatment, we are made fully aware of the isolation of figures and objects. In addition, the two oblique axes of the row of trees and the line of march of the huntsmen clarifies our impressions in this sense – immobility, caused by separation and isolation, is not natural to creatures or to things, but results as a tragic necessity when life is suddenly struck by the paralysis of winter.

Pictorial language, then, consists of relationships of colours, forms, lines and lighting, with this peculiarity – *that these relationships owe their existence and significance to the mutual interactions which they set up in the work's interior economy.* As an ensemble of symbol-images, painting guides us towards a reality of the profoundest kind, but – and this is of capital importance – we must take the first step ourselves. Intuition, however highly developed, only becomes effective when it enters into the spirit of the formal language employed. Formal – or plastic – language is the painter's only means of getting his symbols to accord with one another, and to unite in a single, homogeneous expression. For the spectator it provides the only means of access to the significance and value of the work, in that it imposes a 'disciplined vision', without which the unity of the work would escape him, and aesthetic pleasure would be only partially attained.

As soon as we approach a poem or picture, our consciousness comes into action. We aspire to penetrate into the work, and we ignore all that surrounds it, concentrating upon it alone. This involves a change from our normal *behaviour.* Reading a poem gives a new rhythm to one's breathing, a new intonation to one's voice and a new direction to one's imagination – in short, one embarks upon an experience of which each line establishes a particular condition, and the poem as a whole establishes the general condition. Although the equivalent phenomenon in painting is less obvious, it is of the same kind. The eye does not penetrate to the heart of the work at the first glance,

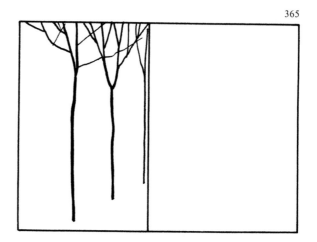

365

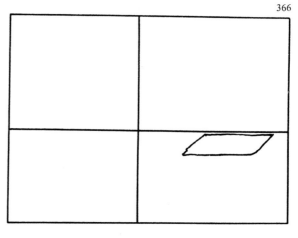

366

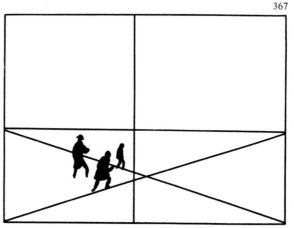

367

but arrives there by a series of evolutions that are suggested by its lines and forms. In this way the spectator comes to *know* the picture, not merely in terms of an image of something represented, but – beyond the mere image – *in terms of the regulated movement of the forms and colours which constitute it.*

Racine's lines require that the actor should put himself into the appropriate mood to speak them, that he should apprehend their fullest significance by paying due respect to their intonation. In just the same way, a work of art requires that the spectator should apprehend its quality by paying due respect to its style. Reading a poem or looking at a picture is a sort of 'dance' – with the poet or painter as choreographer. To go through the movements of the dance until the climax of revelation is reached – this is the height of aesthetic pleasure.

What results from all this, as the reader will have guessed already, is that *the reality of the content,* and therefore also its *quality* on the artistic plane, do not depend upon the presumed intentions of the artist, nor upon his submission to some religious, moral or philosophical rule, nor upon his obedience to any ideal, programme or school, nor upon reference to some 'nature', 'supernature' or fiction, but upon *truth of form.*

Perhaps this is where the secret of beauty should be sought. Beauty is not to be defined; but instead of searching for it obstinately and vainly in such-and-such a type of work, or in such-and-such a theory or criterion, it is surely better and more reasonable to see it in the indissoluble union which the artist establishes between that which he expresses and his manner of expressing it. This is the only field of true discovery for the spectator; and it is living, active discovery because he enters into the spirit of a language whose meanings and resources of expression he can share. Such is the outcome of our quest, but not of our enterprise. If they are to be useful, the conclusions we have reached must be put to the test, so that we can establish valid conditions for their application.

Application, studies
of individual works

Aesthetic evaluation

It is to this end that all my endeavours in this book have been directed. Art exists only through *works* of art, and it is through them that humanity assumes the forms of civilization. Go to the works themselves, refer back to them – this is an imperative that simply cannot be ignored.

Everyone agrees on this point; yet there are innumerable differences of opinion as to the *way* in which works of art should be approached and understood. For the benefit of the sceptics who judge the task to be impossible, I have done my best to demonstrate – in the first part of the book – that most divergences of opinion result not so much from the works themselves as from a variety of prejudices which, often without our realizing it, prevent us from respecting their particular nature.

Aesthetic understanding *is* attainable – even though it is unrelated to other kinds of knowledge, even though beauty defies all attempts at definition and there are no fixed criteria to go by – and the purpose of the second and third parts of the book has been to show under what conditions it is attainable.

Contrary to what is naïvely (not to say complacently) supposed, a work of art never reveals itself in its entirety to a single inspection. Each time one looks at it, some new aspect comes to light, and it will only yield up all its secrets to long and patient contemplation. This effort of penetration cannot be left to chance. Mind and sensibility both want to be guided; otherwise we drift from one impression, intuition or idea to another, without ever being able to gather them all into a coherent whole. To fathom a work of art, one does not have to follow a strict itinerary, but one must adopt an appropriate 'gait' – a real discipline that cannot be ignored without loss. Aesthetic evaluation, as I mean it, is neither an analysis nor a rule-of-thumb, but a *method of knowing*.

Now that we have examined, one by one, the principal factors involved, let us see how they work when we apply ourselves to the particular study of a few outstanding pictures. That is the object of this fourth part of the book.

The merits of a method can only be judged in practice. I do not pretend that the studies which follow are perfect, or that they should be considered as models of their kind. I merely hope that they may be of some use to the reader by showing him the application of those principles which the three previous sections have attempted to establish on a firm foundation.

Perhaps my choice of works may seem surprising. Originally, I intended to include a detailed study of one picture representative of each of the great periods of art, a project which I saw to be less and less practicable as I proceeded with the drafting of the book (it would have called for several volumes!). Therefore I have put this task by for the future, and have confined myself to a selection of paintings which, with the one exception of Titian's *Venus and the Organ-Player,* are all examples of modern art. Modern art, after all, is what people are most reticent about, and so it seems worth-while to concentrate on that, by way of tackling the problem fairly and squarely. The modern pictures we shall study are: *Le Moulin de la Galette,* by Renoir; *The Church at Auvers,* by Van Gogh; *Guernica,* by Picasso; *Movement,* by Kandinsky. Abstract art is not forgotten.

Each of these studies is treated in three phases: the first briefly places the artist in the context of his life and times; the second provides the background to the work itself; the third and most important phase is the aesthetic evaluation of the work, and the first two merely lead up to this.

Contact with works of art is what really matters. No-one can doubt that this is true; and it is also true that in agreeing upon a method of appreciating their worth we can help to bring some order into the confusion that generally prevails. Our love of art can gain by being founded upon reasons and practices that have been tested and proved valid by common consent and in a common desire for truth.

Titian

Venus and the Organ-Player

Titian

'Italian painting interests many of us more than the painting of any other school not because of its essential superiority, but because it expressed the Renaissance; and Venetian painting is interesting above all because it was at Venice alone that this expression attained perfection.'[1] This statement of Berenson's is perhaps a little extravagant. Nevertheless, it exemplifies a state of affairs that is virtually incontestable – that the Renaissance is still of major importance to us, and that Venice played a major part in bringing about the changes in thought and feeling that accompanied it. It is also incontestable that Giorgione, Titian, Tintoretto and Veronese stand in the front rank of the painters who acquired for Venice her pre-eminent position, since all four of them played their part in revealing the lyrical powers of colour to the western world.

Through the rediscovery of antiquity during the Renaissance era, painting – which for centuries had been subjected to the requirements of the Christian faith – responded to new needs and aspirations of mankind, and was led to adopt new themes and new techniques. Turning gradually from fresco to oil, it took up its abode in the sanctuary, transforming the character and spirit of those who dwelt there. As often as not, it turned its back on the holy places to enter private homes in the shape of easel-pictures, on which nobles and merchants prided themselves as they prided themselves on their wealth or on the splendour of their cities.

Titian's output was so vast, and his reputation – even in his own life-time – so great, that legend soon made of him the patriarch of painting, and (with the aid of some juggling with dates) even conferred on him the title of centenarian! Modern scholars have reduced this span to more human proportions, but – surprisingly enough – they have paid back in works what they took from him in years. While they have established that he was born somewhere between 1480 and 1490 (instead of 1476/77, as previously believed), many works that were formerly attributed to Giorgione or other artists have been recognized as his.

Titian did work for Venice, for the Emperor Charles V and his son Philip II, for the Farnese Pope Paul III, for the Duke of Mantua, the Duke of Ferrara, and all the great ones of the age. We have from his hand both religious and secular compositions, portraits, engravings and frescoes, but it was above all as a painter in oils that his genius was

---

[1] Bernard Berenson, *The Italian Painters of the Renaissance*.

expressed – and has been preserved in the principal galleries of the world. The Prado is fortunate in possessing several of the master's most beautiful works.

'The nude' figures fairly prominently in Titian's immense output of paintings. He often returned to this theme, doubtless because he liked to paint feminine beauty, doubtless also because this was the taste of his patrons. Indeed, Renaissance taste shows an equal predilection for works of religious inspiration and works with a more secular appeal.

But although Titian painted many a Venus, it is remarkable to note that their poses differ very little; as Hourticq has observed, they belong to three main types: that of the *Dresden Venus*,[1] to which is related the celebrated *Venus of Urbino*; that of the sleeping nymph in the *Bacchanal*, to which is related the *Venus and the Organ-Player* in Madrid; and finally that of the *Danaë* in Naples.

The picture we are going to study belongs to the second type. According to Tietze it dates from about 1545; it is a large canvas ($53^3/_4$ by 87 inches), painted in oil, and it is in the Prado at Madrid.

[1] Many distinguished art-historians consider the *Dresden Venus* to be partly or entirely the work of Giorgione.

368. Titian (1480/90-1576). *Sleeping Venus*. Dresden, Staatliche Gemäldegalerie. Photo Staatliche Gemäldegalerie.

369. Titian (1480/90-1576). *Bacchanal,* detail. Madrid, Prado. Photo Held.

370. Titian (1480/90-1576). *Danaë*. Naples, Museum. Photo Anderson.

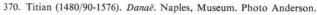

37

371. Titian (1480/90-1576). *Venus and the Organ-Player*. Madrid, Prado. Photo Held.

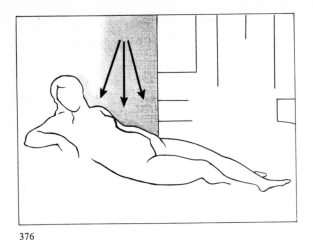

376

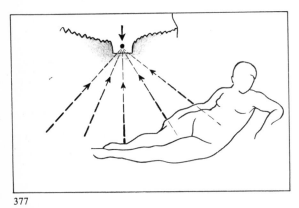

377
378

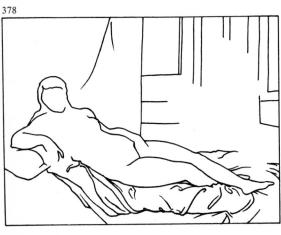

372. Titian (
Photo Held.

371 Venus a

Study of

This bel(
referred to
woman of m
left, dressed
elegant mu:
turned towa
the music, s(
which rears
squirrel. Bey
– a view ov(
among the s
hinds, and a
distance are

379

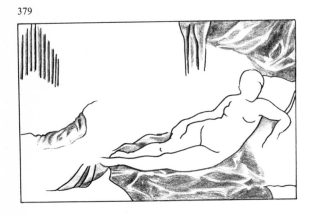

380

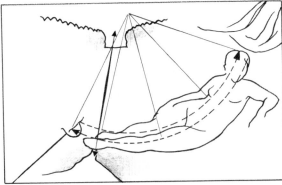

into which the spectator's eye is drawn – a movement made all the more definite by a number of symmetrical 'signposts' (for instance, the musician's nose and the hanging fold of curtain are the same distance from the left and right edges of the canvas respectively). Thanks to this organization, the two poles are not static; the sliding motion of the surface composition causes us to turn continuously from one to the other. In this way the artist has contrived to modify our mode of perception: the Uffizi picture is like an altar consecrated to the grace of youth; the picture in the Prado is more like a reliquary, in the penumbra of which the spectator may discern the sumptuous reflection of autumnal beauty.

The spatial organization of the painting is equally revealing. The right-hand side of the Uffizi picture opens on to a room which is defined geometrically by its walls and window. This prevalence of geometry and straight lines in the décor stresses, by contrast, the supple harmony of the nude, at the same time suggesting, by analogy, its firm internal structure. The treatment of the Prado picture is altogether different: instead of acting as a foil, the background draws the eye into a space of indeterminate depth; instead of asserting her presence through isolation in the foreground plane, Venus is here more self-effacing, in that she yields to the pull of the distant vista.

This has an additional effect. Whereas in the Uffizi painting Venus is confined to a single room, in the Prado picture she occupies a space that takes in the whole park – even to the horizon where the sun is setting: in the one, the space is concentrated to harmonize with the compact forms of the nude; in the other, the open space corresponds to the nude's ampler proportions.

There is the same concern for appositeness in the treatment of accessories. In the *Venus of Urbino,* the curtain is only slightly ruffled in the centre – flexed,

375

376

377

378

380

one might almost say, like a muscle – and the folds of the sheet succeed one another in a tight network, each marked by a definite ridge, like a series of ligaments. The red couch is covered with a smooth fabric, the decorative motif of which conveys the feeling of a fine and firm material.

379 The accessories in the Prado *Venus* are quite different in character. The stiff hanging gives place to a curtain with heavy, billowing folds, the sheet to a sumptuous coverlet – a broad surge of velvet, which sweeps in and dies away in the lapping surf of white linen; the fabric of the couch itself is no longer visible. In each picture, the accessories vary in accordance with the type of Venus; in the one, they accentuate formal structure, in the other, they accentuate musical structure, as if the objects themselves partake of their nature. For the same reason, in the Prado picture, the long broad folds of the pillow and sheet prolong the body of Venus at its two extremities, just as the curtain and coverlet extend it on either side. Organ-pipes, trees and the courtier's sleeve all contribute to this general harmony.

What pains Titian takes to make us feel this grace and charm of ripeness! One cannot fail to remark the soft, milky light which glows at the horizon, and is so tenderly reflected on the surface of the distant water. The late-season sun distils a light which, having touched on the organ-pipes and the musician's sleeve, seems to gather and concentrate in the goddess's body, enveloping rather than delineating it. A comparison with the *Venus of Urbino* will make clear the difference. In the latter, the light accompanies each part of the body like a pure melody, with every note separate: the head, the bosom, the stomach, the legs. The light in the Madrid picture is far less plainly articulated: instead of detailing the various parts of the body, it tends on the contrary to fuse them. Anatomical detail disappears in favour of generalized form.

With the intention, no doubt, of enhancing this effect, the artist has taken certain liberties. He has eliminated the indentation above the hip on the right-hand side of the nude, so that the bust and torso descend in a single flowing curve, which is continued along the leg. This is a pose which emphasizes the width of the torso, consolidates the lower part of the body, and – by stiffening the outlines – compensates for its inward relaxation.

380 The spectator's gaze swings back and forth like a pendulum along the curve of the body, to be checked at one extreme by the heavy brocade of the curtain above the goddess's head, and at the other by the cavalier's sword. In the course of this movement it links – on either side – the light of the horizon and the highlights along the folds of the coverlet. The *Venus of Urbino* invites the eye to pass over her as if along the crest-line of a hill, whereas the Prado Venus suggests a more devious course, with all the charms of a garden-walk (it is surely not mere chance that Titian has painted a park in the background). The receding angle of the right elbow is balanced by the projection of the knee, just as the empty space of the landscape vista balances the volume of the body.

In the *Venus of Urbino,* which celebrates the goddess in the form of a youthful woman, the colours are candidly juxtaposed, differentiating between one object and the next, so that the nude glows in its triumphant flesh-tints between the blue-green of the hanging and the red of the serving-maid, enclosed in a web of meticulous draughtsmanship. There are fewer colours in the Prado *Venus*; involved as they are in the play of light and shade, they mingle to create a coloured atmosphere, dominated by a russet hue which sometimes verges upon red, and sometimes upon greenish-blue. It is an autumnal atmosphere in which colours lose their individual identities, and objects lose their precise outlines. Line, which plays such a predominant role in the Uffizi picture, is of secondary importance, and the colours have to rely more on their own resources, on their thermal values. Thus the bright-burning flame of the *Venus of Urbino* turns in the Prado picture to a glowing ember, incandescent still in the reds of the curtain and coverlet, while – at a distance from the hearth – deep blues mingle stealthily with the greens of the garden trees. Warm and cold colours alike are tempered by the pervading russet, which has a 'deadening' effect on them, although, to avoid their being too thoroughly blunted, the painter has scattered touches of colour here and there, such as the turquoise stripe on the musician's breeches.

One can now, perhaps, more fully appreciate the way Titian has established his forms within a chromatic structure. They do not depend upon linear design or perspective, but grow out of the actual manipulation of colour, enriched by chiaroscuro. This is made quite clear when one comes to examine the modelling, which is neither mechanical nor consistent. On the periphery of the nude figure 381 it is very subdued, but one is rather more conscious of it in the middle of the body, from below the breasts to the thighs, and on the right side of the torso. One finds it again, though very differently treated, in the folds of material, the organ-pipes and the trees in the park, but – and this is a remarkable thing – it conveys less the suggestion of volume than that of rhythm, thus also serving a dynamic purpose.

In the *Venus of Urbino,* the weight and solidity of the nude are made evident by drawing and modelling, also by the serving-women, who echo the mass of the column, and by the little dog asleep on the bedclothes. In the Prado picture, the effect of solidity is modified so as to fit in with the melodic movement of the work as a whole. When one thinks about it, the pose of this Venus is highly unrealistic. The Uffizi Venus seems really to be *lying on* her couch, while she of the Prado has more the air of being placed lightly over the coverlet, in which her body makes no apparent impression. One could almost go so far as to say that she seems to be suspended between the folds of the curtain and those of the coverlet, between those of the pillow and those of the bedding, as if held by springs. This
381 effect of lightness is aided by the little dog, which is painted virtually without modelling, and stands up on its hind legs like a decorative motif intended to support the goddess's torso. The musician's pose is equally unnatural. The twist of his body flattens the shoulders in a manner that is made the more obvious by the treatment of his back in a flat tone relieved only by the chevrons of yellow and brown.
382 Of the same nature, though differently handled, is the painting of his breeches; here Titian very cleverly uses the slashes in the material to produce something of an optical illusion: the breeches give an impression of roundness and volume, but without the sense of weight that would be conveyed if the modelling were obtained by conventional shading.

These are distortions of natural appearance that one might not notice unless one was on the look-out for them, but they show up clearly when one refers again to the *Venus of Urbino.* Needless to say, they are deliberate distortions, their purpose being to ensure that Venus, the musician and the dog – relieved of apparent weight – may take full part in the evocative music of the work.

Note, too, how the artist links his forms, not only by diffusing a dominant tint and a dominant tone-value throughout the picture, but also by means of
381 careful transitional passages at those points where they tend to emerge. For instance, when one follows the outline of the nude, one notices a crimson or pinkish hue running round it – visible from close to,

381. Titian. *Venus and the Organ-Player,* detail.

382. Titian. *Venus and the Organ-Player,* detail.

but not from a distance – and this makes it a zone of interpenetration rather than a clear-cut line of demarcation. The method is somewhat different on the organ-player's sleeve, though the purpose is the same: the material is gathered into a series of wrinkled highlights, which seem to hang in a void when seen from close to, but which give the impression, from a proper distance, of being securely hooked on to and *into* the background.

There is yet another way in which the artist binds his forms to one another. When one looks closely at the colours of the coverlet, the curtain, the musician's doublet or the far end of the park, one finds that they are echoed by complementary tints which permeate them in an effect like that of 'watered' silk. Purplish reds emerge through sombre blues, and ephemeral blues play over the surface of the reds. The painting thus acquires a kind of translucency which penetrates its depths and gives it a crystalline quality, though without the rigidity of crystal. The colours therefore seem mobile, ready to quiver at the smallest breeze.

The *Venus of Urbino* is like some idol upon which our eyes linger, delighted and in unbroken silence. The right-hand side of the picture does not disturb this contemplation, but – like the serving-maids, the little dog and the pot of flowers in the window – serves as a temporary resting-place for the spectator's attention. What Titian understood so admirably in the Prado *Venus* was that he could not possibly present her in the same type of setting as the Uffizi picture; and by a stroke of genius he made a virtue – indeed, an expression of the profoundest truth – out of necessity. The goddess has received from the artist's hands the 'veils' to which his respectful adoration entitles her. We have noted already how he arranges the surfaces in coulisses, how he distributes light and shadow, and how he subdues the colours. Thus far, one could suppose that this is a matter of straightforward consideration, a reserve due to the subject; but this is not the case. With age, new charms come into being, and these are what the artist endeavours to convey. The Uffizi picture is like a mirror, showing us the female nude in the still perfection of her beauty. In the Prado *Venus,* the mirror is exchanged for the multiple cadences of music. The objects no longer 'contract' into formal perfection, but 'expand', and in doing so are not weakened, but draw fresh vitality from their reverberations – like so many echoes – in one another. It is a miracle of rhythm, with the full-blown grace of Venus as its source.

The most obvious point of departure, leading the eye into the composition from the left edge of the painting, is to be found in the organ-pipes. Their bright reflections play an ascending and descending scale, which leads on into the park, where the trees repeat the theme in muted tones. Based on this firm rhythm, which continues to the horizon, are two principal groups of relationships, one of them formed by the curtain, and the other – its concomitant – by the coverlet. The first contains – like sustained musical notes – the three red and pink folds which fan out above Venus's head, and to which the musician's sleeve and breeches, together with the goddess's foot, form a pendant at the other end of the diagonal. The second contains the irregular folds of the coverlet, which have their pendant – at the extremity of the other diagonal – in the disciplined ranks of organ-pipes and trees. Finally, in the interior of this space with its interlocking harmonies and rhythms, there is the unfolding melody of the body of Venus, which completes the composition by giving it its timbre and resonance. Music is not treated here as a mere pastime; it is the very essence of the work. And yet the artist makes us feel this by purely plastic means. Titian does not only divert our attention from the marks of age in the nude body, but – by composition, colour and lighting – he directs it towards a Venus whose charm is musical.

We no longer think of demanding the simple integrity of a younger body; on the contrary, we are captivated by the harmony which emanates from her, and by the orchestral consort which she forms with the musician and the décor. In one picture, beauty is offered to our gaze, unadorned; in the other, it is transformed into melody, and touches that chord within us where the pleasures of seeing and hearing meet and mingle.

383

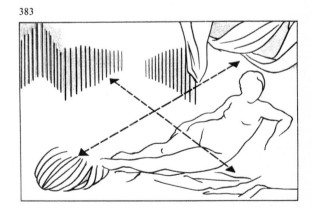

315

The material of which the picture is made plays its part in this effect. On the under-sides of the forms there are gleams which make the light seem here diffused and there transparent, as if it were present in the pigment itself. The paint is laid on in a thin film, which thickens slightly in the interior of the forms, and thins out at their edges, so that the grain of the canvas is visible in places.

However, one must not think of it as an insubstantial thing. The colours which construct the picture are solidly applied. We have already seen the part played by the structural rectangles. As for the rhythm of the work, that is based on the axis of the figures: on the axis of the musician, which is a straight line, and on the axis of the nude, which is a curve; the whole picture space is developed around these in rhythmic waves.

The two figures are linked in addition by an arabesque line which starts from the musician's hand on the keyboard, runs round him, starts again at Venus's leg and ends in the lap-dog's tail. This line describes two great curves like successive waves – the abrupt, breaking wave of the musician and the gentler, rolling wave of the Venus – which provide the vital energy of the painting.

Christianity had reduced the nude to an abstract symbol of original sin. In liberating it from this, the Renaissance restored it to its ancient vigour. Often, too, the Renaissance gave it mythological associations; but apart from such symbolism, which belongs to the period and can be ignored, it is true to say that the nude is still in our own day a fervent song of praise to the glory of womankind, of beauty, and – beyond that – of all nature.

Among the hymns of this kind that have risen in chorus from Italy, few are as splendid as those of Venice. It is to the honour of Giorgione, Titian, Veronese and Tintoretto that they transformed Eve into a matchless Aphrodite, and an art that was in danger of losing its way in imitative techniques into a miracle of visual poetry. Nothing in Titian's long career is more moving than his quest for feminine beauty, a quest that was interrupted from time to time, but to which he kept returning until the very end of his life. This particular hymn to the charms of ripened age – veiled already by the mists of autumn, but full of a secret music that emanates as from a fruit that has been long in the sun – is perhaps one of the most marvellous products of his hand. Itself a garden of light and shadow, the woman's body is revealed to the mysterious park, where – in the soft light of sunset – life has the grave mellowness of the organ's notes, and the tender thoughtfulness of its silences.

Renoir

Le Moulin de la Galette

Renoir

Note on Impressionism

There is something rather piquant in the fact that people have now become so accustomed to Impressionism, which was greeted with howls of derision when it first appeared, that they invoke its authority to refute those painters who still want to do something new. However, there is no need for us to get involved in that argument! The impressionist generation, as is well known, consists of Pissarro, Manet, Degas, Cézanne, Sisley, Monet, Bazille, Guillaumin, Berthe Morisot and Renoir, all born between 1830 and 1841. Concerning the famous exhibition of 1874 all has been told, including the story of how these reckless painters were christened 'impressionists' by the journalist Leroy (in *Charivari,* 25 April 1874) after a picture by Monet entitled *Impression: soleil levant.* Though coined derisively, the word 'impressionism' very soon covered itself with glory.

Generally speaking, there have been two lines of critical approach to these painters. On one side, books such as *De la loi du contraste simultané,* published by Chevreul in 1839, and *Les Phénomènes de la Vision* by David Sutter, which appeared in 1880, together with numerous polemical writings by other authors, have tended to harden into a point of view which sees Impressionism as a school founded upon scientific – and scientifically demonstrable – principles. In opposition to this, many historians deny that Impressionism ever had any real existence as an artistic doctrine, and concern themselves simply with 'impressionists', using the term simply as one of convenience. In their eyes, it is an appellation which covers as many individual destinies as there were painters.

Leaving all such theoretical discussion on one side, I shall limit myself to the statement (which anyone may easily verify for himself) that there are obvious points of resemblance in the works of this period, even though one cannot prove the existence of any scientific system on which they were all based. Even if we take Impressionism to mean only a temporary association among certain artists, it nevertheless has distinctive characteristics to which each of those artists made his personal contribution, producing thereby not a 'movement', as is so often said, but the living art of an epoch.

384. Auguste Renoir (1841-1919). *La Loge.* London, Courtauld Institute.

Renoir

There are numerous anecdotes concerning Renoir, many of them so indelicate that tradition has adorned his ageing features with the goatee of a satyr. Born at Limoges in 1841, he started life in the humble employment of painting flowers on plates. Influenced first by Courbet, he was later associated with Monet, and – being soon converted to Impressionism – he took part in the exhibition of 1874 at Nadar's rooms off the Rue des Capucines. On that occasion, Albert Wolf, writing in *Le Figaro*, made the following comments on *La Loge* and *La Danseuse* – both of which are now among the gems of the Courtauld collection: 'Try explaining to M. Renoir that a woman's torso is not a heap of decomposing flesh, with green and purplish patches that denote the state of complete putrefaction in a corpse!... Some people burst out laughing in front of these things; as for me, I find them harrowing...'[1] Young and active, Renoir gave free rein to his genius, but differed from his companions in that he preferred portraits and figure compositions to landscape. A visit to Italy in 1881 marks a turning-point in his career. His discovery (at the age of forty) of the great Renaissance painters, and of Raphael in particular, made a great impact on him. Giving precedence to draughtsmanship, he subjected his art to a discipline which at times had a somewhat cramping effect on it. But this experience, which lasted about fifteen years, paved the way for its final flowering, when Renoir reverted to a style in which colour is supreme, and entered on the period of his great nudes, which – in spite of the hostility with which they were received – now rank as his most glorious achievements. In love with women and with painting, and far removed from the metaphysical preoccupations of our times, Renoir seems to proclaim man's right to live his life in the sun, and to find it good.

Le Moulin de la Galette

Among all the abundance of impressionist pictures, *Le Moulin de la Galette* is one of the most completely successful; Jean Cassou did not hesitate to describe it as 'the finest of all'. Its merits are of such a sort that to acclaim it as a masterpiece is to pay homage to Impressionism, and even to Monet, who inspired the artist to paint it.

It was painted during the summer of 1876, and – contrary to what one might suppose – it was painted from life, in the open air.

According to Georges Rivière,[1] who knew it well: 'The Moulin de la Galette made no pretensions to luxury... The dance-hall was built of wood, painted a hideous green, which the passage of time had happily obliterated to some extent. At the far end of this room there was a platform reserved for the band, which was composed of a dozen or so poor devils, condemned to blow into their instruments for eight hours every Sunday.

'Beyond the platform there was a garden, or rather a courtyard, planted with stunted acacias, and furnished with benches and tables. Its gravelly surface was firm enough for dancing on in summer, when the dance-hall was open on all sides ... The Moulin was a popular resort of the working-class families of Montmartre. Parents and younger children installed themselves at the tables, eating *galette* and drinking wine or beer, while the girls danced madly until dinner-time.'

Of the circumstances in which the picture was painted, and the models for its principal figures, Rivière has this to tell us: 'The people who appear in the picture used to join us at the Moulin, and we were often quite a large party. The girl seated on the bench in the foreground was Estelle, the sister of Jeanne; Lamy, Goeneutte and myself are seated at the table, with glasses of our usual grenadine. Gervex, Cordey, Lestringuez, Lhote and others were the models for the dancers, and also a painter of Spanish extraction, don Pedro Vidal de Solarès y Cardenas, who came from Cuba. He is the man in trousers of the shade known as *merd'oye,* whom one sees in the middle of the picture, dancing with Margot. The carefree and exuberant Margot found this great hulk of a Solarès rather stiff and starchy, and she used to try to shake some life into him, whirling him round in the polka...'

Le Moulin de la Galette is one of Renoir's outstanding works. It is painted in oil on a canvas measuring 51½ by 69 inches. It belongs to the Louvre, where it is the crowning glory of one of the rooms of the Jeu de Paume. Its state of preservation is good.

---

[1] Quoted by F. Jourdain, *Le Moulin de la Galette.* Ed. Braun.

[1] Georges Rivière, *Renoir et ses Amis.* Ed. Floury.

385. Auguste Renoir (1841-1919). *Le Moulin de la Galette*. Paris, Louvre. Repr., Büchergilde, Zurich.

Study of the painting

Setting eyes on *Le Moulin de la Galette* is rather like being invited to join in the dance. Dresses are swirling, skirts flying, cuffs flapping. Only the music is lacking, one almost feels. But no, the music is not lacking; its beat is felt all through this luminous whirl of animation.

We are at once on close terms with these people, whose enjoyment is so infectious. Some may smile at this rustic fête, open to all comers; others will feel a nostalgic tenderness for this corner of a Paris that has gone and will not return. But obviously we are not primarily absorbed by such moral or picturesque considerations. In contact with this picture, we are filled with a sense of well-being, which is offered, through the medium of painting, for us to share – and we do share it. The joy of living, the fun of dancing and the pleasures of friendly chatter are all mingled in the feeling of contentment which takes possession of us.

If we then turn away from the spectacle to savour our first impressions of it, we quickly realize that Renoir painted his dance at the Moulin in a festive spirit; at all events, it is a feeling of festivity, of enchantment even, that one gets from it. Enchantment; that is not an overstatement: beyond the simple dance which he depicts, the artist transports us to a realm of art where all is changed without our even noticing it.

The picture presents a *scene*. Let us look into it, and first at the *setting*: in the background stands the dance-hall; from this room, which is open on all sides in fine weather, one comes out into the 'courtyard planted with stunted acacias, and furnished with benches and tables': here are the acacias, here are the tables and the benches. On the table to the right, assembled as in a still life, are a carafe, a bottle and two glasses, filled, no doubt, with 'our usual grenadine'.

As for the *figures,* these are men and women, young people, all of them dressed up for the occasion; the men in straw hats or top-hats, Solarès in a very stylish soft hat (only Lamy in the foreground is bare-headed); the women and girls smartly turned out in their fresh, well-ironed finery – beribboned dresses, skirts with stripes and pleats, some wearing hats, others bare-headed with elegantly coiled hair (except for the little girl on the left with the flowing locks).

And the *action?* Most of the figures are dancing. On the left it is Solarès with the jolly Margot (would you not say that they have noticed us, and that she is flashing us a flirtatious smile?). Behind and on either side of them two more couples revolve, while a fourth pair rest on a bench a little further away, and a fifth pair thread their way gently, close to the acacia. But there are also those who are not dancing: at the extreme left, on the end of a bench, is a girl or young mother with a child; in the centre, Jeanne leaning over her sister Estelle; around the table, Lamy, with his back to the spectator, Goeneutte and Georges Rivière, all three of them seated, talking or listening. Behind them, and apparently interested in a similar scene going on further to the right, are a young man, leaning on the tree, and a girl with her back to it. On the right is a couple seen from behind.

The scene is lit by a summer sun, which plays over it in a pattern of capricious flakes and blobs and patches. The sun is very much one of the party, and does not mean to be ignored. Indeed, is it not the host, or at least the master of ceremonies? Setting, figures and action take their cue from the mood of joyful grace which it lavishes on them all; and, if its light has touched the painter's brushes, that, too, is to give them grace.

One may well ask, upon reflection, how it is that, with such a subject, the Moulin with its working men and girls, the picture can produce so powerful an effect. Yet, it is from this vulgar – or, at any rate popular – reality that Renoir has extracted the oasis of freshness and joy which so amazes us. The stunted acacias are transformed into a luxuriant vegetation from which hang – not lamps, but rare fruits, full of nectar. The gravel courtyard is changed to some fleecy substance like a cloud. How can these ordinary folk – workmen and seamstresses, dancing and bobbing about – rival and even outshine the fauns, nymphs and bacchantes, without our sense of wonder being diminished or estranged? How is it that – in this picture without a sky – men and women, trees and benches, all seem to revel in the open air? Or that the earth, to which they belong, seems to grow lighter beneath their feet? This is a thing to make one gasp: the most prosaic spectacle imaginable – the lower classes enjoying themselves on their day off – transformed into a scene of arcadian revelry! At the very least, it is true to say that *Renoir succeeds in converting a commonplace scene into a marvellous spectacle,* i.e. a thing to marvel at, by the unaided power of his lyricism. However, 'lyricism' is only a word, and we must see what it stands for.

Could one imagine a more crowded picture than this one? Customers, idlers and dancing couples everywhere. You can hardly see a square inch of ground. In so far as what it represents is concerned, one may say without fear of contradiction that it is 'full up'. Yet paradoxically, at the same time as we observe this, and expect to receive an impression of weight, of crowdedness, of dust and sweat, we feel on the contrary a sense of lightness and ease, of breathing freely! What mischievous genie is here at work, replacing our normal (and reasonable) impressions with such unexpected sensations? The 'genie' is that of colour, and if I have conferred on it the epithet 'mischievous', that is because it is not a case of colour alone, but of colour collaborating with light – a doubly active and effective genie.

Let us try to track it down, first of all by looking into the picture's construction. In this connection, it is remarkable to find, firstly that it does not appear to possess any definite structure at all, and secondly that it has no weaknesses. No structure at all? Perhaps that is going a little too far, for one can distinguish a few guiding lines – for instance the diagonals, which play quite an important role, establishing other lines of support, such as the table and benches. But these are quite rudimentary indications, though one might add – for the vertical structure – the seats, the trees, the lamp-standards etc., and – for the horizontal – the cross-pieces of the two chairs and the façade in the background. There is no erudite scheme of the kind that was dear to the Renaissance masters; the lines I have mentioned are little more than points of reference which help to guide the spectator's eye from one area to another. This does not mean that the painting has no structure, but that its structure is not based on geometry.[1] It is, in fact, based on light and colour.

It is no use trying to recognize in this picture the kind of space to which one has been accustomed by the traditions of classical art. I am not saying that Renoir sacrifices depth entirely. He reduces the scale of his figures from the trio in the foreground to those in the distance, in accordance with the rules of linear perspective; but he dispenses almost entirely with aerial perspective, its normal accompa-

niment. One can see that, instead of reducing the intensity of colour as he reduces the dimensions of objects, *he maintains it at approximately the same degree throughout.* This has an unexpected effect: in one way, the picture space gives the impression of going back in depth; in another, it appears to come forward towards the spectator. It recedes without seeming to cave in unduly, and it 'stands up' without seeming to be unduly flattened. Let us verify this, to be sure there is no mistake. *Dimensions are reduced* 386 *with distance,* as one can see at first glance: the crowd in the background is no more than a mass of mingled patches of pigment. *Colours are not similarly reduced in intensity,* though it takes a little longer to appreciate the fact: these same little patches of pigment, the columns and the decorations, are noticeably bright and pure in tint.

That is odd in itself, but what follows is even more so. What happens, in effect? First of all, that objects no longer give us the impression of 'going round'. Yet this is too hasty an assumption! It may be true of the faces of Jeanne and Estelle – two similar areas of flat colour, like flowers in full bloom – but it is certainly not true of the various hats or the globes of the gas chandeliers. It would be more exact to say that the objects *tend* not to 'go round', or that – when they *do* 'go round' – *they no longer convey the impression of volume.* Here we have come upon one of the work's fundamental characteristics: while it leaves objects with their everyday physiognomy, *this novel type of space modifies their traditional appearance as solids. Rigidity of outline is replaced by a general plasticity,* as if matter were released from its physical and geometric definition. The rest of our examination will tend to bear this out.

[1] In general, we tend to be very fixed in our ideas. For most people, construction is purely a matter of geometry, and it is a hard struggle to make them understand that geometry is *one of the possibilities, not the only one,* and that any other formal agent – line or colour, or patches of colour – can be the basis of construction. Arising from this, one may point out the intolerable vanity of those who want at all costs to reduce construction to diagrams and mathematical formulae. One should know – and ponder the fact – that construction is not an armature, pre-existent to the work, but that it is arrived at with and through the work.

386

Italian perspective accentuates the separateness of one plane from another. It would be wrong to say that it disappears altogether in *Le Moulin de la Galette,* since linear perspective at least maintains some distinction between planes, if not their separateness. Thus the planes appear both distinct and confused. One may go so far as to say that the latter aspect carries the day, or at least that in this space *the emphasis is on continuity.* What is it that thus manages to interfere with linear perspective? When we examine the foreground figures closely, we observe that, although their stature is relatively larger, their outlines are relatively vaguer, that Renoir has muted their colours, and that he employs here a fairly limited colour range. In the second plane the figures are proportionally reduced in stature, but one notices that they are more firmly drawn, that the colours are heightened with luminous accents here and there (as on the straw hats), and finally that the scale of colours is extended, (for example, in the two different blues of the striped dress). In the background, figures and objects – though reduced to a mass of indistinct patches – are

far from disappearing as one might expect, but – on the contrary – are even more decisively affirmed, not so much by drawing as by colours which assert themselves in a positive way.

Similarly, it can be seen that the paint is rather fluid in the foreground, that it gets somewhat thicker in the second plane (on Margot's dress and the straw hats), and that in the background it is applied in crisp little strokes that really stand out from the canvas.

Thus, by his manner of treating outline, colour, light and pigment, Renoir 'contradicts' the impression of depth without, however, destroying it completely; forms still suggest intervals and distances but they are also linked to each other in continuity. The picture space is not abolished; but its mode of existence is altered.

None the less, this change is so considerable that it causes an upheaval in all our most inveterate habits of perception, thought and feeling. Objects which daily experience has taught us to think of as being distinct from one another, each possessing its own weight, volume and special characteristics,

387

388. Auguste Renoir. *Le Moulin de la Galette*, detail.

penetrate each other; note, for instance, the striking example of the face which peeps out like a bud between the tree and the man who leans on its trunk, or the equally striking example of the little girl on the left, whose hair seems to merge with the texture of the ground. It is the same with *parts* of objects, as in the clothes and faces of the figures (for example: Jeanne's hat and hair, the collar of her blouse and the top of her dress). Drawing has a new meaning with Renoir. His treatment of space is not compatible with linear delimitation. This 'floating' quality and the 'fuzziness' of the forms are not failings; their fusion is not confusion, nor is the weakening of the planes a sign of negligence. *All these are logical necessities;* they are all in accordance with the artist's chosen terms of reference, and are legitimized by a new awareness of reality and by a new mode of expression in painting.

Let us look more closely at Renoir's method of treating the human figure. Where objects cease to exist as solids, it is only natural that the human body should do the same. We are not, therefore, surprised to find that the back of the idler who leans on the tree is raised to meet his straw hat, that the hands of the dancers can scarcely be distinguished separately, or that their fingers merge into each other. We accept, too, that faces will lose something of their individuality in this new sort of space. *As concern for anatomical accuracy is eliminated, so concern for accurate portraiture is diminished.* Of course, Jeanne is different from Estelle, and Solarès from Lamy, but the artist plays down such differences. Only the face of Georges Rivière, on the extreme right, is rather more fully characterized, as if Renoir intended this as the key to the gallery of his friends. Even so, it is only very broadly indicated. In losing their identities, the figures subordinate themselves more strictly to the paint itself, which becomes, in consequence, a sort of enchanted ballet.

In fact, colour is all-important. Renoir has broken away from the colour system of the primitives (there are no flat tints in *Le Moulin*), and he has also suppressed the suggestion of depth, volume and modelling, of convex and concave surfaces. But, in so doing, he has discovered new powers of expression.

In its material aspect, the paint appears as an 388 agglomeration of strokes – long or short, broad or narrow, closely packed or separate, but all in harmony with each other. Treated thus, it is not unlike wool that is being carded, a comparison that

and which Renaissance optics – based on a system parallel to normal experience – has taught us to think of as being solids that occupy a definite geometrical area, are transformed before our very eyes!

388   This is what the *drawing* of the picture reveals right away. No more hard outlines; the forms seem to 'float' – as if in a world where the force of gravity no longer applies. Margot's dress stands out sufficiently from its surroundings, but there is no sharp division between the blue ribbon and the pink material, or between the edge of the dress and the blue-shadowed ground beyond it; nor is there any clear division between the tree and the figures who lean on it. One could trace the outline of Jeanne's hat or Estelle's hair with a finger, but one could hardly do so with a pinpoint. Line, in its function of an imaginary border between two localities, has no place in this picture. One cannot even say that it moulds the contours of objects. In fact, apart from its role as indicator towards one direction or another, it tends to be suppressed in favour of colour. Since there are no longer frontiers between them, the objects *all tend more or less to inter-*

is all the more useful in that it takes account of the impression which is offered to the sense of touch; might one not say that it is full of little tufts of variable thickness, which have not yet been gripped in the loom – tufts which preserve the quirks of the original fleece? The wool is supple and abundant, smooth and fine-textured. This is a tactile property![1]

At the same time as it tends towards a more physical manifestation, colour is emancipated. In Jeanne's hair alone there is a positive hotchpotch of colours – blue-black, yellowish-green, olive, reddish-brown, dark green, pink, a touch of orange, ultramarine blue (above the temple) and traces of violet, while over all there are little dashes of blue-grey.

In all this swirling profusion, the shadows – which act traditionally as retaining 'dykes' for the colours – are swept away; there are no shadows any more; or rather, they are transformed. Instead of canalizing the colours into the forms, the shadows disintegrate and share the fertilizing power of this general state of flux. The picture surface is no longer parcelled out; all is animated by a single shimmering movement which absorbs colours, tones, shadows and reflections. Look at the hat of the man who leans on the tree: yellows and yellowish-whites, bluish and greenish greys, pure greys and greens are mingled in it, crossed by the dark blues and blue-blacks of the ribbon. It is still a straw hat, but it is also the undulation of colour in a form that has broken free from the habitual limits imposed by shadows, or – better still – that has integrated them in its movement. In this world, where volumes interpenetrate one another, where persons and objects lose their outlines, and faces their distinctive features, and where even light and shade are not in opposition, a new presence makes itself felt.

We have seen how Renoir's colour avoids definite outlines at the same time as it frees itself from modelling; its power of continuity is no longer connected with particular tints on particular surfaces, but with the interlacing of its fibres through the picture as a whole. Seen from close-to, these have the 'open' look of separate stitches, but from a distance the fabric is flawless. See how Solarès's hand 'juts into' Margot's waist, how the woman leaning against the tree 'juts into' the trunk. But

388

these are not really clear-cut forms that 'jut into one another'; it is the wisps of colour of which they are composed that are woven tightly together.

Is there not some contradiction here? On the one hand, the objects that are represented are still recognizable; on the other hand, all matter is of a single texture. There is, of course, the fact that the wisps change colour according to the objects concerned, and the surprising fact that, although one outline merges into another, *their limits do not vanish entirely*.

This is due, in great measure, to *touch*. Taken over-all, the paint is fairly thin, a film that scarcely covers the canvas, but this fluid pigment is applied in a very special manner. Note, for example, the brush-strokes on Margot's pink dress and on Solarès's trousers – like handwriting that is sometimes upright and sometimes sloping. In this way the silhouette is expressed without use of outline; by simple changes of angle, the touch of the brush fills it out, without going round it and without compromising the continuity of colour – just as the direction of the threads in certain fabrics produces perfectly discernible decorative motifs.

As for the more extensive areas, such as the space in which the dancers circulate, or the bodies of the foremost figures, they are given a different treatment which recalls a certain technique of ceramic painting, in which the colours are applied with a very pliant brush to obtain a sort of broadly flecked effect.

Proceeding like this, with wisps, firm strokes and flecks of paint, Renoir discovers new material qualities in painting. For him, its purpose is not to evoke the delicacy of woman's flesh, the roughness of bark, the weight of a bench or the soft bloom of a human face; it renounces habitual associations to adopt qualities of malleability, transparency, lightness and fluidity which invite both creatures and objects to enter a new life.

Colour is not alone responsible; light has an equal share in this transformation. Together they lead the dance; but whereas the former displays itself openly, the latter is more secret, more subtle and elusive, since it comes from no identifiable source, and falls in no definite direction. It blossoms, here and there, in *accents* like those on the straw hats, on the carafe and glasses, on the globes of the lamps, and on the little girl's hair. Note also how shirt-collars, cuffs and pockets form so many gleams of luminosity.

Though its presence is obvious in such places as

---

[1] This term has nothing to do with Berenson's 'tactile values'; I mean it not in the sense of volume, but literally of *touch*. The blue, yellow and pink here have qualities of suppleness and softness which add something to our perception of the colours as such.

these, it is much more discreetly in evidence elsewhere. When one's eye ranges from one side of the picture to the other, it meets a quantity of luminous patches, arranged in no apparent order, resembling reflections on water. Look at the blue dress of the girl dancing behind Solarès, with its patches of light blue and white, or at the similar effect on Margot's pink dress. One can see the same thing on the figure in the extreme foreground – his back is literally dappled with light! In specks and flecks like these, a mantle of light is drawn over the whole picture.

Its action upon colour is still more mysterious, as one may judge from a study of Estelle's dress. She sits on the bench, clothed in a striped material of pale blue and pink, merging into green lower down, and one can see how these tints glow brightly or grow darker – as if some current were flowing through them. Outline and volume count for nothing; so far as the painter is concerned, *the objects in his picture are opportunities for the creation of forms which are made to vibrate by the light which passes over them.*

Thus light is not used to localize objects, to define their position, to describe their volume and outline or to evoke their material qualities; it springs up from the ground to the trees like atoms fusing from all sides, or falls in slow flakes like snow to settle on hair and head-dresses and clothes. Light not falling from a fixed point in the sky, but an 'ambient' light, one might say – if the expression did not permit of an irrelevantly naturalistic interpretation; for there is no question here of *plein-air* imitation. Granted, there is some reference to this; but the treatment of light is above all an expression of lyricism, exalting and magnifying reality. Far from being merely additional to colour, the light exists with it *and in it: illuminated from outside and from within, the forms themselves become fluorescent.*

Let us make no mistake, there is nothing degenerate in this, no analogy with Pre-Raphaelite insipidity. This union of light and colour is not an attribute of the forms, or something which merely clothes them; *it is their structure, and therefore also the rhythm of their existence.* See how the colours answer one another at intervals that are sometimes widely spaced and sometimes packed close together.

Their variation in extent, together with the interplay of tone-values, constitute the basic rhythm; for example, in the series of dresses in the left half of the picture (Margot, the dancer in blue, the seated Estelle), or in the succession of light and dark tints within a single locality, as in Estelle's striped dress. Even the brushwork takes part in the effect of rhythm. The individual strokes are grouped now in one direction and now in another, now broad and now narrow, in a thousand separate pulsations; it would be impossible to count them, but – varied as they are – they are all linked in the basic fluorescence, which is the very movement of colour at grips with light.

This is the decisive point. Renoir does not content himself with transporting a studio easel to the courtyard of the *Moulin de la Galette.* He does not content himself with the discovery that light circulates among objects. In persuading us to enter into his work, he reveals that, wood or metal, earth or flesh, bone or foliage, *all is porous to light; all can be transfused by light.* Light is not an abstract principle or a means of illumination, but an infinitely fine *material,* whose differing 'wave-lengths' engender a world of objects which gain in suppleness and iridescence what they lose in weight and solidity.

In the old days, when an artist wished to raise peoples' eyes from the ground, he had recourse, perhaps, to an immensity of sky, which he spread out like a canopy, or perhaps to mythological beings – angels or allegories – fluttering or gliding through the clouds. Renoir sends all such personages and properties about their business – angels, allegories, clouds and cupids – yet nothing could be more ethereal than his *Moulin!* The sky, instead of maintaining its splendid isolation above the tree-tops, or figuratively enrolling in the celestial legions, comes down as light and colour to breathe its grace and lightness into familiar, earth-bound shapes. Does it require any great effort to see how this courtyard – covered, as Georges Rivière tells us, with gravel – is changed to a fleecy cloud of pink and blue, so soft for the foot to tread? But the foot itself no longer leaves an impression on it. Like a new Roi-Soleil, Renoir sets the great festal fountains playing in his own Versailles ... which is the art of painting.

Van Gogh

The Church at Auvers

Van Gogh

How difficult it is to approach his work! Not the man himself – we know all there is to know about him. His life, the subject of one biography after another, has become a symbol, which the cinema has not hesitated to exploit. Yet, what matters is not that Van Gogh was in turn an evangelist, a bookseller's assistant and a vagabond, that his feverish existence burned away in rapture and delirium, or that finally, despairing of everything, he put an end to it with a revolver. Many a poor devil has suffered the same torments! But, where few have left a memory, and most have been forgotten, Van Gogh has left us a great body of work.

There is another source of confusion to be guarded against. In his terribly moving letters, Van Gogh has himself traced the course of his agony. What appalling confessions! Relentless misfortune, consuming despair, the threat of madness... But how many precious passages there are also, which relate to the struggle he carried on for his art! The quotations have become famous – familiar, almost. One can only admire the genius they reveal, both penetrating and prophetic. Nevertheless, they should be put in their proper place, like any other correspondence. Art and life do not exist on the same plane. When Van Gogh opens his heart in his letters, our own hearts beat in sympathy. When we approach his pictures, it is his soul that is laid bare to ours. Before the *Church at Auvers,* we should like to forget that Van Gogh took his own life in tragic circumstances; we would almost like to forget his letters, and even his last words to his brother Theo, who had rushed to his bedside and urged him to take courage: 'It's no use, the misery will never end' – words which posterity has made into his seal and his device.

Van Gogh was born in 1853. After a varied existence, he began painting in 1883, at the age of thirty, but it was not until about 1885 that art became a positive obsession for him. A pupil of the Impressionists, and an admirer of the Japanese, he settled in the South of France in 1888. He was confined in the asylum at Saint-Rémy after a series of violent mental crises, and in 1890 moved to Auvers – where he died at the age of thirty-seven.

Five years – seven at the most – were enough for him to show his worth. It is almost unbelievable that in so short a time, in conditions of hardship which were, admittedly, alleviated by the active friendship of a brother, Van Gogh should have been able to produce close on a thousand paintings [1] (without counting the numerous drawings), or that his work, so misunderstood in his life-time (it is well known that he sold only one canvas), should have become one of the most fertile influences of modern art. By the irony of fate, these are the works to which today's public is most passionately attached!

389 The Church at Auvers

This is one of the painter's last works. Having arrived at Auvers on the 21st of May 1890, Van Gogh committed suicide on the 27th of July. The picture was painted in this interval of two months. It measures $36\frac{1}{2} \times 29\frac{1}{2}$ inches. It is in a good state of preservation.

The painting was originally in the possession of Dr Gachet, whose son presented it to the Louvre in 1951. In a superb speech of thanks to the donor, André Malraux said: 'This picture... is one of the finest Van Goghs in the world, equal to the *Fields under a Stormy Sky* and the *Crows over the Cornfield* (both painted in June/July 1890)... the raging blue of its sky recalls that in the doctor's portrait in the Jeu de Paume, with which it is enigmatically linked... In one version of the Romancero, El Cid – aged and dressed as a pilgrim – returns to his palace. No-one has recognized him in the town. He knocks at the gate, and they want to drive him away. Then one of the children playing in the narrow red street beneath the heraldic sculptures (and who has never seen him) comes to him and says: 'I know you, you are Rodrigo.' It is a fine thing, Monsieur Gachet, to prove to artists (and to others) that there is nearly always someone to whom the unrecognized Cid is known as Rodrigo.'

Study of the work

Is it possible not to feel both perturbation and admiration in front of this picture? Perturbation at the sight of this landscape twisted by heaven knows what torment, of this weird woman at the side of the road. What earthquake causes the upheaval, or rather, what imminent catastrophe draws near? Ideas and feelings flood into our consciousness, and yet – despite their turbulence – we feel that the artist's genius controls and dominates them, and that – if the lightning is about to strike – it will flash from the painter's own hand.

However, this kind of imagery is an obscure route to appreciation of the picture. Let us look at it simply and straightforwardly. There is no difficulty about the *genre* to which it belongs; it is the one which every beginner tries his hand at, the one which is specially loved by the great majority – for nothing is nicer than *landscape*! Van Gogh has painted what thousands of artists in thousands of places have striven to put down on canvas: the village church. So much for the *subject*. But why, when we say this, do we immediately revolt from the idea? Van Gogh a 'landscapist'? The 'picturesque' has no place here. What so stirs us is to sense – beneath the outward appearance of a simple country church – *the presence of some fantastic being*.

I do not use the word 'fantastic' in the familiar sense of something which exists only in the imagination, or something created by fantasy. I can see this church; a woman walks along this road; the silhouette of a belfry cuts across this sky. No visions or phantoms, and yet a feeling of strangeness takes hold of me. This landscape obviously escapes reality, without, however, rejecting it entirely. It is like this in the stories of Edgar Allan Poe, where the fantastic is not a projection of the supernatural, but exists on the borderline between the natural and the supernatural, as if the simplest and most commonplace things – a village church, for instance – can have their share of mystery.

A village church? Yes – the church of Auvers-sur-Oise, in fact. Here is a photograph and here is 390 the painting. The resemblance is striking; there is 391 no mistaking the place or the viewpoint. The painter took up his position a short distance away from the apse, and he included those parts of the building that he could see: here are the belfry, the transept, the apsidal chapel on the right, and the buttresses, of which that on the left, seen in profile, has a sturdy massiveness. He likewise respected the number and the different types of the windows: gothic

[1] *Catalogue raisonné*, J.-B. de la Faille.

389. Vincent Van Gogh (1853-1890). *The Church at Auvers*. Paris, ▶ Louvre. Photo Held.

390. The church at Auvers-sur-Oise. Photograph by Yvan Bettex, Pully.

391. *The resemblance to the photograph is striking. Nevertheless, the picture speaks with a voice that belongs to it alone – the voice of Van Gogh.*

bays in the apse and belfry, romanesque in the side-chapel. Other elements of the building are equally recognizable: the nave between the apse and the belfry, the overlapping eaves of the roof, the clock between the gable and the two bays of the tower. It is all there, even to the details of tracery in the windows. In front of the church, there is the same triangle of grass, with the road branching on either side. Beyond, there is the same great expanse of sky. The photograph does not show the trees and the cottage on the left, nor does it show a woman walking along the road, but in all other respects the picture is at least topographically – if not photographically – correct. Whatever one may say about the artist – that he had just come out of an asylum, that his attacks of insanity were beginning again, that he was soon going to commit suicide – *it cannot be denied that he wanted to paint what he saw.* The accuracy of his observation is proof enough of that.

But, as with any artist, what he sees in front of him is not just a thing or a spectacle, even less an end in itself. The *motif* is a resonant wall on which the painter's spirit reverberates, and which reverberates on him, producing echoes and forms which overlap and mingle like sound-waves to create the work of art whose unique vibration is passed on to the spectator. What is the voice that pervades this landscape? It is a wordless voice, but it has a pronounced accent.

If this landscape can be characterized as fantastic, and if the fantastic dwells at the meeting-point of the natural and the supernatural, one can understand that the dual origin and dual nature of the work will have their effect on the spectator's mind and sensibility. Indeed, the spectator has an oddly simultaneous impression of knowing where he is and of being in a strange country. An insidious change in the relationships between objects results from this unexpected effect; for instance, the woman on the road, instead of claiming the prominence which her human shape would seem to confer on her, is almost completely effaced by the aggressive presence of the church.

Unquestionably, this is a plastically defined space, which means that the forms ('deformed' or not) are no longer represented with topographical realism, but in accordance with the interior image of the work. The sky, one notices, is of a single, continuous hue, a flawless and unrelieved ultramarine, sharply circumscribed by the frame and the outline of the church. A solid sky, bearing down with all the weight, not of air or azure, but of destiny. There is

392

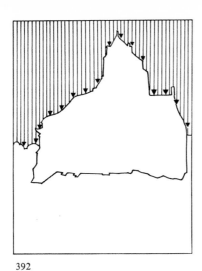

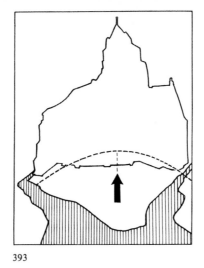

392   393   394

no opening in it, no break of light; without depth and without horizon, it falls with the crushing force of inertia upon the church, which buckles under its weight. [1]

393 In opposition to the sky we have the triangular piece of grass and the fork of the road, with the peasant woman on the left. The form of the roadway is in itself suggestive: its two arms squeeze the church like a pair of pincers. The extraordinary abruptness of the perspective emphasizes the strength of their grip and, at the same time, raises the level of the ground. The building appears to be stable in the photograph, whereas in the painting it looks as if the earth is bulging upwards like a wave. Exaltation, one might suppose – upward movement – buoyancy!... Perhaps, if the grass did not give way so suddenly at the edge of the shadow, or if the shapes of the church were not so painfully twisted.

Van Gogh has placed the body of the church, like an appointed victim, between the weight of the sky and the spasms of the earth. Caught between them, its members crack apart. How does the artist contrive to convey such an impression? Here

394 again, comparison with the photograph is revealing. In the latter, not only does the sky seem weightless, not only does the ground recede normally towards its vanishing-point, but the various parts of the church all have their own distinct volume and, with the intervention of perspective, are articulated one with another as so many solid shapes. In short, it is composed in terms of the physical properties of its elements. Van Gogh turns all this upside down. With him, the sky becomes a rigid, two-dimensional

[1] I do not mean that the dark blue can evoke all this by itself. It only does so in relation to the other elements of the painting.

space, the earth is rent asunder, the impression of *plein-air* is discarded, volumes are not developed in depth, and the church is jammed into a compressed space. Although they are distinct, the planes are subjected to a series of telescoping effects which make them intrude on one another, or at least to appear to do so. The apse is crushed against the nave, the nave against the belfry, the belfry against the sky. But this pressure from front to back is counteracted by a similar pressure in the other direction, from the sky – unyielding as a stone wall – down to the apse. Instead of being moulded in light and shadow, the apse, the apsidal chapel, the transepts and the tower all press in on one another. Van Gogh has suppressed the shadows quite deliberately.

Without them, the planes no longer suggest intervening spaces, and consequently the illusion of volume disappears. Subject as it is to these contracting forces, these pressures from above and below, from front and back, the church does not escape from lateral pressures either. We have remarked how the two roads grip it like a pair of pincers. This almost imitative idea is repeated in the format of the picture: there is only the narrowest of gaps between the walls of the church and the 395 frame on each side (rather less narrow on the left) – a lack of space which adds to the effect of strangulation. Also, in relation to the composition as a whole, the church seems to take up too much room; however, this 'too much' does not imply any misjudgment on the artist's part; we feel it is his intention to put the church at the front of the stage, so as to make clear that it stands at the centre of the drama.

But what right have we to identify ourselves with the lot of an edifice of stone? After all, it is only the church of Auvers-sur-Oise! Yet it is *not* only that; it is also Van Gogh's church. As he has painted it, the church is not just an object which cracks or crumbles under the stress of natural or supernatural forces. By a series of impenetrable analogies, far removed from personification, he gives it *a human character* that brings it closer to us. Let me make this point clear: when a building succumbs to the passage of time, one may be sad and regretful, or even indignant; but when a man *or something that we feel to be equivalent to a human being* suffers misfortune, then our feelings are different: 'sympathy' makes us enter into the sufferings of others. The strange power of this picture is precisely that it gives us this sense of participation through the medium of a landscape – i.e., through a group of inanimate objects.

First and foremost, I think, through qualities of draughtsmanship. Whether we look at the church or the foreground, most of the forms are contained within outlines; the window traceries are indicated by lines; and so on. The dominant lines in the photograph are straight ones which define planes and volumes; in Van Gogh's painting they are mainly curves, juxtaposed in segments of unequal length and thickness, and set in many different directions. The general impression one receives is of a form breaking up, but not in the manner of an inert object – of a mineral, or a piece of architecture. The torsion manifested in these segmented curves shows that the pressures exerted upon the church from outside are answered from within by a force which is not due only to the inertia of its material, but to a substance imbued with energy. Drawing is not used simply to mark the outlines of objects, but to suggest the inward fracturing of forms which are *animated by the will to resist.*

This organic impression is reinforced by the manner in which the *axes of construction* have been warped. We regard vertical and horizontal as the very symbols of stability and equilibrium. That is why they are so naturally associated with our idea of a building, which is by definition subject to the law of gravity. Now, one can see in the photograph that time has interfered a little with verticals and horizontals: the apse leans ever so slightly to the right, the belfry ever so slightly to the left, and the roof is not quite level. Nevertheless, the total impression is not affected; the main axes may be a little bit 'out of true', but they are not bent, and they still convey a sense of the equilibrium of an architectural mass. In the painting, however, the axes are not merely inclined; they bend, and we get the impression of a structure endowed with a certain degree of elasticity – like an organism, in fact. This effect of the axes adds to that of the lines, giving further stimulus to the idea of a living mass that is suffering torture. Gradually the church seems to change from a pile of stone to a body, with all a body's capacity for feeling pain – perhaps also with a soul...

It may seem odd that colour, too, contributes to this 'humanization'. It is true that Van Gogh expressly thought on such lines, as is shown in his oft-quoted sentence: 'I have tried to express with red and green the terrible passions of mankind...' Even so, we should treat this with caution. Anyone may have intentions; but intentions are necessarily vague. What counts is their realization in a work of art.

Let us begin by noting that Van Gogh does not radically alter the colours of objects: the sky is blue,

396 397 398

399

400

395
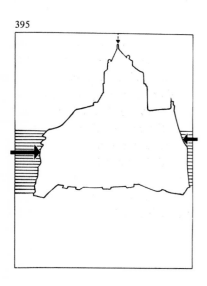

396
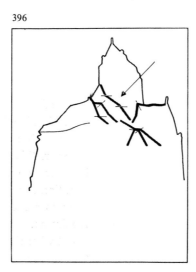

397
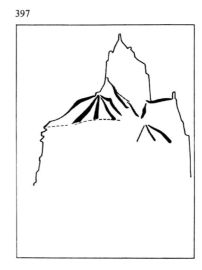

the church roof is red, the windows are blue, the grass is green; but, while local colours are – by and large – respected, they do not strike us as being equivalent to nature's own tints.

His colours are characterized, first of all, by their *homogeneity*. Whether they are spread broadly in the sky, or placed in short, terse strokes on the roadway and the grass, they do not seek to convey the sensations of different material qualities and textures: there is neither lightness nor transparency in the sky; there is no flexibility in the grass, nor rigidity in the stone of the church. Instead of conforming to the objects, the colour imposes its own viscid substance on them, enveloping them with it and kneading them into it. Wherever one looks in the picture, this substance is of the same density to the eye, regardless of whether it is situated in the sky, on the ground or on the church. Nor does it alter in accordance with light. Just as the suppression of shadow on the church prevents its volumes from asserting themselves, so the air, similarly compressed, prevents the forms from breathing. We feel the oppressiveness that hangs over all. Deprived thus of oxygen, it is no use the colours trying to represent grass or stone or sky; all is of the same substance. And what is the reason for this? We have seen that Van Gogh evokes the sensation of something organic through his treatment of forms. His treatment of colour increases the sensation, and even adds something of carnality to it. What is quite certain is that his picture presents not a thing, but a being. A drama, too. But, in this drama, we are aware only of the victim; we know nothing of the malevolent forces by which that victim is afflicted. Van Gogh does not fulminate against pain in general, or against any particular

kind of pain. He simply makes us feel its presence in the body of his church.

The lighting of the scene underlines its cruelty. Seeing the band of shadow along the base of the church, one might suppose the source of light to be high up on the right. Bur not at all. The sky is as hermetically blue and shut on one side as it is on the other; there are no shadows on the building to tell one how the light falls. This is a fantastic light, without natural origin. On closer inspection, one finds that the sky is thick in texture, thinning out slightly here and there, and that it contains very noticeable whorls and twisted circles of dark, almost blackish impasto in the upper right-hand and (even more markedly) the upper left-hand corners. The sun appears only in a simulacrum, a few twisted scraps of burnt-out matter – a black sun with murky rays. But what about the shadow at the foot of the church? Like a wave of the sea – and as tricky as any sea-swell – it stretches from one side of the canvas to the other, forming a horizontal barrier halfway up the grass, as if the rest of the world does not share in the drama, or at least not so intensely. In the throes of agony, the church must also bear the misery of solitude and separation, must resign itself alone to death. There is no sign from on high, no word from below. Light serves no longer to model the forms, to evoke their texture or to fix their positions in space; instead, it acts itself as a symbol. Freed from its normal associations with colour, it breaks the bonds of natural representation to shine in the painter's imagination, of which the picture is a projection.

At first sight, the painting seemed to be the image of its subject, and this we found surprising. But that

398

399

400

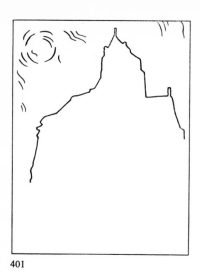

401

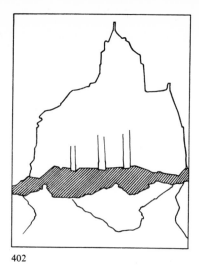

402

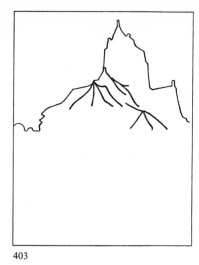

403

was too hasty an assumption. The details are there, but the artist has transformed everything, beginning with the place itself. Auvers ceases to be a geographical reality; in the painting the church's situation is in the midst of anguish and suffering. In their ordinary state, forms acquire a new physiognomy from the looks, the thoughts and the feelings they inspire – that is to say, they are governed by new laws. That is why I was justified in employing the term 'fantastic', even with regard to the colours. Van Gogh makes these converge upon three dominant tints – blue, red and green – and he gives them an astonishing intensity. Nothing shrill, however; he does not force the effect, but *concentrates* it. It is through this carefully considered and controlled transition that the artist's anguish is communicated to us – not by depicting the anguish itself, but through the radiance of his art.

403 Like so many nerve-filaments, the lines of stress formed by the ridges of the roofs are attached to the chaotic arabesque which describes the outline of the church. Subjected to cross-currents from which they do not seem to emerge unscathed, they convey an impression of laceration. With its arteries laid bare, the church lifts up its bloodless and dismembered body. (I need not point out that there is no suggestion of this in the photograph.) Stretched to breaking-point, these ligaments are finally torn apart – and this is the agony we are made to share, as if it were our own flesh.

This participation is made tangible by the artist's touch, by his handling of paint. This is always important in Van Gogh's work, and it is crucial here.
404 See how the movement of the road – not merely its direction – is conveyed by a series of rectangular strokes, placed side by side. In order to reduce the effect of depth suggested by the two narrowing branches of the road, Van Gogh uses strokes of *approximately the same size and value,* regardless of where they are situated in the picture space. The impression of distance is diminished, and the church is thrust forward in such a way that we cannot possibly escape from contact with its torments.

The flowers in the foreground are indicated by 405 jagged strokes of white or yellow, which slash horizontally across the grass in a contrary movement that underlines both the separateness of the various elements and their interior dismemberment. Then notice how the handling changes as it gets near the church! Neither amorphous nor geometrical, as in 406 the flowers and the road, the strokes begin to twist and heave like a mass of wriggling maggots. The handling is not uniform throughout, but follows the dictates of the painter's will to express himself. As soon as it comes in contact with the church, it too becomes organic. This is no view of a ruined church; we are taking part in the sacrifice of a chosen victim. We ourselves suffer, but it must be understood that this is due solely to the way in which pictorial resources are used.

The fact that this basic requirement has been respected is what gives the picture its quality as a work of art. Its over-all *construction* is simple: the 407 foreground occupies one third of its height, and the church two thirds. The grass verge forms a sort of triangle, repeated by that of the road, and balanced by the general shape of the church and by the roof of the apse. Thus each of the main structural shapes is of a fairly simple geometrical form; hence the impression of order which we receive. But it is a

338

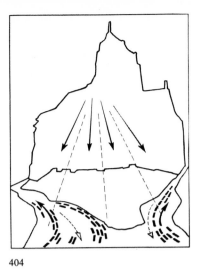

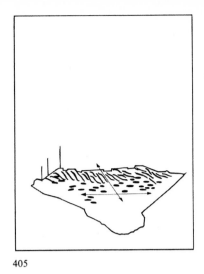

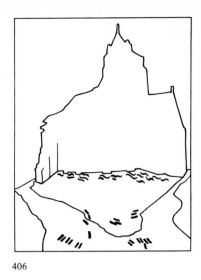

404

405

406

superficial order, and the artist uses it to make the disruption of the church even more emphatic by 408 contrast. Not only are the outlines of these shapes irregular, but they are inwardly distorted: the axis of each triangle is crooked. In addition, they are not 409 arranged geometrically in relation to each other; Van Gogh clearly means to stress their varying orientation and to make them pull in opposite or different directions. Though stable enough so far as the basic structural forms were concerned, the composition now disintegrates once more; every element 'goes wrong' before our eyes.

This character is further emphasized by the *treatment of impasto*. Contrary to one's first impression, the pigment is fairly thin, more especially in the window, the grass and the sky. Elsewhere it thickens in places: on the roof, the flowers and the blackish whorls of the sun. Where the paint is applied in

separate curls and twists of colour the impression of thickness increases, while in those places where it is spread out more evenly it seems to be thinner. In this way the variations in the handling of the medium put us rather unexpectedly on to the track of rhythm.

The rhythm of the picture is manifested principally in variations of colour-intensity and in movement: the vivid blue of the windows alternating with the grey-green of the walls; the light patches of the flowers alternating with the shadow at the base of the 410 church; the hurried movement of this 'wave' of shadow contrasting with the slower, more regular movement of the road; the relative immobility of the roofs contrasting with the slow rise of the buttresses. The pigment gives off a discharge of energy, which is harnessed by rhythm into regular pulsations.

What happens to the peasant woman? Let us look closely: her outline is indicated in broad strokes, her

407

408

409

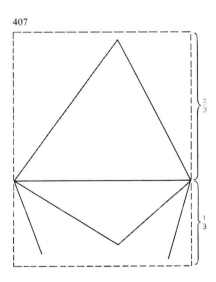

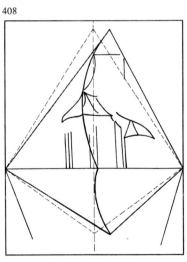

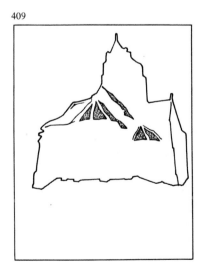

339

410

minute his description of it may be, it goes far beyond the original. Torn from its place in the village square, entering another world where the sky hangs like lead and the very earth heaves, the church – stone, glass, tiles and all – becomes a living being, racked with pain and filling the void of helpless anguish with its cry – the uttermost pinnacle of the forsaken soul. Since one gets this feeling of a trapped and doomed victim, it is possible to believe that Van Gogh is portraying his own situation, a version of his personal Calvary. But, rather than ending up with an image like this, let us marvel that the sheer strength of his art can provide us with material for several such images, all of which have at their heart this theme of the victim's consummation through suffering.

With Van Gogh, anguish is not just a cry that one hears. It takes shape before our eyes in his painting, and takes possession of our very substance. Thus the painter reveals to us – beyond his own agony – the agony of all. Through him, and with him, we are able to take it up and convert it into art. Beyond the world's clamourings, this solitary cry is a part of our human condition.

skirt is rendered with a blue and a green, and her blouse with a very pale blue. As for her head, there is no paint there; it is the canvas one sees. We have already noted that she is represented as walking (she is lifting her right foot), but that, by a curious effect, she alone seems immobile while everything else – earth, sky and church – seems to be caught up in a mysterious commotion. Are we to suppose that Van Gogh put this woman there as an accessory figure, as a bit of local colour? Surely not; so far as the painter is concerned, she has two functions. As is usual in such cases, she serves first of all to fix the scale of the picture: from her height one may judge the height of the church. But that is her secondary role. In relation to the proportions and the forms of the church (and this is her primary function) the peasant woman conveys the notion of an insignificant but complete being, indifferent to the drama which goes on beside her, and *because she is unaware of it* the grandeur of the drama seems all the more potent in its isolation. She stands like a screen between us and the agony that goes on before our eyes, not making us immune to it, but warning us against any tendency to sentimentalize. Paradoxically, she increases the pathos of the picture.

What are we to conclude? That Van Gogh laid bare his heart before he died? Perhaps. But the important thing is not to know the circumstances of his distress or of his madness, but to know how – in spite of madness – he could accomplish the gesture of an artist and produce a work of art. He sees the church at Auvers, his imagination is set alight, and his brushes are charged with feeling. He paints the church most scrupulously. One cannot accuse him of inaccuracy; it is all there. But however

411. Vincent Van Gogh (1853-1890). *Self-portrait.* Gachet collection, Auvers-sur-Oise. Photo Held.

Picasso

Guernica

Picasso

The name of no other painter has enjoyed such notoriety in our time. In contrast to those artists who endeavour to please the public – or, at least, to avoid displeasing it – Picasso seems to go out of his way to shock it. Even the least knowledgeable person on artistic matters – the man who has never entered a museum or an exhibition of paintings – knows that 'Picasso is the man who paints eyes where ears ought to be, ears where the mouth ought to be, and noses where ... etc.'

Others may have struck their blows at familiar appearances, and at that of the human form in particular, but for most people Picasso remains the arch-blasphemer, the man who – against all authority of common sense, science and progress – dares to doubt that we are as we are. Scandalous!

It is also scandalous for an artist not to stick to his course, once he has embarked on it. Being true to oneself is surely the basis of any successful career! But Picasso plays tricks on his 'confreres' and on the public; he starts off in one direction, and has hardly taken the first few steps before he switches to another. One simply cannot keep pace with this terrible man. Not only does he do violence to nature and to humanity, but he even seems to do violence to himself – so outrageously, at times, that one is tempted ironically to conclude that he is faithful only to his infidelity!

Yet (and here words fail one), in his case scandal has turned into success: instead of confounding its author, it has caused him to prosper. Picasso must now be near the end of his life's term, but it would be rash to presume that he is at the end of his career. Each time he sloughs his (stylistic) skin he re-emerges with undiminished vigour, as if – like Deucalion and Pyrrha combined – he needs only to toss a canvas or fragment of pottery over his shoulder to give rise to a new human race, a new fauna and a new vegetable kingdom. Long after he had done with Cubism, the tobacco-packets, bottles and guitars began to flourish everywhere; they still do. Today, one cannot go into a shop without coming across a pot or plate that claims him as its real parent. Can one still call it 'influence'? It is a spell that he has exerted, rather than an influence; and what a spell! 'Pernicious', the pundits call it. Perhaps it would be, if Picasso had tried to sell his magic; but he has never kept shop, and he has never sought to found a school. It is pointless to blame him for all the failures and false steps that have resulted – per-

412. Pablo Picasso.

haps without his being aware of it – from his example. But public opinion does not look too closely into such things. Is it not the height of scandal for scandal to be triumphant? Yet, by a paradoxical twist, the completeness of the triumph has caused the majority of people to accept it. Though opposed to each other in all else, admirers and detractors are agreed on this: that it is impossible to ignore the man. By general consent, Picasso occupies an exceptional, if not unique position.

One cannot say that this is for reasons connected solely with the quality of his work. Painters such as Braque or Matisse are certainly not his inferiors. If their names have not acquired the same renown or the same legendary aura, this is surely because the conditions of our modern world have played into Picasso's hands. Is not the cause of this very possibly to be found in our own sense of uneasiness, which we try to ignore, but which the artist exposes to the glare of day? And have we any right to accuse the artist of provoking or exploiting that uneasiness? People pretend to judge him by his inspiration, and – since they do not care to recognize themselves in the portrait of our age which he offers – they proclaim that it is all a hoax or humbug. This is getting the problem the wrong way round, since one must judge the works themselves, not their origins; no one has any right to evade this basic obligation.

I am now in a position to define my intentions in this chapter: what I want to do is to study a work by Picasso in the same way as we have done with other artists; here, as elsewhere, I have no polemical axe to grind, but desire only that we should see and understand. For our purposes Picasso is neither a demon nor a god, but simply the painter of *Guernica*.[1]

The artist presents an extraordinary spectacle to his contemporaries: a painter at heart, he also produces sculpture, engravings and decorated pottery. But it is not the diversity of his talent that is so amazing; in this respect a Leonardo da Vinci has greater claims to our admiration. The unique position of Picasso is due essentially to the fact that, whenever he sets to work, the basic premises of painting (or sculpture, or engraving, or ceramic art) *are called in question,* and so – by implication – are

art as a whole, the artist himself, and we too, as we should not forget. Whatever he does, he cannot help starting all over again from the very beginning, not out of humbug or a thirst for originality, but from an imperious and often cruel urge in his own nature. This is not to suggest that his work thus acquires a superiority that sets it above all others; it is to say that it receives an imprint that distinguishes it from the rest.

Guernica

Guernica occupies a central position in Picasso's 416 vast and varied oeuvre, and its importance is unquestioned. It marks a crucial stage in the artist's career, and it epitomizes an essential side of his genius. Furthermore, it is a picture inspired by a particular event, which (in this case) redoubles its interest: on the one hand, it presents an opportunity to study a key work of Picasso; on the other, it permits us to see how an artist raises the particular event to the level of art – a rare enough phenomenon in this age of propaganda.

The Spanish civil war broke out in July 1936, producing a chain of repercussions throughout the world. While the dictatorships supported Franco, most artists and intellectuals rallied to the cause of the Spanish republic: many enlisted in the ranks, and many died. Need I remind the reader of Malraux's *L'Espoir* or Hemingway's *For Whom the Bell Tolls?*

Unlike Malraux and Hemingway, Picasso was doubly involved in these events – by his Spanish heart and his republican sympathies. What he must have felt and suffered as a man we may pass over in silence, but we have the right to speak of what he *made* of those feelings and sufferings – *Guernica,* a protest of extraordinary vehemence, *but first and foremost a work of art.*[1]

One of the earliest artistic shapes which his protest took was the *Songe et Mensonge de Franco,* which he engraved at the beginning of 1937, and for which he wrote the text himself. In January of the same year the Spanish republican government commissioned from Picasso[2] a large composition destined for its pavilion at the International Exhibition in Paris. On April 28th the papers reported the brutal bombing of the little Basque town of Guernica

---

[1] I should, however, begin by giving some information about the man, though he has become a familiar enough figure in newspapers and magazines, with his squat form and his black, piercing eyes. He was born in Malaga on the 25th of October 1881. Brilliantly gifted, he soon displayed a precocious talent. In 1904 he went to Paris for the fourth time, and settled there permanently. With Braque he was the co-founder of cubism, and he became the figurehead of what is called the *Ecole de Paris*. He is also the figurehead of what is more vaguely called 'contemporary art'.

[1] I do not mean to belittle the force of Picasso's protest, but simply to point out that our concern is with the picture's place in the world of form.

[2] He had been nominated as director of the Prado in 1936.

by German aeroplanes flying in Franco's service. This event, which affected Picasso profoundly, was the origin of his composition of that name. On May 1st 1937, two days after hearing the news of the tragedy, he put down his first ideas on paper. After numerous sketches and preparatory studies, the picture as we know it was completed by mid-June.

'The first state of the composition dates from the 11th May', Maurice Jardot informs us in his catalogue (*Picasso*, Musée des arts décoratifs, Paris, 1955). 'At this stage', he continues, 'the right-hand part of the work already contains the elements and approximately the structure that one sees now. The expiring horse in the centre has its head turned to the ground; the warrior, lying with his head to the right, raises an avenging fist high in the air. On the left, the mother holding her dead child already has more or less her final appearance, but the body of the bull will be turned the other way, from the fourth state onwards, without the position of its head being altered. The third state sees the reclining warrior turned with his head to the left, face downwards; at the same time the sun against which his raised fist was silhouetted takes the shape of an almond – or an eye – a shape it will retain, even when it becomes a modest electric lamp (seventh state). The fourth state sees the raising of the horse's head, and the seventh, penultimate state sees the warrior's face turned upwards. A certain amount of collage appears in the fourth and sixth states.' [1]

Of course, it would be fascinating to follow the stages of this genesis, but we cannot do so here, partly because it would take up too much time and space, and – even more – because it would not be within our terms of reference, which are to follow the stages by which we get to know the work as it stands.

Guernica is an oil painting on canvas, measuring 11ft. 6 ins. by 25ft. 8 ins.; it was shown at the Paris International Exhibition in 1937. A souvenir postcard, produced on that occasion by the Spanish government, bore these words: '*Guernica*. The great Spanish painter Picasso, who founded cubism and who has so powerfully influenced contemporary art, has sought to express in this work the disintegration of a world afflicted by the horrors of war.'

[1] For this side of the question, one should refer to *Cahiers d'Art*, Nos. 4 & 5, 1937, which reproduce the principal stages of the picture's development, and also Juan Larrea's *Guernica* (New York, 1947), which contains all the photographic documentation. According to Barr *(Picasso, Fifty Years of His Art*, New York, 1946) it appears that Picasso made a number of related studies both before and after *Guernica;* the latter are not the least revealing.

Study of the work

One cannot help feeling astonishment and dismay when one stands for the first time before this huge canvas. In the presence of these barbaric idols, with their grimacing features and their menacing eyes, one feels both afraid to draw nearer, and incapable of tearing oneself away. Beyond the horror, there is a strange fascination: *Guernica* casts a spell over the spectator, and one cannot depart from it unscathed.

'But, after all', one says to oneself, 'it is a picture, not an idol.' It is even a figurative picture. On the left, a mother bewails the dead child in her arms, in front of a bull which turns its head back sharply over its shoulder. In the centre is a horse which collapses in agony, transfixed by a spear, its mouth open, its tongue protruding like an arrowhead. On the paved ground lie the dismembered remains of a warrior, his left hand outstretched, his right hand clenched on a broken sword. On the extreme right, a woman transformed into a living torch falls, with arms outstretched and head thrown back, from a burning house. Below her is another woman, with distorted feet, and arms that hang down at her sides, whose head and neck so prolong her forward movement that she almost touches the horse's chest. From an open window leans an apparition with head thrust forward, hair that streams on the wind and breasts with nipples like nails, holding out an avenging lamp over the carnage. An electric bulb – like some cyclopean eye – dominates the scene, shredding the shadows round about it; four blade-like flames echo it sombrely on the right. Between the horse and the bull is a table on which a bird with extended neck and open beak utters its last cry, its body slashed by a livid light, sharper than any razor. There is no colour in this picture. It is composed entirely of black, grey and white.

'Can this be called painting?' some astonished spectators ask themselves. Some of them, indeed, turn away. 'Incomprehensible!' mutter those who are least ill-disposed.

But among those who remain (always more numerous), admiration is not unmixed with discomfort. 'For me', says one, 'the stricken animal signifies the death of War itself.' 'No', says another, 'it's the death of Franco.' And so the interpretations multiply and vary, their principal virtue being not really that they say something, but that they make some noise that may relieve the mind from its disquiet. Some of the more knowing and more cautious ones

413
414
415

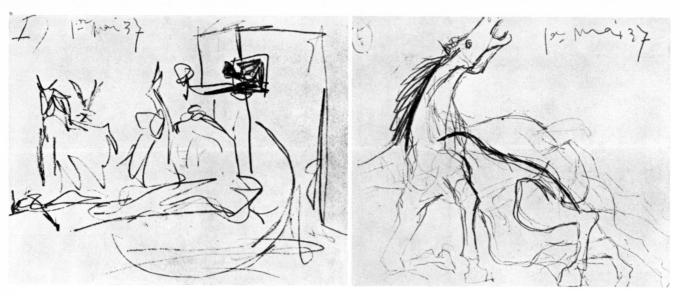

413. Pablo Picasso (b. 1881). First drawing for *Guernica,* 1st May 1937.

414. Pablo Picasso (b. 1881). Fifth drawing for *Guernica,* 1st May 1937.

415. Pablo Picasso (b. 1881). *Guernica,* first state, 11th May 1937.

remark that Picasso must have explained himself somewhere, and, if they happen to have Maurice Jardot's catalogue with them, they open it full of hope – only to find this sentence: 'It is not easy to elucidate the symbolism of this scene, which evidently touches on many aspects of the crime of Guernica, and *Picasso has never supplied any information to throw light on it* . . . ' [1] Since the artist has remained silent, it is useless to look to him for enlightenment. But, if he has chosen to stay silent, it is for the good reason that he felt that the work itself is enough. That is where we must start from.

However, we need not ignore the lesson that has emerged from this. To interpret a work of art is one thing; to understand it is another. In the first case, whether one trusts one's own powers of divination or is guided by the artist's evidence, one is still judging probabilities. Thus Maurice Jardot very pertinently finished the sentence I have quoted above ' . . . even supposing it to be in his power to supply it.'

Shall we follow the paths of criticism? Maurice Raynal, one of the best judges of modern painting, has written as follows of this picture [2]: 'In the avenging ardour that animates him, he is going to transform the plastic expressionism of his earlier figures into dramatic expressionism, in which the urgency of his message will ruthlessly override any complacent preoccupation with style or technique. He will even forget colour: black, white, a little grey; that will be all. He thinks no longer as a painter, but as a man overwhelmed and agitated by pain, fear and hate. His work will instinctively obey the passionate lyricism which governs him when his inspiration comes more from his heart than from his hand. With *Guernica*, it is no longer a question of composing a picture: no premeditated scheme, no formal researches. . . there is no longer any room for the deliberate and more or less drawn-out construction of a pictorial entity. This is not description, but a cry prolonged by plaintive echoes.'

Enthusiastic criticism – but full of pitfalls! Certainly, not everything that the author says is wrong; his culture and sensibility break through in flashes, as at the end of the quotation, but the passage as a whole is fatally influenced by the romantic misconception that a scene which expresses violence must have been painted violently. 'Sympathetic criticism', founded on emotion, pours forth a mixture of true judgements, attractive conjectures and downright errors. [1] I shall not discuss Juan Larrea's interpretation. His book, valuable for its documentation, seems to me to be the very type of the dangers we want to avoid: starting out from psychoanalysis, the author makes discoveries which do honour to his talent as a poet, but which seem to have, at the most, a tenuous connection with Picasso's picture.

I do not wish to generalize, but – having rejected the path of interpretation – let us not be drawn on to that of a certain other critic, whose enthusiasm is too much for his discernment. I intend no irony; I only permit myself these references in order to get the problem into its proper perspective.

Our starting-point was the spectator's justifiable astonishment. Now, starting from this astonishment, let us see in what terms the question is posed. What does one *want* to explain? What *can* one explain? These are the two basic requirements to be kept in mind and reconciled; otherwise one will fall into excess of one sort or another.

Going back to our first examination of the picture, we can say this much:
— *Guernica* represents a scene of carnage;
— it moves us through the suffering of the creatures it represents, and through the suffering it expresses;
— beyond the immediate emotions which it evokes, it is like some kind of a warning. Not that Picasso preaches; he plucks a particular chord in our imagination, strikes it with horror, and our whole being is shaken with a thrill of protest;
— finally, the transposition into art of so horrible a spectacle fills us with silent admiration.

One cannot deny that this is a scene – and what a scene! Lacerated bodies; hands twisted, clenched or outstretched; eyes, ears and mouths distorted; burning houses; cries of the wounded; a deathly light on the corpses . . .

But what has become of the real Guernica? Were it not for the title of the picture, we should hardly recognize any allusion to the bombardment of that little town which the Spaniards held so dear. We realize that Picasso is not attempting a historical picture. There is nothing here in common with Goya's famous *Third of May*, 1808; indeed, there is 418

---

[1] My italics.

[2] Maurice Raynal, *Picasso*. Ed. Skira.

[1] How can Raynal declare that with *Guernica* it was not a case of composing a picture – in view of the fact that he knew the studies and preparatory drawings? This is clearly a case of someone allowing himself to be carried away by feeling, instead of sticking to the work itself.

nothing that would permit us to date or to identify the event.

Yet perhaps Goya can provide a more relevant comparison. Every page of his terrible series, *The Disasters of War*, is dedicated to carnage. Are these subjects really datable? Occasionally, perhaps, where one can recognize the uniforms of the French soldiers; but in general there are only the vaguest indications of time and place. How many of the scenes are set in a plain, bare landscape, with a tree or two to serve as gibbets for the victims! But it is on this point – the treatment of the victims – that the difference shows up clearly. With Goya, they retain their individual human characteristics; though not strictly realistic, Goya's art remains closely in touch with visible reality. With Picasso – and this fact is important – *the forms are in revolt against visible reality*. One is so immediately aware of this that no-one would think of attaching names to the faces in *Guernica*, or of trying to see them as belonging to recognizable categories of human beings. One can hardly say that the animals are more particularly characterized; is this creature in the centre of the picture exactly a horse?

We have now hit upon one of the work's essential characteristics: *Guernica* is an *allegory*, and – as in any allegory – beings and objects are intended to lead our minds towards something other than what is represented.

One sees, in fact, not only that Guernica avoids precise historical reference, but that it is not strictly a 'war picture'. [1] As we have noted already, one cannot infer the date or place of the event from the internal evidence of the painting, and one may add that even the setting of the scene eludes one. Are we inside a house? The half-open door at the right, the ceiling and the electric light might lead us to think so, but then the roof-tiles above the apparition with the lamp make us think again.

Strange though it may seem, we have to conclude that we are both indoors *and* outside. It is even less possible to decide what time of day it is; the scene exists as independently of the sun's movement as of its rays. Where does the light come from? From the window? Or from the lamp? Certainly, we can still distinguish human beings and animals, but only through an approximate resemblance to their natural appearance. It is an allegory, then; but not in the usual sense of that term: there are no personifi-

417. Pablo Picasso (b. 1881). *Head of a Weeping Woman*. 13th June 1937.

---

[1] Compare it with the picture which Picasso painted on the subject of the Korean war (pl. 420), in which reference to reality is far more apparent.

419

418. Francisco Goya (1746-1828). *The Third of May, 1808*. Madrid, Prado. Photo Viollet.

419. Francisco Goya (1746-1828). *I Saw This*. Etching from *The Disasters of War*. Photo Viollet.

420. Pablo Picasso (b. 1881). *Massacre in Korea*. In the artist's possession. Photo Marc Vaux.

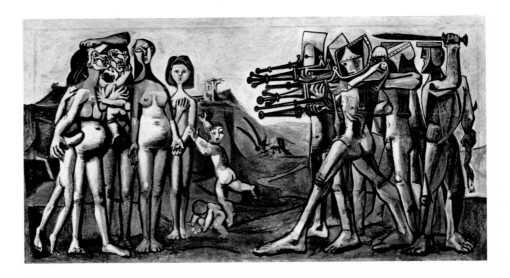

421. Pablo Picasso (b. 1881). *Three Women at the Spring*. New York, Museum of Modern Art. Photo Giraudon.

cations here – no Mars and no Bellona. [1] This allegory has its roots in the painter's imagination.

The effect of this method of composition is to diminish the representational character of the scene, but not its *truth*. One can understand how much the painting gains in consequence. For one thing, by avoiding direct representation of bloodshed, it prevents our feeling the unwholesome shock that results when one is suddenly confronted by a horrible spectacle (remember one's reactions when certain documents were published during and just after the last war). For another, by wrenching the forms from their normal external appearance, and by releasing them from the bonds of time and space, it tends to elevate them to the level of *symbols*. Pathos is transformed (we shall shortly see how), and – above all – *the work assumes a new dimension*. Concentrating each individual aspect of the truth, the forms combine to become *a universal and timeless formulation of that truth*. We cannot yet say what that truth is, but we can already say in what terms it is expressed, and how far it can be expected to reach.

Let us make no mistake, it is not the mere fact of the forms being emptied of their substance and torn from their context of situation and circumstance that makes them into symbols, *but the fact that they are given new substance, new situation and circumstance*. Allegory is a means to an end. If that which gives it shape has life, then the allegory is alive; if not, then it is only a lifeless integument.

Having made this point, let us continue with our examination. The expression 'approximate resemblance', which was useful a moment ago, is worth going back to. We have seen that the forms, while tending to be converted into symbols, do not break away entirely from visual reality; thus we could justly refer to figures of women, a warrior, a bird, flames, lamps, and so on – though we may have had some hesitation in recognizing the horse and the apparition at the window.

Now, as soon as we start considering them from this angle, the appalling expression of suffering which they convey (except for the bull) hits us in the face, and the artist's manner of rendering it rouses resentment in most spectators: 'How can Picasso thus exaggerate the horrible? Isn't it enough that a mother has lost her child, that a man is cut in half, that a woman is turned into a living torch? ... Could he not have done without all these distortions that

[1] It is not that Picasso ignores this tradition; note, for instance, his *Three Women at the Spring,* which would appear to be a sort 421 of allegory of Fontainebleau, where he was living in 1921.

are almost unbearable to look at? It is perversity...'
The resentment is premature, but the questions are none the less legitimate. On the artistic plane, they amount to asking if Picasso has not made ill use of an inferior brand of expressionism.

By 'expressionism' one means a tendency displayed by certain artists, who resort to what may be called 'shock tactics' in order to express themselves: extravagance in composition and colour, and distortion – of the human figure especially; certainly the impression made on the spectator is one of shock. Is that not exactly what happens with *Guernica*?

Here one must be particularly attentive, if one really wishes to understand rather than to condemn. Instead of painting the *individual suffering* of *a* mother, *a* warrior, or *a* woman, Picasso retains *what is sufficiently general* in the suffering of each to represent the anguish of *all* bereaved mothers, *all* vanquished warriors, *all* women burned alive. On the one hand, he endeavours to reduce each kind of suffering to its archetypal expression, while at the same time trying not to lose contact with the intensity of the individual situation; on the other hand, he endeavours to reduce each kind of suffering to its archetypal situation, while trying not to lose touch with its individual expression.

A fantastic gamble! Nevertheless, Picasso takes this risk in creating what one could call 'expressionist symbolism' – or 'symbolic expressionism'. Is this not a contradiction in terms? Perhaps, but theoretical considerations are of small importance; all that matters is the pictorial realization. The risks are formidable. If the forms incline a little too much to one side or the other, then the picture will be nothing more than a meretricious production, an admixture of two irreconcileable elements. But the measure of Picasso's genius is that he *has* succeeded in combining them so that Guernica attains the limits of range – in *universality*, and the limits of intensity – in *expressive emotion*. The forms are subjected to a dual elaboration, which appears in the finished work as a new sort of unity.

On the left is the *agonized cry* of the mother who howls at death like some animal robbed of its young. On the right is the *terrified cry* of the woman who falls like a blazing torch – the scream of the burning flesh and of the mind unhinged by panic. On the left again is the *cry of rage* of the stricken warrior. On the right, the extraordinary forward movement of the woman with bared breasts, emptied of all that is best in her, expresses the *tremendous questioning* of the panting flesh. Above her is the apparition's *shock* of horror. And in the centre is the *fear* of the mortally wounded horse, contorted by a pain which it does not understand.

In each case it is the *type of suffering* that is given visible shape. It should be understood, however, that *the symbol is not obtained simply by a series of abstractions, but – on the contrary – by keeping as close as possible to the individual creature which it shapes, and from which it derives its own shape*. That is to say, the 'distortions' cease to be felt as such, since *each has its reason and function*.

Eyes shift from their anatomically correct position, and take varied forms *according both to what they represent and what they signify*: tear-like eyes of the 422 bereaved mother, which seem to trickle across her head like moisture; eyes cruelly displaced of the 423 warrior, wide open still, in spite of the severed head and mangled body, as if the fury of battle and the rage of impotence blaze on in them after death; rivet-like eyes of the horse, which, in this battle of 424 human kind, loses even the sense of its animality (does it not subside like some carcase of iron?).

We cannot pursue this examination in detail, but the principle which I have indicated above explains the other instances of 'distortion' equally well. With what terrible and perverse insistence (one might

422

423

424

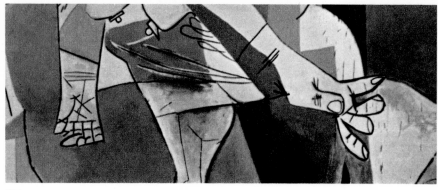

425

426

think) Picasso degrades the natural appearance of humanity! He obliterates the distinction between left hand and right (for instance, the woman advancing on the right); he changes the order and position of the fingers (for instance, the hand holding out the lamp, where the little finger is reversed); he ignores proportion (for instance, the dead warrior, whose left hand is far larger than the right, which pathetically clutches the broken sword); he even suppresses some features altogether (for instance, the shoulders and – in the case of the falling woman – the whole torso). Not only is the impression of suffering increased, but we begin gradually to feel that war affects the nature of things, that it is not a temporary disorder, something incidental, an episode of history, but an *anti-nature* – an infernal emanation which is not content with mutilating creatures, but takes pleasure in *deforming* them.

Thus it is that Picasso, through his hatred of war and his artistic genius, rediscovers the meaning of monstrosity. I am not referring to the common definition of monster as a being whose conformation differs from that of its species. Certainly, this aspect is present in the creatures of *Guernica*; but the monster which is only the exaggeration or distortion of some human characteristic – an ogre, for ex-

425

426
427
428

429

ample – is ultimately something to laugh at (even Bluebeard!). Behind its show of strength there is always a simplistic mechanism at work, and so this kind of monster, for all its fierceness, can only inspire us with a short-lived thrill of fear. Picasso, however, reintroduces the monster which – as in the ancient myths – is a celestial portent, coming from on high or from the beyond, a type of prodigy which is meant precisely to *show* [1] us something. Expressionism is well able to create a phantasmagoria; but it is only when it attains the level of symbolism that the Scriptural 'Mene, Mene, Tekel, Upharsim' [2] shines forth in letters of fire.

And now these creatures, which seemed at first sight to be so disconcerting, become intelligible – profoundly so! We are scarcely tempted now to say that they move us to pity them. Do they bear testimony against war? Yes, they do, but they operate on a level beyond the reach of testimony and emotion, since it is ultimately through their prophetic significance that they assert themselves and impose their fascination upon us.

[1] *Translator's note.* The author's play on the French word «montre», referring to the Latin derivation of «monstre», cannot be rendered literally in English.
[2] Book of Daniel.

427

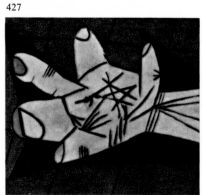

428

429

430

We must be careful, though; too much has been said of the prophetic nature of Picasso's works. It is pointless to enthuse over the fact that he painted the carnage of the last war several years before it came to pass; this, at the most, is a talent for prediction.

But we are talking of prophecy! Through the medium of these monsters, the painting transmits a warning to us, reminding us of that evil of which war is a symptom. There is a very real difference. Popular opinion regards *Guernica* as a presage, a sign to throw light on coming events, and as such it figures on the stage of history. For us, it is a 'prodigy' – a vision thrust before our eyes to throw light upon ourselves. To anyone with an open mind it is inescapably evident that *Guernica* attains a metaphysical grandeur and eminence. Such is the force of truth in this work. If one fails to grasp this at once, the bull will set one right. One is amazed at this 'imperturbable', 'impassive' creature, but how can one fail to see that he turns his head with such power (and such effort!) in order to make us take notice of him. Once one has encountered his magnetic gaze, it is no longer a scene or a spectacle that one contemplates, but a vision, which – even when we close our eyes – stays with us, because we are in it and it in us. The final impact of *Guernica* is an undeniable act of communion.

But a vision is not a picture; no more, indeed, than a prophecy is a book. Nevertheless, the Bible contains the Book of Daniel. In the same fashion, *Guernica* is both a vision and a picture. Its formal economy testifies to this.

The spatial composition of this picture is of a complex kind. One finds indications of depth in it, such as the foreshortened angles in the upper corners, the table and the squared pavement. However, there is only an allusive suggestion of the third dimension. The human figures and animals are given no volume at all (except for the shadow on the horse's neck), and consequently bring the eye back into the surface plane. Is it, then, a composite space? No, for the forms do not give an impression of 'bitty-ness'; on the contrary, we are struck by their cohesion, which means that the space which the artist has created accords with their nature.

We know that Egyptian painting employed a perspective in which the human form was represented in a manner designed to preserve as much as possible of its intrinsic character, so that the deceased person might find his double intact and entire in the afterworld: a purely imaginative perspective. Similarly, Picasso's space is contrived so that the forms may

355

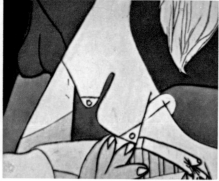

431 432 433

realize to the full *their expressive and symbolic character*.

431   In the mother on the left, planted on the ground like some classical stele, the accent is placed on the profile view of the head and neck, since this gives the greatest possible intensity to the cry which she emits (the broken outline of the face, the agonized gape

432 of the mouth). As for the bust, we see one breast in profile and the other full-face, both pointing at the little corpse to show how it has been cut off from the

433 nourishing springs of life. Since the rest of the body can contribute nothing to this forcible expression, it is reduced to a striped dress, flat and rigid, forming a kind of plinth on which maternal grief is displayed in its emblematic character.

434   Let us look at the horse again. As Picasso has painted it, it presents its right side to the spectator – and also its left side, which would normally be hidden. Thanks to this folding back of space, we see simultaneously the gaping wound in its left flank, the spear stuck squarely in its body and the hole in its right flank from which the blood flows. This may seem to be an arbitrary brand of perspective, but when one thinks about it one realizes how fully justifiable it is. Human beings like ourselves are well accustomed to recognizing the marks of pain or suffering in a human face, but it is not so easy to read the expression of a horse's head; it is therefore not surprising that the contorted mouth of Picasso's horse, when seen in isolation, should be perplexing. But when one considers it in relation to the animal as a whole, one feels that the artist has succeeded – by means of this folding over of space – in conveying the animal's capacity for suffering pain by displaying as much as possible of its 'area of vulnerability' – i.e., the surface of its body; and this is emphasized by the numerous little strokes which, far from alluding to the texture of its coat, are so many virtual wounds and incisions. The

anguish of a mother who has lost her child is essentially a mental state; the anguish of a wounded horse is essentially physical. *For the expressive and symbolic character of each type of suffering to be displayed in its fullest degree, a special treatment of form and space is needed for each individual case, according to its nature.* That is the fundamental principle upon which *Guernica* is composed. The picture space is not constructed according to optical laws, but according to the intellectual need for each form to be granted its own appropriate style of revelation; consequently it is sometimes stiff and flat, sometimes curved and pliant, sometimes folded over or opened out; and it is moulded throughout by the artist's expressive purpose. It is the same with the other pictorial elements.

Let us turn to the *lighting*. One can see straight away that the light does not fall from the left or the right, from above or from below; it is no natural daylight, then. How about artificial light – the electric lamp and the paraffin lamp? Apart from the former's jagged aureole, neither produces the least radiance. Nevertheless, light and dark zones are clearly distinguished. The dark parts appear to belong mainly to the setting – to what is *inanimate* (background, walls, door, table, pavement, etc.), while the light areas belong mainly to the *human figures* and the *animals*. A premeditated division, for it means that neither sun nor lamp, neither natural nor artificial light, has the strength to pierce the horror of the vision, and that consequently *it is the vision itself that converts its power into light*. The light does not come from outside; it emanates from the intensity of the subject. Thus one need not be surprised to find that the places where the horror is greatest are those which stand out most sharply – heads, hands, arms and legs.

The absence of colour is to be explained by the same reasoning. It is not that Picasso 'forgot' it in

434   435

the fever of creation; he omitted it deliberately, which implies a considered choice. When carried to its extremes of intensity, colour reaches the two poles from which it originated – white and black – and therefore also reaches its extremes of contrast. That is why *Guernica* has such dramatic power, and why the experiments with colour of its early stages were dropped. [1] Moreover, the opposition of white and black corresponds to the inherent dichotomy of the forms. It is not exactly that each form is divided in two; but, when it is not so divided, something in it nevertheless makes us aware of an internal fracture. Whether one looks at the horse or the bull, the mother or the warrior, the apparition at the window or the falling woman, they all convey this sense of disruption – either in terms of light and dark (the bull), or of plain and worked-over surfaces (heads, hands, the horse's body). Under the explosive pressure of black and white the forms disintegrate, and the whole picture-space becomes a kind of inferno.

However, the lighting does not throw the picture into disorder. Two greys (not one, as is frequently said) – a dark and a light grey – are introduced into the scheme; by their distribution, and by their variations of intensity, these serve to regulate the contrasts of black and white, and to turn them into 435 movement. One can see this plainly in the arm of the apparition, which is divided into three bands, and the same thing happens on the body of the woman below her. The impression of dislocation remains, but – thanks to these two tones of grey – the forms are not shattered in pieces, but are articulated with one another to maintain the continuity which the picture requires. Though expressionism and symbolism pull them this way and that, the forms are still conscious of the demands of the surface plane; they

---

[1] Picasso also very quickly renounced the use of collage, which is a round-about way of introducing colour.

even draw additional strength from this consciousness. The powerful impression of chaos is not produced by chaotic design, but by *controlled expression*.

This concern for order is evident in the *composition*. Picasso's heart may be filled with rage and hatred, but his hand retains its composure.

An initial characteristic of the construction comes 436 to light in the way the subject is arranged: it is like a triptych, with the horse, half of the warrior, the apparition and half of the advancing woman in the centre panel; the bull, the grieving mother and half of the warrior in the left wing; the falling woman and half of the advancing woman in the right wing. This is an aspect which stresses the ternary arrangement of the painting, but one should note how Picasso securely fastens the wings to the centre by means of the half figures, which act like hinges. In this way the masses are evenly distributed, and – with the help of a traditional scheme of design – the composition is made easier to 'read'.

The second characteristic of the construction is not quite so obvious, but it is still plainly visible, having the form of a triangle – like a central pediment for the composition: the horse is in the middle of it; its left side passes through the warrior's open hand to the horse's tail and mouth; its right side forms a tangent to the figure of the advancing woman. This primary triangle has another inscribed within it, of which the apex is at the flame of the paraffin lamp. On each side there is a further triangle, that on the left occupied by the mother and the bull, that on the right by the apparition and the woman in flames. On the one hand, the action is inscribed in a shape which permits one to grasp it at once; on the other hand, the constriction of the forms within the triangular scheme increases the sense of latent power, and therefore also increases the effect of tension.

This effect, which paradoxically risks being stifled by an excess of violence, is enhanced by the rhythm that animates it and sets it moving. This rhythm, which consists of alternations of straight lines and curves, of solids and voids, of black areas and white, of figurative and geometrical forms, produces an effect of syncopation so powerful that – in this work which is dumb with the weight of horror – one seems no longer to hear the beating of one's heart, but to hear the silence of death between two heart-beats.

There is so great an intensity of feeling that – not surprisingly – qualities of handling even dissolve in it: there is no trace of brushwork in *Guernica*. The white shapes are sharply silhouetted; the blacks and greys are subject to an equally clear-cut demarcation. It makes no difference if you bring your eye close to the surface; everything is smooth and sharp. With fierce lucidity, Picasso consigns his brush to anonymity, so that *Guernica* may shine forth of itself in all its prophetic clarity.

What are we to conclude? Monsters, as such, are part of the tradition of painting; expressionism belongs to all ages, as is witnessed in our own by Munch, Kokoschka, Soutine or Ensor; but the decisive thing is that Picasso's expressionism is never merely a nightmare vision, nor do his monsters belong to the troubled regions of the dream world or the subconscious. *Guernica* affects us through our sensibility, it is true, but it does more than that – it fills us with holy awe. At a single blow it raises the expression of pathos to the status of tragedy, and its monsters, while they frighten us, 'instruct' us also, by showing us the tokens of our destiny.

A strange painting, alien to our confident age – at least in respect of what we can do, if not in respect of what we are. What can man do in these days? Everything – or nearly everything. What *is* man in these days?... Does not Picasso's work stand between these two questions – between the answer and the lack of an answer – in the place where our modern conscience should be standing? Is this not why it seems so strange, and why we want to escape from it? Is this not why it also seems so familiar, and why we succumb in the end to the fascination of its message?

To raise us, *as we are*, so that we can take the measure of *our* truth, is the work of a true painter, of a great artist. Are there many artists who have a stronger claim to this title than Picasso? In his hands the modern myth becomes an Apocalypse.

436. *A scene of carnage, but how rigorously composed!* Pablo Picasso (b. 1881). *Guernica*, 1937.

Kandinsky

Movement

Kandinsky

Note on abstract art

The term 'abstract' covers a vast artistic movement which began in Russia (or at least in eastern Europe) in the early years of the century, spread through Germany into France, and thence throughout the world. Though its origins and early evolution are still not fully known, it was soon so widespread that there is no uncertainty about its subsequent development or importance. It is a movement which embraces not only painting, but sculpture and even music also, and it has provoked the most hostile reactions. To all appearances, it marks the extreme point of the artist's alienation from the public. And yet, it is curious to note that abstract art still forges ahead, that posters and publicity placards, wallpaper and textile designs have all hitched themselves to the wagon, to an extent which makes it fair to ask if we are not witnessing (and unconsciously promoting) something very like a revolution in human thought and taste. The situation is complicated, and painting is only one aspect of it. Consequently, the remarks which follow are intended only to throw some light on the question, without hoping to dispel all the obscurities which surround it.

Let us begin at the beginning – with the term 'abstract'. To avoid confusion, one is tempted to replace it with some other term, such as 'concrete', but agreement upon the term to be used is less important than agreement upon what it means. The expression 'abstract art' appears to have become so solidly established by custom that we shall continue to use it.

What should we take it to mean? According to popular opinion: 'Anything that looks like nothing at all.' That is a simple and forthright formula, and it is not far removed from the definition given by Michel Seuphor, who has recently written a history of the movement [1]: 'Abstract art is that which contains no trace or evocation of observed reality, whether or not that reality was the artist's point of departure.'

Thus the layman's view and the historian's have much in common; but one needs to beware of superficial resemblances. For the layman, what looks

[1] Michel Seuphor, *L'Art abstrait*. Ed. Maeght.

437. Wassily Kandinsky (1866-1944). *Water-colour*, 1910. Paris, collection of Mme Nina Kandinsky. Photo Galerie Maeght, Paris.

438

439

440

438 to 441. Theo Van Doesburg (1883-1931). *Abstraction of a Cow*, 1916. Meudon. Photo Mme Van Doesburg.

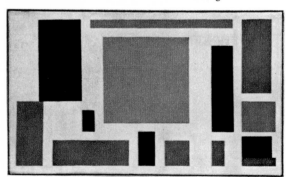

like nothing at all is equivalent to 'something incapable of looking like anything at all'; hence his derogatory tone and his general suspicion of abstract art, which he regards as something half-formed and unfinished – a sort of sub-art. For Michel Seuphor, on the contrary, it is a perfectly valid form of art. Which proves that the same words may mean two quite different things and express two diametrically opposite points of view!

It appears to be historically established that Kandinsky was the real initiator of this new art. His earliest non-representational water-colour, a 437 series of coloured patches linked together by dynamic draughtsmanship, dates from 1910. Recent researches have endeavoured to demonstrate the priority of a Lithuanian artist, Tchurlianis, who is said to have started experiments of this kind as early as 1906/07. For our purposes, to fix a name or date is of less importance than to understand the nature of the phenomenon. On this point, it seems that there were two distinct stages: in the first, which lasted from 1910 until about 1918, abstract artists were primarily attempting to make a *progressive distillation of reality*, as can be seen in the analyses of Van Doesburg and Vantongerloo, and in the early 438-441 works of Piet Mondrian. The visual experience of reality serves as the starting-point for a series of abstractions which lead to the final composition. In the second stage, which begins with the foundation in 1917 of the review *De Stijl*, and especially with the publication of articles by Mondrian, *the abstraction itself is the starting-point*. In a text which was published later, but which sums up his ideas very well, Mondrian wrote: 'Unconsciously, every true artist has always been moved more by the beauty of lines and colours and by their mutual relationships than by what they represent . . . Consciously, on the other hand, he has followed the forms of objects . . . Nevertheless, unconsciously, he has made flat planes, has increased the tension of lines and has purified colours. Thus, in the course of centuries, he has progressively led pictorial culture towards the exclusion of limited form and specific representation. In our time, art has been set free from all that prevents it from being plastic.' (New York, 1942).

The first stage represents what is properly called 'abstract art', while the second stage might more properly be called 'non-figurative art'. But, even if the creative process differs in each case, the fact remains that both have the same end in view: 'pictorial expression from which all allusion to reality is excluded.' This is the important thing to bear in mind in order to understand this new art form, which – for all that it matters from this point of view – can be called abstract or non-figurative as one pleases.

Wassily Kandinsky

Of Russian origin, Kandinsky was born in Moscow on December 5th 1866. Although he loved painting 'more than anything else', he first studied law and political economy; it was not until the age of thirty that he devoted himself entirely to his art. In 1898 Monet's picture *The Haystacks* impressed him forcibly: 'I had the impression', he said, 'that here the paint was in some sense the subject of the picture, and I wondered if it would not be possible to go much further in the same direction. After that, I looked at Russian ikons with new eyes, that is to say, I had eyes for the abstract element in this form of art.' Nevertheless, it was only after several years of unremitting labour that he found what he was looking for. Going through an Impressionist and then a Fauve period, Kandinsky travelled, exhibited and – above all – matured, until a new experience suddenly opened his eyes. This is how Kurt Leonhard describes it in his book, *Augenschein und Inbegriff* [1]: 'One day, when he had been working in the open, Kandinsky returned to his studio at Schwabing. He was tired after his long walk, deep in thought, and he was gnawed by doubts and dissatisfaction: would he ever succeed in interpreting the mysterious language of nature? On the threshold of his studio he was brought to a halt – suffering, he supposed, from a hallucination. Before him was an unknown picture, the most beautiful he had ever seen. One could recognize no object in it; but in its harmonies, in its melodies of forms and colours, he felt again the enchantment of Moscow nights and the magic of music, such as he had been seeking so long in vain. It lacked neither the charm and power of the Russian ikons, nor the language of pure painting which Monet had led him to believe in as a possibility. Now this was one of his own pictures, placed upside-down on the easel, so that one could not recognize its subject.

'Next morning, turned "right side up", the picture instantly lost all its charm, which was dissipated by

[1] Deutsche Verlags-Anstalt, Stuttgart.

the unmysterious representation of commonplace objects.

'It was then that the precise and long suppressed question was formulated in Kandinsky's mind: "Are not the objects in my paintings perhaps an obstacle in the way of their effect?" This was quickly followed by a second question: "If I am bold enough to remove this obstacle, what must I put in the place of the demands of the object?"

'The anwser to the first question was (in 1910) the first abstract water-colour.'

Kandinsky played a major role in the movement known as 'The Blue Rider', of which the exhibitions in Munich, in 1911 and 1912, were notable events for the future of painting. He spent the war in Switzerland, returning to Moscow after the Russian revolution. There he was entrusted with important official duties, organizing several museums and founding the Academy of Arts and Sciences. He then returned to Germany, where he taught at the Bauhaus, one of the most fertile centres of the arts in the inter-war period – until it was closed on Hitler's orders in 1933. Having settled in Paris, he worked there until his death in 1944.

These brief notes do not pretend to cover his life story, but are intended simply to present the picture of a man's efforts and an artist's researches, both calling for infinite patience and forethought. For this is what characterizes this painting: it evolves slowly, smoothly, constantly controlled by a critical intellect. In the manner of Descartes, Kandinsky starts from an intuition, which his pictures develop into 'chains of reasoning'.

Preliminary note: the approach to an abstract painting

At first sight there would seem to be nothing in common between a figurative and a non-figurative work of art; the one term is apparently the negation of the other. Nevertheless, there is not really any incongruity in the comparison which I propose to make here between *The Burial of Count Orgaz* and 442 the abstract composition entitled *Movement*. El 446 Greco's picture is a celebrated masterpiece; Kandinsky's is known only to a small circle of admirers. But we are not concerned with the hierarchy of works of art, and – to my mind – the confrontation of these two paintings should help us to tackle the enormous problem of the relationship between art that is called 'figurative' (or 'representational') and that which is called 'abstract'.

With one or two things explained to him, the spectator can grasp the subject of *The Burial of Count Orgaz* without difficulty: in the lower part, Saints Stephen and Augustine carry the dead man's body (that two saints should take it upon themselves to perform this task in person is a measure of the miracle!); above, the count's soul enters heaven, guided by an angel; higher up again, the Virgin holds out her right hand to him; on the clouds to the right, St John the Baptist intercedes for him before the throne of Christ, who dominates the scene among the host of saints and angels. The composition unfolds in accordance with the phases of the event, and so the spectator follows, stage by stage, the ascent of the soul to God. Thus the picture contains an edifying element, before which the faithful bow in reverence.

Kandinsky's work, by comparison, seems strangely impenetrable. What do they represent – these wandering lines, these gridded circles, these curling ribbons that perform their stately dance? If one is at all prejudiced or impatient, one is almost prepared to suppose that they are cabalistic signs, taken straight from a book of magic, or that they originate in a brain of a kind far removed from our own.

Yet, when one looks more closely, the differences are less radical than they seemed at first. There is a narrative element – doubtless edifying and sublime – in *The Burial of Count Orgaz*, but for us it exists primarily as a picture, and the crowds who make the pilgrimage to Santo Tomé in Toledo do so not out of veneration for the miracle which occurred in that church, but to pay homage to the 'miracle' of painting performed by El Greco.

Now this picture, like any other, is composed of lines and colours arranged in a certain order. From the point of view of pure form, there is no essential difference of principle between a 'figurative' and a 'non-figurative' work.

What is different, above all else, is the appearance of the forms. This difference affects the average spectator so strongly that he fails to notice all that these two types of work have in common, and tends only to be aware of their differences. This is a serious failing, since it implies also a failure to see and think clearly.

442. El Greco (1541-1614). *The Burial of Count Orgaz*. Toledo, church of Santo Tomé. Photo Bulloz.

364

443-444-445

What does the difference really amount to? Supposing I look at a detail of *The Burial of Count Orgaz* – the priest with raised arms on the right, for instance; and supposing I look at one part of the priest in isolation from the rest: all that I can say is that I see a patch of colour, a painted area, in which there are curves and straight lines, and in which white, grey and blue are mingled in varying degrees of transparency. If I now consider this area in relation to the whole figure, I see at once that it is an alb – a white vestment worn by Catholic priests in their ceremonies. There is nothing mysterious in this; it is the commonplace process of identifying the whole from the part – a thing we are always doing. But, when that process is applied to a work of art, it has far-reaching consequences. So long as I consider the detail in isolation, I regard it as a 'patch of colour' – that is to say, I do not relate it to any particular object, but to the painted surface of which it forms a part. When, however, I consider it within the picture as a whole, I immediately relate it to a specific object – an alb, or at least the image of an alb – and I no longer think of its existence as 'a part of the painted surface'. *It is the spectator's attitude which changes, according to whether he is considering a detail as part of an object or as part of a painted surface, and to whether he is considering the whole as an ensemble of objects or as an ensemble of plastic forms.*

With this point established, the position becomes unequivocally clear. Figurative painting arranges lines and colours in a certain order upon a given surface with the aim of creating a whole which exists on the aesthetic plane, and which also *refers* to identifiable objects, real or unreal, which form its subject: women, flowers, angels, rocks or monsters.

Abstract painting arranges lines and colours in a certain order upon a given surface with the aim of creating a whole which exists on the aesthetic plane, *without reference* to identifiable objects – i.e., to the exclusion of any subject *in the accepted sense of the word*.

Except for the last part of each sentence, those two definitions are identical. Nevertheless, the second requires some amplification. To say that abstract painting excludes all reference to identifiable objects does not mean that it dispenses with a subject; it means that the subject – a necessary and integral part of the whole – is in no way related to objective reality.

We have learned already that the quality of a figurative work does not depend upon the real or imaginary scene which it represents, but upon the manner in which line and colour are arranged in the picture where the scene takes shape. In other words, the pictorial quality of *The Burial of Count Orgaz* depends neither upon the miracle which it portrays, nor upon the glimpse of the heavens opening, with all the crowds of the elect gathered around Christ and the Virgin, but upon the manner in which El Greco has tied all these elements together as a work of art. If one were to remove the figure of St John

445

the Baptist, the result would not merely be a gap, which could conceivably be filled by a prolongation of the cloud; the whole composition would be put out of balance: the figure of the Virgin, isolated now, would make it 'tilt' to the left; the lower zone would lose its terrestrial stability; the celestial zone would be thrown off its axis. Pictorial quality, as we know, derives from the internal demands of the forms – *all* the forms.

That being so, it is clear that an abstract work can have pictorial quality in just the same way as a figurative work. It is only necessary for its forms to obey these internal demands, so that they appear to the spectator to be an indivisible whole, and not merely a sum of separate elements.

But, if we grant that abstract painting can have pictorial quality, may we not still expect that it will only be on the level of decoration, and that it will consequently be unable to express any profound human significance such as we find in the great masterpieces? The problem comes down to this: when El Greco paints *The Burial of Count Orgaz*, he produces a masterly work in which we admire the interplay of line and colour – and, above all, of light, which irradiates the picture with a celestial brilliance; but, over and above this, the work expresses something else which can be felt and described. There is no denying the mysticism which breathes from this painting.

Thus, in figurative painting, the character of the work is always linked on one side to representation and on the other to the artist's style. In other words, it results from the interaction of the 'exterior' and the 'interior' world. In *The Burial of Count Orgaz* the painter combines figures and objects (gentlemen, angels and saints; torches and clouds) with his own personal mysticism, which he expresses through his art. It is thus that the 'exterior' objects are elaborated into forms, and that *representation is incorporated in the work's artistic constitution.*

But how can an idea or a feeling be expressed without some element of representation to sustain and explain it? This is where the originality of the abstract revolution can be appreciated. Lines, colours and shapes are considered, traditionally, as *means* of expression, in association with some representational usage; thus, yellow may take the form of a mitre here, or of a flame somewhere else. Now, the abstract painter thinks as follows: instead of associating lines and colours with this traditional usage – i.e., subordinating them to an 'exterior' subject – *is it not possible to regard them as the subject*

itself of the picture? This is to say that, while lines and colours are still 'means' of expression, as in classical painting, they also replace nature's 'repository of images' – they supply their own, since they have no other end than themselves. That, in its full theoretical garb, is the first postulate of abstract or non-figurative painting; of 'pure' painting, one might rather say, by analogy with 'pure poetry', which has had a similar history since it was first heralded by Baudelaire – a critic who saw deeper than most into the modern mind. [1]

Of course, all kinds of compromise are possible, which proves that we are not dealing with two distinct and watertight worlds. Nevertheless, the novelty of abstract painting is quite distinct from the abstract decorative art of former periods. It is a new form of pictorial thought that has been brought to light in our times, and it has nothing to do with the question of stylisation.

But can it have any meaning? Yes, *on condition that a new mode of expression is found for it.*

A word – beside the fact that it designates something – has also a resonance which it owes, not to the thing it designates, but to its own phonetic conformation. [2] Without elaborating this idea, it

---

[1] '...Crowds of people suppose the aim of poetry to be some kind of instruction, that it should strengthen the mind, improve manners, or at any rate serve some useful purpose... Poetry, if one will only look into oneself, question one's soul and remember one's enthusiasms, *has no end beyond itself;** it cannot have any other, and no poem is so great, so noble, so truly worthy of the name of poem, as that which has been written solely for the pleasure of writing a poem.' *(Notes nouvelles sur Edgar Poe*, 1857.)

[2] Kandinsky analyses this phenomenon with such penetration that it is worth quoting the passage in full:
'...A word is an interior sound. This sound corresponds in part (perhaps principally) to the object which the word serves to designate. If one does not see the object itself, but only hears its name, an abstract image – the dematerialized object – is formed immediately in the hearer's brain, and produces a simultaneous vibration in the 'heart'. Thus the tree in the meadow – green, yellow or red – is no more than a material 'case', a fortuitous, materialized form, of the tree we feel in us when we hear the word 'tree'. The judicious use of a word (in the poetic sense), and the interior need to repeat this word, twice, three times, several times in succession, do not only amplify its internal resonance: they can cause other powers of the word to appear. *A word constantly repeated (a game one enjoys in childhood, but later forgets) eventually loses all reference to its exterior meaning. The abstract quality of the object designated disappears; only the 'sound' of the word remains.** Perhaps we perceive this 'pure sound' at the same time as we perceive the object – either real or as an abstraction. But now the sound comes into the foreground to make a direct impression on the mind. The mind feels a pure vibration of a kind more complex – I would almost say 'more supernatural' – than that which it receives from the noise of a bell, a taut string or a falling plank, etc....
Consequently a word has two meanings – an immediate and an interior meaning. This is the pure material of poetry and art, the only material which art can use, and by virtue of which it touches the soul...'
Kandinsky, *Du Spirituel dans l'Art.*
* My italics.

can be understood by analogy that *colours, lines and shapes, when they renounce their representational function, lose nothing at all of their own suggestive qualities, which become the basis of a new form of expression.* This is the second postulate of abstract painting.

Painting is not to be confused with music, but it is true to say that plastic elements can combine their non-representational qualities into a complex and diversified whole, according to their own inherent system of notation. In exactly the same way as figurative painting, abstract painting is intended to make us experience something by creating a new attitude which will bring us into contact with our own realities. The one does it through the medium of a subject which relies on a representational image; the other does it through the medium of a subject which, *though still an image*, dispenses with representational characteristics in order to exploit the internal resources of language.

Will abstract art oust figurative art altogether – or is it destined (as some people insinuate) to disappear very shortly? We cannot say. But no-one can deny that an artistic revolution is taking place. And if works of high quality endeavour to satisfy the conditions of a new sensibility, it is one's duty to forestall the misunderstandings that may arise, by trying to show the legitimate basis on which a new language is founded.

446 Movement

Kandinsky painted this picture in 1935. In his preceding 'Bauhaus' period he had been concerned mainly with geometrical experiments. In his final period (Paris, 1933-1944) he progressively laid aside geometrical constructions, and invented a world of his own forms. The picture which we are studying is one of those which mark the transition from one period to the other. It is painted in oil on canvas, measuring 45½ ins. by 35 ins. It forms part of the collection of Mme Nina Kandinsky.

Study of the work

The differences between figurative and abstract painting leap to the eye at first glance: no objects, no space, no light – in short, nothing recognizable or familiar. Certainly, one can see forms: vague shapes, ribbon-like shapes, circles, sorts of grid, and so on; but the use of the words 'like' and 'sort' show how approximate this identification is. When one tries to relate the elements of the painting to something known, one only half-succeeds; their forms always elude one's grasp, as does the manner of their grouping.

This is a point of some importance. When one examines the skin of one's hand or a section of some plant through a magnifying-glass, the eye is unfailingly surprised; it all looks so different. But there are limits to this surprise. Since all the elements are modified simultaneously by the conditions under which one perceives them, it will be found that, in spite of the change, the mind still recognizes a general order, existing on a minute scale, which helps in identification.

There is nothing of that sort here: Kandinsky's picture is neither a 'magnified view' nor a 'reduced view'. The elements which compose it refer to art, not nature. Neither microscope nor telescope influences the painter's vision.

This is a necessary point to make, owing to a common tendency to believe that scientific progress influences art directly. Of course science is reflected in art, but only through the creative sensibility of man.

The question which immediately arises, in front of this picture which has absolutely no relation to visible reality, is this: has it a meaning? Has it quality? If so, how is one to set about looking for them?

The first stage of our examination has produced only negative information: no objects, no space, no light. Nevertheless, we must be careful to note that these negatives are not absolute. The painting is neither chaos nor a void. The negatives which we pronounced contained only a *relative truth,* which means to say that there are no objects, no space and no light *in the sense that these words designate elements of the reality to which we are accustomed.*

Now, disregarding *that kind* of reality, one can see that there is no lack of forms; it is even easy to count and classify them:

large patches of colour in the form of irregular circles, purplish-red, blue, green and greenish-brown;

hollow geometrical forms, reminiscent of watch dials, grids or cages;

solid geometrical forms, such as discs and rectangles;

multicoloured dots of various sizes;

ribbon-like forms, like strips of paper;

446. Wassily Kandinsky (1866-1944). *Movement*. Paris, collection of Mme Nina Kandinsky. Photo Laniepce.

all of them being arranged on a brown background.

Does this get us much further? Not if one is thinking only of a simple catalogue (which is anyway incomplete); but we soon realize that these forms are not just a heterogeneous collection scattered at random over the canvas; *they have definite relationships.*

Here are some of the more obvious of these relationships:

relationship of *solids* (the coloured patches) and *voids* (the grid-like shapes);
relationship of *geometrical* and *non-geometrical* shapes;
relation of *broad* (patches, discs) and *narrow* (ribbon-like and wire-like forms);
relation of *large* (patches) and *small* (dots);
relation of *long* (ribbons) and *short* (dots);
relation of *dense* (patches) and *scattered* (dots);
relation of *opaque* (the solid patches) and *transparent* (where patches overlap).

This liaison of the forms is rendered more apparent by a further series of relationships, based on colour:

Five major patches of colour emerge from the background, and one notices that they do not 447 merge into one another at the points where they interpenetrate, but that they change colour. The area where the red and the blue patches meet becomes violet-blue; the area where red and green meet becomes greenish-blue; and the area where red and greenish-brown meet becomes grey-blue. It is not a matter of one form simply overlapping another, but of *plastic interaction.*

448 The same thing happens to the 'ribbons'. Take, for example, the one on the extreme left: not only does it change shape, swelling and contracting like some huge primitive organism, but each time that it crosses another element it changes colour too, sometimes as if we were seeing it through the other form, sometimes as if we were seeing the other form through it. When one has noticed this effect of mimesis – at once active and passive – one realizes that the ribbons are linked formally to each other, in the same way as the coloured patches. They are not just a number of scattered pieces, but a fluid and ductile substance, which has its articulations, its spurts of energy and its zones of transition. Thus, confining ourselves to these two examples, patches and ribbons form a definite texture.

And this is a demonstration of the truth of a fundamental law of abstract painting – one that

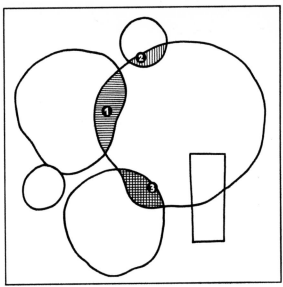

447

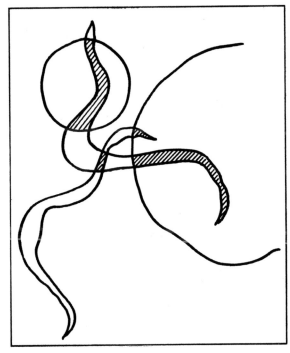

447-448. *Colours and forms interact upon each other to give rise to the work's inward life.*

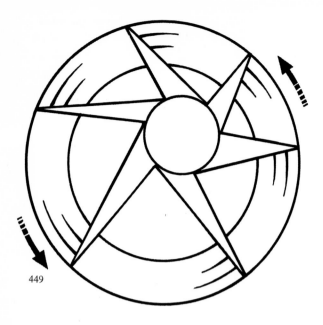

449

cannot be too strongly emphasized: although they do not refer to known objects, the elements of the picture can attain *formal consistency,* and can act upon the spectator as a *coherent whole.*

Even though there is no 'lighting', as such, in this painting, one cannot say that light is entirely absent. Of course there is no question of any source of natural or of artificial light, but still, the colours are clearly distinguishable, and so are the contrasts of dark and paler tones. One can see, too, how light affects the picture space, though here again there is no question of depth or volume. It is a space which has nothing in common with what goes by that name in classical painting; there is no horizon, no foreshortening, no vanishing-point. The cubic construction of the Renaissance masters has been well and truly demolished! However, while we cannot really even speak of aerial perspective, we have seen that some elements pass 'over' or 'under' others, so that there is, if not distance, at least an interval between the forms. This space, to which no limits are set at the top, at the bottom or at the sides, which seems even to have no major axis from top to bottom or from left to right, is not unlike the expanse of the sky, whose depth we perceive not by relative distances but by the progression of clear and tenuous masses towards darker and more concentrated masses, giving us the sense of infinity. Thus light is not absent, but is used in a different way.

Freed from all limits, the picture space communicates a feeling of infinitude. Simultaneously,

the forms which inhabit it are divested of all appearance of corporality. A new world is opened to us.

In his surprise, the spectator wonders at first if he is not being fooled: 'Movement'! Isn't it more like a firework display? Rockets tearing across the night sky through showers of coloured sparks, while the stars are studded with catherine-wheels and roman candles. Fortunately, reflection cuts short such digressions, but – since it is impossible to talk about a picture without recourse to some sort of visual notation – let us use this comparison for a start. When the initial surprise has passed, the eye is caught by the six-pointed star in the centre, which draws it into its rotary motion and propels it by centrifugal force into the extraordinary labyrinth of the ribbons. Here the interest lies not in tracing the hidden pathway, but in 'living' it – that is to say, in savouring the ideas and sensations which one experiences in following it. Ceaselessly beckoned onward, the eye goes on its way; according to the track it chooses, it slides or climbs or marches steadily. The corners, and the points where the paths widen or grow narrow, add touches of the unexpected, producing a variety of impressions. Think of one's sensations when riding in a motor car: here the countryside 'closes in', one says; then suddenly, at a turn of the road, it 'opens out' again, and the traveller's soul, which has been shut in upon itself, perhaps even oppressed, expands all at once in a sense of well-being. The effects of speed are no less varied. Such feelings are of everyday occurrence, yet are scarcely describable, since we retain only a fugitive recollection of them.

Now, the country which Kandinsky invites us to explore is no ordinary one, and the eye is no ordinary traveller. Forgetting our terrestrial journeyings, we set off into a complex space in which the road turns back on itself – sometimes underneath itself – as if we are permitted to escape not only from precise locality, but also from time itself (there is nothing to indicate what season it is, what day or what hour of the day). We have cast off our two main physical servitudes!

Drawn onwards by the road ahead, we pass through strange cities of glass, spun in flawless threads of translucent geometry. They are not to be thought of, however, as purely geometrical figures. They do indeed describe circles, squares, rectangles and parallelograms, but they are neither 'planes' nor 'in space' as the geometry books say. They are neither surfaces nor volumes, but ambiguous shapes which 'cave in' or 'swell out' as if from the elasticity of the fluid in which they are immersed. It is an extraordinary sensation to move among these fragile constructions, which – behind their apparent inertia – permit one to perceive the breath of life.

And we come to more strange places – for instance, these broad patches that have drifted from heaven knows what deeps of night, slack and stagnant – yet dimly alive. The eye only pauses momentarily to take note of these weird aerial fabrics, so heavy with foreboding, since it is dazzled by the tiny dots which – in vivid contrast – dance wildly before it.

Would it be true to say that the colours are used simply to fill in these curious shapes? They are indeed confined within the outlines of the forms, but their choice and their distribution contribute materially to the overall movement of the composition. The blue, the wine-red, the green and the greenish-brown of the larger patches convey an impression of infinitely slow rotation, like that of the large wheels of a clock, while the gridded circles, because of the thinness of their yellow framework, suggest a much quicker movement. As for the white or pale blue ribbons, they introduce an element of vagrancy into the calm, well-regulated movement of the composition as a whole. And the calm is also disturbed by the hail of brightly coloured dots of all sizes, which add a sort of frenzy that becomes almost strident to the ear.

The spontaneous nature of the journey is stressed by the picture's rhythm. Instead of presenting too obvious echoes and similarities, the forms exploit their diversity. Nevertheless, each type of relationship that we have seen them to possess is clearly conveyed to the spectator. Note how the artist animates the solid forms – the ribbons, for instance; widening or narrowing, they mark 'down-beats' and 'up-beats' of a kind which one can also recognize in the relationship of the grid-like discs to the opaque patches.

Kandinsky's handling, like that of the primitives, is extremely smooth. One can scarcely speak of impasto in connection with this polished film of paint. There are no accidental features to divert one's attention; even the grain of the canvas is invisible. The eye slides over its surface. Thus all sensuous pleasures are renounced, and one looks at the picture with a more inward gaze, that delights in the contemplation of forms without feeling a desire to touch them or to refer them to tangible things; painting has become a 'mirror of the mind'. A new relationship is established between the work and the spectator. Like Baudelaire in his preface to the *Petits poèmes en prose,* Kandinsky seems also to dream of 'the miracle of a poetic prose, musical without rhyme or rhythm, supple and hard enough to adapt itself to the lyrical movements of art, to the undulations of reverie, and to the sudden bounds of the consciousness' (1869).

Perhaps one can now more readily understand how abstract art has come to light, and how it has brought to light a new reality. With his customary genius, Baudelaire foresaw it long ago: 'It is above all from living in huge cities, from the intersection of all their manifold relations and proportions, that this obsessive ideal is born', he continued in that same preface. It would be rash to assert that Kandinsky had the same idea, but it is none the less true that the conditions of modern life have profoundly affected our world and the structure of our thought.[1] This is not to say that man has lost his soul, but that in our age it is manifested – in the arts, at least – in different ways from those that were used by our forefathers. Since man's idea of the world was formerly relatively stable, it is not surprising that it served for so long to sustain his spirit; to-day, when science and history constantly remind us of the complexity and instability of our knowledge, it is not surprising that artists should seek a secure foothold in language itself – the last bastion of humanity, when all else is swept away.

Only the future will tell whether man can find in the internal resources of language as rich a response as he found in his thousand-year-long commerce with nature. But the work of a Kandinsky, or of any worthwhile abstract painter, gives proof that even now a new sensibility has been born, and that humanity, in forging a new means of expression, is seeking its new face – the face of our times.

---

[1] 'What happens when our gaze, endowed with new powers of penetration, searches beyond habitual appearances for the mechanism of a development, a growth, a transformation, and when those are the aspects which impose themselves on our mind, and demand to be expressed? In other words, what happens when the interest aroused by the sight of a river, a tree and a flower, crystallizes round a vocabulary that is concerned with the dynamics of their existence: flow, growth, flowering? Now, this shift of interest is imposed on us by a sharper awareness of the relationship between our knowledge and the reality.' (Extract from the lecture *Art in the 20th Century,* given by Werner Haftmann at the inauguration of *Documenta,* international exhibition of modern art at Kassel. See *Cimaise,* December 1955.)

Conclusion

Art has assumed a vital importance in our times. We need still to recognize that our attitudes have changed, and that the change has given it a new role and a new meaning. Of old, when a Christian looked up 450 at the tympanum of Vézelay, it was not to admire the sculptor's genius, but to feel the rushing wing of Pentecost pass over him. Carved or painted, images were for him the symbols of his destiny. Angels and saints formed a family that was the projection of his own, and in contemplating them he learned to recognize his own features and those of his neighbour. Thus, in Christianity, was accomplished the union of his natural existence and his divine calling, and the mission of art was to make this manifest.

Man's situation has changed, but his human condition remains. It is useless for television to treat us like gods, broadcasting our image all over the planet; the sight of our own features – or those of our fellow-men – repeated to infinity is no answer to our secret agonies, to the beating of our hearts, to the silent questionings that are summed up in Gauguin's admirable: "D'où venons-nous? Que 451 sommes-nous? Où allons-nous?" [1]

[1] 'Where do we come from? What are we? Where are we going to?'

450. Romanesque art. *Pentecost*. Vézelay, 12th century. Photo E. Janet-Lecaisne.

451. Paul Gauguin (1848-1903). *D'où venons-nous? Que sommes-nous? Où allons-nous?* Boston, Museum of Fine Arts. Photo Bulloz.

Science and technology do not and cannot answer such questions. They establish *facts*, and can do no more than that. Man searches for a *meaning*. And even when all the facts which science presents to him are added together, it is he, and he alone, who co-ordinates them and gives them direction. Man can no more fulfil himself in positive reality than in pure imagination, and – with or without gods – there is no instance of his being satisfied with the former of these; nor does it seem that he could ever be so, since it is in his nature to transcend nature. Wherever one follows him, one sees him striving to unite the two parts of his being. Only *human reality* is capable of responding to that which is his own – his soul.

For a long time the great religious myths effected this union. It is not for me to say whether or not they do so still. But it is a fact that men no longer look exclusively to religion for that *tangible certainty* which we need in order to live, and that they turn more and more to art and artists. Men who no longer believe in Christ revere the *Resurrection* of Piero della Francesca. Deprived of religious reality, the picture is a fictive creation; but fictive creation is not sham. *In our time, aesthetic quality has acquired the validity of a special reality.* This is surely the major event of our age – an event of which we are only beginning to be aware.

Thus knowledge of art is no longer solely a means of satisfying a religious need, or of satisfying a taste for luxury – as it was a century ago; it has become a necessity, linked to the actual quality of our life. The categorical tone in which art is discussed is revealing. Would people show such lively interest – or such asperity – if mankind did not feel the certainty that art has an absolute value for our world?

Our epoch no longer accepts the methods of investigation that have hitherto sufficed. To-day we know that philosophies and aesthetic theories have only an indirect bearing upon our need to 'understand'. Even the history of art, indispensable though it is, is gradually taking its place as an auxiliary field of study. For what the public demands – in the name of this new need of which it is conscious – is a method of knowing that is suited to its purpose and to the conditions in which contact is made with a work of art.

This is what I have endeavoured to bring to light in establishing:
the requirements of the aesthetic approach:
any reference that is not based on aesthetic values prevents the work of art from fulfilling itself in our eyes, and prevents us from fulfilling ourselves in it;
the requirements of aesthetic experience:
aesthetic revelation is only attained through a state of awareness in which our being is transformed;
the requirements of aesthetic judgement:
understanding can only be reached through a form of thinking which abandons normal intellectual processes and adopts a method of its own.

This method, as I have attempted to elaborate it, is not theoretical; it is closely bound up with the means by which it is applied, though this practical aim should not at any time be interpreted as a tendency towards simplification. That is why I have

452

confined myself to suggesting certain *requirements* to the spectator, and have avoided preaching any doctrine.

Art is language, as we have seen. As is the case with everyday language, its purpose is to communicate; but, unlike everyday language, it is not limited to that purpose. In other words, the work of art is not expended in the act of communication; it keeps its power and, what is more, gives the communication a quality such that the spectator – if he is disposed to receive it – experiences a feeling that it alone can give him, and apprehends a meaning that it alone can create.

This book – as I have made clear from the beginning – is not concerned with the psychology of artistic creation. It is not concerned with the relationship between the work and its creator, but with that between the work and the spectator. This is the viewpoint to which I have adhered; other view-points are not necessarily wrong or useless, but the one I have chosen is perhaps the most

452. Piero della Francesca (c. 1410/20-1492). *The Resurrection,* fresco. Borgo San Sepolcro, Palazzo Communale. Photo Held.

neglected, and it is certainly the most essential in these days when the public aspires more and more to understand art better – in order to like it better.

Aesthetic understanding progresses by successive and varied movements. Instead of following a dead-straight line, we take a step now to the left – in the direction of form, and now to the right – in the direction of content, employing simultaneously all our powers of perception, reflection and sensibility. *It is the paradox of our human condition that we have to proceed by oblique and indirect steps in order to march straight to our goal.*

Having now come to the end of our enquiry, one is entitled to ask: can any such method, even though it be supported by studies of actual works, show *why* a picture is beautiful? A fundamental objection! And if it could be sustained, my whole edifice would collapse – which would be unfortunate for me and even more so for the success of my undertaking. Either we are so many separate cells of consciousness, cut off from one another, or else – despite the walls which divide us, and which we cannot demolish – we have the means of understanding one another *across the walls.* That is the stake which I put down!

Now, has anyone the right to assert that humanity cannot do for aesthetic knowledge what it has done – at the cost of immense effort – for intellectual knowledge, by the establishing of language and of methods of thought?

Beauty, it is true, cannot be defined as a concept, any more than it can be isolated in the manner of a chemical element. It is revealed much more in the form of an enjoyment that takes possession of one's whole being. But, if it is something to be enjoyed, one must acknowledge that it is no less something to be understood (not, however, something to understand in the normal or scientific sense). This means that, even if we cannot share our experience, we can still hope, if we try hard enough, to share *the conditions in which we have the experience.*

That is the article of faith of this undertaking.

Experience of the beautiful cannot be communicated. Only knowledge of some kind forms matter for discussion; it is through discussion that one can begin to look for certainty, and only through discussion can one hope to find it. Feeling and discernment are not blunted by discussion; on the contrary, they are sharpened. The result of their co-operation is to feel truly.

As I have defined it, aesthetic appreciation is a method of understanding. It can never claim to exhaust the work of art, which is – by its nature –

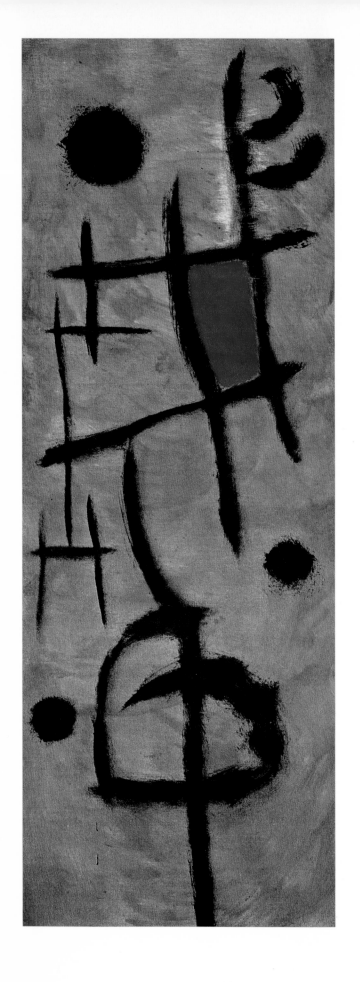

inexhaustible. The virtue of explanations, however brilliant or ingenious they may be, is not to cover the work with a sort of parasitic shell, but – like scaffolding – to permit us to get nearer to it, *and then to disappear when their help is no longer needed,* for in the last resort the work of art is revealed by its presence, by its presence alone. When all such support is withdrawn, then the mystery of contact with the work, which is always a new beginning, comes into operation.

Each time that we approach it, the face of the work is made new – as ours is also – and it is important that the circumstances of this contact should be securely ascertained. Rather than a pleasure or an emotion, we are offered the *chance* *to perceive ourselves in our condition as real and imaginary beings.* To experience this joy, to recognize ourselves in and through the beautiful, we need to be in a state *to respond to the work's presence at its highest level by giving it the highest level of our attention.*

In an age which seems doomed to misunderstanding and confusion, it is surely our duty – in the domain which provides us, if not with our health, at least with a reason for our existence – to do our best to replace the opinions that divide us with a means of understanding one another. In this hope I have undertaken this discussion, and I thank all those who – from the love of art and of mankind – have had the patience to follow it with me to the end.

◄ 453. Joan Miró (b. 1893). *Painting,* 1953. Lausanne, private collection. Photo Held.

List of illustrations
Bibliography
Index

List of illustrations

Italic Numbers at left are plate numbers, numbers in roman type are page numbers. The list is arranged in alphabetical order according to name of artist, school or type of art.

387

Bibliography

If we are to know and understand a work of art there is no substitute for direct experience. But this is not to say that books cannot help us. In the course of writing this work the author has drawn on numerous books, and many more have contributed to it indirectly over the years. Faced with the impossibility of listing them all, the author has compiled what is more in the nature of a select guide than a bibliography.

For the English language edition the English editors have wherever possible given works in translation, and have selected from the author's list the works which are obtainable in Great Britain or the United States. They have also supplemented the author's list, with his approval, with useful and relevant English language titles.

I Philosophy of Art

Croce, Benedetto, *Brevario di estetica* (Bari, 1924).

Focillon, Henri, *The Life of Forms in Art* (New Haven, 1942, Yale History of Art, Vol. IV).

Gombrich, E. H. J., *Art and Illusion* (Phaidon Press, London; Pantheon Books, New York, 1960).

Huyghe, René, *Art and the Spirit of Man* (Thames and Hudson, London; Abrams, New York, 1962).

Discovery of Art (Thames and Hudson, London; Abrams, New York, 1959).

Malraux, André, *The Voices of Silence* (Secker and Warburg, London; Doubleday, New York, 1954).

II History of Art

(1) General

Arts of Mankind Series, ed. André Malraux and Georges Salles (Thames and Hudson, London; Golden Press, New York, 1960 –   ).

    Parrot, André, *Sumer. — Nineveh and Babylon.*

    Ghirshman, Roman, *Iran: The Parthians and Sassanians.* (*Persian Art: The Parthian and Sassanian Dynasties,* Golden Press, New York).

    Guiart, Jean, *The Arts of the South Pacific.*

Bazin, Germain, *A Concise History of Art* (Thames and Hudson, London; Houghton Mifflin, New York, 1958).

Encyclopedia of World Art (McGraw-Hill Book Co., London and New York). 15 vols. 5 vols. published (1959 –   ).

Gombrich, E. H., *The Story of Art* (Phaidon Press, London; New York Graphic Society. New York, 1959).

A Handbook of Western Painting (Thames and Hudson, London; Tudor Publishing Co., New York, 1961).

Huyghe, René, ed., *L'Art et l'Homme* (Paris, 1957).

Jansen, H. W., *A History of Art* (Thames and Hudson, London; Abrams, New York, 1962).

Newton, Eric, *The Arts of Man* (Thames and Hudson, London; Doubleday, New York, 1960).

The Pelican History of Art (20 vols.) (Penguin Books, London and Baltimore, 1953–60).

Read, Sir Herbert, *A Concise History of Modern Painting* (Thames and Hudson, London; Praeger, New York, 1959).

(2) Particular Periods, Movements, Subjects

Brion, Marcel, *Romantic Art* (Thames and Hudson, London; McGraw-Hill, New York, 1960).

Cassou, J., Langui, E., Pevsner, N., *The Sources of Modern Art* (Thames and Hudson, London; McGraw-Hill, New York, 1962).

Chastel, André, *L'Art Italien* (Larousse, 1956).

— *Humanist Europe* (Thames and Hudson, London; McGraw-Hill, New York, 1963).

Clark, Sir Kenneth Mackenzie, *The Nude* (John Murray, London; Pantheon Books, 1956).

— *Landscape into Art* (John Murray, London, 1949; Beacon Press, Boston, 1961).

Dorival, Bernard, *Les Etapes de la Peinture française contemporaine* (3 vol., Paris, 1948).

Gould, Cecil, *An Introduction to Italian Renaissance Painting* (Phaidon Press, London; New York Graphic Society, New York, 1957).

Kandinsky, Wassily, *The Art of Spiritual Harmony* (Constable & Co., London, 1914).

— *Concerning the Spiritual in Art* (Wittenborn, Schulz Inc., New York, 1947).

Mâle, Emile, *The Gothic Image* (Collins, London, 1961; Harper & Bros, New York, 1958).

Pater, Walter, *The Renaissance* (Macmillan & Co., London, 1924; Modern Library, New York).

Rewald, John, *The History of Impressionism* (Museum of Modern Art, New York, 1949).

— *Post-Impressionism: From Van Gogh to Gauguin* (Museum of Modern Art, New York, 1956).

Rosenblum, Robert, *Cubism and Twentieth Century Art* (Thames and Hudson, London; Abrams, New York, 1961).

Ruskin, John, *The Lamp of Beauty* (Writings on art, ed. Joan Evans) (Phaidon Press, London; New York Graphic Society, New York, 1959).

Schonberger, A., and H. Soehner, *The Age of Rococo* (Thames and Hudson, London; McGraw-Hill, New York, 1960).

Seuphor, Michel, *Abstract Painting* (Abrams, New York, 1962).

Wölfflin, Heinrich, *Classic Art: An Introduction to the Italian Renaissance* (Phaidon Press, London, 1952).

III Dictionaries of Artists, Techniques, Etc.

Bénézit, E., *Dictionnaire des Peintres, Sculpteurs, Dessinateurs et Graveurs*.

Thieme and Becker, *Allgemeines Lexikon der bildenden Künstler von der Antike bis zur Gegenwart*.

Fernau, Joachim, *Encyclopaedia of Old Masters* (Thames and Hudson, London; Praeger New York, 1959).

Seuphor, Michel, *A Dictionary of Abstract Painting, preceded by a history of abstract painting,* (Methuen & Co., London, 1958; Tudor Publishing & Co., New York, 1957).

The Art Index (H. W. Wilson Co., New York, 1929–   ).

Index